FIELD OF VIEW

Film Criticism and Comment

By Stanley Kauffmann

Novels

The Hidden Hero
The Tightrope
A Change of Climate
Man of the World

Criticism

THEATER

Persons of the Drama
Theater Criticisms

FILM

A World on Film
Figures of Light
Living Images
Before My Eyes
Field of View

Editor

(With Bruce Henstell)
American Film Criticism: From the Beginnings to *Citizen Kane*

Memoirs

Albums of Early Life

Stanley Kauffmann

FIELD OF VIEW

Film Criticism and Comment

PAJ Publications
(A Division of Performing Arts Journal, Inc.)
New York

All rights reserved under the International and Pan-American Copyright Conventions. For information, write to PAJ Publications, 325 Spring Street, Suite 318, New York, N.Y. 10013.

Library of Congress Cataloging in Publication Data
Field of View
Library of Congress Catalog Card No.: 85-63862
ISBN: 0-933826-87-7 (cloth)
ISBN: 0-933826-88-5 (paper)

Graphic Design: Gautam Dasgupta
Printed in the United States of America

Publication of this book has been made possible in part by grants received from the National Endowment for the Arts, Washington, D.C., a federal agency, and the New York State Council on the Arts.

J. S. K.

1892 - 1954

Contents

Preface

Early in 1958, uninvited, I sent a film review to *The New Republic*. They published it. Herewith, in consequence, is the fifth collection of my film reviews and articles. Most of the contents of the four previous books was drawn from *The New Republic*; fittingly, perhaps, this book comes entirely from that journal. I have had the privilege through these years, rare and valued, to write in a sense of community and continuity.

As before, I have chosen material that, because of subject or comment or both, may have continuing interest. Many of the pieces have been slightly revised, but none has been substantively altered. Within each section the order is chronological by date of publication, except that the first review of a director's work is followed by any other reviews of his work. Occasionally, because of these groupings, a subject is mentioned that is treated later. Some postscripts have been added, along with some footnotes that may be useful for cross-reference.

Deep gratitude, happily acknowledged, to: Martin Peretz and associates at *The New Republic*; to Carl Brandt, agent and friend; to Bonnie Marranca and Gautam Dasgupta, publishers and friends. Thanks, again and ever, to L.C.K.

S.K.

New York
April 1985

Reviews

Monty Python's Life of Brian

(September 22, 1979)

"Roman Catholic, Jewish, and Protestant spokesmen have joined in con-demning as blasphemous a movie produced by the British satirical group known as Monty Python . . . . *Life of Brian*, an attempt to spoof the life of Christ, is the story of a contemporary of Jesus who is mistaken for the Messiah." (*The New York Times*, September 4, 1979.) Wrong. He is mistaken for *a* messiah, in an age that is visibly hungry for messiahs and has many can-didates. (Nothing like us, right?) What's more, Brian, whose last name is Cohen, continually denies that he is a messiah and, unlike Jesus, flees those who want to be his disciples. What's even more, the story of Jesus is kept quite separate from Brian's, is glimpsed only twice, and is in itself never mocked. Brian is born in a manger across the way from the Holy Family's, and the Three Wise Men call at the wrong manger first, that's all. Our one glimpse of the right manger, from a distance, is pure Christmas-card. Later on, in 33 A. D., Brian and his mother go to hear the Sermon on the Mount and are on the far edge of the crowd, where they misunderstand some of the words and get caught in a squabble that breaks out among some of the onlookers. I thought the incident was funny because it was possible, and because it was a retrospective forecast of just how much peace the Sermon has brought to mankind in the following cen-turies, particularly between Christians.

And what's even more, the religious spokesmen above seem to me to be shortchanging Jesus himself, who demonstrably had a sense of humor, shown in wordplay. "Thou art Peter, and upon this rock I will build my church." (Mat-thew, 16:18.) "And Jesus . . . saw two brethren . . . casting a net into the sea: for they were fishers. And he saith unto them, Follow me, and I will make you fishers of men." (Matthew, 4:18, 19.)

The many who (I hope) have seen Monty Python on PBS may suspect that they are at their best in short bursts. But in their feature film, *Monty Python and the Holy Grail*, they sustained their invention and insolence very well, and, with the help of witty anachronisms, they reamed the stupidities and cruelties of the Middle Ages, particularly those with contemporary resonances. They did not destroy the spiritual-intellectual legacy of the Middle Ages. (How could they, even if they'd wanted to?) In *Monty Python's Life of Brian*, they use the same invention-insolence-anachronism to ream the stupidities and delusions of religiosity. They will not destroy true, unpompous faith. (How could they, even if they wanted to?) If you like, you can read the script in a plentifully illustrated, oversize paperbound (Grosset and Dunlap), which also contains some additional sketches on the subject, and decide for yourself whether you want to see the picture. If you've stuck with this column so far, you'll probably want to see it. I read the script after seeing the film and doubled up all over again. My only objection to the film has nothing to do with any of the above: the dialogue is so fast, in ultra-English throwaway style, that I missed a bit from time to time, and (as the book shows) little of it is missable.

The screenplay was written by Python regulars, Graham Chapman, John Cleese, Terry Gilliam, Eric Idle, Terry Jones, and Michael Palin, all of whom play numerous parts, including females; and it was directed by Jones. A layman's blessing on the lot of them. Even when I wasn't laughing, I was happy, which to me is a sign of really good comedy.

The story as such doesn't need summary: Brian keeps fleeing messiahdom, unsuccessfully, that's the core. At last he is brought before Pilate (who lisps on the letter 'r'). He is sentenced to be crucified along with that day's batch—no nails, just ropes. In the last shot there hangs Brian on a cross, surrounded by a dozen others on crosses, all trying to keep cheery. One by one they join in a song, kicking their legs in unison as far as they can. The film ends as they sing:

And always look on the bright side of life . . . .
    (whistle)
Always look on the right side of life.
    (whistle)

The camera pulls back and pans up into the sky.

If I had to pick a favorite moment, it would be the one in which Brian, escaping the idolatrous crowd, loses his right shoe. The crowd seizes his shoe as a sign and, through the fevers of iconography, they hold up right shoes thereafter as symbols of belief. It reminded me of H. G. Wells's remark that if Jesus had been hanged instead of crucified, the symbol of Christianity would be the noose.

Monty Python's The Meaning of Life
(April 18, 1983)

It's time to take Monty Python seriously. This may sound ungratefully grim, but these six men have brought it on themselves. They have been heading toward serious consideration ever since their first film, *And Now for Something Completely Different* (drawn from their first five years' work on BBC-TV); they pressed onward with their medieval mockery, *Monty Python and the Holy Grail*; and they virtually sealed their fate as important figures with their pietistic satire, *Monty Python's Life of Brian*. Now, after two feature-length collections of live-performance tapes, which contained some of their best recent TV work and some sketches that would frizzle TV tubes, comes *Monty Python's The Meaning of Life*—and they are doomed. They must be called significant comic artists. I can't add "of the first rank" because there's no one else in their particular rank: they are unique.

The Meaning of Life is not their most consistently funny film, but it's the one that is most free in fantasy and most savage, with the special MP savagery that blends humane rage with cruel means, under the license of comedy. (The copiously illustrated screenplay has been published by Grove Press, with, inevitably, some slight differences from the finished film.) This is true even though the picture begins rather weakly, with a ten-minute "short," separately titled, which has only a few engaging visual effects and comic ideas. Then *The Meaning of Life* itself begins, and it quickly does much more than allay our fears.

It's not a continuous story: there are sections, so labeled, going from birth to death, containing discrete bits of material about the section subjects. I suppose the material must be called sketches, but the term isn't always quite right. Many of them *are* Monty Python sketches, well up to their lunatic mark; but some of the material, though it has sketch shape and tone, pushes beyond.

At the middle of the film—which, too, is labeled—Michael Palin sits at the side of the screen as a refayned TV hostess. (Yes, that's the gender. In customary MP style, many of the women are played by them. Palin here is dressed and coiffured and sounds like a lady-in-waiting to H. R. H.) The hostess announces an interlude. At the very end of the film, again so labeled, the hostess again appears. She opens a large envelope that contains the meaning of life, and she reads off a message with sound advice but flies off into audience abuse.

Out of the plentiful sketches, here are two samples. In the section called "Growth and Learning," John Cleese is a schoolmaster. The others of the group and some other men, dressed in British schoolboy garb, are his students. Cleese, a martinet, behaves as if he were drilling a dull Latin lesson into these bored sullen kids, but the subject is in fact sexual intercourse. (Teacher, bullying: . . . . "No doubt you can tell me what the purpose of foreplay is . . . Biggs."

Biggs rises reluctantly and looks at chums for help: "Don't know, sorry, sir.") Cleese pushes a button that lets down a huge bed; his wife comes in and strips; they engage in sex before the class. Cleese didactically describes every move to the apathetic boys and has to reprove them for inattention.

In a section called "The Third World," which turns out to be Yorkshire, Michael Palin, as a weary factory hand, comes home to face his saggy wife, Terry Jones, and their small army of kids, from infants to teenagers, and reports that the mill is closed. "We're destitute." He's going to have to sell the children for scientific experiment. When they protest, he says, "Blame the Catholic Church for not letting me wear one of those little rubber things." He then breaks into a song with the lines, "Every sperm is sacred, every sperm is great," and the picture explodes into a gigantic musical number, through backyards and streets, with dancing kids and clergy and nurses and neighbors, with crane shots and cute cuts, in punitive parody of the heartwarming orphanage numbers in *Annie*.

The jabs are so sharp that I began to remember the old saw about anti-Catholicism being the anti-Semitism of liberals. Just then, the number ends, and we cross the street to a stuffy parlor with a stuffy middle-aged couple. The husband deplores the Catholic fecundity across the street. He can wear a rubber sheath and keep his wife from being impregnated. "That's what being a Protestant is all about." He can even wear French Ticklers if he likes. He can walk into a shop, with his head held high, and say, "Harry, I want you to sell me a condom. In fact today I think I'll have a French Tickler, for I am a Protestant . . ." (And later on the punch line of a song jabs the Jews. Nobody gets off unjostled.)

But in some wonderfully eruptive ways, the film goes past the usual Monty Python form, the anthology of sketches. Some sequences flow from an initial idea into a shape that resembles a musical fantasia on a theme. For example, in the "Death" section, the Grim Reaper, complete with cowl and scythe, arrives at a posh cottage. The sequence continues through a sharp sketch in which he announces their doom to hosts and guests, then the Grim Reaper conducts them all to heaven, which turns out to be a lush, crowded, Caribbean-style hotel with a huge cocktail lounge in which Eric Idle, wearing ascot and brocade jacket, is seated at a piano accompanying himself as he sings, in clipped Coward accents, a clipped Coward song about his penis. Is it possible that heaven is hell?

And the contents of some sketches, even when they are rounded-off in shape, go past the funny into the disquieting, then keep going. And going. One such is in a luxe restaurant with John Cleese as the Frenchified headwaiter. In comes the fattest person ever constructed for play or film, Terry Jones in a blimp-size dinner jacket. As the headwaiter fusses over him, the man announces that he is going to be sick, a bucket is provided, and he continues to be sick and sick and sick while the headwaiter keeps his aplomb, while an immense meal with oceans of drink is ordered and served. If the sicking-up has any humor at all, it's soon over. But if you grant, as I do, that we are dealing here with some of the wittiest men alive, you must also grant that they know the scene has ceased to be funny, that they are not interested here in being funny. Clearly they want to burn through the joke and look back at it. Satire on grossness, on the need of a rich man to cram his money down his gullet in food form, on the thin servilities of a headwaiter pretending affection for a guest—these patent targets are left behind as the scene tears past the possibility of laughter into disgust and anger. The same is true of another sketch about a company that deals in liver transplants.

Most social satire is by now contained cozily within the society it satirizes. Instead of scathing, it flatters—by testing and proving the broadmindedness of the audience. "The hell with that," imply the Monty Python crew in these sketches, as they push into the intolerable. Some of the audience at the press screening thought these scenes tasteless, failed humor. I thought them differently intended and entirely successful. They make the purported frankness of Woody Allen's *Everything You Always Wanted to Know About Sex But Were Afraid to Ask* look like japery at an adult summer camp. They make the so-called anarchism of Buñuel's *The Discreet Charm of the Bourgeoisie* look discreet and charming. The Monty Python people are telling us that, in the Great Contest of Life, neatness does not count. They have set foot on Blake's road of excess, hoping that the old man was right, that it will lead to the palace of wisdom.

Terry Jones, who directs, can no longer be called the member of the group who directs, as if he were the goodhearted sucker who is willing to do the dirty work for the group. His eye, his rhythmic sense, his instinct for attention—where to be looking at every moment—show him to be a genuinely able director in his own right. He and his five fellows are flawless performers, with uncannily precise ears and versatility. As devisers and writers, they are breathtakingly ingenious—most of the time, anyway. I can think of no other filmmakers, from the gravest to the giddiest, whose future work I anticipate more eagerly. They are the most dangerous madmen at large, ruthlessly perceptive and torrentially gifted, who are angry at everything improvable in human behavior that is not being improved. On the basis of this new film, I'd guess that their anger is beginning to include their own work and its success.

The Ballad of Orin

(December 8, 1979)

It's risky to single out cinematography for praise. It makes a film sound otherwise dull, particularly in these days when gorgeousness is pretty general and pretty cheap. Yet a new Japanese film, *The Ballad of Orin*, gives me no alternative. In terms of its script and acting and direction, the film is perceptive, moving. But the cinematography—I'm trying to speak carefully—is the most subtle color work I've seen. It's not a visual sauce poured on a plain or less plain dish: it sustains and fixes the gravity of the whole work.

First, the other elements. Orin is a girl born blind, in the early part of this century. At the age of six she is apprenticed to a group of *goze*, itinerant blind woman singers, and with them, the child travels about the countryside. Apparently *goze* have a quasi religious status and are expected to be chaste. When Orin matures, she is seduced and expelled from the group. She meets a man, who turns out to be an army deserter, with whom she has a long platonic relationship. He commits a murder for her sake. They become lovers. He is caught and executed. Orin wanders off into the forest to die.

The director is Masahiro Shinoda, also the co-author of the script. Shinoda, born in 1931, began as assistant to the great Yasujiro Ozu and has been making his own films since 1960. *Double Suicide* is probably his best-known work in this country. A few years ago he said in an interview (Mellen, *Voices from the Japanese Cinema*):

> I must categorize the films of the world into three distinct types. European films are based upon human psychology, American films upon action and the struggles of human beings, and Japanese films upon *circumstance*. Japanese films are interested in what surrounds the human being.

Often the most helpful aspect of such categories is not their reliability in themselves but what they tell us about the persons who made them. Shinoda treats Orin as the product of a culture: in the way that her society has devised a profession to care for her, in the character of that profession, and in the fact that she is destined to be victimized by men, who seem to take her victimization as due part of her fate. The film moves in several time tracks and the editing is a bit more virtuosic than it need be, but Shinoda understands dramatic force, how to restrain it, how to loose it. The performance of Orin by his wife, Shima Iwashita, has both sweetness and passion.

If *The Ballad of Orin* were photographed with the usual Japanese competence, it would be worth seeing. The camera of Kazuo Miyagawa raises it higher.

When I read Miyagawa's name on the screen, it meant (I confess in shame) nothing to me. After I saw the film—at a theater, not a press screening—I stayed to see the credits again and get his name straight. Later I looked up Miyagawa's record and saw how much he had done for my filmgoing life. Born in 1908, he began work in 1935 and has made dozens of films. Among those on which he has been cinematographer: *Ugetsu* and *Sansho the Bailiff* for Mizoguchi, *Floating Weeds* for Ozu, *Odd Obsession* for Ichikawa, *Rashomon* and *Yojimbo* for Kurosawa. A staggering career.

Here is what Donald Richie says (in *The Films of Akira Kurosawa*) about Miyagawa's camera—black and white—in *Yojimbo*:

> Miyagawa's style . . . consists of almost perfectly balanced framing, though this framing is rarely symmetrical; the creation of a pattern which is often based upon the lateral (objects and or people) which lends a two-dimensional aspect something like a stage-set; the insistence upon an unusually deep focus which brings the very near and the very far into visual alignment; and a fondness for the kind of lighting which will fill (or even obscure) a portion of the wide screen with a dark, partially lighted object (usually a person) against a fairly light background, thus directing our interest to two planes at the same time.

Sixteen years later these are still Miyagawa characteristics, but the addition of color makes them even more striking. In that last-mentioned two-plane mode, for instance, a single object or person in the middle distance of an outdoor winter scene will now be brushed with not-quite-golden sun, while a branch in the foreground is velvet black and the snow itself is a delicately connecting greenish-gray.

The control of colors and the integrity of their scale are wonderful. Only a few moments are show-off shots. (One scene begins with a close-up of a surveyor's instrument in the sunlight, abstracted against black. Then a cut to a long shot, and we see that the instrument is standing outside the mouth of a tunnel. That sort of bravura touch is atypical.) Mostly the color choices are gentle, highly intelligent, and exquisitely stated. The whole spectrum is seen not so much through a cinematographer's temperament as through a sense of fate. It makes the shadows softer, the sun precious, the tint of everything a touch muted, unpredictable yet right.

The colors of course cannot be separated from the compositions, made by the same miraculous eye. For instance, a marketplace where the lover is waiting for Orin. The first view of it is a long shot of wide steps teeming with people. I can't remember seeing so many people on screen at once since the Babylonian mob sequence in *Intolerance*—not just a mob but an infinitesimally articulated beehive of individuals, compacted but individually mobile. Or, after the lover's arrest, the first shot of military headquarters: a complex of low gray-brown wooden structures, interconnected with one higher building at the right. High, just inside the frame at right, standing at an upper-floor window, is a lieutenant, smoking, before he turns to begin interrogation of his prisoner. In that first shot, order and indolent power have replaced freedom.

I've argued more than once against the concept of cinematographers as independent, whole artists: I'd still maintain that view. If I knew all of Miyagawa's work, I'm sure that, as in Sven Nykvist's, I'd find instances where his talent had been squandered on material that made it *look* squandered, under a director who presumably was hoping that the camera would redeem all shortcomings. But in *The Ballad of Orin*, with the collaboration and kinship of Shinoda, Miyagawa has exalted a film that in any case would have some interest and weight into one that must be seen. The cinematography is not "lavish," as some have said. This is not *Barry Lyndon* or *Days of Heaven*. For the most part, the eye is taken by vision, not by exhibition. Miyagawa has confirmed that, in the right instance, the right visual texture can be more than supportive: it can be transformative.

Kramer vs. Kramer

(December 22, 1979)

Kramer vs. Kramer, based on a novel by Avery Corman, was written by Robert Benton who also directed. I don't know the book: the script tells, in supple dialogue, the story of a New York couple who split. The struggle is not about the divorce, which as such is never glimpsed, it's about the custody of their small son. The drawing of the characters is adequate, possibly excepting the wife who is off screen a good deal of the time. Her inner crisis, which is why she leaves, and her recovery are more matters of report than enactment. All the people go through expected difficulties the way that runners take the hurdles in a track event: no surprise in it, it's just a question of how they do it. The anatomy and engagement of the script are those of a television drama bellying up to reality.

But the actors make it more. It's an old plaint of critics that good actors do much of the writing for lesser authors, fleshing out characters that have only been sketched. That's not quite the case here. As written, Benton's characters are clear enough but are a set of samples. The actors provide the dimensions of travail and grief, and of humor, that turn commonplace incidents of fictions in-to unique yet representative experiences.

Dustin Hoffman, the husband, is back in form—a new and better form, in fact. Early in his film career he was splendid in *The Graduate* and *Midnight Cowboy*; then he began to seesaw between sleeping and waking—comatose in *Papillon* and *John Loves Mary*, for instance, awake in *Lenny* and *Agatha*. And in *Straight Time* he leaned on a kind of screen presence, strong and silent, that he doesn't have. (He does have his own kind.) In *Kramer* his role is uncomplicated, a man of likes and dislikes carefully arranged to make him both individual and "average"; but Hoffman burns through the givens into the unknowns even in this "average" man. His playing with his child; his patience, true and enforced, with his child; his "office" affection for his boss; his genuine affection for the woman in the apartment below who helps him; his fight for his child, in an emergency operating room and in court—all these and more stab deeper than mere credibility to the community that good acting provides. Hoffman unites us with him and with one another, tacitly but well. And all of this is based on a furious energy, as it was in *Lenny* and *Agatha*: what I'd call the drive of a talented small man. It's an energy that both James Cagney and Edward G. Robinson had in their own ways, an energy that probably has its source in psychic compensation but, in gifted men, it quickly becomes authentic in itself.

To continue the old-star comparison: Meryl Streep, the wife, is today's Bette Davis, or could be if there were now an equivalent film industry. Streep is first an actress, a much less mannered and self-centered actress than Davis but with Davis's qualities of unconventional beauty and of reliance on acting as much as on starriness—the woman star who really acts and does it in differing roles. Think of Streep as the airy southern rich lawyer in *The Seduction of Joe Tynan* and as the supermarket worker in *The Deer Hunter*, sitting in the stock room stamping prices on items and crying softly. Age allowing, Davis could have done things like that.

But I vastly prefer Streep. In *Kramer* she plays a somewhat neurotic woman whose dissatisfaction with marriage drives her out, leaving her son, ten minutes into the film and who returns—about a film-hour later, I'd guess—when she has herself in hand and wants to reclaim her son. Obviously the brief appearance at the beginning had to be strong enough to make her a continuing presence and to give her a foothold after she returns. Streep handles this difficulty easily, by concentrating on the truth of the woman and by having the talent for that concentration. I've been waiting for some years now—nastily, I guess—for Streep to make a false move on stage or screen in widely varied characters. I'm still waiting. So much for nastiness.

There's a traditional role in the theater dubbed "Charles, His Friend," which of course has a female counterpart—the confidant(e) of the protagonist. Jane Alexander seems born to be an extraordinarily good "Charles." I've seen her in a lot of plays and films, romantic or strident or maturely feminine roles, and in all of them she has lacked sex and shine—central and centering power. What she can supply is intelligence and, within domestic limits, reliable sensitivity. She has never been better than as the woman downstairs in *Kramer*—no standard soap-opera understanding "Charles" even by the new soap-opera standards, a reinforcer of the drama though not one of its pivots.

Howard Duff is a late bloomer—re-bloomer, really. He reappeared (for me, anyway), after long absence, as the family doctor in *A Wedding*. Here, as Hoffman's lawyer in the vicious custody fight, he enriches the screen. With gray wings on his head and an elegant gray moustache, with juicy voice and silver-headed cane, prowling the courtroom or sitting in a bar with an absolutely apt tumbler of neat whiskey before him, Duff embodies the Irish-American histrion who, in life even more than in the theater, has done much to brighten the landscape.

Even the small part of a woman in Hoffman's advertising agency who spends a night with him is well cast. The attractive Jobeth Williams has a comic scene to play naked: on the way to the bathroom she encounters Hoffman's small son who is supposed to be asleep. Williams does it wittily.

And this brings us to a recurrent mystery/miracle. All through film history, some directors who have nothing else in common have been able to get good performances from children. I don't mean from child stars like Rooney, Garland, Temple, O'Brien—small monsters who apparently were professional prenatally, I mean directors who got good performances from children under 10 who never did anything else: Benoit-Levy (*La Maternelle*, *Ballerina*), De Sica (*Bicycle Thief*), Truffaut (*The Wild Child*), Ritt (*Conrack*) to name a few. Now Benton's name must be added. Justin Henry, about six when the film was started, had not acted before. With Benton's help, and surely with Hoffman's and Streep's help, the boy goes through as wide a range of scenes as he could possibly be asked for, and he is true, absolutely true, every moment. He's enchanting. And the mystery of how it's done—which probably begins with a very acute casting sense, a "smell" of possible response and imagination—that mystery goes on.

Nestor Almendros, a master, did the cinematography, but he didn't need to. Outside of the exquisite opening sequence, which begins with a burnished close-up of Streep, the cinematography could have been done adequately by any competent man. The music is mostly a Vivaldi mandolin concerto which is "planted" in the film by a shot of two New York street musicians playing it and which dresses the sound-track neatly. (Did you know that, in nice weather, Fifth Avenue at night is now a series of recital halls? In one shop doorway after another, soloists and various small groups play, for contributions.)

Benton's direction must first be praised for his choice of actors and his collaboration with them. This is his first serious film: previously he directed *Bad Company* and *The Late Show*, both heavily comic. Here he's dealing with heartbreak, even though it's seen through a temper of quick comedy, and his hand is right. He does well with the interiors of scenes, the movement of actors and camera, the internal cuts. My one quarrel is with the overall editing, the joining of sequences. I'm always conscious of his cutting away for time-lapses, beginning with an early insert of garbage trucks—after Streep walks out—to tell us that a night has passed. And too often, at the end of the sequence, Benton cuts or fades to black. This device, once common, is now relatively rare and should stay rare. No one wants to be jolted to consciousness of the screen itself while watching a film, unless that moment of black, that consciousness of the screen's existence, is itself part of the film, as it sometimes has been in Bergman. I can't remember any instance of black in *Kramer* where the film couldn't simply have cut ahead to the next sequence, perhaps holding the opening shot of the new sequence a few frames longer to let us get our bearings.

But Benton has made a good vernacular film that, because of its acting and its urban detail more than its story or writing, is what I'd call a time-capsule work. Compare it with Woody Allen's *Manhattan* which—funny lines, lush photography, and all—made an attempt at a large embrace of New York, an attempt to enclose its current styles and behavior in a paean to the city; and failed because of the script's flickering vision and the cast's inadequacies (except Meryl Streep, who was in that one, too). Benton's film makes no attempt to sing the city, but it fastens so tight a grip on some city lives that the city they live in can't escape. Put *Kramer vs. Kramer*, not *Manhattan*, in the time capsule, and if it is dug up centuries from now, it will report some truth about the city today—flavor, quirk, pain, and maneuver, and the wry comedy in which they all seem to be set.

Places in the Heart

(October 1, 1984)

Christian belief is both the foundation rock and the irony of *Places in the Heart*. At the start we hear a hymn as we see houses and streets in Waxahachie, Texas, 1935. At the end, in a symbolic scene, almost all the characters of the film are seated in church, taking communion and murmuring "Praise God" to the sound of another hymn. In between we have seen greed, cruelty, murder, and natural disaster, all of them interwoven with lives of genuine faith.

That faith and its contradictions are what Robert Benton remembers most forcefully about Waxahachie, where he was born in 1932. After a varyingly effective career as a screenwriter and director—his best work was *Kramer vs. Kramer*—he has made this picture about the place where he grew up. Still, filled with reminiscent detail though it is, it can't be strictly autobiographical: Benton is six or seven years younger than the boy in the picture, and in any case that boy couldn't have seen everything that happens—wouldn't have understood it, anyway.

Several story strands are followed: the struggle of a suddenly widowed young woman (Sally Field) to raise her two small children; the love affair between her sister's husband (Ed Harris) and another man's wife (Amy Madigan); the travail of a black Depression vagrant (Danny Glover). I don't argue with the truth of these stories—how could I? But I note that Benton has hampered his telling of them with filmmaking clichés.

The main story is of Sally Field and family. All of them are having lunch one day when some men come for her husband, the sheriff, to take care of minor trouble. He gets up, straps on his pistol, and says to his wife: "I won't be gone long." So we know he's going to be killed. (Especially since the role is cast with a lesser actor: a "name" actor would not be expendable.) To pay her way, Field puts in her first cotton crop. She is told that she must get her cotton to the gin by a certain day or lose the money she needs and that she can't possibly do it. Fields sets her toy-bulldog jaw, and we know we're going to see a montage of hardships, bleeding hands, and so on, but that the job is going to be done. Madigan goes to a party at the home of her lover and his wife, and when Madigan walks into a darkened room, we know her lover is going to be waiting for her. When the Ku Klux Klan forces Glover to leave Field's farm where he has become a beloved aid to her and her children, we fear that he will walk off into the night like Paul Muni and Bette Davis – and he does.

And that usually superb cinematographer, Nestor Almendros, here leans on the pretty. The result is less the softening vision of memory than the softness of the calendar illustrator.

Most of the acting is good, some of it better. Field gives all possible tenderness and gumption to the brave-little-woman role. Harris and Madigan do what they can with the illicit lovers, but the characters are undeveloped. (Where are the big parts that Madigan deserves, as she proved in *Love Child*?) Lane Smith plays intelligently the town's sanctimonious banker. Better than the rest, in some measure because the roles are better, are John Malkovich, nervous and proud as Field's blind boarder, and Glover, sweet and strong and resigned, as the harassed black man.

Benton's best accomplishment is his vision of the basic conflict in the town's life: between Christianity and human limitation. But all the elements in his film move either to neat uplift or neat poignancy, and his very familiarity with film conventions makes him skid on triteness while he tries to travel toward truth.

Angi Vera

(January 19, 1980)

Angi Vera is a Hungarian film about a young woman named Vera Angi – the order of names is, as you doubtless know, the reverse of English so the effect of the title in Hungarian is not quasi bureaucratic, like *Lacombe Lucien*, it's simply normal. Simplicities and normalties are the theme of this succinct film. Made in a communist country, it nonetheless examines the way that a totalitarian government can shape the ethics of a growing person. If there is such a thing as grace with which we are born (saving only original sin), then this is a story of the corruption of that grace, or at least its re-definition. The device under which such a film can be made is a familiar one in communist countries: the story is set in the past under a superseded regime. "How bad things were back there in 1948," this picture can seem to say, "under the cult of personality." There are two reasons for making historical works: one is to show how much things have changed, the other is to show how much they haven't. Hungarian and other viewers can decide for themselves which was the reason here.

The director is Pál Gábor who was born in 1932 – thus only 16 in the time of *Angi Vera* – who made his first feature in 1968. I've seen one previous film of Gábor's *Horizon* (1971), and I remember one moment vividly. The subject was adolescent disaffection. The scene is the manager's office in the factory where the seventeen-year-old protagonist has been summoned on charges of laxity. The manager, a middle-aged veteran of war and revolution, tells the slouching boy that a lot of people died to give him his opportunities. The boy shrugs and says something like "Who asked them to?" The manager can't help slamming the boy alongside the face and knocking him to the floor, realizing even as he does it that his action is counterproductive and the situation tragic.

Inquiry into moral status in the new society is thus not a new theme in Gábor. The screenplay of *Angi Vera*, adapted by Gábor from a novel by Endre Vészi, begins with a statement by Vera at a meeting and ends, virtually, with another statement by her at a later meeting. In the first meeting she is a nurse's aid—a scrubber—in a hospital. Unlike the cautious co-workers at this political assembly, she rises to voice objections to some hospital conditions when the local party leader asks for comments. Her frankness pleases the leadership, and she is sent to a political re-education center for training and for better employment. In that re-education, her independence is subtly transmuted into fealty. Her action in the meeting at the end *seems* the same sort of honesty as her action at the beginning: that, precisely, is the great corruption.

The shape of the film is perfect, which is to say that it does what it has to do without waste or wobble; and what it has to do is to touch profundity through concise plot motions. The characters are sharp and immediate: the ex-miner who drinks too much because of the contrast between what he fought for and what his future holds; the political teacher, an indoctrinated but guileless young man, who falls under Vera's well-meaning axe; a healthy, stubborn woman trying to advance without losing herself; an older woman whose proselytizing of Vera has some suggestion of a madam recruiting a girlie. Gábor's direction matches the script in taciturnity, yet the texture has the symbiosis that is often visible in films from Eastern Europe, the persistence of the older culture in the new order. The café to which these Marxists resort is, in look and in its life, pure Franz Josef.

I have only two substantive criticisms. A number of interior scenes are shot, by Lajos Koltai, with a kind of burnt umber overlay that makes a sentimental/nostalgic atmosphere. I couldn't see why. Second, the casting of Vera. She is played by the doe-eyed Veronika Papp who never does anything overtly false but never seems what she is said to be. We are told of the horrors that Vera and her mother underwent before they arrived in the hospital where the mother died and Vera was given work. It's hard to believe it of the delicate Papp. A sturdier girl, more peasant than displaced university student—a Hungarian Eva Mattes—would have given more presence to the character and more poignancy to the way she is used. Still, *Angi Vera* is a small barb of a picture that brings after it a long thread of truth.

Our Hitler: A Film From Germany

(February 2, 1980)

The most important fact now about Adolf Hitler is that he was good—in the eyes of many, many millions of people. To think of him and his friends as gangsters who took over an innocent country (which is what Brecht says in his bad play *The Resistible Rise of Arturo Ui*) is to miss or conceal this important fact. Most people in two nations, Germany and Austria, along with plenty of sympathizers elsewhere, thought that Hitler was a rigorous, inspiring god who dispensed good. Kenneth Burke said, when he reviewed *Mein Kampf* on its American publication, "Above all, I believe, we must make it apparent that Hitler appeals by relying on a bastardization of fundamentally religious patterns of thought." The Hitlerian zealots, party members or not, believed that they were doing right.

If that point is missed, if Hitler is seen only as a drooling homicidal maniac at the head of millions of other drooling maniacs, the enormity of what happened is slighted. It is tucked away, wrapped, disposed of. If the point is grasped, then caverns of mystery and despair and fright, great and appropriate, open within us.

It is this hardest of horrors—the fact that Hitler was *loved* by millions, that he was not a murderous careerist who struck it lucky but the embodiment of vast frustrations and hates and desires who was adored for his incarnation of them, that the people who adored him were not Martians but members of the human race to whom we all are tied—it is this horror that Hans-Jürgen Syberberg addresses in his seven-hour work, *Our Hitler: A Film from Germany*. Please note: *this is not a documentary*. I emphasize this point because it was not clear when the film was shown, in three installments, on the BBC last summer: I was there at the time and read reviews that treated it as an oddly failed documentary. The picture has no smallest ambition toward historical summary or completeness: only in the last of its four sections are there even a few feet of newsreel film (although there is much interweaving of recorded historical voices throughout). *Our Hitler* is a work of the imagination—a vaulting, fearless, sometimes foolish, sometimes bloated but essentially vigorous imagination.

This film, though mammoth, is the last part of a Syberberg trilogy. I haven't seen the other two parts, one on Ludwig II of Bavaria, who appears as a puppet and a child in this film, and one on Karl May, the German author of Westerns who was a Hitler favorite. I've seen one previous Syberberg film, *The Confessions of Winifred Wagner* which was condensed here from its original five hours to 104 minutes and was subsequently shown on PBS. This *was* a documentary, staggering: and its chief theme, the relation between Wagner and Hitler, obviously has bearing on the new work.

Our Hitler is symbolic, figurative. It was made in a studio with a dozen actors including Syberberg's small daughter. All the men play several parts; several of them play Hitler at different times. The settings are abstractions or bald film studio or junk-piled film studio; many of them have slide projections behind them which change during a sequence; much of the lighting is deliberately theatrical. Syberberg sometimes moves a single actor or two through a group of mannequins, sometimes uses superb puppets of Hitler and friends together with actors. Each of the film's four sections consists of a number of episodes, connected only in overall theme, each a kind of rhapsody on an aspect of that theme. Music, mostly Wagner, flows throughout, as do those voices of actual persons, all identified. Syberberg's actors speak German, which—like the historical recordings—is subtitled, and there is much voice-over narration done in English, well.

This leads to another important point. Syberberg, a uniquely gifted filmmaker as such, is also a writer of considerable power. From the subtitles of his script and the English narrative sections, I got a feeling of size, strength, metaphor, and forthrightness perfectly consonant with his visual gift—in fact, his gifts match so well, both in strengths and overextensions, that they can't be considered separately. The film opens with the camera moving out into the starry firmament; it might be, in itself, the opening of a sci-fi film, but the *words* accompanying the shot convince us that what we are about to see is a grave matter of human history seen under the eye of eternity.

The four sections of *Our Hitler* are called "The Grail," "A German Dream," "The End of Winter's Tale," and "We Children of Hell." Intermission after the second section. (I gather that the work was designed for serial showing on TV: it was financed by German, British, and French television.) I can't see that the four sections are intrinsically separate: the materials seem interchangeable, and the whole film is cumulative only in terms of further exploration, further imaginative use of factual materials, not in chronology or dramatic growth.

As a schematic sample, I'll quote a bit of the synopsis in the program. After the starry opening:

> A little girl dressed in black, a figure recurring in the four parts of the film, is playing with dolls, puppets of Ludwig and of Hitler hanging from a gallows. She rises and wanders off into the distance with a toy dog that bears the face of Hitler. Against a Caligari projection she lays the toy Hitler in a cradle. The devil appears, bends over the cradle and turns into a black eagle.
>
> A circus director announces the greatest show on earth, the rehearsal of the end of the world. In a monologue in the Black Maria (Edison's first film studio and symbol of the world of our inner projections), the puppet of Ludwig II asks, "Where would we be without this guilt?" from Jesus to Hitler, the Jews . . . . One by one all the actors come on, as in a circus, in various roles: as audience, as Hitler: Hitler as painter, as Nero, Frankenstein, Chaplin.

These are a few of the joints of the armature. Omitted are the language, the sweep of the music, and, above all, the images. The torrent of images that Syberberg puts before us is overwhelming: they are wonderfully conceived, individual, strong and—through the first two sections at least—breathtaking in their incessant freshness.

The sample above gives some idea of the quality of the progress, but little of the range, the ruthless insistence on German guilt and also on the non-innocence of others: how so many, other than Jews, wanted Hitler before and since. (Jews are not left untouched: for instance, treating the postwar years, Syberberg reminds us that some Jews in Hollywood, some of them Hitler refugees, supported the persecutions of McCarthy.)

But the sample above shows one major element: the film's self-consciousness as film, its film references. For instance, at one point Hitler (played in this scene by Peter Kern) is in uniform with a chalked M on his back, turns, sinks to his knees, and speaks Peter Lorre's wonderful closing lines in Fritz Lang's film. Later an actor speaks a passage presumably written by Hitler's private film-projectionist, telling us that Hitler, who had been a voracious film-buff, would see only newsreels after the war started; he looked at them every night before they were publicly released as if they were daily rushes from a picture he was shooting. "He was the greatest filmmaker in the world," says the projectionist.

Hitler's valet, too, and Himmler's masseur, and Himmler and Goebbels (only a glimpse of Goering) are dealt with. Many others. If I had to sum up the film's theme—which is risky, because its being is as much textural as it is thematic—it would be that *Our Hitler* says to Germany: "Professions of anti-Nazism today don't settle things. Renouncing Hitler and his works is not enough. We made him because we loved him." To the world *Our Hitler* says: "Anti-Germanism won't do. Look into your secret heart." That is the core of the most magnificent scene. Hitler's spirit, in Roman toga, rises from the grave of Wagner and, played here by Heinz Schubert, he relentlessly presses home, in an iron voice, his charge: he was wanted. He cannot be denied. He may still be wanted.

The film has excesses, numerous and sometimes silly. An imagination that keeps leaping for such a long time is almost certain to stumble occasionally, and Syberberg certainly does. One silly moment comes early: as a proof that butchery is in the world, is not confined to Hitlerism, he cites Erich von Stroheim's difficulties with Hollywood moguls. Even in a film-centered film, this is ridiculous. A sequence near the end in which a speaker tells the Hitler puppet that he has conquered posthumously—Germany today is snared in money-placidity and the Wandering Jew whom he hated is now settled in Israel—is worse than ridiculous. Syberberg's sheer pictorial invention flags in the third and particularly the fourth parts. We get a sequence in which an actor sits at a desk and reads a lengthy monologue on Hitler as a phenomenon of thousand-year German history, while slide projections change behind the speaker. After about six hours of film-watching, the sequence is not tolerable.

And the final moments get soft. What has been a salvation throughout the film, even at its worst, is its unsentimentality. But near the close, the text gets cautionary and explicit: the sound-track quotes the one music I hoped not to hear, the "Ode to Joy" from Beethoven's Ninth; the little girl (who wears bits of film as a headdress) clasps her hands in prayer and looks upward. The very last thing we hear is the trumpet call from *Fidelio* that, in the opera, announces rescue. It contravenes the film.

If all of *Our Hitler* were at its highest level, which is inconceivable, it would still exceed the psycho-physiological ability of a viewer. Seven hours! After the first two parts, at intermission, I was elated. Despite some shortcomings, those first parts are lofty, immense, unsparing, majestic. Watching the second half is a matter of finding the bits that are up to the first half. But you can edit this film yourself: see the first half, plus as much as you like. It's the first half that will live for me. Syberberg knew that he could not explain Hitler, but at its best his film contributes to our understanding of the impossibility of explaining Hitler: which increases our understanding of, at least, the size of what Hitler did and still threatens.

One closing irony. This film that reminds us of German horrors is itself "A Film from Germany." And Germany is today without question the most vital and innovative filmmaking country in the world. The so-called New German Cinema includes Fassbinder, Wenders, Handke, Schlöndorff, and Herzog. (One of the life-size cutouts in some scenes is of Klaus Kinski in Herzog's *Aguirre*.) High in the ranks must be placed the forty-four-year-old Syberberg. If it's argued that the West German film renaissance is due to relative ease of financing there, the right reply is to repeat the argument. The present subsidizing of film is only the latest aspect of the old German tradition of subsidizing theater and opera and other arts, more generously than almost any other country. German generosity to the arts is itself part of the irony and the heartache.

Parsifal

(February 14, 1983)

If you know Wagner's *Parsifal* and if you have seen Hans-Jürgen Syberberg's *Our Hitler: A Film from Germany*, you will not be surprised that Syberberg chose to make a film of Wagner's work; nor will you be surprised by the director's general approach. But this *Parsifal*, among its fascinations, does have a surprising new aspect.

Syberberg's obsession with Wagner is now familiar. The first film of his to be shown in the U. S. was a 104-minute condensation of a five-hour interview, made for German TV, with Winifred Wagner, the composer's daughter-in-law. Wagner, musically and otherwise, is present in several other Syberberg films. One of the most vivid images in postwar German cinema is in *Our Hitler*: the toga-clad Hitler rising from a grave that has a stone marked RW. And in Syberberg's view, *Parsifal* must be the most representative of Wagner's works, the most beautiful/silly, exalted/pretentious, noble/vicious—all the contradictions that Syberberg patently finds in German character and behavior. The score, which (I think) he uses uncut, is a succession of marvels that coalesce into a grand marvel; yet the libretto, or poem as Wagner called it, is less than completely cogent. The atmosphere is as spiritual as anything in Wagner; yet he explicitly intended the work as an Aryan, anti-Semitic allegory. (More contradiction on that point: the first conductor was a Jew.) *Parsifal* idealizes again Wagner's view of male innocence beset by the temptations of woman (Tannhäuser enslaved within the Venusberg, Siegfried cutting open the armor of the sleeping Brünnhilde and exclaiming naively, "*Das ist kein Mann!*"); yet the Parsifal-Kundry encounter in Act Two is one of the most perceptive rites-of-sexual-passage in drama. (Kundry entices Parsifal by speaking of his mother—more than a decade before Freud.) Writing from Bayreuth in 1889, Bernard Shaw said:

> And that long kiss of Kundry's from which he learns so much is one of those pregnant simplicities which stare the world in the face for centuries and yet are never pointed out except by great men.

No wonder, then, that Syberberg, only the latest in a long line of German artists who have loved and loathed their country, should respond to *Parsifal*. Still a question persists, one that leads to the surprise mentioned earlier. Why did he film a work that was already famous in another medium? His previous films have been entirely his creations. Here he began with a new recording of *Parsifal*, and, except for bits of the music rehearsals under the credits and a few snatches of random voices after the finish, he simply supplied "visuals" to accompany that recording. Why?

The answer begins to be suggested by a statement of his:

> Just as the composer was inspired by a legendary evocation of the Middle Ages in his desire to express ideas which were of his own time, I am basing my approach on the fact that the work is one hundred years old and that I can therefore describe its significance throughout time.

Ascribe the last phrase to the energy that an artist needs in order to do anything at all—no one knowingly creates just for next week—and his approach becomes clearer while we watch the film. This view of *Parsifal*, as a classic text chosen by a later artist for contemporary definition, puts Syberberg's film in a *theater* tradition, not a cinematic one. That is the surprise. His film derives, fundamentally, from Adolphe Appia.

Appia (1862-1928), the Swiss theater visionary, had revolutionary views of production that have hugely influenced Western theater in the twentieth century. His strongest love was for Wagner; all his life he worked on designs for Wagnerian productions. Few of them were ever realized—he participated in only six actual productions of any kind in his entire career—but they changed the theater's ways of seeing. Appia was shocked by the old-fashioned staging and design at Bayreuth, which had been prescribed by the composer; he wrote:

> Wagner made but one essential reform. Through the medium of music he conceived a dramatic action whose center of gravity lay inside the characters and which at the same time could be completely *expressed* for the hearer . . . . But he did not know how to make his production form—his *mise en scène*—agree with his adopted dramatic form.

In 1892 Appia sent a package of designs to Wagner's widow, Cosima, the guardian of the Bayreuth shrine. She returned the package unopened, but Appia continued to dream-design for a theatrical revolution of Wagner that would fit the revolution in the music. He got only three Wagnerian production chances, half of his whole practical career: one of them was *Tristan and Isolde* for Toscanini at La Scala in 1923, and neither of the others was *Parsifal*. But his designs for *Parsifal* figure prominently in the treasury of his work.

Syberberg's film does not in any detail come from Appia, but ideationally it is the result of an intent that began with Appia and has since flourished. Appia was the first conceiver of productions who recreated the inside of his head on stage, rather than reproduce the world outside classically or romantically or realistically. What he wanted to reify on stage was his imaginative response to a work. That, exactly, is Syberberg's basic intent, though of course his response is his own, nothing like Appia's.

Syberberg puts before us, not just a film of the opera, however symbolic or impressionist, but absolutely everything that *Parsifal* evokes in him: about art and politics and history, about film and theater, about the possible exorcism of the demon Wagner himself. While the rich, almost extravagant music floods our hearing, Syberberg feeds our eyes with as much as he can crystallize of what that music has done to him.

The *Parsifal* story gets told well enough, but this is not a consistent eccentric version, as a modern-dress or science-fiction version, for example, might be. We watch a cascade of connections, the play of associations hauled out by other associations. Some of the elements in the film are easily understood, perhaps too easily. When Gurnemanz leads Parsifal to the castle in Act One, they go backward through German history as represented by an alley of flags, beginning with the swastika. Behind Klingsor in Act Two, the watchtower of a concentration camp can be seen. The waxworks-museum heads of Marx and Nietzsche and Wagner are sometimes part of the décor; so is a three-dimensional facsimile of André Gill's famous caricature—Wagner inside a huge human ear, hammering away; at one point Parsifal is seen against a ridge that turns out to be Wagner's face in horizontal profile. Amfortas's wound is an entity quite separate from his body, so that it seems a possession more than an affliction. Syberberg represents it by a thick folded napkin on a pedestal next to the ailing king's couch: in the napkin is a bleeding gash. (It suggests a vulva. The wound, which he got from Kundry, may be a figure for carnal seduction.)

Most of the film's actions and details, however, must be taken only as phenomena that affect us or don't. Two of the performers we see are also singers on the soundtrack; most roles are mimed with lip-sync. That in itself is neither novel nor troublesome. But Syberberg chooses to have Parsifal mimed first by a stripling adolescent boy, then, after Kundry's kiss, the role is mimed by an even younger girl, with Reiner Goldberg's strong *Heldentenor* coming out of each Parsifal in turn. At the end the boy and girl embrace chastely. I don't believe that this device "means" anything: it's intended to jar preconceptions and provoke new scrutiny, not to fill any pattern, Freudian or otherwise. Dolls are suddenly used as characters, then discarded. The Flower Maidens are posed immobile against rocks while they sing of caressing Parsifal. The penultimate image is a skull, crowned with a bishop's miter, lying on the ground. The last image is of Kundry, with her arms and long hair embracing a small wooden model of what I take to be the Bayreuth Festspielhaus. And much more, all of it intended only to represent Syberberg's visions, for us to use if we can or will.

Contrapuntally, as in *Our Hitler*, Syberberg insists on a kind of Brechtian candor, to keep us aware that fabrication is in process. Everything is played against a black cyclorama, on which slides are often projected. The lighting of a scene often changes while we watch. Almost all the scenery is meant to look like scenery. Sometimes we see the board floor of the studio. Near the end, projected on the cyclorama behind a scene, is some film footage of the conductor, Armin Jordan, shot during the recording session.

Yet in the midst of this torrent of images combined with "exposé" of image-making, most of the acting performances are quite traditional. The Gurnemanz is much younger than usual, but he is the poem's Gurnemanz, beautifully played by Robert Lloyd. (Lloyd also sings the role beautifully. The other singer who appears is Aage Haugland, the Klingsor.) Amfortas is feelingly mimed by the conductor, Armin Jordan, to the good baritone of Wolfgang Schone. Yvonne Minton sings Kundry powerfully, while that miraculous actress Edith Clever mimes this problematic role with an intensity that holds it in fiery focus.

Jordan, who conducts in many European opera houses, here leads the Monte Carlo Philharmonic Orchestra and the Prague Philharmonic Choir. The text is sung in German, with subtitles. The recording is, fortunately, in Dolby stereo. Syberberg uses the "old" screen size, one-third wider than high.

The most significant previous film of an opera that I know is Bergman's *The Magic Flute*, and a comparison with Syberberg brings out a paradox. To Bergman, Mozart's opera was a *cinematic* challenge: he combined a conventional stage performance with the presence of the audience and with backstage data to create a purely filmic locus for the work. (Coincidence: backstage, during the intermission, Sarastro studies *Parsifal*.) Bergman, a veteran of the theater, transmuted a theater work into a true film. On the other hand, Syberberg, who has never worked in theater as far as I know, strives here to make film into theater. Distant from Appia yet evolved from him, Syberberg puts his "definitive" theater performance on film because, in several senses, it would not be possible in a theater. Aided by designers of exceptional talent, he has created a sweepingly personal vision of *Parsifal* that places his film in a theatrical line—a director's "statement" of a classic. With a camera that is almost always slowly moving, in or away, panning or travelling, this is much less like pure cinema than a superb TV film of a production in a hypothetical theater.

Syberberg's final comment on *Parsifal*—possibly it's where he started—is the fact that he filmed it at all. *Parsifal* has a unique history. Beginning with the première at Bayreuth in 1882, it was zealously guarded as a sacred work, to be performed only in the hallowed atmosphere of Bayreuth, not on profane stages elsewhere. Except for some concert versions, this held true for twenty-one years. Then the Metropolitan in New York took advantage of the inexact international copyright law to produce it, despite German cries of profanation, on Christmas Eve, 1903. (A chartered Parsifal Limited train came from Chicago; the *New York Evening Telegram* published a *Parsifal* extra.) Other "profanations" followed in other cities, here and abroad, until 1914 when the Bayreuth copyright expired and *Parsifal* became unrestrictedly available to all opera houses. And now, a hundred years on, Syberberg makes a mere film of it, something that can be shown anywhere at any time.

But this fact, too, holds a contradiction. By making his film, Syberberg has utterly destroyed any remaining fake pieties about *Parsifal*. At the same time he has tried, through belief in the pertinence of his vision of the work, to consecrate it anew, for the protean, present-and-future theater of film.

My Brilliant Career

(February 9, 1980)

Australia! What a resounding plunk that name arouses in the filmgoer's breast. The plunk has lately been deepened by a campaign for Australian pictures, headed by something called *Newsfront*, a clumsy item about an early Aussie newsreel company, and two duds by Peter Weir, *Picnic at Hanging Rock* and *The Last Wave*. Apparently Weir is being hustled to become for his country what Andrzej Wajda is for Poland. I think Weir is well on the way: he's equally arty and imitative.

But—a big, cheery but. Here is a lovely film from Australia, a film of wiry, sensitive, humorous strength. *My Brilliant Career* is based on a 1901 novel of that name, unknown to me, by a woman named Miles Franklin. All the principal members of the filmmaking team—except the excellent cinematographer, Don McAlpine—are women: the producer, Margaret Fink, the costume and production designers, Anna Senior and Luciana Arrighi, the production supervisor, Jane Scott, the screenwriter, Eleanor Witcombe, and last but possibly best, the director, Gillian Armstrong. I can't remember so female a list of credits on any feature film, and we're not yet at the stage of sexual equality where the phenomenon can, or should be, ignored. Hurrah—down around the globe—for them all.

And I haven't even mentioned the bearer of their combined standards, the principal member of the cast, Judy Davis. A separate, ringing hurrah for her. How straightaway and completely winning she is. Davis plays a budding teenager out in the Australian bush in 1897, the daughter of a well-bred woman and a lower-class farmer, a family scratching a livelihood in grim, windstormed surroundings. The daughter is a stubborn dreamer and aspirer. She won't settle for the life available or even for a "good" marriage that would lift her out of that life. She wants to make her own life, somehow, she wants to discover herself. This hunger—internationally familiar and perenially important—is conveyed by Davis with a sureness that shows, in musical terms, absolute pitch. She has talent, intense and trenchant, something like Jane Fonda's: she and the role become absolutely congruent, as with Meryl Streep. Her performance is full of unconventional yet absolutely right "choices" in reading and movement and interplay; and she brings all the details into focus—which is to say she makes them all disappear—through her force of spirit.

The film starts with Davis starting her autobiographical novel, *My Brilliant Career*, in a school notebook on a farmhouse table. At the end she mails it to a Scottish publisher. (A final note tells us that it was published in 1901, but there is no note about the author's difficulties in living an independent life thereafter.) As she writes, the heroine's adventures take her to stay with her wealthy maternal grandmother, a visit from there with wealthy neighbors including a marriageable young man, proposals and refusals of marriage, a teaching job with scrubby kids, and a final resolve to make her own way. She "very nearly" loves the young man—attractively played by Sam Neill, a sort of young James Mason—but she doesn't want to tag her life with a Mrs. label. She acts out of resolve, out of obligation to herself and to the secrets that made her different.

The role could have slipped over into nuisance, a cartoon of the headstrong, poetic madcap that Katharine Hepburn sometimes played forty-five years ago. But there's no archness in Davis, only—fundamentally—awe: awe of the fire and dissatisfaction in her and of the responsibilities they entail. And all of this is thrust along with high-spirited delight.

Surely collaborating with Davis, and meriting the same hopes for the future, is the director, Gillian Armstrong. Davis was trained entirely in Australia; Armstrong, except for a six-month tour of observation elsewhere, likewise: at film schools in Melbourne and Sydney and with local companies. Her work here speaks for her training as well as her talent. She knows every shot she needs and how to get it, with minimal fuss, without eccentricity, but with flavor. One or two moments, like the reappearance of Neill at the end, could have had more impact, but on the whole this is smooth, unhackneyed direction. And every sequence shines with Armstrong's sympathy, her understanding of all the characters. She stacks no cards, not even with the silly-ass visiting Englishman, and she deals fairly with the difficulties that the heroine's determination makes for others.

My only real complaint about this film is affectionate. Everyone keeps commiserating with the Davis character because she isn't pretty. Beats me. I thought her highly appealing in a touching, funny, intelligent way, and McAlpine's camera does nothing to glamorize her. McAlpine also knows how to handle inarguable beauty (Wendy Hughes, as Davis's aunt), wonderful "character" faces, the rawness of the open country, and the sanctuary of the Anglicized wealthy homes.

No large statements about expectations from Australia on the basis of one very good film. But at least now there has been one very good film.

The Left-Handed Woman

(March 8, 1980)

"The soundtrack invented silence," said Robert Bresson. It's proved yet again in Peter Handke's The Left-Handed Woman, which he directed in 1977. The woman's silence is a chief component and must be audible. She isn't mute like Elisabet in Persona: she is just quiet most of the time. Her quiet affects the voices of those who speak to her, except her child, the person to whom she responds most readily and warmly. Her quiet affects the sound of the railroad trains below her house.

Handke's novel of that name was published before the film was made—in the U.S., Farrar, Straus & Giroux did it in 1978 after its complete appearance in one issue of the New Yorker—but Handke said recently that he conceived the work as a screenplay and wrote it first as such. Subsequently, with apposite changes, he made it into narrative before filming started.

An exceptional sequence. How many serious writers think of material in film terms? Most screen writing is done for hire, by writers of more or less talent who adapt someone else's play or novel or develop someone else's idea. The amount of serious writing done originally and impulsively for the screen, so far as it shows up there anyway, is minuscule.

The woman, unnamed, lives with her husband and eight-year-old son in a Paris suburb. All are German. The husband works in Paris and, at the beginning, comes back from a business trip to Finland. He is glad to be home with his wife, whom he loves more and more; takes her out for dinner that night; stays the night with her in a hotel above the restaurant so that they can be only with each other.

Going to the airport to meet him, she is enclosed in silence. We have seen her in it from the start, sitting at a window sewing while her son reads a school composition aloud. Her very first words are not spoken until the morning after the hotel, and they are "voice-over" on the soundtrack. The first words she actually addresses to her husband, after their night of marital reunion, are to tell him that she wants him to leave, to leave her alone.

In most of the film she is alone. Her child is with her, she moves about the neighborhood and encounters friends, her husband comes to visit her and the boy. But her being is solitary. She has gone into silence as to another place where she can be visited or telephoned but which is nevertheless away. She has to be by herself: to *be*, by herself.

No overt reason is given for her decision to ask her husband to leave, no quarrel, no cooling—on his part, quite the reverse. (This last causes his outbursts of anger when he visits later, which she understands and accepts.) Nor is it a modish quest for identity: she seems to know who she is. Nor is it a "retreat" from the world through aversion to it; presumably she has withdrawn in order to reconsider engagement. The world laps at her, like waves at a rock: a young woman with a baby whom she sees recurrently in the streets; an old couple sitting happily on a bench in their small garden; the games of her son and his chum. Contradictions abound: a man passes her on horseback, when she is out for a walk, riding along a ravine edge under which a passing train roars; her house is lovely in a grim neighborhood. (It's a house that Handke lived in for a while, in Clamart. The novel is set outside a German city, where Handke was living when he got the idea for the work, but the film is set outside Paris, where he was living when it was made.) There is no romance of old Paris here; it is old-and-ugliest-new Paris that surrounds her, puzzles, attracts, and freezes her.

What does she want? It would debase the film if she uttered a word about it. Still it seems clear she doesn't want, will not get, change: in herself or anything else. The film goes through three months—March, April, and into May—by which time she gives a small party. What she has wanted, it seems, is the power, the orientation, *to go on exactly as before.* Margaret Fuller said, after some contemplation, "I accept the universe." When Thomas Carlyle heard this, he said, "Gad, she'd better." For Handke's woman, her three months of inner solitude serve as her simple but necessary Carlyle.

The tension in the film—not suspense, of which there is none, but surface tension like the top of a too-full glass—comes from several strong elements. First, there is Handke's understanding of the people, what the actors must concentrate on, what they must omit. Then there is his eye, wonderful, wonderfully aided by Robby Müller, the cinematographer of Wim Wenders's films. (Wenders was the producer of this film.)

Handke, with Müller's help, frequently uses lighting that suggests Vermeer: the window on the world, the window *as* the world, affording light that touches the interior gently. This Vermeer-like lighting works in two ways: a tension between Out There and In Here; and a tension between this classicism of light and the heterodox drama of the whole.

Also, Handke electrifies space, physical space, with charges from the innermost beings of people in that space. His model in this is the Japanese master Ozu, as Handke tells us explicitly. At one point the woman is watching, on TV, a Japanese film in which a withdrawn wife is coerced into a family game by her scowling husband, who smiles after she complies. I assume that this is an Ozu film since Ozu's photograph is on the wall of this Paris house.

And there's a reminder of another master who reveres Ozu—Antonioni. A publisher who comes to give the woman an assignment (she translates from French into German) is played by the Swiss actor/director Bernhard Wicki. Anyone who knows *La Notte* will recognize Wicki as the writer who dies early in that film; and Wicki, to my knowledge, has not been in a film since then. Handke must have been aware of this suggestion of Antonioni.

Many of Handke's references in the film are just as obvious as the Ozu photograph, obviously intended to be so. The woman lives on rue de la Raison, near the corner of rue Pascal. When she walks down the rue Elise, we hear a piano playing Beethoven's *Für Elise.* The publisher wants the woman to retranslate that tale of acceptances, Flaubert's *A Simple Heart.* This isn't symbolism on Handke's part, it's humor about symbolism. So much bombards us every day that bits here and there are bound to be emblematic, just as, because we dream every night, an occasional dream is bound to be prophetic.

Patterns, non-symbolic, concern Handke more. For instance, there's an early view of the city seen through a lateral aperture. Later, the woman walks at dusk past a shop just as its white shutter is coming down. The second parallelogram reinforces the first. Handke uses Paris as unsentimentally and pithily as Godard did in *Two or Three Things I Know About Her.*

But the strongest element is Edith Clever. Finally and fundamentally, she is the film. Handke shows a gift for direction that makes the head spin after our experience of his other gifts. Bruno Ganz, as the husband, is his customary *sérieux* self. Bernhard Minetti, a famous old actor of the Schiller Theater in Berlin, lays in endearing colors as the woman's father who comes for a brief visit. They are both fine, but the film is or is not the woman, and the woman is: is Edith Clever.

She is the leading actress of the Theater am Halleschen Ufer in Berlin, reputedly the best theater in Europe, and was first seen widely as the Marquise of O. in Eric Rohmer's superb film. A power that was present in her as the marquise now flowers as Handke's woman, the power of inner suggestion: the conviction that what we see and hear of her are the phenomena of a private cosmos, a cosmos like that in each of us which, as Wittgenstein spent some time in reminding us, is ultimately doomed to isolation. The conviction of that inner cosmos is virtually the whole of *The Left-Handed Woman*. (The title has no literal application. It merely indicates some difference from the usual, without really rare anomaly. I take that to be Handke's point. She is not like everyone; nevertheless, we know there are many like her.)

Nothing that Clever says or does in this film is of first importance. What is important is that unheard, unseen self. Without a conviction in us of that self, the woman would be only a neurotic or a poser. The question never arises.

Recently I saw *The Wrong Move* (1975), directed by Wenders with a script by Handke freely adapted from Goethe's *Wilhelm Meister's Apprenticeship*, made contemporary. The structure and harmonics resemble *The Left-Handed Woman*, but the film is much less successful than Handke's own. The behavior of most of the characters is capriciously elliptical, in a post-modernist way, rather than implicative, and the leading actor, Rüdiger Vogler, who is often Wenders's leading actor, is inadequate. (Vogler has a lesser role in *The Left-Handed Woman* as an unemployed actor who is attracted to Clever.) He does not convey the inner world. He is merely a man who is taciturn, even affectless, neither a hero nor an anti-hero, a non-hero. Without our certainty of his secrets, he becomes something of a contemporary cliché.

No danger of that with Clever. The woman in this film is alive—remote, listening, waiting, even (as we later infer) faintly hoping—alive. The time that the picture covers is the time that it takes her to rearrange the world around her like a garment that must be made to fit. The picture closes with a line from a poem by Vlado Kristl: "Have you noticed there's only room for those who make room for themselves?"

Another quotation. Handke wrote some years ago:

> The progress of literature seems to me to consist of the gradual

removal of unnecessary fictions. More and more vehicles fall by the wayside, the story becomes superfluous, invention becomes superfluous, what matters more is the communication of experiences, linguistic and non-linguistic ones, and for that it is no longer necessary to invent stories.

By this credo, he has written some of the best novels and plays of our time. In this first film that he has directed, the risk is, paradoxically, less. The film of *The Left-Handed Woman* is more crystallized than the novel. Not because I learned after I saw it that it was first conceived in screen idiom. Before I knew that, it was clear that Clever and Müller, under Handke's guidance, were realizing what was more distantly admirable in the prose. They were communicating more immediately the "non-linguistic" experience.

Other preeminent writers have directed films, notably Cocteau and Malraux. Now Handke. He is becoming one of the relatively few artistic forces who make this a time in which it's interesting, culturally, to live.

The Tin Drum

(April 5, 1980)

Why, why, why? The question echoes down the centuries. Well, one century. Why do film people adapt important novels, about which there is no special best-seller incentive, without (a) a way to reproduce the novel cinematically or (b) a way to deconstruct it and reconstruct it authentically in cinematic terms? Wim Wenders did (a) with *The Goalie's Anxiety at the Penalty Kick*; Harold Pinter did (b) with his as-yet-unproduced screenplay of Proust. Volker Schlöndorff, that earnest German mediocrity, has done neither with Günter Grass's *The Tin Drum*.

Schlöndorff's past promised little, it's true. I've seen *Young Törless*, from Musil, *Michael Kohlhaas*, from Kleist, *The Sudden Fortune of the Poor People of Kombach*, *A Free Woman*, and *Coup de Grâce*, all of which were tedious. (To make *Michael Kohlhass* tedious is no tiny accomplishment.) Most of them panted in that miasma of artiness that seems to thicken as one moves eastward through Europe—a bit worse, admittedly, in Czechoslovakia and Poland but bad enough in the Germanies. It consists of nineteenth-century bourgeois smugness about culture transmuted into contemporary filmic terms. The taste that took Bruckner and Wilhelmine architecture seriously, now modernized, takes Schlöndorff seriously—along with the Czech Véra Chytilová and the Poles Andrzej Wajda and Wojciech Has.

In Schlöndorff's films from Musil and Kleist, failed though they were, he seemed to have at least some idea of the work. With *The Tin Drum* Schlöndorff discloses no comprehension of the work's essentiality; thus it isn't treated in either the (a) or (b) vein mentioned above. Schlöndorff does more or less what John Huston did with *Wise Blood*: he follows the story (up to a point) and uses much of the original dialogue. The result is like a fuller version of Lamb's *Tales from Shakespeare* in place of the plays. I know that Grass himself collaborated on the screenplay—most of which was written by three people, including Schlöndorff—but this turns out to mean no more, in quality, than the fact that Nabokov wrote the screenplay of the unsatisfactory *Lolita*.

To begin with, Schlöndorff's film uses only the first two-thirds of the novel, until the end of World War II. This is ridiculous. If the novel was too long to handle as an organism, that was a prime reason for leaving it alone—not only because of narrative but perspective. The whole novel is recounted by Oskar Matzerath in a mental hospital where he is taken near the end of the book. Without those events at the end, you can't put him in the hospital at the beginning; and if he's not in the hospital from the beginning, the entire texture is damaged.

Second, and very difficult (a problem that was insoluble even for Pinter with Proust), is the subjectivity of the narrative. Oskar tells the story in two constantly changing voices, first and third persons, but always as Oskar. This is intrinsically impossible in film without removing Oskar from the screen and making him the camera, which is not film, it's a film stunt.

Third, connected with that, virtually everything that happens in the novel leaks into the story tangentially, is not dramatized, is figuratively seen out of the corner of Oskar's eye. For example, the discovery of the body of the suicided Markus, the toy dealer, is given coolly, naively, in the book. The film treats it head-on, conventionally, with a close-up of the dead man's face on the desk. Tonally, this is false and destructive.

Then, connected to *that*, is the matter of point of view, which is quite distinct from subjectivity. How could the boy Oskar have seen his mother and Jan Bronski whacking away together in a hotel bedroom? The omniscient-narrator eye of the camera further hurts the essential tone.

As does the absence of the book's rich saturation in history, the German-Polish-Kashubian memories and references that recreate the past of the city of Danzig where most of it takes place. Grass's novel intends, among other things, to be a saga-epic, a locus by which a culture may represent itself to the future. Oskar is the bard-hero of the work, with a voice and eye very much his own. Not a wisp of any of this in Schlöndorff. The events of the film happen in present tense, that's all, with Oskar involved in most of them. Critics have noted some resemblance between Grass's novel and *Ulysses*. The film has about as much resemblance to Grass as Joseph Strick's wretched film of *Ulysses* has to Joyce.

Contradictorily, many of the film's components are first-rate. Igor Luther's cinematography is perfect—chilly, precise, positing. Every member of the cast, without exception, is good. Mario Adorf and Angela Winkler as Oskar's parents, the Polish star Daniel Olbrychski as Jan, Berta Drews as the old grandmother. Even Charles Aznavour, patently dubbed though he is, has the adoring sadness of face and manner for Markus. Fritz Hakl and Mariella Oliveri, the two midgets whose troupe Oskar joins for a while, are splendid, the first full of friendly wisdom, the second full of charm. And Schlöndorff's decision to use a boy as Oskar, instead of a midget—since Oskar throws himself down a flight of stairs at three in order to stunt his growth—proves apt, since it differentiates him from the midgets he meets later. The boy, David Bennent, is a laconic, mysterious, explosive little madman.

I suppose that not much of the film was actually shot in Danzig since the old city was smashed in the war, but the locations have the right quasi-claustrophobic feeling. Schlöndorff's direction varies from the adequate to the laborious. The troupe of midgets, on a tour of the war front, dancing on top of a coastal pillbox—that's a shot etched cleanly. But much of it is ordinary and some of it obtrusive, like the iris shots and the focus-racking. And why, of all moments, was Oskar's birth made subjective? We come out with him, but that's where subjectivity ends.

The Tin Drum has not been filmed. Grass created Oskar as a refuser of responsibility (he stunts his growth but gets involved in history nonetheless); as a protester (his screams can shatter glass, but this ends as only a vaudeville trick); as someone who refuses adulthood (but he fathers a son); as a drummer trying to drown out the world around him (but drumming is just a nuisance that alters nothing). That much of the book is synopsized in the film. What is lost is any sense of Oskar as a German artist's symbol of disgust and rage and agony about Germany, a pre-Syberberg anti-romantic romanticism, deluged in a virtuosic mélange of styles. The film is a reduction, nearly a travesty. It's only the story of an odd little freak moving through some by-now familiar history.

Swann in Love

(July 30, 1984)

The advance word on *Swann in Love* has been bad, and, for once, the advance word turns out to be true. Still, the wrong person is made the culprit. Blame has been heaped on Volker Schlöndorff, the German director of this French film, and certainly Schlöndorff has done no better than one would expect from the earnest, pedestrian director of *The Tin Drum* and *Coup de Grâce*. But the real clod of the affair, the bungler and butcher, was the author of the screenplay, Peter Brook.

Originally Brook had agreed both to write and direct his adaptation of Proust, but after he had finished the screenplay, he opted to move on. No wonder. His screenplay concentrates on the *Swann in Love* section as a way to solve the problem of transferring the seven-volume work to film; futher, Brook condensed the action of that small section to twenty-four hours, plus a brief epilogue with the dying Swann. (Schlöndorff, with the help of others, subsequently altered Brook's script "slightly.") Brook says that "all Proust's obsessions" are in the *Swann in Love* section. If you can survive the word "obsessions," Brook goes on to say, "I wanted to prove that in a single day it's possible to reflect eternity." A brilliant percept. Pity that James Joyce never thought to prove it. Pity, too, that Proust had an utterly different view of the function of time in his novel. Brook's screenplay, from a man who wants, but only doubtfully deserves, status as a premier theater/film artist, is Filmland hackwork at its most facile and insensitive.

I write out of strong prejudice. First, Brook's statements seem to me self-exculpatory hogwash: no section of Proust's gigantic work can represent all of his "obsessions." Second, Harold Pinter recognized this truth, and in his grand screen adaptation, tried "to distill the whole work, to incorporate the major themes of the book into an integrated whole." The Pinter screenplay has been published; Roger Shattuck, no mean Proustian, wrote of it: "It enlarges the language of film in order to encompass one of the most sustained products of the human imagination." But Nicole Stéphane, the producer who commissioned the Pinter screenplay, despaired of raising the money to film it—it was published so that it wouldn't be completely lost—and at last she persuaded Brook to take on a version for which financing could be found. With all (or some) respect for Stéphane's "obsessions" to get Proust on screen in some shape or other, I think the decision was ludicrous. The story of Swann and Odette is, as such, banal—a cultivated man enslaved by an intellectually and morally inferior beauty. Much of the episode's weight in the novel comes from the fact that it takes place in the "past": we already know a good deal about the young Marcel and something about Gilberte, the daughter of Swann and Odette. Therefore the Swann-Odette story is exponential to the whole work's central subject, the weavings of time. Pinter, whatever the flaws in his transmutation (Shattuck has noted them), understood the central subject and was not to be dissuaded by pressures of expediency, not even when lacquered with Brookian rhetoric. Brook, however, a high priest of high art, was quite willing to snip out and restitch some bits of one line of an immense counterpoint, before moving on to matters loftier than Proust. Schlöndorff can be chided for accepting the Brook version and for his own executant limits; but the basic barbarity was committed by Brook.

Yes, the costumes are sumptuous, but that's no rare achievement. Good designers are not rare, and this one—Yvonne Sassinot de Nesle—surely is gifted. (The clothes were made by Umberto Tirelli, who had been tapped for the job twenty years ago when Visconti was mulling his own Proust project.) The settings are by Jacques Saulnier, whom I've admired ever since Chabrol's *Landru*. Sven Nykvist was the cinematographer, so all is well in that department. A more sympathetic composer than Hans-Werner Henze could have been found; and it was certainly a mistake to let us hear Henze's idea of "the little phrase by Vinteuil which was, so to speak, the national anthem of [Swann and Odette's] love." This is a clear instance where unheard melodies are sweeter.

But if these elements had all been better than they are, they couldn't compensate for the acting any more than for the script. Jeremy Irons cannot play Swann. Not only does he lack Swann's "aquiline nose" or any suggestion of the Jewishness that makes Swann's presence in high society continually extraordinary, he lacks the elegance that Swann must easily embody. Irons had touches of romantic sweep in the historical sections of *The French Lieutenant's Woman*, but here he is just an English actor over from London to do a film. The soundtrack compounds the trouble, with what can only be called dementia. In France Swann's lines were dubbed by a French actor. In the U.S. version Irons speaks Swann's lines after a three-month Berlitz course in French. You don't need to know any more French than I (a modest requirement) to hear Irons's bad accent and to wonder why it provokes no comment from Swann's Parisian friends. Irons is hardly so famous a film star in this country that another, similiar voice would have been unacceptable. The present effect is mad.

Ornella Muti, the Odette, *is* dubbed, but so clumsily that we're constantly aware of it. She is wrongly cast, anyway. "Her profile was too sharp, her skin too delicate, her cheekbones too prominent, her features too tightly drawn" does not describe Muti's rounded, doughy face. She seems ostentatiously vulgar from the start.

Michel Piccoli was first talked of for Charlus, then Michael Lonsdale. As it comes out, the wicked Baron is played by Alain Delon, a performance that has been hailed by some as the film's saving grace. But the film is not saved, and Delon has no grace. He does well enough with the satanic leers of the cruising pederast, but he is not remotely an archetypal dandy. There is more of Charlus in Boldoni's portrait of the Comte de Montesquiou, one of Proust's models for the character and also the model for Delon's makeup, than in all that the actor does.

Swann in Love falls with repellent neatness between two stools. Those who know the novel can only be irritated by the film; those who don't know the novel will see only a tedious film. But this picture makes two matters crystalline. Peter Brook's screenplay is in every way reprehensible. Pinter's screenplay will now certainly not be filmed. This last is one of the grievous cultural sins of our age.

As this is written, news comes of Joseph Losey's death. It was through Losey, who had been approached by Nicole Stéphane, that Pinter took on the writing of the screenplay; and as Pinter says in his introduction, he was advised all along by Losey—together with the Proustian authority, Barbara Bray. (The published script is dedicated to them.) Losey was meant to direct the film. I was not by any means a consistent admirer of Losey's work, but this script would have brought out the considerable best in him. It's grimly apt that he should die just as the *Swann in Love* abortion appears and finishes off the Pinter screenplay forever.

The Long Riders

(May 31, 1980)

"What makes Peckinpah's violence so disturbing, ambiguous, and subversive . . . is that he is able to render [it] so terrifyingly, so graphically, with such raw and unflinching power, yet *still* to respond, and make us respond, fully, even exultantly, to the joy, passion, and exhilaration these men experience when fighting . . . ." Thus writes Paul Seydor in the chapter on *The Wild Bunch* in his new book *Peckinpah: The Western Films* (University of Illinois Press). He goes on to say that "Peckinpah is absolutely aware" of "the changes that history inevitably brings to artistic conventions," that when "he resurrects the epic warrior in the form of the outlaw-hero . . . his prodigious sense of irony . . . expresses that awareness."

It's precisely the lack of subversive exhilaration and of irony that makes *The Long Riders* abhorrent when it isn't boring. Directed by Walter Hill, this Western was written by four people, including Stacy and James Keach who were also executive producers and who are in it as the James Brothers, Frank and Jesse. There have been a lot of previous films about the James boys, but *The Long Riders* didn't remind me of the James films I've seen as much as *The Wild Bunch*, of which it's clearly derivative. So is a lot of subsequent Peckinpah. More and more, as time goes on, *The Wild Bunch* becomes a landmark.

Of what? Between the time that I wrote my review and the time that it appeared I got a letter from a well-known novelist, typed (he said) just after he had seen *The Wild Bunch*, hoping that I would stand against the praise that the picture was getting. I had to reply that my review was going to disappoint him; but because of his letter, I went to see the picture again—and liked it even more. What happened in that film was, I think, significant. Without losing one jot of historical veracity, Peckinpah moved the Western out of John Ford's domain of retrospective myth-exaltation into the contemporary sensibility of Antonin Artaud, out of veneration and idealization of the past into rowelling of the present. Artaud, in "The Theater and Cruelty," wanted "to resuscitate an idea of total spectacle by which the theater would recover from the cinema . . . a spectacle addressed to the entire organism . . . space thundering with images" that would crack psychology and literature and open the audience to the long-suppressed elemental in itself. Many have tried it in the theater, a few with success. Peckinpah, who may never have heard of Artaud, seemed impelled by the same hot drives in his own field: he "resuscitated" spectacle for the cinema, reclaimed violence from the balletics of the gun duel and from anaesthetized, remote, random butchery. He made violence hurt and thrill; and he did it through conviction of *fulfillment of being* by bloodshed and by the expression of it—the only word—beautifully. So he was able to strike the Artaudian blow, past our civilized disdain, to the animal in us that wanted waking—at least to test our civilizing.

But the trouble, as subsequent Peckinpah and his imitators have proved, is that sheer Artaudian ecstatic violence is not enough. Conditioned as we are, if the violence is to work, then the irony that Seydor mentions is nearly essential, and the characterization that Artaud despised is absolutely essential. Without them, we find ourselves merely looking, or not looking, at the violence. Unsupported wild killing is unsupportable. It's bad enough in latter-day Peckinpah, where he has floated to his surfaces; it's worse with Walter Hill who never reached depths and who is just a shopper. He got a lot of praise for his most recent film *The Warriors* because it treated New York street-gang fights in a stylized manner. This seemed to me a bankruptcy of praise and vice versa. Because a director had actually read a book (in this case the *Anabasis* from which Hill took the sketchiest framework) and because he could do velour imitations of *West Side Story* with touches of Bertolucci splashed in, he became a Hollywood genius. With *The Long Riders* he keeps plodding down Memory Lane.

He got a cinematographer (Ric Waite) who could imitate the Almendros and Wexler of *Days of Heaven*, even to the long shot of a train cutting black across the green. He put in all the frankness about brothels from Venus-knows-how-many modern Westerns. But mostly he piled on, as he thought, lots of Peckinpah: much explicit violence, much of it in slow motion—shootings, of course, but also sequences like the one in which horsemen fleeing a bank robbery crash through a large shop window, ride through the shop, and come out through the window on the other side.

What makes the picture abhorrent finally—and "finally" means long before the end—is, first, the triteness of the materials, including the train robbery and the Northfield, Minnesota, raid: not just because they're trite but because we assume that Hill must have known that, too, and must have had some special treatment in mind. It never appears. Because of this and because there's no true characterization or cogent irony, we soon feel that we are being asked to sympathize with the estheticized idiocy of homicidal degenerates. There's some attempt at moral "tone" by providing these men with sweethearts and wives. It fails, because the women are not kept in sheltered ignorance like the Mafia wives in *The Godfather*, they encourage the criminality of their men. The excuse for the criminality is, as usual, the Civil War, its dislocations in lives and goals, but this is never made remotely credible and it isn't even dragged in substantially until just before the finish.

The picture's gimmick is to have three sets of bandit brothers played by brothers: the James boys by the Keaches, the three Younger brothers by three Carradines, the two Miller boys by two Quaids. If you want to see the film that has the most brothers playing brothers, this is it. The exceptional talent of Stacy Keach is, apparently, one more such talent destroyed because it was given to someone without will and ambition. His brother James did actually change expression once in the picture but was better stone-faced. Of all the others, only David Carradine is notable. His "romance" with Belle Starr, sassily played by Pamela Reed of the New York stage, has some spice, and because he is the only one who draws a moderately interesting character, his knife fight in a bar has some excitement.

Fame

(June 7, 1980)

Explosion time. About five minutes after *Fame* began, I began to feel the pressure building in the big theater where I was seeing it. I hadn't felt anything like it since the first production of *Hair* at the Public Theater in 1967 where, long before the intermission, I thought the walls of the high-ceilinged hall would simply *go*. Not with noise, with young energy. *Fame* threatens the walls of its theater the same way: not with the stereo sound, not with the rock beat—not alone, anyway—but with young energy. I'll make a deal with the rest of the world: you keep *Star Wars* and all the sequels, with their special-effect, lab-coddled cosmic powers, and I'll take the real cosmic powers of these kids.

The High School of Performing Arts in New York accepts students with gifts in dance or music or acting and trains them in those fields at the same time that they get the standard four-year education. *Fame* begins with the entrance auditions, then has a section for each year as it follows some students through, and concludes with graduation. The opening has echoes of *A Chorus Line*, therefore echoes of that show's antecedent, Joseph Chaikin's *Mutation Show*, where prospective performers delve into themselves. Christopher Gore's screenplay is decked with plastic curls. When a girl applies as a dancer and says that the fellow with her is not applying, that he's just partnering her for the audition, we know he's the one of the pair who's going to be accepted. When a student (that same dancer, by the way) has a running fight with a woman English teacher through the film, we know they're going to end up in friendship. A Puerto Rican boy, an acting student who is the least engaging character in the picture and has the most screen time, makes a hit in his debut as a stand-up comic in a small club and later bombs out; and he goes through the stock letdown in the stock dingy dressing-room.

But all that stuff, and more, has the same relation to *Fame* that *recitative* has to 19th-century opera: it connects and makes possible the numbers. The film has a double point: the talent of these students, the ambition of these students. (None of the leads is actually a student: they're all young professionals.) Those two qualities are like the poles in a carbon-arc spotlight: they make the picture flare.

So we hear Irene Cara singing "Out Here on My Own" with nuance and heart; we see the hot kinetics of Gene Anthony Ray's body, so sexy that he turns on the women teachers who audition him; we see the flowing gold-and-pearl of Antonia Franceschi's ballet work; we see and hear dozens of other young musicians and dancers, all bursting. Louis Falco, choreographer for Alvin Ailey and others, has devised "extemporaneous" outbursts of dance—in the school cafeteria and the street outside (not the actual school building) that are rock at its most infectious. The implication of these numbers is that rock underlies the beings of all these young people, chamber musicians and Shakespeareans, too: it's their *lingua franca*. Falco makes it believable and fine. The good score is by Michael Gore, with a smashing graduation number built on Whitman's "I Sing the Body Electric."

The art in this high school that comes off the worst in terms of display is, inevitably, acting. Of the three arts involved, acting is the hardest to learn, master, and show: the acting equivalent of, say, Franceschi's dancing doesn't often come at Franceschi's age. Bits of plays are seen, including one funny scene of the rehearsal of a Russian play in the snowy schoolyard, but the director, Alan Parker, doesn't try for virtuoso splashes of acting as he does with music and dance. This obviously has nothing to do with the acting in the film itself, which is mostly better than competent—especially Anne Meara as the embattled English teacher and Maureen Teefy as a duckling who becomes a swan. In counterpoint to the roller-coaster feelings of the students is the steadiness of their teachers, particularly Jim Moody, the acting teacher, and Albert Hague, the musician, who impress us as strong, patient, and basically very happy.

Not many pictures depend so openly on their editing as *Fame* does. Parker and his editor Gerry Hambling developed an editing and shooting vocabulary that soon becomes clear but that always clicks: a loud scene followed sharply by a quiet one and vice versa; mosaics of work around the school spliced between major sequences, often over the soundtrack of the next upcoming major sequence; a cut to a close-up that's unrelated to the sequence ahead of it—an object or face—then a pullback by the camera as we slide into the next phase. The interweavings—a dozen or so stories go forward at the same time—are tight because all those stories have the same centers, literally and figuratively: the school and the drive.

Parker and his producer, Alan Marshall, are long-time collaborators, veterans of over 500 TV commercials before they made their first feature. I didn't know their background when I saw their last film, *Midnight Express*, which was about a young American imprisoned in Turkey on drug charges and which I thought was hyped-up false agony. Doubtless I'd have used their TV-commercial background as a club against them. But it's just that shorthand hustle, the lush laying-it-in-your-lap that gives *Fame* its fortune. It's nothing like a vertical film, even in those moments when it weakly tries to be; it's horizontal, a forward-motion storm.

What's especially interesting is that Parker and Marshall are English. (So is David Greene, who did the spirited Manhattan film of *Godspell*.) It's long-exploded nonsense that only a native director can use a location. The point here is that two Englishmen have understood a film that couldn't possibly have taken place anywhere else. There may be similar schools in other cities, in other countries, but *Fame* is not just American, it's New York. These two men understood that: understood something of what this city means to the rest of the country, to the world.

The New York theater world as it is today comes out of New York City as it is today—brawling, dirty, dangerous, fiercely and combatively vital. The WASPs and Jews and blacks and Puerto Ricans and Chinese in this school are statistically available elsewhere but not dynamically. Very shrewdly Parker puts the school (against the fact) on a side street off Broadway: when the kids pour out for their street rock number, Broadway is only half a block away. It's afternoon, and the whole district looks like the world capital of Clutch. It's also still the world capital of adolescent show-biz ambition and fantasy, even in the aged.

Fame is absolutely about its title, not about the arts it's dealing with. Almost all the talent in the picture is revving up for a zoom to the glitzy top. The film opens with a close-up of a photograph of Olivier as Othello, then the camera pulls back to reveal the acting auditions, but that photograph is from a different planet. Little in this film has anything to do with what made Olivier what he was. Little in this film has anything to do with anything except Making It. (I mean the film, not the real New York high school.) That's what gives the picture hustle. That's what makes it corny and slight when it tries to create character. And that's what makes it truthful—maybe more truthful than it set out to be—about the performing arts in Fever City.

The Shining

(June 14, 1980)

Stanley Kubrick's horror film *The Shining* has two good shots in it, and he spoils them both. Before the credits, a helicopter shot follows a speeding car on a mountain road. Suddenly the camera stops tracking the car and flies out over the landscape. Thus we're told that this isn't a conventional shot in which the emphasis is on the car. Here the emphasis is on the camera, the watcher, a presence of some sort that can follow the car or not as it chooses. But his good effect has already been marred because in the preceding shot, the first of the film, that helicoptered camera sped over a mountain lake. By the time we get to the car shot, the camera's independence is already debased into trickery. If the car tracking-and-departure had opened the film, it would have been eerie.

Later there's a shot of Shelley Duvall snooping around the writing table of her author-husband Jack Nicholson to see what he's been working on for weeks. The camera is in front of the table, low, and her head comes into view over the top of the typewriter. It's not only a new angle on a commonplace action, it heightens the sense of illicit peering. But this feeling of scared intrusion into her husband's madness—the evidence is in the machine and in finished pages—is blown away when Kubrick shoots Nicholson's discovery of her intrusion with Nicholson in the foreground, watching her in the background. Because we see him seeing her, we're not scared when he speaks. If the camera had been on Duvall and her husband's voice had cut in, Kubrick would have peaked the suspense that the opening shot of the sequence had begun.

Nothing else in the picture's cinematics is good enough even to be spoiled. This fact is the biggest among the many disappointments. At Kubrick's most torpidly inbred in the past, the inbreeding has at least consisted of bravura visual work. In *The Shining* there's nothing but strain, most of it platitudinous. A lot of furious traveling shots, following people down corridors, telegraphing the fact that surprises await them around the corner—though sometimes there's no surprise and the traveling is a telegram undelivered. A lot of fast zooms to and out from something purportedly frightening, though this is the most common and mechanical of dodges. And once Kubrick uses it stupidly. We have seen a man murdered, we know he's dead, but when someone else discovers him, Kubrick zooms to and out from the body, which is no news to us, when he ought to have played the discoverer's face. Kubrick doesn't have much sense of shock—what is new to *us* at the moment and how to handle it. It's a sense that Hitchcock, whatever his other failings, had tuned to a fine edge, the shooting and editing of surprise. Kubrick hasn't a clue.

The impreciseness of the filming reflects the random thrill-grabbing of the script. It comes from a best seller by Stephen King, adapted by Kubrick and Diane Johnson. I haven't read the novel and don't know whether the TV banality of the dialogue—or the ritual sprinkling of gratuitous profanity—is King's or K-and-J's. It's about a writer, with a wife and small son, who gets the job of caretaker at an immense Rocky Mountain summer hotel that's closed down for the long winter. (The hotel reminded me of the great lodge at Jackson Hole, Wyoming. The basic situation reminded me of *Seven Keys to Baldpate*.) Ten years earlier a man in the same job had gone crazy during the long snowbound isolation, had murdered his wife and two little daughters and himself. When we hear this story at the start ("I think you can appreciate that I had to tell you this," says the manager to Nicholson but really to us), any surprise in the film is pretty well smothered right off. But that information isn't planted any more lumpishly than: the huge hedgerow maze on the hotel grounds; the large, well-bolted food locker; the racks of butcher knives on the kitchen wall; the forbidden Room 237; or the fact that Nicholson's little son has an imaginary pal who speaks to him in a different voice that comes out of the boy's own mouth.

All of this—the laborious filmmaking and story structure and dialogue—might be endured, might even be surmounted, if the script made some ground rules for itself and followed them. One of the reasons why *The Exorcist* scared me was that it defined its territory and governance and stuck to them: the power of Phenomenon X or Y did not vary from scene to scene. The worst, least effective way to make a horror film—or fantasy or science fiction—is just to slap on effects as they occur to you. If the writers seize anything that may scare, without internally consistent sense, we know we're being held up for random punches, which is tedious.

The Shining is a grab bag of spook stuff, with no rhyme or reason of its own. For instance, it's carefully set up at the start as the story of a hotel haunted by the ghosts of a prior caretaker and family. Then who is the beautiful young woman in the bathtub? Who is the old woman she turns into? Who are the skeletons in the cobwebbed ballroom? If a ghost could let Nicholson out of a well-locked room, why couldn't the same ghost have opened two much thinner, simply locked doors that he has to chop his way through with an axe? If, as his wife discovers, he has typed several hundred pages of drivel, when did he go crazy? If he was crazy when he arrived—which he would need to have been because that insane typing must have begun many weeks before—then what's the point of the story? And there's a closing touch, a close-up of a photograph that's been hanging on the wall all the while (a reminder of the end of Polanski's *Repulsion*), which is supposed to give us a final chill but which is only a last desperate grab at *frisson* that makes further hash of the story.

There's one more lack, a fundamental one, in the script. *The Exorcist* gave reasons, in its own terms, for its evil. *The Shining* has nothing but "motiveless malignity." (Thank you, Coleridge.) The one vague theme is facile: death is awful, the dead are jealous of the living and want to kill them. That's the basis of most summer-camp bunkhouse ghost stories, and it's pretty feeble by now.

Kubrick scents this, I think, or else he wouldn't sweat so much. From the outset, under the shots of the gorgeous mountain scenery and the bland scenes in offices and homes, music howls and screeches on the sound track. All I could think was that, if Nicholson and family could hear the music that was accompanying their talk, they wouldn't go up to the hotel. How hammy that use of music is. But then virtually every device in *The Shining* is the multi-million-dollar enlargement of the vocabulary of creaky old B horror films.

The one good performance is from the boy, Danny Lloyd. Kubrick's best accomplishment in the film is his work with the child. He had less luck with Shelley Duvall, who is scrawnier than Marisa Berenson of Kubrick's last film *Barry Lyndon* and not much more of an actress. Admittedly, Duvall has to spend a lot of her time in that ineluctable cliché of horror films – staring at the camera wide-eyed and open-mouthed in fright. Still, Kubrick's casting and use of her is a reminder that, excepting *Lolita*, he hasn't had much interest in women or skill in handling them. In *Paths of Glory*, *Spartacus*, *Dr. Strangelove*, *2001*, *A Clockwork Orange*, and *Barry Lyndon*, women have been male appurtenances and adjuncts.

The disgrace among the actors is Jack Nicholson, just because he is so gifted. His eyebrow-arching, mouthy work here makes the late Bela Lugosi look conservative.

As for Kubrick himself, there's little left even to deplore. Since *Dr. Strangelove*, his work has seemed to me an abandonment of true cinematic imagination for preening photography, for hermetic exercises in the deployment of space and light, but I could manage to see why some serious people thought otherwise. Now, to choose to do *The Shining* at this stage of his career is not the exaltation of a genre, it's a confession of vacuity. One proof of this is that he has done it badly. The film's imaginative and syntactical shortcomings – many more than I've cited – are not academic: Kubrick hasn't flunked an abstract exam. He has flunked the elemental test for a horror film: *The Shining* doesn't scare. The only pang in it is that it's another step in Kubrick's descent.

The Chant of Jimmie Blacksmith

(September 20, 1980)

In American history there are Indians and blacks. In Australian history, apparently, the social place and function of both those races are filled by one race, the black aborigines. Like our Indians, they were the first inhabitants; like our blacks, they are the largest, needed/hated, cheap labor force. That double aspect is the ground of *The Chant of Jimmie Blacksmith*, an Australian film based on a novel by Thomas Keneally which in turn is based on fact. Jimmie is a half-white black youth, at the turn of the century, who tries very hard to be a "good boy," takes his orders and does his work, suffers his exploitations and insults, and cheerily slogs on, but is at last abused over the edge into murder – mass murder.

The screenplay is by Fred Schepisi (pronounced Skepsee) who directed. Schepisi is forty-one and has been working in film for sixteen years; *Jimmie Blacksmith* is his second feature, his first to be shown here. Lately there's been a push to put Australian films on the American map, with most of that push wasted on overblown, fundamentally provincial pictures. Many of them are set at the turn of the century: *My Brilliant Career*, easily the best of the previous lot, *Picnic at Hanging Rock*, *The Getting of Wisdom*, and now *Jimmie Blacksmith*. I can't explain this plumping for period, except that in general the costumes and customs and cinematography were engaging even when the films weren't.

Jimmie Blacksmith charts its terrain in its first two minutes. Somewhere out in the country a minister and his wife wonder where their charge, Jimmie, is. We see Jimmie, then about thirteen, off with his black relatives and friends, going through a tribal initiation rite that includes scarring of his chest. Later he returns to the minister's house in Western clothes. We soon skip to Jimmie as a young man, setting out in the world with the minister's reference, and we know that we're going to watch the tugs of Jimmie's double heritage.

I note here, as I must, that I didn't understand a good deal of what was said throughout, because of accents, native and white, and vocabulary. I know I didn't miss any important points or links, but surely I missed a lot of nuances. Occasional subtitles would have been a good idea for U. S. audiences, though nothing is muddy in major story or character development.

Step by step Jimmie makes his way unknowingly toward the brink. He is bright, hardworking, and not naive—he expects to be cheated and insulted. He expects to find drink and sex only in black shanties and tents. He expects to be skinned out of pay. But he also expects, when a pregnant white kitchen maid marries him, that he is the father, which he has reason to believe. (The minister's wife had encouraged him to marry a white farm girl. By the time his grandchildren came, she told him soothingly, they would be only one-eighth black.) The baby comes out all white.

He cherishes his wife and her child. Buffets continue until a point when he and family have nothing to eat and the farmer for whom he works denies him credit as a stratagem for driving away Jimmie's black relatives. Jimmie snaps: with an ax in his hand. A black uncle who is with him joins in, not so much out of fury as loyalty. They flee, accompanied by Jimmie's full-black half-brother. Jimmie says he has declared war, though obviously this is after-the-fact rationale of his explosion. More killings follow, until the inevitable happens. All three men are wiped out, Jimmie last.

The story breaks at the moment of the first murders. Before that, tension; after that, nothing but doom. And the second part, at least a third of the film, is a long time to await the foreseen. That last third is just protracted, narrowing flight, with Jimmie's story taking on some political freight, with some moments of poignancy and pain. The end of Jimmie, his jaw torn away by a bullet, captured in a convent, carted off to jail with soldiers protecting him from a mob, then—the night before hanging—talking in his cell with the minister of his boyhood who says he takes the blame on himself—all this is more completion of the form than iron grimness, more whimper than bang. It has only a touch of what ought to suffuse it, the sense that death has caught up with a man who has been dead for some time.

But this obligatory feeling in the last third is the defect of the picture's virtue: we expect more because so much of what has gone before is so good—well modeled, rich, humane. An American viewer will recognize that Jimmie's experiences are virtual duplicates of what an American black's would have been. (If you imagine an Indian, the irony is fuller.) And, admittedly, part of the interest of *Jimmie Blacksmith* is as travelogue: the "same" film about a U.S. black c. 1900 would be less engrossing. Still Schepisi works for intrinsics. The film's texture is woven out of terrible universal incompatibilities.

Ian Baker's cinematography is in the post-1970 ultra-gorgeous vein which tends by now to make me suspicious that vacuity is being varnished. Not here, though some of the compositions, like windings around great trees, are arty. And in many outdoor shots the close plane is focused and the farther planes are unfocused so that the actors seem to be performing in front of a huge misty backdrop. Brian Kavanagh's editing, doubtless done with Schepisi, includes too many inserts of worms and leaves and insects to make us remember the theme of the Natural; and Schepisi himself can lean a bit. Did we need a close-up of the horse manure that Jimmie shovels? Or a close-up of his feet when he breaks spontaneously into an aboriginal dance at the birth of the baby? Bruce Smeaton's music leans even more heavily.

But these flaws, not negligible, are carried in sum by this broad-shouldered, genuine film; and I come now to what really makes *Jimmie Blacksmith* as good as it is. The performances. Every part, without exception, is well cast and acted. Ray Barrett, a brutal policeman, and Peter Carroll, a schoolteacher whom Jimmie takes as a hostage, do particularly clean-lined work. They are actors. Tommy Lewis, who is Jimmie, Freddy Reynolds, his black half-brother, and Steve Dodds, his black uncle, are not actors, I think, and are wonderful. This speaks to the casting, which was done by Schepisi's wife, Rhonda, and of course the innate gifts of these performers. But, for me, the work Schepisi did with his actors, professional or not, is the strongest talent that he shows in the film. I don't expect to forget Reynolds's ease in nature, the wilting of hate in him through natural sunniness; or the stunning moment after the first murders when Dodds sits shivering, or his brief speech in the dock after his sentence. Tommy Lewis, who carries the film, is enchanting, graceful, heartbreaking. His strength and beauty in the first part, his hatred of *everything* after he starts killing, his numbness after his jaw wound, are all like movements in music.

Violence? Yes, *Jimmie Blacksmith* gets to a lot of it, with axes and guns, though no more explicit than necessary. Compare these killings with those in a current violence-peddling film. The razorings in De Palma's *Dressed to Kill* are the reasons for its existence: everything before and after is trumped up with glossy psychologizings, to make the razors possible. Nothing is trumped up in *Jimmie Blacksmith*: the violence is grounded and ordained, and Schepisi is careful not to revel in it. "Where your treasure is, there will your heart be also," says the Gospel. De Palma's treasure is razors; Schepisi's treasure is Jimmie.

Stardust Memories

(October 11, 1980)

All through Woody Allen's *Stardust Memories*, I was clamped by two contrary feelings. The first was compassion—for Allen himself. How desperately he wants to be more than he is. Most of the film, from start to finish, hangs in method and in manner on 8½. (The opening sequence also has a touch of Bergman, the ticking of a clock.) The protagonist is a film director named Sandy Bates, born Sidney Finkelstein in Brooklyn, and some of the scenes with women are straight Allen; but all the rest clings to Fellini's masterwork. Free-flow and dream-like continuity, a flood of vivid faces seen close and briefly in what could be called silent-movie makeups; black and white cinematography by Gordon Willis openly inspired by Gianni di Venanzo, just as Santo Loquasto's costumes get their exaggerations from Piero Gherardi—all these visual aspects proclaim their source. And there's more. Besides the fact that it's about a film director's private and professional troubles, it also takes place at a spa, sort of; it has an ornate railroad station; his mistress visits him; it has teasings about priests and nuns; and it ends with the director's mock death.

Now ten or twenty minutes of this might be good parody, a super Johnny Carson skit—Fellini in Flatbush, and After. But an hour and a half make it slide out of the funny into the desperate. Satire becomes parasitism. Allen isn't kidding Fellini or even revering; he's saying that he wishes he were Fellini and by the very act of persistent imitation confesses that he knows he never will be. Every once in a while there's a faint hint of mockery of his master, but it's like a feeble gesture of control by an embarrassed man who finds himself riding a tiger.

The story's occasion is a film weekend at a hotel—modeled on actual weekends run by a well-known reviewer—where there's a festival of Bates's films for paying guests with Bates on the premises. So there are plentiful chances for oddball characters with odd requests, clips of films, flashbacks, and fantasies. As *Stardust Memories* went on, one of my conflicting feelings, compassion, deepened. It went past Allen himself because he's not only talking about his own limitations but those of American film, therefore of American culture. What postwar American director could he have envied and imitated —recognizably? The only defined and significant new film styles in the postwar era, Allen's era, have been European. (Or Japanese.) When Guido, the director in Fellini's film, stagnates, some reassurances out of his life and his society—crystallized for him by a very "continental" magician—come to his rescue. But nothing comes out of Bates's life, crystallized by any cultural manifestation, to help him. Everything in his past and his present only drains him more. One salient difference between 8½ and *Stardust Memories*: Guido's mock-death is suicide; Bates's mock-death is murder by a demented admirer. It confirms my sad feeling that Bates is much more a symptom than a suffering romantic hero.

Lately I saw another American imitation of Europe, Paul Mazursky's *Willie and Phil*, which opens with the close of *Jules and Jim*, then deals with two New York men and their love for one woman. But all three of the actors were so repellent and their characters so flatly written—Mazursky has a laundry-list mind that thinks, if he checks off every modern problem, he has dramatized it—that the picture is an always-remote bore. (Besides, the three characters, all of whom have seen *Jules and Jim*, never seem to realize that they're trying to live it.) At least *Stardust Memories* is keen enough to cut closer than that. Mazursky's film is about trying to be Truffaut; Allen's film is about not being Fellini.

But conflicting with my compassion was some anger. Almost all the subsidiary characters in *Stardust Memories* are stupid and/or ugly. Allen hasn't grasped the core of Fellini's caricature: the human race is deplorable and silly and even vicious but he's one of them and can't completely shed fellow-feeling. Allen's trouble isn't that he thinks he's prettier or better than these characters: it's exactly the reverse. He's trying to equate the world with his own view of himself, smearing dat ole debbil Jewish self-hate all over everyone. This peculiar brand of egotism, a hypersensitivity that breeds insensitivity, made me angry.

One notable change from previous Allen films is in the main women. Cyril Connolly said that one benefit of success for a writer is that it gets him into interesting society and enriches his work. The advantage of success for Allen, apparently, is that it has enabled him to meet more glamorous neurotics. The Brooklyn background is still there, vividly etched in flashbacks, but now he knows internationals. Marie-Christine Barrault (of *Cousin, Cousine*) is Bates's French amour, seemingly a mother-earth type but a bit wacky; and Charlotte Rampling is his English amour, an out-and-out neurotic, subject to episodes. (The viewer must decide personally whether it's credible that they want Allen as a lover. I still think his pictures would be better, exactly as written and directed, if someone else—say, Dustin Hoffman—played the leads. But I know I'm in a minority. In Trieste, this August, Allen's pictures filled the theaters.)

Rampling is in the film's two best moments, non-imitative moments, Allen's own, fine. During one of her episodes she is seen in her hospital room, in a tight closeup, telling the off-screen Allen that her doctor has fallen in love with her, asking Allen whether he is "seeing" anyone. The scene was shot a number of times, obviously, because Allen has used a lot of the takes of the brief moment, snapping on one after another in mimesis of Rampling's mental state and his feelings about her. Excellent. And there's a lazy Sunday morning with Rampling in his apartment. She is lying on the floor on her stomach, reading. He is sitting at a table, eating. She glances up idly, he looks at her. Nothing happens. He tells us on the sound-track that this was one of the rare moments in his life when he was completely happy. It's lovely. In fact, the use of Rampling, the feeling for her face that—with the help of Willis's camera—he gives us, is Allen's best sheerly cinematic achievement to date.

The smoothness of the direction as a whole may come from following a model closely, but smooth it certainly is. There are some funny lines: Allen is a funny writer. And some funny sights. (In one film-studio sequence, Allen is in the foreground, in priest's garb, arguing with Rampling. Far in the background, three nuns come in and start to practice a tap routine. It's Fellini fiddled—one of the few truly satiric bits.) The worst moment is, as usual, when Allen attempts the physical: in one "film clip" he's in top hat and tails, dancing as one of a vaudeville trio. Mel Brooks understands these things; Allen doesn't.

Fundamentally, finally, *Stardust Memories* washes out. It isn't good satire. Of Fellini? To what end? From what standpoint? It isn't good bitter comedy about success; it adds nothing to that subject. Any one of us could have written the story-conference dialogue or the lines about wanting to get away from it all. It isn't even an effective cry for help; the cry is so insistent in the crier's own ears that he's deafened to what he might possibly hear around him.

A Midsummer Night's Sex Comedy

(August 16 & 23, 1982)

As Woody Allen has gained in some skills, he has weakened in others. *A Midsummer Night's Sex Comedy* is easily his best-directed film, much better than his *Stardust Memories*, which finished last in the Fellini sweepstakes. He apparently continues to study closely the film artists he admires, such as Bergman and Renoir—I'd also venture Rohmer and Ozu—but now he's not imitating, as he did with Bergman in *Interiors* or Fellini in *Stardust Memories*; he's ingesting and learning.

One evidence is his comfortable use of the screen-frame as theater: holding a shot for a minute or a minute-and-a-half—which is a long time in a film—and letting characters move in and out of it. No cuts. He does this several times in *Comedy*. Confidence in such a shot, for what must still be a moving picture, shows more confidence in actors, in his own discretion, in film itself. Compare it with the skittery early stuff like *Bananas* and *Sleeper*.

Then there are a lot of totally opposed shots, cursive, flowing. One character comes through a wood to meet another, they converse, then leave together—all in the same continuous camera motion, without cuts. Again Allen is showing greater sensitivity to the relation between what is going on in the scene and how it is filmed.

On the other hand, there's Allen's script. As his career proceeds, he seems to be straining harder and harder to find ways of employing his "character," who by now needs no description. This time, besides Shakespeare's solstice, Allen has drawn on the time-worn theatrical convention of the country-house weekend, with its enforced isolation and amorous complications, which he flavors with Bergman (*Smiles of a Summer Night* and *Wild Strawberries*) by setting it at the turn of the century.

Santo Loquasto's costumes are excellent, but they are the only really authentic period items. After dinner, a guest says to his hostess, "Dinner was super." C. 1900! A stuffy old bachelor professor spends the night before his marriage in the same guest-room as his fiancée. C. 1900! Allen, whose house this is, plays a cranky inventor—flying bicycles, etc.—who makes an evidently good living on Wall Street. If you can imagine this post-Jules Feiffer persona existing before World War I at all, it certainly wouldn't be in even a moderately important Wall Street job.

The script gets into the clairvoyant, spirit manifestations and so on, with no atmospheric grounding, only because Allen wants a particular (heavily) ironic conclusion. It's not a conclusion, really: just an escape hatch. And though Gordon Willis's cinematography is lovely, often overlaid with gentling sepia, Allen uses some of the most trite pastoral symbols, and not parodically: a rabbit, a leaping deer, an owl on a branch swiveling its head as humans below argue. All that's missing is a huge close-up of a dewdrop falling from one leaf to another.

On the *other* hand (who's counting?), the film glides easily, no excitement, no great amusement, but many pleasant-enough scenes and an occasional chuckle. Mary Steenburgen, as Allen's wife, is clearly being groomed as a new Diane Keaton—the same repertory of broken sentences, broken gestures, broken smiles. Tony Roberts, a lecherous doctor, continues his smooth but null career. Julie Hagerty, his nurse and doxy, is much more pretty than competent. Mia Farrow, the professor's intended, is strangely colorless. José Ferrer, the professor, is strangely colorful. The opening credits say that the music is by Felix Mendelssohn, and the *Midsummer Night's Dream* music is used a lot. But two of the songs that Ferrer sings as after-dinner entertainment are by Schubert and Schumann.

Zelig

(August 15 & 22, 1983)

What a good idea for a film Woody Allen has in *Zelig*. His screenplay is something like a story that John Collier might have written after reading Melville's *The Confidence-Man*, followed by a dose of Borges. The mode is personal transformation; the theme is more than establishment of identity, it's proof of existence. And, since these matters are in Allen's hands, the tone is comic. In the late 1920s and early 1930s a mysterious man named Leonard Zelig becomes visible in such an inconsistent way that he's almost invisible. He keeps turning up in different guises with different names and actually in different physical forms. News photos and newsreels show this Zelig as (presumably) himself, as a black man when he is with blacks, as a Greek when he is in a restaurant, as a sparring partner with Jack Dempsey, as a WASPy companion of Herbert Hoover, and in many more "roles," including the ultimate transformation of the early 1930s which I won't, probably don't need to, describe.

Zelig assembles the "documentary" evidence on this metamorphosing man. Most of what we see is "old" film, carefully manufactured by Gordon Willis and colleagues much in the way that Gregg Toland and colleagues manufactured the newsreel shots of C. F. Kane. We also see clips of Zelig's sessions with his psychiatrist, Mia Farrow, because her cousin hides in a closet with film camera and sound equipment to record some of their conversations. This "past" material is supplemented by interviews with some present-day survivors who give us their impressions and memories. (Note: The name Zelig seems a variant spelling of *Selig*, a German and Yiddish word that, as noun, means "the departed" and, as adjective, meaning "blessed," is spoken by religious Jews after the name of a deceased person as one might say "rest in peace.")

Also included are a number of interviews with well-known contemporaries of ours: Saul Bellow, Bruno Bettelheim, John Morton Blum, Bricktop, Irving Howe, Susan Sontag. The ostensible purposes of these interveiws are (a) to buttress the "documentary" texture of the film, and (b) to parody the string of interviews in *Reds*.* They accomplish the first aim more fully than the second. In *Reds* the speakers were discussing a real man. Here the interviewees discuss a fictional character as if he were real. This fact bends their comments back on themselves in good-natured self-parody. When Howe speaks seriously of a fictitious man as if he had been factually the epitome of the American Jew's wish to assimilate or when Bettelheim seriously describes the same figure as the "ultimate conformist," each speaker knows that he is displaying an intellectual characteristic of his own without real reference, thus is caricaturing a feature of his mind as David Levine might caricature a physical feature.

Further, Allen—need I say that he directed the film and plays Zelig?—has embroidered the picture with 1930-type songs about his hero and with dance crazes inspired by his legend. The finest touches of all are the clips from a 1935 Warner Brothers biopic about Zelig which has about as much to do with the "reality" we have seen as *Pride of the Yankees* had to do with the real Lou Gehrig. (We see a newsreel clip of Gehrig, in connection with Zelig, and I felt a pang again for my favorite baseball player of all.)

The skill with which the film is made is so clever as to approach brilliance. I ignore dozens of gifted artists and technicians when I single out Santo Loquasto for costume designs that combine accuracy with slyness. Allen, as director, shows a keen eye for the way people looked, and thought they looked, in the period: the way they glanced at cameras, posed themselves for photographs, or invented "business" for newsreels. Behind all this is not only a careful study of period materials, which many directors have done, but a sensitivity to cultural change. Allen, looking back from the present, perceives that this c. 1930 mo-

---

*See p. 140.

ment is a point of transition from the film camera as an ornament of civilization to a central component of consciousness. Compare people in 1930 newsreels with people in the newsclips on TV tonight.

In effect the star of *Zelig* is not the hero but the making of the film. It is dazzling. Allen, as actor, is not. But then he doesn't need to be: he has almost no acting to do. We see him in newsreel shots, wearing different costumes and makeups as Zelig's incarnations are traced, but virtually the only times that Allen really has to act Zelig are in the filmed discussions with the psychiatrist; and these are the weakest moments because Allen just gives us more of his customary hesitant, apologetic, nervously insistent performance. From Allen's view as actor, this film is a perfect protection device. It allows him to be on screen a great deal without doing much more than pose for pictures.

The concept of Zelig, the "chameleon man" who becomes like the person or persons he's with, is of course intended as satiric social commentary, not as an isolated comic gimmick. He can be seen as a hyperbolic extension of Arthur Miller's American-salesman dictum: it's not enough to be liked, a man must be well liked. In fact, responding to the psychiatrist's question about his reason for his multiple changes of personality and appearance, Zelig says, "I want to be liked." Or we can take him as a metaphor for our century's pressures on individuality, diabolically counterpointed by the growth of hype. As that much-mooted Common Man gets more and more mass produced, the exceptions to commonness get more and more publicized. Isherwood could at least be a camera. Zelig can only be a mirror; but if that's all he can be, at least he can reflect famous people.

It's a fascinating premise for a film, yet as Allen treats it, it's no more than a premise. Where's the film? He uses wit and insight to describe a character, to prepare him for engagement—and then he quits. He never *employs* Zelig: to any narrative, dramatic, or thematic point. After we begin to hunger for the story in which Zelig is going to be involved, all we get are some fast closing titles. (And the paradox is that, after attracting attention by his ability to be like other people because he feels he's nothing, Zelig sinks out of sight when he stops feeling that he's nothing.) Zelig is a scintillating idea, picked up and examined and shown to be full of promise, then put away.

Zelig confirms that Allen is the most valuable sadness in American films today. He's valuable because (as I've noted before) he's the only filmmaker in these constricted times who is given freedom, for work at a budget level where first class technical quality is possible; and because in several ways he justifies that freedom. As director, he has grown immensely. As screenwriter, he has developed the wit that he showed before he entered films, and he pushes into areas opened both by his imagination and by his power in the film world.

The sadness is in the recurrent incompleteness of his work, in his willingness to settle for a good premise and a good launch. *Zelig* is a particularly painful example because it starts so well and runs along so well—until Allen runs out of steam and has to find an escape hatch, as he did in *A Midsummer Night's Sex Comedy*. Neither he nor anyone around him asks sufficiently rigorous questions of his scripts before he begins. (And then there are the apologists who come along later to tell us that failures such as *Interiors* and *Stardust Memories* have been mistakenly judged: they were parodies.)

Well, even a valuable sadness is especially valuable in the current American film scene.

Broadway Danny Rose

(February 20, 1984)

Six months having gone by since *Zelig*, it's of course time for a new Woody Allen film. Some people argue that he is now the best American filmmaker; what is inarguable is that he is the most prolific and most personal filmmaker now working in our major leagues of production and distribution.

The new one is an exercise in nostalgia, updated. The title, *Broadway Danny Rose*, hints strongly at what the film fulfills: it's Damon Runyon time, with a contemporary difference. Imagine *Guys and Dolls* written and directed by someone with *Angst* who is ethnically hyperconscious and who adores Fellini. Viewed as another installment of Allen, *B. D. R.* further displays his drive to do something different every time. I can't recall a previous film of his about show biz seen from the gritty inside. He handles that aspect with atmospheric exactness. In aid of verity, he shot a good deal of the film in, or in a good reproduction of, the Carnegie Delicatessen on Seventh Avenue. He even got a top executive of the Shubert organization, Gerald Schoenfeld, to play a top talent agent.

But the film is a curious mix. Runyon's Broadway has two main components. Broadway is taken seriously as the habitat of show-biz people, gamblers, mobsters, and others whose "time of day," as Frank Loesser put it in *Guys and Dolls* is "a couple of deals before dawn." Second, manners must be rough, but the hearts must be of gold. The trouble is that Runyon's Broadway is no longer fact or fiction, it's fantasy: Broadway is now a locus for junk shops, sex shows, and drug dealers—with a scattering of theaters among them. Further, Allen has no syrup: with his people, the manners are rough and so are most of the hearts. So we have the paradox of a nervous realist writing about a sentimental domain that no longer exists and dealing with it harshly.

A group of nightclub comics—all of them real-life comics—sit around a table in the Carnegie, reminiscing. The subject of Danny arises, a very small-time talent agent whom they all know or knew. One or two memories are recounted, which we see in flashback, then one of the comics launches into a long story about Danny, which in flashback is the film. The shape is nice, a tale told by a pro about a pro to other pros sitting around a delicatessen table, but what comes out is, substantively, an in-delicatessen story.

Danny, played by Allen, is a fast, if not especially confident, talker who has talked himself nowhere. After failing as a stand-up comic, he has become an agent for bedraggled, lowest-rung performers. His biggest chance to score is with a boozy, beefy Italian-American lounge singer, once mildly popular, now virtually passé, but with a hope of a return via the craze for 1950s figures. (Nick Apollo Forte is the singer.) Danny gets him a shot at the Waldorf, then must bring the singer's girl friend to the opening, or else the singer will booze himself away and ruin the chance that could lead to more chances. Since the singer is married and his wife will be present, Danny is to be the "beard," a cover to conceal the woman's relation to the singer: she will seem to be Danny's date.

He calls for the young woman, Tina, at her New Jersey apartment. She, too, is Italian-American. She is angry at the singer because of a supposed slight and refuses to accompany Danny to the Waldorf. He learns that the singer, hearing of this, is starting to hit the sauce. Danny has to persuade Tina to come to the opening. She goes to a big Mafia party; he follows her there. This leads to a mess of Mafia complications. It also leads to a pure Runyon ending that, just because it is pure Runyon, is tonally out of kilter with the film.

Allen's directing continues to grow in control, though he sinks to one more rerun of a shootout in a warehouse of huge figures. The tough, tight-trousered, blonde-wigged Tina, a Mafia widow, is played by Mia Farrow, for whom the part was written. Any actor knows that it's easy to play a part completely unlike one's self, easier than finding a part *in* one's self especially if the dissimilar part is stock. (Katharine Hepburn would probably be more effective as a Mafia mom than in one more of her variations on gentility.) But the fact that it's relatively easy doesn't mean it can't be done badly; and Farrow does it well. As for Allen's performance of Danny, the cosmos divides into those many who never tire of his same old angular, high-strung, cowardly but brave, transparently shrewd New York-Jewish operator; and those few who, like me, do tire of it. Once again he has made a film that would be better if someone else had played his part.

That, however, wouldn't have erased my chief reservation. Every Italian-American in the film is shown to be some kind of bum or grotesque. I'm not a member of any ethnic defense group in the arts, intent to suppress *The Merchant of Venice* or *The Birth of a Nation*. I'm not plumping for a return to Runyon's sugary realism. But Allen is relentless. He tries to balance matters negatively by showing us elderly Jews at a Catskill hotel who are equally grotesque—in appearance anyway; and I noticed a fair sprinkling of Italian names in the credits, possibly as a group buffer in case of attack. The fact remains that Allen, with Gordon Willis's rather cruel black-and-white photography, peers at a group of people—not actors, I'd guess—as if they were inmates of a menagerie. The point is not that no Italian-Americans are ugly or stupid or criminal or that some good and beautiful Italians ought to be included as balance. The point is that Allen has mishandled satire, has misunderstood Fellini. Fellini's use of odd faces is, as I've noted before, humorous and humane; basically, he says, "What a curious species you and I belong to." There's no humor in Allen here: just mockery and dislike. Instead of Fellini's mischievous embrace, we get an extension of Allen's self-hate.

Kagemusha

(October 25, 1980)

Akira Kurosawa's genius has been manifold all through his long career. Prodigally, prodigiously, he has moved with ease and mastery from the most mysteriously interior to the most spectacular. *Ikiru* is about a dusty civil servant in postwar Tokyo doomed by cancer; *The Seven Samurai*—one of the great art works of the twentieth century—is a historical epic about honor as a predestined anachronism. Contrasts from his filmography could be multiplied.

The last decade has been bad for Kurosawa. In January 1972 *Newsweek* reported that he had attempted suicide. His latest work before that shocking news was *Dodeskaden*, a rather soft film about a modern slum boy; his next film was *Dersu Uzala*, a Russo-Japanese co-production which was like a 1930s Soviet paean to peasant simplicities. But now with *Kagemusha*, finished when he was seventy, Kurosawa is back, really back: seizing us with his vision that seems to transform the screen before us into different shapes and depths and rivers of force, with stillness and with blaze. "Yes," I kept thinking as I watched, "yes. Yes." I don't know precisely what I meant, though I could speculate, but I kept thinking it.

Kagemusha, translated as *The Shadow Warrior*, is set in sixteenth-century Japan, like *The Seven Samurai*. It tells the story of a "double," a man who looks astonishingly like a reigning war lord and is constrained to appear in public as that lord, as a decoy and safety measure. The true leader is killed, and the double, a criminal whose life has been spared on condition that he take over this role, must carry it on, at the insistence of the dead man's brother and colleagues: to deceive two other war lords with whom they are battling. The deception fools virtually everyone but not the dead man's horse. The horse throws the impostor, and when he is treated, it's discovered that his body doesn't have the scars of the true war lord. He's no longer useful, and he's kicked out. The lord's son then makes a foolish military decision, and the impostor, now in rags, unnecessarily insists on joining the battle and is killed in the defeat.

Kagemusha is not at the level of *The Seven Samurai*: it lacks the intricacy and interplay of characterization, the majesty of contrapuntal themes in that earlier masterpiece. (At the end of *Kagemusha* there's a faint suggestion, too, of Rossellini's *General della Rovere*, but again, the script lacks the depth of that fine film.) But what Kurosawa has done in his new work, extraordinary in anyone but stupendous in a man of seventy, is to center his film in immense military action: to make that action the sea on which individual lives sail, to make the rush and clash of masses of men, on foot-or on horses, the ground of the whole 160-minute work. In the battle sequences one inevitably thinks of Eisenstein's *Alexander Nevsky*, but Kurosawa's battles are his material throughout, not his climax only. Some of the lines of distant panoply recall Jancsó's *The Red and the White*, but Jancsó uses battle beautifully as philosophic-political instrument. Kurosawa uses battle as battle, uses men's hopes and trickeries and braveries as the root and fruit of battle. These men live for war and take their beings, as well as their deaths, from it.

The very first sequence, before the credits, deliberately does not prepare us for the tone of what follows. With the camera at the Japanese *tatami* level, we see three men seated on the floor: the war lord on a low dais, his brother to his right, his double—just now brought before him—nearer us on his left. (Both the lord and the double are played by Tatsuya Nakadai, who was the handsome young man with the pistol in *Yojimbo*. His performances here, very vivid, seem modeled on what Toshiro Mifune might have done in the roles.) The discovery of the double is explained to the lord by his brother, and the lord agrees to his use. The scene runs surely over two minutes, a very long time, and it's done without a camera movement, without a cut. Three figures in a history are introduced as in a frieze. Then, after the titles, the action pours, figuratively flowing around the islands of quiet scenes that occur thereafter.

Part of the impact of *Kagemusha*, battles included, comes from the cinematographer, Takao Saito, who, with his operator Asakazu Nakai, has worked for Kurosawa over 25 years. The color scheme is enriched, heightened, to keep the film out of realism and in "ballad," though much of the specific action is graphic. But, of course, most of the impact comes from Kurosawa's imperial grip, particularly from his complementary deployment of two fields of motion: that of the camera and that of his actors. This does something that only film can achieve—a ballet in which the spectator, through the moving camera, himself participates. Kurosawa has long been celebrated for his tracking shots. Examples: the woodcutter striding into the forest in *Rashomon*; the opening ride of "Macbeth" and "Banquo" in *Throne of Blood*. In *Kagemusha* there are many, many tracking shots of furiously galloping riders, most of them bearing banners fixed to their backs, the flags fluttering above their heads. The sweep of these shots is marvelous, especially as Kurosawa sometimes blends one into another going a different way.

Often the motion is made by the men only, with the camera still, with the men hurled across our vision in strong, startling patterns. Soldiers will pour down from (say) the upper right corner of the screen diagonally while another stream moves from the middle of the lefthand edge and bends away as it meets them. Battles are battles, not flubberings of extras, because of the director's eye for the rhythms in realism and because of the way he lights the encounters. In one attack an army is surprised in a defile, dark, while the attackers are in profile on a ridge against the sky. Occasionally the pulse of motion is carried by one man alone among many still ones: early in the film a messenger runs frantically through an encamped army, through loafing and sleeping soldiers, bearing a messsage to the lord. As he plunges ahead, the men he passes come awake or start up, and in this simple strophe—his feet pounding past the resting or sleeping men—is a whole conviction of being in an army in a war, with the lulls and starts of service. (It's helped by the sound track, which is always incisive.)

Sometimes a touch of prettiness seeps in: for instance, a file of soldiers moving past a setting sun or a dream in which the dead lord comes back to haunt the sleeping impostor—rather too estheticized a dream for the impostor to be having. But mostly the film strikes and strikes again with grand compositions, grand gestures: the stoicism of the loyal as certain death approaches; the vistas that turn the engagements of armies rolling away over hills into terrible excitement; the frozen gestures of the corpses. In the very last sequence, we see the slow-motion death agonies of fallen horses, and though they don't scream, we hear them.

If *Kagemusha* is not nearly Kurosawa's fullest picture in human and spiritual compass, it is up to his height in cinematic purity. The thrust of the film is not to eulogize war but to see it: an event that men *want*, whatever they may say, in which their totalities are engaged as in very little else that is possible on earth; a universal continuum, still flourishing. To understand what men have been and done, Kurosawa says—to understand, paradoxically, some of the noblest and most beautiful of what they have done—we must look at war. By the might of his vision, by his imaginings of motion, he has rendered war as a great subject, the ancient traffic of nations and of men. In this sense, *Kagemusha* is Homeric.

From the Life of the Marionettes

(November 29, 1980)

"Language is, of course, a problem," said Ingmar Bergman, interviewed recently in Munich where he now lives and works. "However fluently you speak German, you cannot explain to an actor precisely what the emotional meaning of a play is, and what your ideas about it really are." In principle I agree—I've been agreeing for years before he said it, about him and other directors and certainly about actors working in non-native languages: so I went to his new film a bit apprehensively because it's set in Munich and is in German. (No Swedish-German translator is credited; did he write it in German?) I can't judge Bergman's direction of the German dialogue because my own knowledge of the language is feeble, but I do have some response to the "emotional meaning" of the film, and it seems to me perfectly comprehended by the cast—quite unlike the cast of *The Serpent's Egg* (1978) which Bergman made in another foreign language, English.

Let's stay with language for a bit. Seeing *Persona* again last spring I was struck with an injustice that has been done Bergman because he is a great director. Perhaps out of fear of making him sound too literary (one of the curse words in film discourse), perhaps out of simple myopia, he has been scanted as a dramatic author. The sheer *writing* of *Persona* is the work of a great film dramatist: an artist who has mastered the needs and opportunities of film's verbal elements in the service of the whole art in which he works.

It's as writer that he seems to have moved to his latest film, *From the Life of the Marionettes*. The two leading characters, a married pair called Peter and Katarina, appeared previously in the first episode of *Scenes from a Marriage*, where they were Swedish. They were dinner guests of the leading pair, and the evening ended with the visiting wife throwing brandy in her husband's face. They were, says Bergman, "lunatics to be pitied." He has pitied them sufficiently, these "two furious and disastrous persons," to transpose them to Munich, alter them somewhat, and give them a film of their own.

But the key for me is that it's not their film. It begins with, centers on, the murder of a prostitute by Peter; his previous relations with his wife are explored and are important, as is her behavior before and after the crime; but these matters are only the territory of the story, not its being. The film has no protagonist; Bergman has designed it to be about several people: the married pair, Peter's mother, a psychoanalyst, and Katarina's male homosexual partner in her fashion business.

The structure moves both ways from that opening murder, with scenes before and after; each scene is introduced—sometimes just after it's begun—by a title that places it in time. Here are some of the building blocks. There's a scene between Peter and the analyst, not many weeks before the crime, in which Peter, a highly successful businessman in his thirties, reveals his obsessive dream-fantasy: to kill; to kill his wife. He has no reason. They get on well, in bed and elsewhere; they both know that the other has been unfaithful but that's no matter; Peter is simply haunted by this obsession. The analyst is not upset. He asks Peter to come back in a few days when they can have a longer talk: now a visitor is coming to the office. After a hint that he knows who the visitor may be, Peter pretends to leave but hides in the doctor's large office suite. The analyst phones Katarina to come over at once. She does; the analyst tries to seduce her and nearly succeeds. She declines finally because she loves Peter very much and senses that the analyst is trying to hurt that relationship. Peter, hidden, hears all this but is not visibly moved or reassured.

There are two long scenes for the gay partner. One, between him and Katarina—the closest to platitude in the film—is before the murder, in which the gay discloses his fears, of aging and loneliness, his self-loathing about the degradations in his sex life; the other—much keener—is after the murder, an interview between the gay and the police investigator. There are substantial scenes with Peter's mother, a widowed ex-actress who lives in a huge, slightly run-down mansion. Of course there are also substantial scenes with Peter and Katarina: an excellent one in which both can't sleep, get up and drink and talk; a letter of Peter's describing dreams of Katarina in which we see, hauntingly, his torment; a scene in which a male friend of Peter's tries to get Peter down off the roof of his apartment house (an echo of a mention in *Scenes from a Marriage*), which ends in a nasty encounter between Peter and Katarina. And there's an epilogue in which Katarina peers through the window in Peter's door at the mental hospital where he will presumably stay forever, while a nurse, standing behind her and facing us with her (a typical Bergman shot), describes his punctilious and aloof behavior. And the film ends with a closeup of the childhood teddy bear in Peter's hand as he lies on his hospital bed.

The weight of the film seems distributed too much to other characters—mother, analyst, partner—for it to be about Peter and Katarina. This contradiction is echoed in the structure, which by moving back and forth on both "time sides" of the crime, has the air of unraveling a mystery, of explaining a psychosis. And this air of explanation is heightened by the penultimate scene in which the analyst tape-records his clinical report on Peter's case, piecing (as he thinks) everything together—Peter's upbringing, marriage, fear of homosexuality, venting of rage on the prostitute, and anal brutalization of her after the killing. The analyst purrs on, quite satisfied.

But the film does not explain. For me that taped explanation is Bergman's height of irony. The analyst smugly thinks he understands, as he also believes (so to speak) that the film is about Peter. It's really about all the people in it, brought into focus by Peter's crime. The idea of the film could hardly be plainer: it's in the title. They are all marionettes, including the analyst himself, manipulated by forces they know or don't know but which are irresistible, and it's the more frightening because all of them are intelligent and successful, and two of them have what "ought" to be a happy marriage.

That is the terror at the heart of the film. Do everything you can and want to do; have much that the world can envy; and still the Furies inhabit. Peter, a controlled man—we see a scene in which he dictates a detailed business agreement that shows us how controlled he is—is increasingly trapped in fear. ("All roads are closed," he says several times.) Katarina, beautiful and busy, is beginning to drink a great deal out of growing frenzy-cum-impotence. Peter's mother, who ought to be proud and happy, has competed incessantly with Katarina for her son. The gay partner is a man in an upholstered hell. And the analyst! (Bergman always has a knife out for analysts.) Smooth and hieratic, he lies to Peter about the gravity of his condition in order to get him out of the way because Katarina is coming, lies to Katarina about Peter's condition in order to keep her mind on bed, lies to the police after the crime about Peter's condition beforehand in order to keep himself in the clear—and then purrs a clinical report into his microphone, without realizing that he is part of both the story and the condition. That last is Bergman's worst indictment of him, worse than his deceptions.

Bergman's chief subscription is to a belief in dark forces within us. This belief, patent also in many of his previous films, is the closest he comes to the supernatural, a belief that we can contain forces that cannot be exorcised by modern knowledges or even by love. One might even say that Bergman is not mainly interested in character as such, in the dossier of motivations, in psychological study: he makes some root assumptions about a commonalty of resident darkness that we and his people share, and sooner or later he concentrates on that darkness. And his films affect us as we do or do not recognize that commonalty. The tone in this latest film is of Chekhov, in that these are people who, by the standards of their time, have what is prized yet are in anguish; but it's Chekhov laced with Strindberg because what is troubling them is demonic.

Bergman extends this tone with his direction. I can't remember a prior film of his so largely composed of close-ups, some of them intense. The effect is more than intimate, it's almost awesome, as if the intimacy were freighted with a sense of hovering. This effect is fulfilled by his excellent cast. Robert Atzorn, immediately and unwaveringly true as Peter, looks like a Hamlet who would rather not have the role. Christine Buchegger, humane and poignant as Katarina, has a lovely face that itself seems to be modeling the lights and shadows on it. Martin Benrath, the analyst, looks like the Devil, appropriately; but the homosexual, Walter Schmidinger, is cast against type—a quite commonplace face so that his sensitivities won't seem comically precious. Lola Muethel, the ex-actress mother, has a face that looks theatrical, a face used to dealing with emotions and now concentrating on her own.

Bergman has also cast with his ear. The voices of these actors are wonderfully orchestrated. Often, though my attention was never tempted to wander, I was bound even more closely to a scene by the sheer sound of it. (Those who think the German language always harsh might have their opinion shaken by this film.) Along with the voices, Bergman integrates sounds by Rolf Wilhelm, hardly a score: drum beats, piano chords, isolated electronic tones.

The cinematography is, as usual, by Sven Nykvist. Adjectives are superfluous. I'm puzzled, however, by one device. The picture opens and closes in color: most of it is in black and white. If Bergman-Nykvist felt that they wanted black and white through most of the film—especially for the "floating" dreams—then why the color at start and finish? I can't see its need, even as an intensification of the murder.

About Bergman's direction, too, no adjectives. I'll single out just one moment for comment. In the early scene with the analyst, Peter is seated to the left of the doctor's desk, talking. While talking, he gets up, wanders through an open door into the next room, with the camera remaining still; then he returns, still talking, and sits in a different chair, facing the analyst. It's not a movement one is meant to notice as such: I didn't notice it until the second time I saw the picture. It combines, in real Bergman style, theatrical and cinematic gifts. The walk, as an external expression of an inner state of unease, is a felicitous stage movement. (The camera is fixed, remember.) But it also deepens the screen for us and freshens the eye without change of shot. And it also takes us into the room where, very soon, the analyst will try to seduce Peter's wife. It's Peter himself who "reveals" the room to us.

From the Life of the Marionettes was made to involve us through its very making. Because it has no central agonist with whom we are meant to identify, because therefore we understand it intellectually and emotionally rather than empathize with it, it's not as powerful as *Autumn Sonata* (to cite only the most recent Bergman). Its grip is almost phenomenological, experiential, rather than traditionally dramatic. But that experience is so beautifully wrought, so beautiful in itself, that one comes out of the film feeling privileged: initiated into a society that is paradoxically open to all.

Fanny and Alexander

(June 27, 1983)

The best news about *Fanny and Alexander* is that despite the valedictory hubbub about it, it is not Ingmar Bergman's last film. The next one, called *After the Rehearsal*,* is already in post-production. That announcement is very welcome. An artist's final work proves nothing about past accomplishments or eventual stature, but *Fanny and Alexander* would be a weak finish to a magnificent career.

The worst news about *Fanny and Alexander* is that apparently Bergman conceived it, and kept thinking of it, as his last film. It's chock-full of retrospect, of "exit" atmosphere. To ensure that we don't miss this air of Prospero's farewell to his art, he begins with a curtain going up—on a boy's puppet theater—and concludes with two theatrical sequences: a "philosophical" speech by a member of a theater family at a baptism banquet and a scene in which an actress reads a few lines from Strindberg about the power of imagination. But more disturbing than the heavily underscored farewell are the intrinsic qualities of the film: the sentimentality of composition and editing, of lighting, of character and discourse, even of menace and ugliness. Most disturbing of all is the feeling of willed affirmation that lacquers the whole work.

Whence cometh the film's wistful poignancy? Bergman's previous four features were hemispheres away in tone and interest: *Face to Face, The Serpent's Egg, Autumn Sonata,* and, last and bleakest, *From the Life of the Marionettes.* Certainly no artist need sign a long-term contract with either "L'Allegro" or "Il Penseroso," as Bergman's own past shows, but the change in *Fanny and Alex-*

---

*See p. 71.

ander has so adversely affected the texture of the film that the altered mood, the uplift, seems fabricated, unsettling to him, like an unskillful and therefore insistent falsehood. That suspicion is heightened by a passage in Peter Cowie's new (and pedestrian) biography of Bergman:

> This film was conceived as Bergman pondered a comment from his friend Kjell Grede. . . . Why, asked Grede, when Bergman so obviously loved life and found parts of it so amusing, did he consistently produce gloomy and depressing movies?

To this philistine and obtuse question, Bergman seemingly felt he had to respond—with *Fanny and Alexander.*

As the center of this smile-and-tear adieu, Bergman chose a theater family in a provincial Swedish town in 1907. The town, though unnamed, is Uppsala, where he was born. The period gives him chances for nostalgic décor and for the statement of hopes that are fraught with amiable rue. The theatrical sphere fits a man who has spent most of his career there. The first two elements, town and décor, he handles well; the theatrical ambience is a disappointment. It could have been done by someone who has never set foot in a theater. Bergman gives us clichés about the private lives of actors versus their public personae, the great world versus their little world, the more achievable reality within a smaller, controlled universe. Not one word spoken about the theater, not one scene of rehearsal or performance (there aren't many) carries fresh insight.

The film is more than three hours long, plus intermission, which is a bad sign to begin with. Bergman, at his best, works succinctly; epic length suggests inflation, rhetoric. *Fanny and Alexander* is only partially the story of Fanny and Alexander: it's about them *and* their family and the family's friends. The head of the family is Grandmama, who is a widowed actress, her three sons and their wives, and her two grandchildren, the title characters, who are about nine and eleven. The children's parents are Grandmama's oldest son, a theater manager and actor, and his actress-wife—though it's only at the end that we learn about her acting.

Grandmama herself is a pastiche of innumerable matriarchs. Her first son is a good manager but a bad actor; his wife is virtually uncharacterized. Her second son is a failed professor of some kind with a German wife: Bergman's attempt to characterize him is hothouse Chekhov and the misery in this marriage is hothouse Bergman. Her third son is a businessman who revels in the theatrical environment of his family and who loves life. I've rarely seen a man laugh so much in a film. He has a buxom, compliant wife and a buxom, compliant mistress, one of the housemaids, who is lame. These four family groups occupy separate apartments in the same huge, palatial building. Provincial theater folk evidently lived extremely well in turn-of-the-century Sweden.

Two other characters figure prominently. Isak Jacobi, an old Jewish dealer in antiques, is an old friend of the family and was once Grandmama's lover. (According to the screenplay published by Pantheon—which, as usual, differs markedly from the finished film—her maiden name was Mandelbaum, not mentioned on screen.) Edvard Vergérus, who bears a familiar Bergman surname, is the bishop of the town and gradually slides into the center of the story.

Fairly early in that story, the theater manager, father of the title characters, dies after a stroke. (What happened to Bergman's subtlety? The man is stricken while rehearsing the Ghost in *Hamlet*.) In a year or so, his widow marries the bishop and, with her two children, moves into his house. The bishop, his mother, and his sister are piously domineering, and their house is furnished with aggressive spareness. (In fact the bishop's house, rather than seeming austere, as intended, is almost pleasant after the overstuffed rooms of the theater family.) The central drama is the encounter between the new environment and the actress and her children, the collision of a rigorously moral world, built on absolutes, and people used to a good-hearted, accommodating world. The climax of the story is Isak's rescue of Fanny and Alexander from the bishop's house and the subsequent escape of their mother. Much of the material before, during, and after these episodes is heady stuff, deriving more from Gothic romance than theatrical melodrama.

The film is as egregiously upholstered as the theater family's residence. The sighing scene between the aged ex-lovers; the thunder-and-lightning at appropriate moments; the shots of a rushing stream to cover time lapses; the scene in which the old lady looks at old photos; the scene in which Alexander walks at night through Isak's shop hung with grinning scary puppets—these are all shocking platitudes. The autobiographical bits are there to be noticed: the bishop (Bergman's father was a clergyman in Uppsala), the statue of the female nude that moves for Alexander (which Bergman once said he imagined as a boy), the puppet theater and magic lantern (things he has often talked about). Bergman also employs the mystical, which he has done before but not so arbitrarily. The dead manager reappears to his mother and to his children, and they·converse with him as if they expected him. When Isak abducts the children from the bishop's house, he invokes some sort of magic which fools the bishop and which the children's mother understands. I didn't. And I didn't understand why Isak's two nephews are made to seem homoerotic toward Alexander or why the younger, demented nephew is played by a woman.

The casting has other problems. The manager is Allan Edwall, a long-time Bergman colleague, who is not a fount of appeal. The possible pathos in his death and ghostly return is damagingly muted. His sybaritic younger brother is Jarl Kulle who played the leading male roles in two of Bergman's poorest films, *The Devil's Eye* and *Now About These Women* and is still conceitedly phony. Bergman's latest discovery, Ewa Fröling, who plays the manager's widow and the bishop's wife, has been called the new Liv Ullmann. *Magari* (which is Italian for "She should live so long").

Erland Josephson and Gunn Wallgren are pleasant as Isak and Grandmama. Jan Malmsjö is directly, and aptly, out of Dickens as the wickedly righteous bishop. Pernilla Allwin and Bertil Guve are all right in the title roles. (But why is the boy made up to look like wax fruit in closeups?) Harriet Andersson, whose Bergman career began in 1952 and has grown and varied as she has grown and matured, plays a crabbed, spying maid in the bishop's house. Andersson is vividly cranky, but her performance is helped by what we know of her.

At a testimonial celebration for a distinguished filmmaker, they often show a collage drawn from his works. In a way Bergman has done the job for himself here, by assembling new treatments of old themes, by interlacing a lot of self-references. It's almost offensive to stipulate that much of *Fanny and Alexander* is made with consummate skill; it's more pertinent to mourn that so much of it is flaccid (like the long wanderings of Alexander in the first sequence), that so much is bloated or stale, and that Sven Nykvist's cinematography, often miraculous in the past, is here not much more than competent. I'm glad that this is not to be Bergman's last film, not because it is far from his best—his career has always fluctuated—but because it introduces a jarring element in his work: insincerity.

After the Rehearsal

(June 25, 1984)

Only Ingmar Bergman could have made *After the Rehearsal*, and that's precisely the reason it exists. He had announced that *Fanny and Alexander* would be his last picture, but even before that disappointing film was released, he had almost finished this subsequent work, a seventy-two-minute piece for TV. Allow Bergman his implied distinction between theater films and TV films. Certainly he has contradicted it in the past by releasing TV work as theater film, but in this case the TV piece is intrinsically different—in fact, different from anything he has done before. Bergman has often worked with small casts in relatively limited space: *Persona*, for prime instance, has only two important characters and takes place mostly in a seaside cottage and the surrounding grounds. *After the Rehearsal* has three characters (two children appear who don't speak), but it is limited to one place; what's more, excepting an occasional long shot seemingly to let us catch our breath, the camera stays close, much of the time on faces only. This method, almost frighteningly rigorous, contains a wry contradiction: the closeness is employed, not in a conventional room but in the large space of a relatively empty theater stage in front of a large, empty house.

Let me first enlist this review as, in part, a postscript to the one of *Fanny and Alexander*.* For me, *After the Rehearsal* refutes the inflated cinema rhetoric, the carpentered cheer, the trite poignancies of the previous film. The difference is not that *Fanny* was a period piece full of nostalgic warmth while the new piece is modern and more somber, therefore *echt* Bergman. (*Smiles of a Summer Night* manages to be good though neither contemporary nor somber.) The difference is elemental. In all its elements, *After the Rehearsal* is genuine. Unlike *Fanny*, no line of dialogue, no composition, no cut is forced, is anything but authentic.

Bergman's script is an act of quiet daring: it dares to be something other than a drama, of whatever color. It is a meditation, by a theater director, on the life and work of a theater director. Yet it is done on film!—by a theater director of world fame who is also a film director of world stature.

Bergman hasn't told a story, he has constructed an armature for his meditation. Three characters sustain it: a middle-aged director, Henrik Vogler; a young actress, Anna Egerman (both of whose patronymics recur in Bergman scripts); and her mother Rakel, also an actress. The film starts with Vogler dozing at his work table on the empty stage, as he often does after a rehearsal. In comes Anna; as he wakes, she explains that she has lost a bracelet at the rehearsal just finished. A long scene follows between them, with voice-over privacies from Vogler establishing that this is *his* film. Then, while Anna is sitting on a sofa, her mother, Rakel, walks in, looking for her shoes. (She says that she had left mistakenly in her rehearsal shoes.) We learned in the first scene that Rakel has been dead for five years, but she is not treated as a revenant: she simply walks in and the scene with Vogler occurs—at a time when Anna was about twelve. When there is a cut to Anna on the sofa during this scene, the young woman has been replaced by the child, who sits mute and motionless. Rakel leaves for her apartment behind the theater, expecting Vogler to follow. In a transitional moment, Vogler comes back to the sofa and strokes the hair of the silent child; then, with the magical simplicity that marks all of this work, the film continues seamlessly with more of that opening scene between the grown Anna and Vogler. Those three sections constitute the whole.

The time warp, treated as if it didn't exist, harmonizes with the play that Vogler is rehearsing, *A Dream Play*. In Strindberg's words, he attempted "to imitate the disconnected but seemingly logical form of a dream. . . . Everything is possible and plausible." (Remember that Vogler was dozing at the start; perhaps the whole film doesn't "really" happen.) "But," says Strindberg, "one consciousness is superior to [all the other characters]: that of the dreamer." Here the dreamer is Bergman's vicar, Vogler. It would be silly to assume that this film is a veristic memoir, even the memoir of a dream; it would also be silly to assume that Bergman doesn't know what he's talking about.

Anna, who is the same age as Vogler's daughter, knows that the director lov-

---

*See p. 68.

ed her mother. (But he tells Anna that he never had an affair with Rakel. Later, with Rakel, he recalls that both he and Mikael, her husband and his friend, had long been her lovers.) From Anna, we learn that Rakel, who was greatly gifted, went to a premature death through alcoholism. In Rakel's own scene, she is already in physical decline and has only a small part in the production Vogler is then rehearsing—also *A Dream Play*. Rakel virtually begins by asking Vogler to make love to her in his office; gets around to wondering whether he no longer trusts her with major roles; eventually leaves with his promise of a rendezvous in her apartment. When Vogler and Anna resume their scene, they play a dialogue game in which they trace the course that an affair between them might take. Obviously there can't be perfect analogues between the Anna-Vogler and Rakel-Vogler scenes because of the difference in his age-relationships to the two women, but there are some parallels.

Those parallels relate to the two main themes on which the film is meditating. (Additionally Bergman includes acute observations on acting and directing.) The first of these is theater mystique—the mode in which even the most intelligent theater people can romanticize about backstage atmosphere, about the auditorium silently echoing with past passions, about the agonized ecstasy of the actor's emotional nakedness on stage, and so on. That mystique truly exists, but it is still twaddle, the inflation of an art that uses the artist's being as instrument and resource. Bergman indulges the mystique quite knowingly but affectionately, because "it goes with the territory." He understands how work in the theater makes that mystique unavoidable yet also, if used discreetly, possibly helpful.

Second, sex. The theater thrives on sexuality, even in many of its apparently chaste manifestations. An art that lives by the summoning of its performers' emotions, in deliberate reproduction, must sensitize those people in ways that, say, working in a bank does not. This is patently not to say that acting equals depravity (or that bank employees have no sex lives). Yet it's easy to see why actors were long thought to be ipso facto immoral. Bergman is not so much searching out hidden truths about the alerted sexuality of the theater as he is drenching his film in its musk. The moment that Anna returns ostensibly looking for her bracelet, Vogler knows that it's only an excuse—for some kind of skirmishing. When Rakel enters, somewhat high on more than drink, she wastes little time in asking Vogler to make love, and she insists over his demurral that he really wants her. It's relevant that in the middle of his scene with Anna, Vogler helps her with her acting—a passage in her Strindberg role; and that, in the middle of Rakel's scene, she launches into a speech from a play. (From *The Bacchae*, of all plays—a literally Dionysian speech.) Both of the acting moments, and all three of the scenes in the film itself, are wreathed in sexual vapors that seem to be simmering out of this very place, a theater.

Neither with these themes nor in plot does the film move to a conclusion. It is all just Bergman meditating on what it would be like to be sitting at his work table after a rehearsal when certain things happen, as (allowing for differences in detail) they presumably could; and he perceives how even these encounters, "undesigned" in the traditional dramaturgic sense, could not avoid the two main themes of this piece.

Cinematically the film depends on three faces. (The two children, young Anna and Vogler-as-boy glimpsed backstage, are not significant.) I've previously expressed reservations about the resident interest in the face of Erland Josephson, the veteran Bergman colleague who plays Vogler, but age is improving it, sculpting it clean, not making it baggy. Now it is a face of patient secrets. Anna is Lena Olin, who had a small part in *Fanny*. Her chief asset is her voice, which is expressive, rather than her face, which is less so. Olin is certainly quite adequate, but the role could have used more than adequacy. A shock, for those who know her, is the appearance of Ingrid Thulin as Rakel, and that shock is intentional. She hasn't made a film with Bergman since *Cries and Whispers*, 1972, but other films have shown that Thulin is aging differently from Josephson. Here she figuratively wears a sign saying "Formerly Beautiful," and she speaks a number of lines to underscore that idea. But Thulin is as good an actress as ever, even stronger than she was, and she fulfills exactly what Bergman wants in this role: a woman who no longer *can* care about appearances but who is (therefore?) all the more passionate: for her work, for sex, for a cherished place in at least some minds. The combination of her looks and her heat makes Vogler uncomfortable—and us, too. In time, he becomes embarrassed by his discomfort and finds compassion; and we share those feelings, too.

The cinematographer was Sven Nykvist, of course, not much challenged here. The art direction by Anna Asp could be more delicate: Anna in a solid red jersey and Vogler in a tan corduroy jacket sit on a green sofa. But *After the Rehearsal* is a unique accomplishment. Nothing in it is greatly moving, nor is meant to be; we are enveloped in a master artist's reverie on some aspects of his life in art, and when it's over, it's over—that's all. Yet when we "awaken," we remember.

(July 16 & 23, 1984)

Postscript. In the second of the three long scenes that compose *After the Rehearsal*, Ingrid Thulin and Erland Josephson converse frankly about sex, past and planned, while her twelve-year-old daughter sits nearby. Only much later did I really become aware of the fact that, technically, the child is present; and then the effect was not distaste but admiration for another power of film. Bergman keeps his camera so close to the two adults that we forget the child is present: in any operative sense, the child is *not* present—except, at cooler moments, when Bergman reminds us of her with a glimpse, in order to fix the "pastness" of the dialogue between the adults. Oddly, when he cuts to a shot of the child, or gives us a long shot of all three persons, it seems a different, interwoven scene, not as if the child had been added to the previous intimate scene.

A filmmaker can of course remove a person at will without that person's actually leaving the scene. But that is not merely a fact of editing: it is an aspect of cinematic mystery, the way a scene becomes a *different* place according to what is included of the very same place. The theater can do this by means of lighting in nonrealistic plays; in fact, today's film-conditioned theater audiences cry out for the theater to do it at times. When I last saw *The Bacchae*, I pitied the actress playing Agave who had to lug Pentheus's head around the stage for the final twenty minutes or so while a lot of things went on. Film made me wish the director could have cut away from her until she was needed, to disembarrass us and her of her continuous presence with that fake head in her hand.

In *After the Rehearsal* Bergman uses that quasi-metaphysical asset of film in a work about a theater director that is set on a stage. This usage underscores the quality of Bergman's meditation here: on the faculties of both the theater and the film and his love of both.

Raging Bull

(December 6, 1980)

Seeing Martin Scorsese's new film is like visiting a human zoo. That's certainly not to say that it's dull: good zoos are not dull. But the life we watch is stripped to elemental drives, with just enough décor of complexity — especially the heraldry of Catholicism — to underscore how elemental it basically is.

Scorsese specializes in the primitive aspects of urban life, with an emphasis on Italian-Americans. American films have developed a latter-day line in this vein: *Rocky*, both *I* and *II*, which twined Movieland braids around its primitivism, and *The Godfather*, also *I* and *II*, which aggrandized a family's bestiality into a saga. Italian-Americans may very understandably be tired of this canted concentration on gutter and crime, but they had better brace themselves: because here it is again and — which may irritate them further — done better than ever, done excellently. Scorsese has filmed the life of the boxer Jake La Motta, his rises and falls and eventual retirement, and this time Scorsese's work is purged of heavy symbolism, of film-school display, of facile portent. His directing is imaginative but controlled; egregious mannerisms have coalesced into a strong style. Some of *Raging Bull* is shocking, but all of it is irresistible.

The screenplay, based on a ghosted autobiography, was written by Paul Schrader and Mardik Martin, both of whom have worked with Scorsese before. La Motta is played by Robert De Niro, another Scorsese veteran, and obviously the whole enterprise was built around him. Previously De Niro played demented animalistic characters for Scorsese in *Mean Streets*, written by Scorsese and Martin, and *Taxi Driver*, written by Schrader. Here they have found the best beast for De Niro in La Motta, best because free of patent psychopathy, a "normal" man capable of overpowering fury but still answerable to some social canons and therefore accessible to pathos rather than to clinical category.

They have also constructed the film — probably with fidelity to La Motta's life but who cares? — so that the boxing ring, which occupies a lot of screen time, is almost indistinguishable in temper from much of the man's personal life. De Niro's La Motta is a fount of rage, a man who lives by rage or the threat of it or the tension of controlling it, a man in whom quiet means the absence of rage, but a man who has the cunning of an animal and enough capability for guilt — inculcated by family ties and implicit religion — to give him moments of remorse for his rage. All of these qualities except the last are present both in the living room and the ring; and the key achievement of the picture is that the four makers, director and writers and star, have made this zoo creature unfailingly gripping.

Partly this is because they were clever enough to start in the "present," 1964, long after La Motta has retired from boxing, then go back for the events leading up to this point. Thus the first La Motta we see is middle-aged and fat — De Niro put on a well-publicized fifty pounds for these sequences — in a dinner-jacket, rehearsing a humorous poem for a nightclub appearance. And thus we know all through the picture that he survived and in some ways grew, because there isn't much humor or humanity in him until the fighting stops. Throughout most of the story La Motta seems to have as simple a set of motives as one could have and stay out of a real zoo. He wants to hit and to screw — to *own* a woman more than to screw, apparently — and he wants peer approval by winning the middleweight championship more than he wants to fulfill any ideal of being champ. That opening glimpse helps the bulk of the picture.

But it would hold anyway, because of De Niro. Behind his false nose, he assaults us with force, engulfing force so sheer that it achieves a kind of esthetic stature. Whatever subtlety is in the performance comes from De Niro rather than the role. For instance, his use of his body. In the otherwise barren film of The Last Tycoon, De Niro gave Monroe Stahr kinetic patterns that completely expressed a man whose body was of little concern to him, whose center was in his mind and his secrets, a man who was almost reluctantly attended by his body. La Motta of course lives through his body. De Niro expresses it immediately and exquisitely.

Even more cheering is Scorsese's growth. Little Italy, the conflict between the support and the restrictions of Catholicism, the alliances and counteralliances of family and of the Mafia are still his home ground. He tells us in the sequence under the opening credits that he is dealing with provenance and struggle: while La Motta — in slow motion — prances around a ring in a robe, warming up, the sound-track lays on the "Intermezzo" from Cavalleria Rusticana. It's a splendid *fixing* of the film.

Contradictorily Scorsese has both purged and complicated his filmmaking. *Taxi Driver* was better made than *Mean Streets* (I'm ignoring his films out of this vein), and *Raging Bull* is a huge leap. He is still avid to move film all the time, eager to energize his screen, but instead of his former frantic cutting from long shots to closeups and back, with some reverse shots thrown in, he now more subtly cuts to shots in which the camera is already moving forward slowly. In the fight sequences, he sometimes creates the effect of putting the camera in a glove, inside a battered head, and he always keeps prime the feeling of complete physical collision. (Some of the fight shots are horrible, but they're not out of place.) He has solved the visual problem of chronicling many fights; sometimes he varies with slow motion, sometimes with a series of stills, sometimes with isolated successive frames like the ones of astronauts on the moon. Never does he let us anticipate wearily that there are more fights to come; he never lets the matter get near tedium, and he never uses trickery that distracts. These sequences are interesting variations, like a good composer's variations on a theme.

There are some bumps in the story line, and they may be connected with Scorsese's filmmaking process rather than the script. For instance, La Motta throws a fight for the mob and gets into trouble with ring authorities; his subsequent reinstatement is badly skimped. Later we see him at his expensive Miami home and the nightclub he owns, yet moments later, when he needs $10,000 bail, he can't raise it. Scorsese fell so in love with the making of this film, I think, with the actual shooting of scenes and sequences—such fine small touches as a scene with an Irish gambler at a bar, with a sports official in a tunnel under a stadium—that he found himself with more of a jigsaw to assemble in the editing room than do most directors. What holds this picture together more than its story line is its stylistic consistency, and style here means more than cinematic syntax, it means fire and personality. I've a hunch, too, that the result owes a great deal to its editor, Thelma Schoonmaker, that she found ways to fuse the fiery particles into a flow and to make an organism out of what may have been digressions and lingerings in the shooting.

But one laurel must rest on Scorsese's head alone, praise for the acting—that is, for the casting and for the guidance of the actors. Many scenes are played in a very low key, not as patent Paul Muni preparations for outburst but to draw us into privacies, to take us beneath the skin. The timing of the dialogue is excellent: note the meeting between La Motta and his future (second) wife. Or a later scene when she urges him to telephone his brother and make up a quarrel. They are standing together silently after a boxing match. After a moment she suggests the call; another pause; she suggests it again. De Niro doubtless could have felt the timing on his own, but Cathy Moriarty, who had never acted before, must have needed help. Some of it, I'm sure, came from De Niro (people who have worked with him have talked about his generosity), but there must have been real help from Scorsese.

Moriarty is physically perfect for the part and conveys the precise sense of a girl who is sufficiently bright to know that being petted and desired isn't enough. As La Motta's brother, Joe Pesci is perfect: feisty, street-honorable, glumly humorous. The many, many fast exchanges between the brothers sound to me like improvisations based on a script—sharp pickups, repetitions and overlaps, quiet and loud amazements. (From first line of the film to last, the language is as it ought to be—vile.) And all the Mafia figures, who are not explicitly called such, are lushly handsome and have voices like top-grade olive oil.

Inevitably De Niro's role has covert reminders of Brando, plus two overt ones. After the worst battle between husband and wife, she begins to pack, preparing to leave. Subdued now, La Motta appeals to her, mostly with body language, and they embrace, like Stanley and Stella, in A Streetcar Named Desire. And just before the end, the obese La Motta, rehearsing his act in a nightclub dressing room, does Brando's "I coulda been a contender" speech from On the Waterfront. Of course it's not as good as Brando—it couldn't be, De Niro is playing La Motta playing Brando—but it's a nice goodbye wink at the audience.

I have to hope that De Niro will make more films with other directors: though he and Scorsese clearly work well together, they stay within a relatively narrow spectrum, and the limits are demonstrably Scorsese's, not De Niro's. But within these limits, Raging Bull is electrifying.

Except for a flash of color in the credits and some color "home movies" used as a bridge, the film is in black and white, shot by Michael Chapman with plenty of evocative shadows, except for the ring which is drenched in scary glare. Some verses from John IX, 24-26, are appended at the end, but I don't grasp their relevance. More, I think it may be misguided to try to crystallize what the film is "about." Attempts have already been made to explain La Motta's character as reactive to the Italian-American atmosphere, but the script wouldn't have to be much different fundamentally if the protagonist were a black or an Irish Catholic or a Jew. La Motta is to be taken as given, a chunk of temperament like a character in a medieval morality play.

Finally Raging Bull is "about" what we see and hear, elevating its rather familiar materials through conviction and the gush of life. After the socio-psychological explanations have limped on, this film, like some (though not most) good art works, is finally "about" the fact that it incontrovertibly exists and, by existing, moves us.

The King of Comedy

(March 28, 1983)

The screenplay of the *King of Comedy* is by Paul D. Zimmerman, a former film critic of *Newsweek*. Martin Scorsese, the director, has usually worked with scripts by himself collaborating with Mardik Martin or Paul Schrader, and most of those scripts have been conceived as naturalistic torrents, meant to sweep us with their turbulence. Zimmerman's script is a concoction, a match-stick construction naturalistically colored but close in concept to the gimmicky Hollywood and French comedies of the 1930s. This may explain why the picture is virtually bare of Scorsese style, such touches, heavy or helpful, as the opening manhole shot of *Taxi Driver* or the opening prize-ring sequence of *Raging Bull*. I saw nothing in *The King of Comedy* that couldn't have been done by any competent director. Cinematically, it's flavorless.

Scorsese's lack of liftoff here may be due to the nature of the psychopathy with which he is dealing. Yes, his central figure is once again a psychopath, but, unlike his other films, the pretense here is that the man is only eccentrically obsessed. Neither Zimmerman nor Scorsese really faced the facts that they themselves put forth in the film, never came near realizing the character they were dealing with. In fact they never create a character, only an immense running gag of gray (not black) humor. No wonder the resultant film makes us feel that, for the first time, Scorsese seems untouched by what he is doing.

Robert De Niro, too, once again Scorsese's leading actor, seems somewhat hamstrung by the pasteboard ninny he consented to play. De Niro doesn't need violence in order to be excellent: remember his performance in *The Last Tycoon* (under another director). But basically he, like Scorsese, seems to have been partly anesthetized by infatuation with the *idea* of the script and hasn't perceived that the protagonist, as written, is only an arrangement of actions to make that idea possible.

That protagonist is named Rupert Pupkin: and the name itself ought to have been a warning to all concerned that they were dealing with a self-conscious "little man" attitude. Rupert, apparently in his thirties, is a messenger who idolizes a talk-show host named Jerry Langford. Rupert wants nothing but to be a stand-up comic and talk-show host like Jerry. He, along with others, hangs around the studio stage door. He lives (to judge by one exterior shot) across the river in New Jersey with his mother, and he has furnished the cellar of their house like a studio, with tape equipment, with three chairs—a life-size cutout of Liza Minelli in one, of Jerry on the other side, and a place for himself in the middle. As he fantasizes aloud, his mother calls down to him from above to lower the taped sound effects.

By the time that place and character have been established, the film, intended to be socially surgical, has itself been established: as myopic, false, and forced. At his age Rupert is still a messenger. How intelligent can he be? Much less shrewd and smooth, surely, than he is here. He seems to have all the time he needs at his disposal every day. Then how does he earn a living? Especially, how does he afford the expensive equipment in his cellar and his spiffy, if not tasteful, clothes? On the salary of a messenger who apparently works very little?

Rupert is so pasted together of incredibilities that he isn't even convincing as the demented person he would be if he were credible. And he couldn't be lovably pathetic, as intended, even if believable. His persistence *isn't* persistence: it's a mixture of inability to recognize reality and ability to fantasticate. He doesn't perceive how he's behaving in Langford's offices when he tries to see the comic or what is being done to get rid of him. He doesn't know that his taking a girl out to Langford's suburban home, after he has persuaded her that they have been invited for a weekend, is psychotic. Well, psychopaths don't always know of their affliction, even in lucid moments. But this ignorance seems as much De Niro's as Rupert's: the two ignorances combine to make the character a puppet. (His last name is clearly meant to suggest that word. Leave the filmmakers out of it: if Rupert Pupkin himself were minimally sane, he would know that his name is ludicrous and would either alter it or exploit it.)

His girl friend, played by the gorgeous and engaging Diahnne Abbott, is black. Would Rupert have a black girl friend? Not likely, in his environment. Would she, a bartender drawn as world wise, have picked up so congenially with a fellow she hasn't seen since high school and didn't much like then? Would a smart girl have believed that he had been invited to Langford's country home, had been asked to bring a guest? Would Langford, whose city quarters are carefully guarded, have no security at all in the suburbs? If Rupert had made a nuisance in the office and then intruded in the suburbs, wouldn't Langford without hesitation have called the police? And even if he *had* talked Rupert into leaving, wouldn't he then have told the police as a precaution, against the sort of action that indeed follows?

Involved in that action is another Langford groupie, a rich New York Jewish girl, a role cast by Scorsese to show, I assume, that he is no slave to film cliché but which shows instead a desperation to give his flimsy script a touch of old-time Scorsese verism. This girl assists Rupert in the film's climax, a sequence by now so publicized that I'm not spilling any beans. The two kidnap Langford and use a death threat to get Rupert a chance to tape a comedy sequence for the show. Rupert makes a hit, goes to prison, is much celebrated, and comes out after two years to comedy success. (What happens to the girl who was his accomplice? No word about her.) The finish was presumably intended to be wry, à la Preston Sturges; instead it's mechanically benevolent, like diluted Frank Capra.

Only one moment in the whole picture struck me as truthfully scathing, the tone that apparently was the hope for all of it. After Rupert threatens his way into taping his comedy bit in front of a live audience, he comes out and tells some weary jokes. *The audience laughs.* I believed that. You can hear almost every night on TV that audience response is conditioned by more than the Applause sign. Has there ever been a comic, however dismal, who came out before a TV audience and never got *any* laughs? Not in my experience. The audience is as hype-happy as Rupert, is excited by being there, and seems to feel some deep obligation to do its part. And the only way it can be in the show is to laugh. Responses vary in warmth, of course: the good comics do better than the lesser ones; but an audience never completely lets the show down. That scene of Rupert's seemed to me valid, so it was the only scene that was satirical.

Faced only with a framework hung with tags, aware of this fact or not, De Niro does his extraordinary best to transform the mechanics into a man. He conveys Rupert's basic hearing block: the man never really hears the denials, rejections, put-offs that come his way. De Niro tells us this with half-smile, with glinting eyes, with assumed svelte superiority. He also gets the unrhythmical quality of Rupert's movement and gesture, epitomized in that one TV appearance. De Niro knows that Rupert has studied Langford and other comics, that he thinks he has learned how to do the stuff. But all Rupert has acquired is some of the mannerisms—the Bob Hope run-on, for instance. He doesn't have central ease, his delivery is a collection of remembered inflections, he hasn't a clue about what to do with his arms. Because that scene is the best in the script, De Niro, one of our best film actors, is able to blend Rupert's imitation of professionals and his residual amateurishness into a spot of horror. But the rest of the script, with its faked characterization and flabby dialogue, its unrealized insanity, gives De Niro troubles.

Jerry Lewis plays Jerry Langford, and I'd guess he had a good deal to do with his own dialogue. Now past zaniness, Lewis presents a hardened old pro, quiet, a bit tired, very sure. Would any "straight" actor have been as good as Lewis in this role? I doubt it. Lewis's life has written the part, and, with Scorsese's help, he has managed something much harder than it sounds: to be himself.

A chance was missed in this film, a chance that Susan Seidelman grasped in her small-scale *Smithereens*: to show the harrowings of hype in little lives, lives that might have been much happier if left unteased. The most quoted remark on the subject is Andy Warhol's line that, in the future, everyone in the world will be famous for fifteen minutes. What's terrible in that remark is not that it's possible, not that media of the future may even more ruthlessly exploit and cast aside, but that, in our culture, publicity has replaced sex and even success as the dirty little secret.

Breaker Morant

(December 27, 1980)

Bruce Beresford is an Australian director, previously represented here by *The Getting of Wisdom*, which was a well-directed, exquisitely photographed, platitudinous film about the rites of passage of an adolescent schoolgirl at the turn of the century. *Breaker Morant* is a better-directed, more exquisitely photographed, equally platitudinous film about military injustice at the turn of the century.

Films about the harshness of wartime tribunals are so familiar that, especially because crispness like Beresford's implies intelligence, we look for an increment; we feel that Beresford must know that his material is essentially trite and must be bringing some addition to our experience. Not perceptible. Like Kubrick's *Paths of Glory*, like Losey's *King and Country*, *Breaker Morant* just winds through a court-martial—this one a historical case—that shows another military need for a verdict of guilty despite the facts.

Harry Morant, called Breaker because he was a breaker of wild horses, and two fellow-officers are Australians fighting in the Boer War. Obeying orders from Lord Kitchener, they kill some Boer guerillas whom they take prisoner. This wouldn't have caused much fuss except that they also kill a German missionary who could have spread the news. The German government is ruffled, and as the British government is eager not to provide an excuse for coming in on the side of the Boers, all three officers must be tried and punished even though they were obeying (unwritten) orders. A younger man gets a life sentence; Morant and another lieutenant are shot.

The strophes of irony and prejudice—English gentry accents deployed against the colonials—are followed faithfully. The cast is good. Beresford and his editor strive imaginatively against the stasis of a courtroom story, with flashbacks of course but also with sudden closeups that are like quick slices of intimacy. But the picture remains more predictable than grimly inevitable.

A special word for Don McAlpine, the cinematographer, who did two Beresford films and *My Brilliant Career*. It's time to acknowledge his world rank in his profession.

Tender Mercies

(April 11, 1983)

Horton Foote's first play, produced in 1941, was *Texas Town*. His new screenplay, *Tender Mercies*, is about Texas towns, the people in them and around them. (A lot of the picture was shot in the country between Dallas and Waco.) Much of Foote's writing has been concerned with Texas subjects. He has had fluctuating success in the theater, film, and television, but his new screenplay is a beauty.

A few of the elements in *Tender Mercies* are just good enough to be true; most of it is quietly fated. Its central character is a man who has been through rough weather and has been seasoned by it. Luck and talent brought him success—in country music—then success brought him weakness and failure. "I don't trust happiness," he says at the end, but he is grateful for the happiness he ultimately finds.

Because screenwriting is a collaborative art even more vulnerable to the collaborators than playwriting, Foote would probably be the first to say that the splendid realization of this film helps to form our high opinion of his script. Begin with the leading actor, Robert Duvall. (He has been in at least two previous Foote screenplays, *To Kill a Mockingbird* and *The Chase*.) Anyone who has seen one Duvall film knows that he is a striking actor. Anyone who has seen three Duvall films—say, *The Eagle Has Landed* (Duvall as a German officer in World War II), *The Seven-Per-Cent Solution* (Duvall as Sherlock Holmes's Dr. Watson), and *True Confessions* (Duvall as a tough L. A. detective)—knows that he goes past mimetic wizardry to an almost metaphysical territory of multiple personae. Anyone who has also had the luck to see him on stage—say, in *A View from the Bridge* and *American Buffalo*—knows that the quality of Duvall's ambition is all that keeps him from greatness. Nothing stands between Duvall and a fine Macbeth and John Gabriel Borkman and Colenso Ridgeon (in *The Doctor's Dilemma*) and Con Melody (in *A Touch of the Poet*), if he chooses to do them. And on screen, if he can't film any of the above or comparable works, if worthwhile original film scripts are not forthcoming, he could reach for good adaptions of novels. Melville's *The Confidence-Man* and Hardy's *The Mayor of Casterbridge* and Bellow's *Henderson the Rain King* are only the first three titles that come to mind.

To speculate so wildly about Duvall after *Tender Mercies* is a special tribute to him because of the character he plays here. The man is a former country singer who drank himself out of performing and composing fame, out of marriage and fatherhood (a daughter), into an anonymity that he now enjoys. (Note: in the course of the picture Duvall sings a number of songs, and it's really he who sings them. He even wrote a couple of them.) Except for the daughter, he has no regrets about his losses even though he is now penniless and lives as he can. After a drinking bout with another man in an isolated shabby motel, the pal (never seen) deserts him. A young widow, whose husband was killed in Vietnam, runs the motel and lives there with her nine-year-old son. Duvall asks if he can work around the place to pay the bill with which his pal has left him. Reticently but sympathetically she agrees—and at least some of the story is foretold: but with a pleasant sense of mesh, not staleness. Foote provides neatly crystallized dialogue and well-modeled scenes; and his story has twists that come simply from verity. A reporter tracks Duvall to his snug retreat as the husband (yes, he marries the widow) of the motel owner. When the reporter keeps pestering with questions after Duvall says he wants to be left alone, we do not get the expected movie outburst and sock on the jaw; Duvall just walks out the back door of the house. Much later, when he does get upset about something, he piles into the pickup and barrels off, leaving his worried wife and stepson. We assume that he's going to dive back into booze. He stops in a bar and a liquor store. Eventually he comes home and tells his wife that he bought a bottle but poured it on the ground: that he had spent hours driving up and down past their house, glimpsing his wife and her boy watching TV. (Pronounced "tee-vee.") Foote is concerned with what is really happening in this man, not with mechanical climaxes, and Duvall has realized it all perfectly.

The whole picture is wonderfully cast. Tess Harper, a Texan actress, gives the young widow pride and gentleness. When Duvall's presence around the place first causes sexual stirrings in her, she conveys it subtly: her increase in dignity is her declaration of interest. Her boy, Allan Hubbard, reflects her upbringing and example. Ellen Barkin, who was in *Diner*, plays Duvall's eighteen-year-old daughter who visits him against her mother's wishes. In two scenes Barkin creates a troubled life. Wilford Brimley, as a manager who used to manage Duvall, has patience that covers gnarled stubbornness. Betty Buckley, as Duvall's ex-wife, still a country music star, gives a more conventional performance than the others, but it's the most conventional role.

All the acting certifies the understanding of the director, Bruce Beresford, the Australian who made *Breaker Morant*. First and least, *Tender Mercies* is the best of the American debuts made in the past year by Australian directors. (Others were Fred Schepisi with *Barbarosa*—also set in Texas—and Peter Weir who made *The Year of Living Dangerously* under American auspices.) Did Foote help Beresford with the casting of small parts? The youngish choir conductor in the town church, a plump man whose jowls wag fervently, seems a youthful memory revivified. Still, Beresford has directed as crisply and confidently as he did at home, with as keen a sense of phrase and silence.

Certainly he was helped by the cinematographer Russell Boyd, also an Australian, who looks for essence in landscape rather than for lushness. With Boyd, Beresford fixes the spirit of the place. As many have noted, the Australian outback and this Texas terrain have similarities; perhaps those similarities sharpened Beresford's perception that, in huge flat landscape, visual experience tends to be two-dimensional. Cars and trucks shear across the screen like scissors through paper. The lonely motel, seen in long shot, is like a cardboard cutout. Beresford and Boyd carry this linear spareness indoors: many shots are framed in doorways, sometimes in doorways seen one behind another. The vertical and horizontal lines of nature and of buildings frame the flow of characters' feelings.

And what editing! Beresford's touch, strengthened by his editor, William Anderson, is masterly. One instance: the film opens with the sounds of a drunken brawl that is then seen in lamplit silhouette behind the drawn shade of a seedy motel room. The boy, in his bathrobe, comes out of the motel office behind which he lives, and his mother comes out to join him. Both watch and listen apprehensively. In between shots of the window and of the watching pair there is one quick close-up of Duvall's head hitting the carpeted floor of the motel room. Why, I wondered, had Beresford and Anderson shoved one interior flash into this exterior sequence? The answer came quickly. We go back to Duvall's sleeping head on the floor as the credits roll, after which the picture continues with *him*. That opening sequence established place and atmosphere, showed the mother and son in their vulnerable loneliness, but it also flicked in a bit of the future by showing us the protagonist. That one quick insert is the filament that leads out of the (essential) mother-son view into the rest of the film: it connects the "prologue" with the work.

Beresford also shows delicacy in what must be called his staging. In one sequence, five young musicians drive up in a van, ostensibly to get gas at the motel pump but really to meet Duvall whom they revere through his old records. Duvall, informed by his wife that they are waiting, comes out carefully. He and the five men keep their distance, but the space between them is filled with their admiration and his reluctant pleasure. Near the end, Duvall is hoeing the small vegetable garden behind the motel at sunset. He has "recovered" sufficiently to write some songs, to sing a little, to record a little, but he has no wish to leave this place and this life. And he has just had some terrible personal news, sudden but not surprising. His wife is at the edge of the garden. Beresford keeps the camera back most of the time, a little distance. The film just watches and listens as this man, in this small garden with evening immensity behind it, quietly tells his wife how battered and baffled he feels. He keeps on hoeing, will keep on living and working with this woman and her son whom he loves, a woman who has seen her own considerable share of suffering. If he doesn't trust happiness, it's not because of her. We know that he has been baptized in the town church for her sake. Apparently he has some belief in the religion he has professed, but the tender mercies he has found don't seem to come from the one who giveth and taketh life. Duvall is willing to settle for some crevices, some refuge in the mercies of human beings.

That distancing of the camera through much of this sequence is the tonal signature of the film. Foote and Beresford want distillation, not saturation. Every step in the story that can be inferred is left to inference, like the elision that goes from Duvall's first suggestion of marriage to their married state. Almost all the violence we might expect in a Texas small-town story of saloon dances and drunkenness is kept on the edge, is felt more than seen. The result is quasi-theatrical, almost a modern version of a medieval morality play. The characters are very much richer than pageant figures, but *Tender Mercies* is more allegory than story—a cry for some understanding of mysteries or at least some solace for ignorance. Motels and guitars and booze are only the surface phenomena.

Tess

(January 3 & 10, 1981)

Roman Polanski's *Tess* begins beautifully. The camera is high over the Wessex landscape (shot in Normandy actually), then pulls back slowly, comes down, and picks up a lane running toward us at an angle. A small procession approaches slowly up the lane—musicians leading a group of girls in white, bearing branches. They pass by us, close, and as the camera turns to follow them, it picks up a farm laborer coming along a road that joins that lane. The camera stays with him and soon picks up a horseman ambling toward him. It's a "sequence shot" in the best Renoir tradition. The two flowing movements, of the people and of the camera, combine to begin the story at the heart of its milieu, with a suggestion of ballad, with a sense of the coursing of narrative, of fate.

In camera choices and movements, the film continues beautifully. *Tess of the D'Urbervilles* has, in those terms, brought out the best in Polanski since *Knife in the Water*, his first feature. *Tess* has the same strong simplicity, the same inviting compositions, the same contained intensities, with none of the failed meretriciousness (the worst kind) of much of his intervening work. Polanski has had some perception of the rhythms of Hardy's tragedy and has respected his perception.

The picture is not a failure. I put it that way because it isn't a success and I don't want to make it seem a disaster. But, though not tedious or trifling, it falls short. The trouble is not that the screenplay, by Gerard Brach and Polanski and John Brownjohn, omits and compresses a great deal: that was inevitable. In fact, it's surprising how much this film, at a mere 170 minutes, retains. The trouble lies elsewhere.

First, the casting. Lovely Nastassia Kinski, daughter of the celebrated Klaus Kinski, is credible, but it's not quite Tess that she's credible as, it's a different character. Oddly, she seems to fit Hardy's description: "a fine, handsome girl—not handsomer than some others, certainly" (Polanski doesn't make her the one swan among crows), with a "mobile peony mouth and large innocent eyes." But her temperament and flavor are very much more Brontë than Hardy. No conviction of being rooted in the earth comes from her, though we often see her laboring; and thus the killing of Alec seems more of a boulevard scandal than the result of primal forces working through a natural woman. Peter Firth, as Angel Clare—a character name that ranks in daring with Dickens's Rosa Bud—is hopeless: a petty face further diminished by whiskers, a presence of no impress, a figure of nullity. Firth looks even worse because so many of the faces and performances in small roles around him are trenchant. Leigh Lawson, as Alec, is adequate but without much depth.

(Still, Lawson is good enough to revive my qualms about Alec. Certainly he seduced Tess with brutal egotism; but certainly he didn't know that she became pregnant and, when he found out, he helped her and her family in real remorse. Then, when Tess wants to rejoin Angel, she murders Alec: not because she couldn't leave him if she chose but to purge herself in her own and Angel's eyes. It does seem a bit hard on Alec.)

And there's the trouble that recurs in films of great literature: no cinematic equivalent for the prose. I cite, again, a successful example: Eric Rohmer's *The Marquise of O.*, which in its texture achieves a metamorphosis of Kleist's texture, thus gives the film a vertical as well as horizontal being. But Polanski has merely extracted the story, much of it anyway, from Hardy's novel, as one might extract the plot of a thriller. One result is that the major transitional moments don't hold. The wonderful density of Hardy's writing, its complexity, its almost palpable "feel," create the world in which his story's events exist. But the texture of Polanski's film doesn't support key moments: when Angel cannot accept Tess's past and leaves her; when he returns after some years and expects to be welcomed; when she joins him at last and tells him she has killed Alec. These moments seem either stuffy or slightly comic because, without a prose-equivalent film texture, they are pressed against *our* standards of behavior instead of the standards in that world.

The cinematography by the late Geoffrey Unsworth and Ghislain Cloquet doesn't help. It's so gorgeous that it heightens the romantic feeling generated by Kinski. There is an opposition in Hardy's depiction of Wessex. His drama is hard, but his prose is not. Hardy's land pulses. ("Amid the oozing fatness and warm ferments of the Froom Vale, at a season when the rush of juices could almost be heard below the hiss of fertilization, it was impossible that the most fanciful love should not grow passionate.") But it is not merely pictorial. Two summers ago I spent a few days in Dorset, which is most of Hardy's Wessex, three miles from Marnhull, which is Tess's Marlott; and, no doubt influenced by Hardy, I saw that wonderful countryside as *living*—busy in its thriving and its cycles—rather than as a set of postcards. Polanski and his cinematographers show some rough farm work, but when they look at the countryside, it becomes picturesque, which is not how the characters often see it or what the tragedy needs.

Polanski is better with cycles of narrative than of earth. For instance, when Alec first gives Tess lunch in the lawn tent, he cuts a slice off a ham with a large carving knife. Years later, when she comes up to their rooms in the seaside place, after seeing the returned Angel, Alec is at breakfast, with a ham and a knife just visible in the frame—the knife she then presumably uses to kill him. It's Polanski's devising, and it's good.

. He ends the film at Stonehenge where the police catch up with the fugitive Tess and Angel. A next-to-last shot of the sun rising behind the ancient ruins gives us the implied sacrifice of a victim on a culture's altar. But there is no mention of her subsequent trial and execution, and thus we miss what may be the most terrible line in Hardy—after her execution—which could have been spoken or inscribed: "'Justice' was done, and the President of the Immortals . . . had ended his sport with Tess." The absence of that line, or at least its idea, is typical of what saps the film, for all its merits.

Man of Marble

(January 24, 1981)

A kind of moral terrorism flourishes in criticism these days. This is a delicate subject to raise because inextricably mixed with the terrorism are true terrors; and because the artists involved are not themselves responsible for the terrorism. Here is the nub: art about Eastern Europe, produced by people under Soviet domination or recently escaped from it, is grievously overrated in the West by critics who are moved, or cowed, by its provenance.

Since I'm raising the matter, let me use myself as counter example with neither true nor false modesty. I know very well that I could not endure for one week what Solzhenitsyn endured for years in the Gulag archipelago: but that doesn't alter my belief that he is at present the world's most overrated novelist. The Czech playwright Pavel Kohout is, on the evidence, a heroic man, but, also on the evidence, he is a sententious and laboriously metaphorical writer. Nikolai Erdman's play *The Suicide*, written by and about a Soviet citizen of the 1920s, has lately had a number of U. S. productions and was widely praised. I saw two of the productions and thought the play a two-hour spin-off from one bitter joke, and suspected that the critics might have been weighing in Erdman's grim fate.

At least one contemporary writer from Eastern Europe seems to me established in the highest rank: the Hungarian novelist George Konrad, whose novels *The Case Worker* and *The City Builder* place him with the utterly dissimilar Peter Handke among the best living artists. But the immensely gifted Milan Kundera is apparently to be forgiven his flecks of cuteness by critics who might have slated them in Western writers, because he comes from brutalized Czechoslovakia and is writing about the brutality.

Even Western writers who attack Soviet tyranny benefit critically from their opposition. Look at the praise heaped on Tom Stoppard's commonplace TV play *Professional Foul* and on his atrocious theater piece *Every Good Boy Deserves Favor*—performed with a full symphony orchestra—because they are both against oppression of Czechs. (And everyone knows that Stoppard is Czech-born, so it's especially touching that he hates injustice there, isn't it?)

Inevitably, when this matter of critical moral terrorism is raised, so is the question: shouldn't judgment take into account the sufferings of these artists, the risks they have undergone and may still be undergoing? My answer: no. I, who tremble when a customs inspector goes through my luggage, would maintain that we insult part of what those men and women are suffering *for* if we overpraise their work because they have suffered to produce it. This seems to me very far from a small or smug or overly neat point.

Now here's a film from Poland, *Man of Marble*, made in 1977 by Andrzej Wajda and already celebrated. It's about repression and subversion of thought in the Stalinist days of the early 1950s. Add to our feelings on this subject the fact that part of the picture takes place in Gdansk, scene of the 1970 revolt; add further what happened in Gdansk and elsewhere in 1980, what is hanging in balance at this very moment, and the picture acquires, without slyness or manipulation, something of the ambiance of a sacred object. But every painting of the Madonna is not a good painting, and *Man of Marble* is a mediocre, overlong, confused film.

First, as I've said before about Wajda, he is a windy film rhetorician, mannered and pretentious. The central character of *Man of Marble* is a young woman working on her diploma film for a film-school degree, and at one point her supervisor says to her, "Shoot it straight. Nothing arty." This after about eighty minutes — half the film — of Wajda's own artiness: floor shots upward past crossed legs, handheld intrusions, distorting pans.

Second, the performance of the filmmaker by Krystyna Janda is a gallery of muggings and posings.

Third, deeper and more delicate, this is one more film from a communist country about how tough things once were — under Stalinist regimes. *Angi Vera*, the very much better Hungarian film, used the same device.* Either as an oblique way to comment on the harried present or as a way of boasting that things have improved, the device is questionable. But it was sufficient to slide *Man of Marble* past the Polish censors — for the most part, anyway. Bits of the film, including the finish, are nebulous. This isn't Wajda's fault; censors scissored.

Janda, in the 1970s, is making a documentary about a Stakhanovite bricklayer of the 1950s who set a production record, was hailed, was even commemorated in a statue — and then was suddenly dethroned. Janda wants to find out why, and her search, through interviews with survivors, takes us through a story convoluted with police-political paranoia. The bricklayer began with genuine revolutionary fervor; he ended as a character out of Koestler. Janda is prevented from finishing her film, although there's an ambiguous hint at the end that she may eventually continue. Wajda, too, was prevented from showing his whole film, and there's no hint that we'll ever see it. But what we can see of it confirms that he is no more sharp and discriminating than ever. By the time this review reaches print, tensions in and about Poland may explode. The least important truth about that possible horror is that it won't improve Wajda's film or talents.

---

*See p. 24.

Man of Iron

(December 23, 1981)

The Polish filmmaker Andrzej Wajda has, among other attributes, a gift for embarrassing his critics. He digs so courageously into touchy issues in his country that skepticism about the results may seem to scant his courage. (Not to mention the courage of many others associated with him who may, in fact, be more vulnerable.) Who could feel pleased to write adversely on *Man of Iron* on the day when there is a front-page story about the Polish politburo ordering the government to seek legislation banning strikes?

Still *Man of Iron*, in my view, is a muddled, vastly protracted film, with Wajda's artiness once again splotching the sincerity of his concern and the urgency of his themes. This new film is a sequel—written, in a sense, by events—to *Man of Marble*, which he made in 1977.* The earlier film was about a young filmmaker, a woman, who wants to do a picture about the mysterious downfall of a Stakhanovite bricklayer of the 1950s who had first been hailed, then toppled. Her search for truth takes her to Gdansk in the 1970s. *Man of Iron* is about an older filmmaker, a man known for his TV work, sent to Gdansk to snoop out materials that will smear the leaders of the shipyard strike. The picture weaves the present with three time-levels of the past—1968, 1970, and the mid-1970s—distinguished (poorly) by different film tonalities. Wajda wants to emphasize the increment of events, the multi-layered texture, beneath the current unrest; this is his chief success in the film.

The son of the dead Stakhanovite, now a young leader in the shipyard strike, is the same actor who played his father, Jerzy Radziwilowicz. The former young filmmaker, played by Krystyna Janda, is now his wife, a mother, and an aide in the strike. Radziwilowicz is authentic, just as he was as his father; Janda is improved, much more restrained and convincing. Lech Walesa is seen in newsreel footage, but he also takes part in Wajda's film, as a witness at the wedding of the young pair in church. (The force of Catholicism is a recurrent theme.) The older TV correspondent, badly overplayed by Marian Opania, winds through all the present-day material, half-sodden most of the time, following the half-smoked cigarette in his mouth as if it were pulling him along. His inquiries are what instigate the flashbacks.

In the British journal *Sight and Sound* (Autumn 1981), Gustaw Moszcz writes:

> The moral reversal between *Man of Marble* and *Man of Iron* is not only that the first showed defeat . . . whereas the latter is mutedly optimistic about the precarious and limited success so far gained, but centers on the differing functions that journalism plays in both films. In the earlier, [the young woman] had desperately searched to reveal

---

*See preceding review.

> the unsavory truth . . . In *Man of Iron* . . . [the TV correspondent] is
> set the task of distorting the truth . . .

It's extremely pertinent to add that in the earlier film Wajda was talking about past oppression; now he's dealing with the present. The catalytic center of the new film is a government stooge; and after Walesa signs the agreement with the government, an official tells the TV man wryly that it's only a piece of paper, signed under duress.

These points may contain a clue as to how this new film got made. Wajda and colleagues could have ten times the courage they undoubtedly do have; still the picture could not have been made without the censors' approval. Why did the Polish government allow the making of a film that shows contemporary government slyness, injustice, police harrassment? One amateur guess—strengthened by the latest news cited above—is that the government approval of this film is an oblique anti-Soviet move. "See? These are the conditions of governing forced on us by Soviet pressure. Our sympathies are really with our brother and sister Poles, but what can we do with Big Brother on our backs?" The only direct reference to Big Brother is the statue of Lenin in a dining hall, but the government's sweat can easily be inferred as Soviet-induced.

Moszcz saw the film on Polish TV and notes one significant cut in the version being shown abroad, a shot of the body of a man murdered by secret police. In the light of what *is* shown, the cut is incomprehensible. Moszcz also reports that Walesa, interviewed on Polish TV last summer, called *Man of Iron* "too radical," "too aggressive," "untrue." Again these comments are incomprehensible without considerable inside knowledge of tactical positions. In any event, the film exists. It's muzzy, marred by the zooms and hollow enigmas of cutting and fancy angles that mar much of Wajda, but the impact of its very existence can't be denied.

Danton

(October 17, 1983)

Danton was directed by Andrzej Wajda, and after the first minute or so, I found this hard to believe. In the opening sequence, Danton and his wife are returning to Paris from the country in the spring of 1794, and their coach rolls past the shrouded guillotine in the Place de la Révolution. Here's Wajda yet again, I thought: pointed prognostication. Not only that, he throws in a few close-ups of the guillotine blade itself. I was resigned to one more trip to Wajda-land, the home of heavy symbols. But I was utterly and delightedly wrong. After that beginning, *Danton* is excellently directed, by far the best work of Wajda's that I know.

Two elements contribute strongly to this difference, this refinement. First,

Wajda has here the collaboration of the Czech master cinematographer, Igor Luther. I'm aware of Luther's work with the German director Schlöndorff and in France with Robbe-Grillet. (Luther left Czechoslovakia around 1970.) I think this is only his second film with Wajda — the first was for West German TV in 1972 — and, from the start, his camera establishes a unique and striking texture: history as *insistence*: the past insisting that it is quintessentially immanent. Luther uses colors with a discriminating "modern" restraint, and he ranges to what seems high-contrast black-and-white. Sometimes the close-ups of Danton look like news photographs done by an artist, as if Danton had been caught in unguarded moments but the object was understanding, not surprise. Faces and faces and faces throughout, along with a sense of architecture as drama (splendid sets by Allan Starski), are used by Luther to create a quasidocumentary feeling without any facile updating. Certainly the look of *Danton* is stratospherically beyond the usual portentous shadows or pretentious atmosphere of most Wajda films.

Second, Wajda's extensive theater experience. He exploits it to more advantage in this film that in others. *Danton* is based on a play by Stanislawa Przybyszewska. I have a photograph of a Warsaw production in 1975 that Wajda directed and for which he did the sets, with the film's Robespierre in that role. The film adaptation provides Wajda with two kinds of theatrical opportunity: the set pieces for individual virtuosities (the Danton-Robespierre private supper; Danton's self-defense before the tribunal), and the crowd scenes. Wajda "gives" the set pieces to his actors as Bergman has often done, relying on their talent and his understanding of it, rather than directing the cinematic blazes out of such sequences. The crowd scenes are as good as any I can remember in films, whether the camera is moving around them where they stand or racing around with them through galleries and streets. When Gance shot comparable scenes in *Napoleon*, he gave us the feeling of a master conductor controlling an orchestra. Wajda sees his crowds as molecular, not capital-M Mass but a lot of individuals who happen to be in the same place at the same time. Yet the seeming individual freedoms are integrated with the movement of the camera. All through those many, vivid crowd scenes, I thought that Wajda was at last fulfilling something he had felt about the play on the stage. I imagined that in the theater Wajda had kept muttering to himself, "If only . . . if only . . . ." Here he was able to do it.

I don't know of any other Wajda film adapted from a play that he has done in the theater. Possibly what has inflated his past work was a feeling of escape from theater discipline, which resulted in the overdone. With *Danton* his film seems the ultimate and just realization of a previous work. The "touches" that he supplies here, instead of being exhibitionist as they have usually been in the past, help the validity. Examples: the wooden floors of the assembly halls creak under the weight and passage of the crowds; Danton, famous for his big voice and generous with it, grows hoarse after long, impassioned speeches.

Danton is played by Gerard Depardieu, ferociously. At least two previous films have been made about Danton, both German: one with Emil Jannings in 1921, one with Fritz Kortner in 1931. I haven't seen the latter; the former was a silent film, so comparison is clumsy. Still Jannings's force in the trial scene stays in the mind, and I'm sure Depardieu's force will do the same. The French actor, marked especially by his vitality, his gusto for food and women, slips into this role like a quick-change artist slipping his arms into the sleeves of a jacket as he walks on stage. I assuredly don't mean that Depardieu glides through the role, only that it fits him like a measured garment. We believe both in Danton's sensuality and his vision. One of Depardieu's dubious appetites as actor is that, apparently, he'll take on anything. Sometimes he ends up in witless roles in witless films, like Beineix's *The Moon in the Gutter*; sometimes his voracity for acting leads him to a role like Danton where he is better than he has given us the recent right to expect. Depardieu's stage experience, touched surely by Wajda's help, enables him in this larger-than-life role to make the screen a theater without leaving the domain of film acting, and, in the rhetorical scenes, it enables him to wield language both for meaning and for intoxication.

In a smaller role but trenchant and fine is Roger Planchon, the famous actor-director of the French theater. When Planchon appears, he not only takes command: he implies antecedents and forecasts futures.

Robespierre is played by Wojciech Pszoniak, who has previously played it for Wajda on the Warsaw stage. I have no idea of what he sounds like: here he is dubbed in French. He looks and behaves well enough, though he's a somewhat more physical being than one imagines for Robespierre.

About half the speaking roles—Robespierre's supporters—are played by Polish actors who are dubbed. One role (Lucile Desmoulins) is played by a German, Angela Winkler, and she, too, is dubbed. *Danton* is a French-Polish production. There were both financial and political reasons for using the Polish actors, but the result is a film half-full of two-part performances.

The screenplay was adapted from the original by Jean-Claude Carrière, Buñuel's old friend, assisted by Wajda and three other Poles. Comparison with Büchner's *Danton's Death* is both inescapable and overwhelming. Let's note only a few differences in the treatment of Danton's character. The screenplay gives us almost nothing of Danton's past actions in the revolution and of his recoil from them. That last is the spiritual locus of Büchner's Danton, the man who, for instance, ignored the September Massacres of 1792 and can no longer ignore them. The increase in enjoyment—of everything from light and air to wine and women—that grows in Büchner's Danton as his faith in political action wanes, this too is absent from the film. (We see only a brief meeting, in public, between Danton and some whores.)

I don't cite Büchner's play as historical gospel, which it is not, but as a genius's use of history to large purpose. The screenplay uses the story to smaller, polemical purposes. Everyone who sees the film knows that Danton is meant to suggest Lech Walesa, that Robespierre is a stand-in for General Jaruzelski. (When Robespierre goes to the studio of the painter David, he orders the painter to delete from a gigantic canvas a man now out of favor.) Poland's present agony is a gigantic fact; but the honing of the Danton-Robespierre story to fit that situation not only results in a script that is pigmy compared to Büchner—which might not in itself matter if the film helped in contemporary terms—it produces a work that is too neat, too patly applicable, too transparent. The result, as I've heard, is that the French are not happy with what happened to an important moment in their history, and the Polish regime is differently unhappy about showing the picture in Poland.

Still, *Danton* is not to be missed. Script aside, the making of the film (I can hardly say "execution") is almost incessantly, intelligently exciting. The Wajda who made it is refreshingly genuine.

Let There Be Light

(January 31, 1981)

In May 1946 James Agee wrote:

> John Huston's *Let There Be Light*, a fine, terrible, valuable non-fiction film about psychoneurotic soldiers has been forbidden civilian circulation by the War Department. I don't know what is necessary to reverse this disgraceful decision, but if dynamite is required, then dynamite is indicated.

Attempts at dynamiting were headed by the admirable Arthur Mayer, the dean of American film exhibitors, but without success. This one-hour documentary, made by Huston when he was an officer in the Army Signal Corps, was withheld from public view on the ground that it was an invasion of the patients' privacy—even though the patients had signed releases. Huston's previous documentary, *The Battle of San Pietro*, a grimly immediate record of combat, would also have been bottled up except for the personal intervention of General George C. Marshall. Huston quotes Marshall as saying—it was typical of the man—"Every soldier who knows he is going into combat must see this picture, and the country should see it in order that they know what a soldier is going through in battle." "But," adds Huston, "there was no General Marshall with *Let There Be Light*."

Now, at last, the government has reversed itself, and *Let There Be Light* is made available to the public, who can buy prints from the Public Affairs division of the Defense Department. The first theatrical showing was at the Thalia in New York in mid-January. (Paradox: the complete script, except for some deleted names, has been available since 1962 in *Film: Book 2*, edited by Robert

Hughes, published by Grove Press.)

The script was written by Huston and Charles Kaufman, who subsequently worked with Huston on *Freud*. The camera work was by Huston and Stanley Cortez, who had already shot *The Magnificent Ambersons* for Welles. The look of the film is unexceptional, as is the editing. The lighting is like that of every other wartime documentary; the editing is in shot and reverse shot for conversation, quick cross fades for time lapse, etc. The exceptional quality of the film is not cinematic: it's in the concern of the filmmaker and the nakedness of the subjects.

A group of combat soldiers arrives at a U.S. army hospital suffering from various kinds of shell shock, as it used to be called. One man can't speak without heavy stuttering, one can hardly walk though physically uninjured, one is emotionally uncontrolled, and so on. Each one gets an interview with an army psychiatrist in which sodium amytol is injected or hypnosis is used to relieve stress and enable him to talk. Each one is "cured"—at least to the point where, six weeks later, they are all playing softball and then are discharged from the hospital.

To my knowledge there had been no previous documentary on this subject. Everyone knew there had been casualties of this kind; they had been part of fiction films. (E.g., Donald Cook, as James Cagney's older brother in *The Public Enemy* (1931), came back from World War One "nervous.") But this film really confronted the "casualties of the spirit," as the narration (spoken by Huston) calls them; and so soon after the war, the army apparently was reluctant to publicize these facts. It's more than moving to see these men, in these quiet surroundings, still dazed by the battles they carry within them.

But today the film is something less than Agee thought it in 1946. Since then there have been, of course, many films—documentaries and fiction—about the treatment of psychoneurosis; as I recall, there's even a sequence about the treatment of psychoneurotic soldiers in Susan Sontag's documentary about Israel, *Promised Lands*. One reason that Huston's film is now released, I suppose, is that the patients in it are, for differing reasons, out of danger of embarrassment. Another, perhaps, is that we are all now so accustomed, in film and TV, to disorders of this kind and their treatment that there is no longer any shock in the picture. In comparison with what we've been flooded with since *The Snake Pit* (1948), *Let There Be Light* is no hair-raiser.

But there's another reason why it may have been released, a disquieting one. The film is misleading. It says nothing about the possibility of recurrence in these men; and, worse, it says nothing about the sufferers with combat psychoneurosis who took longer to leave or who never got out of hospitals. Huston is sensitive on this subject. In a 1962 interview he said: "We tried scrupulously to avoid any suggestion that these men had been rendered the way they were simply by their experience in battle, and that now they were completely cured." It's hard to find support for this statement in the film. There is no instance in the film of a soldier who did not respond fairly quickly to treatment: and no hint that there were others in worse shape who could not have been discharged.

I don't impute craftiness to Huston—at the time of making the film, anyway. He took a giant first step, as large as he was presumably permitted at the time, maybe even a bit further. Milestones are honorable, essential: his film is a milestone. But—and it's not the first instance—suppression has helped its reputation.

Under the Volcano

(June 18, 1984)

"A procession of thoughts like little elderly animals filed through the Consul's mind . . . ." When I reread Under the Volcano recently and came to that line, it heightened my apprehension about a film of the book. Luis Buñuel said in his autobiography that he had read eight screenplays of Malcolm Lowry's novel but had found none of them convincing. "If you confine yourself to the action, it's hopelessly banal, because everything important takes place within the main character, and how can inner conflicts be translated to the screen?" Of course they can be translated—Buñuel himself often did it—but he was right about Under the Volcano: it immensely increases the problem of interiority. Everyone who has wanted to adapt the book must have perceived this problem, yet many have attempted it. And it was a newcomer to screenwriting, Guy Gallo, who wrote a version that persuaded a renowned director to proceed, although that director, too—John Huston—had declined previous versions.

So this film is a special case. After a vast history of attempts discarded because of a difficulty that can't be avoided, it seems unfair to ask complete success of Huston and Gallo. The just question is: How far do they succeed? Even then, the melancholy answer is: Not enough. Gallo's script shows how clearly he understood the problem, and it also shows the steps he took to compensate. But many of those steps are counterproductive. Gallo has of course condensed the book (for example, the entire prelude/postlude first chapter is gone); he has quarried out much of the action, amplified some elements, and put it all in chronological order. The result is not "hopelessly banal," particularly because of two superlative performances, but it doesn't compensate for what is lost. Worse, what is done underscores what can't be done, emphasizes that we are missing the very qualities in Lowry's novel that make it important: not only the "inner conflicts" but the prose in which they exist.

Just one instance: the sodden Consul runs from his wife's bedroom embrace when he can't perform (a scene transposed acceptably here for dramatic compression) and staggers out into the street, where he sprawls, face down, in the middle of the road in broad daylight. It's a rightly horrid sight, but in the film, that's the end of it. What we miss is the interior monologue that blisters through the prone man's mind, along with the fact—even more important—that he cannot turn off his mind, no matter what happens to his limbs and speech.

The action takes place in Cuernavaca and environs, on the Day of the Dead, November 1, in 1938. Geoffrey Firmin, the lately resigned British consul in the Mexican town, has also lately been divorced by his wife Yvonne, whom he adores and who has gone to New York. For this and complicated other reasons, the Consul, a man of intellect and sensibility and despair, is now boozing himself out of the torpid world around him into a busy inner world. (See the opening quotation.) Yvonne suddenly reappears, repentant. Present, too, is the Consul's half-brother, Hugh, a journalist back from the Spanish Civil War. In the course of the day, several themes figure strongly: the consul's agony because of his love for Yvonne and his inability to sustain it, sexually and otherwise; his torment because he knows Yvonne and Hugh once had an affair and he knows that this can't stop his loving them both; Hugh's political concerns, intensified by his Spanish experiences and by his discovery of fascist activity in Mexico subsidized by the Germans. Of the political matters, the Consul is not much more than a wry, grieved observer. At the end, driven by his contradictory anguish and acedia, both awash in drink, the Consul visits the lowest brothel-bar in the vicinity and is murdered by fascist bullies. The shots frighten off a horse that had been tied to a rail nearby—a horse that, as the Consul knew, had been stolen by the fascists from a peon they murdered. The horse plunges into the woods through which Yvonne and Hugh are searching for the Consul. The horse tramples Yvonne and kills her.

Thus the film. Two points illustrate the script's troubles with matters other than interiority. First, chronological order. In the novel we learn of Yvonne's death before we learn of the Consul's, though in fact he was killed earlier. Yvonne's death seems suspended, an open chord, until the closing pages of the book resolve it, making clear that, in effect, the murder of her husband—which caused the horse to bolt—also killed *her*. Gallo must have worried that Lowry's reverse sequence would be confusing, but the film's "correct" time order robs Yvonne's death of appropriate mystery, makes it pat, and robs the Consul's death of the reflexive quality it has in the book, the awesome quality of a fate foreknown and fulfilled.

Second, the political matters in the novel, voiced mostly by Hugh, have largely been retained when much else was dropped and have been underscored. Gallo apparently thought that these political matters would give the film dramatic energy, to offset the long slope of the Consul's alcoholic decline. But the political matters are the book's weakest element, a framework imposed to give the book a larger relevance (which it does not lack anyway) and to give the Consul's murder an added irony. In my view, this imposition of the political is what keeps the book, despite its wondrous writing, from greatness. Lowry didn't trust his own gifts enough. If the Consul had gone down the drain for his own personal reasons, had met his senseless death at the hands of ordinary brigands, the book would have lain more securely within the author's grasp, unmarred by enforced obeisance to topicality. And it's precisely those weakest matters in the novel that Gallo expanded to give the film more action.

Huston has directed with the deftness that one expects of him but with the touch of the meretricious that one also expects. Puppet skeletons of various sizes are made by the Indians for this Day of the Dead, and, beginning with the footage under the credits, Huston exploits them blatantly. In that last saloon, an Indian woman puts a small skeleton on the bar in front of the Consul shortly before his death. Lowry touches this action glancingly, thus tellingly; Huston slams it at us. Visually, the picture is predictably "Mexican"—nothing that we see through Gabriel Figueroa's camera gives us any Mexican imagery we haven't seen before, much of it through Figueroa's camera.

However, Huston engaged Alex North to write the score; and North, veteran composer for theater and film (he did the music for *Death of a Salesman*, still used), has worked freshly and well.

And Huston gets fine performances from two of his three principals. One of the three is weak. Anthony Andrews, who was Sebastian in the *Brideshead Revisited* TV series and was inadequate there, is even more inadequate as Hugh, quite pallid. But Albert Finney as the Consul and Jacqueline Bisset as Yvonne are perfect. When I read that Finney had been signed, I was afraid that he might be too beefy, too much a mere drunk instead of (in Walter Allen's words) a man "more in love with damnation than with being saved." In proof, Finney is magnificent: acute, deep, a creature of echoing caverns in which he tries to hide. Bisset, whose career hasn't matched her talent, immediately makes us believe that she is indeed the woman whom the Consul adores and needs; then she goes on to create movingly a woman in love with her husband who is trying to rescue him from his romance about her. The acting of Finney and Bisset is all that holds the picture together.

But they can't save the enterprise. This film of *Under the Volcano* diminishes the novel drastically. Gallo and Huston were evidently motivated by reverence for Lowry's book and a wish to serve it cinematically as best they could, despite its manifest problems. But, sad to say, they have ended by proving what many have feared: this darkly lustrous novel cannot be filmed.

Napoleon

(February 14, 1981)

Every art has artists who are influential without being widely known. In the film world Abel Gance, now ninety-one, has exemplified that condition through the century. There he has been, alive and well in Paris and sometimes working; and there were his films, known to some of the profession but not to many others.

In 1957 Jean-Luc Godard wrote: "The modern cinema owes Abel Gance as great a debt as the automobile owes to André Citroen . . . ." But the modern cinema is only now getting around to pay it, or some of it, and in great measure this is because of Kevin Brownlow, the English film historian and filmmaker. For many years Brownlow has been scavenging and retrieving and patching and has at last come up with as good a version as we are likely to get of Gance's *Napoleon*, a four-hour silent film first shown in Paris in 1927 and subsequently ravaged.

Earlier versions have been shown here. I saw a fairly substantial print at the New York Film Festival in 1967. Brownlow's is the fullest and has just been shown in New York at the Radio City Music Hall, presented by Zoetrope Studios, Francis Ford Coppola's company. His father, Carmine Coppola, composed an orchestral score—with acknowledged assists from Beethoven, Berlioz, and others; Coppola senior conducted the orchestra and organist in the music that accompanied the huge film throughout, the organist coming in solo once in a while to give the band a rest.

Gance began life as a law clerk to please his father and became an actor at nineteen to please himself. (He plays Saint-Just in *Napoleon*, a proud, scalpel-sharp performance.) He entered films as an actor in 1909, soon began writing and directing short films, made two features and then was drafted into World War I. Right at the end of the war he made a pacifist film, *J'Accuse*, which he remade as a sound film in 1937; the latter was released here as *That They May Live*. (It's merely speaking accurately to say, more than 40 years later, that Victor Francen's performance in the leading role is unforgettable. He plays a war veteran driven mad by the approach of another war, and I can still hear him calling the World War I dead of every nation in their own languages to arise.) The only other Gance film I've seen is *Beethoven* with Harry Baur, which I remember as the best in that dubious genre of life-of-a-composer films.

But those two, plus others that could be cited, make *Napoleon* an anomaly in Gance's career as well as in the film world. His broad and fervent worship of the moral hero—the pacifist and the composer, for instances—was utterly swept away by adoration of a military-political genius and by an infatuation with La Gloire that makes De Gaulle seem reticent. (De Gaulle saw *Napoleon* in 1927 and responded as one might expect.) The film takes its hero only up to his marriage with Josephine de Beauharnais and his appointment to command the army of Italy; despite its mammoth size, Gance intended it to be the first of six films on the life of Napoleon. Nothing more was done, but the patriotic zeal that sparked the project burns through the first part. The boy Napoleon's pet eagle is the key symbol, and at times we even glimpse La Belle France herself, waving her sword and inspiring her children.

Gance chose good collaborators. His chief cinematographer was Jules Kruger, already well known, later better known for such films as *They Were Five* and *Pepe le Moko*. Some of the photography was done by Léonce-Henry Burel, who had done much work with Gance and later worked for Robert Bresson (*Diary of a Country Priest, A Man Escaped*). One of the assistant directors was Anatole Litvak, later to make *Mayerling* and a lot of American films. The art director was Alexandre Benois, one of Diaghileff's chief designers here doing his first film work. The designs for Napoleon's Paris lodgings, the Club des Cordeliers, and the Convention are only three examples of Benois's mastery.

The cast is Napoleon. The dozens of others (not to mention the massive crowds) are all right, with one exception, but the film is sustained by Albert Dieudonné in the title role. Dieudonné, who had often worked with Gance earlier, seems at first as if he's going to be grotesquely intense, but soon we're convinced that this is Napoleon's intensity, the almost manic singlemindedness of the man born under a star who believes in his destiny. Along the way we get a glimpse of the sixteen-year-old Annabella, making her debut four years before she did Clair's *Le Million* and went to Hollywood. The only really bad performance is by Antonin Artaud, mugging away like mad as Marat—nothing like the work he did for Carl Dreyer the following year in *The Passion of Joan of Arc*.

The film was made by the same temperament that wrote the script, that chose the symbols and saw Napoleon in a secular halo. The picture begins with prophecy. In a schoolyard snowball fight the boy Napoleon is undauntable. Point One. When a geography teacher gives the class a lesson on islands and mentions St. Helena, something vibrates in the boy. Point Two. When some other boys spitefully set Napoleon's pet eagle free, the bird returns from the sky to join the disconsolate boy. Point Three. What keeps us gripped through all this nineteenth-century previsionary corn is the passion of the director. Though the filmmaking came from the same fount as the script, the direction is fresh and vigorous—with lithe tracking and editing—where the script is mechanical. At one point during a dormitory pillow fight, the screen bursts into subdivisions until there are nine panels. (I couldn't help thinking of the dormitory pillow fight in Vigo's *Zéro de Conduite*, made six years afterward. Vigo had tried, unsuccessfully, to get a job of some kind on the Gance film.)

The next sequence is some ten years later in Paris, 1789, at the Club des Cordeliers where Rouget de Lisle sings his new song, "La Marseillaise," and young Lieutenant Bonaparte congratulates him on doing more for the Revolution than some armies will do. There's no longer any question that we are in the hands of a romantic director of high power. The crowd picks up the song, the cutting accelerates from face to face, and at the last the figure of La France is superimposed over the singing mob. This pattern recurs—a speed-up of cutting toward the end of a sequence with superimpositions as capstone—and it works every time.

Napoleon's visit to Corsica and his escape to the mainland in a small boat through a stormy sea; the concurrent forensic storm in the Convention; the siege of Toulon; the marriage to Josephine; the visit to the empty Convention hall; the assumption of command in northern Italy—all these come in for full-blooded, explosively imaginative treatment. And as Napoleon rallies his army for the invasion of the Po Valley, the frame opens to what we have been waiting for—Gance's famous triple-screen panorama. Originally there were three other triptych sequences, now lost. The one that remains makes a fine climax as the bedraggled army rouses itself and begins to march with—can you believe it?—the eagle at last superimposed and the three screens colored blue, white, and red.

Overwhelming is the word. All through the film, no matter how easily we can discern the contrivances to make Napoleon a stoic master who never errs, the sentiments from recruiting posters, the revived Byronic swirl, they sweep us along. Much has been written about Gance's daring with the camera—mounting it on a pendulum or on a horse or on an actor's chest—and certainly his insistent cinematic ingenuity makes the picture pulsate. So do the splendid compositions and images, the (seemingly) thunderous deployment of crowds. But what is really conquering us here is the cinematic use of nineteenth-century theater, the popular theater being exploited to the full in a new medium by a master who knows both theater and film—which is also the key to much of D. W. Griffith.

Who could help responding? Who would want not to respond? But even before the cheering fades, questions come. First, are we cheering cinematic ingenuity or cinematic chronology? The audience shouts when, in the long-shot triptych, horsemen suddenly cross the screen in foreground, or when the screen subdivides into nine cells, but what's being cheered, in an age when those matters are the daily bread of Cinerama and TV commercials, is the fact that they were done *then*. It's the date that is being applauded, more than the accomplishment or its intrinsic value. As for the latter, Godard wrote:

> On the center screen, a battalion on the march; on the side screens, Bonaparte galloping along a road. . . . After a few minutes we feel we have traveled all the thousands of kilometers of that prodigious Italian campaign.

Then Godard adds:

> So the triple screen . . . may in certain scenes provoke supplementary effects in the sphere of pure sensation, but no more; and I admire Renoir, Welles or Rossellini precisely because they achieve a similar or even superior result by more logical means, breaking the frame but not destroying it.

I'm not out to derogate the pleasures of "pure sensation," nor was Godard, I'd guess. I just want to look carefully at the terms that are now flying in Gance's direction, among which "genius" is the coolest.

There's still another reason why we cheer *Napoleon*. We're cheering for the future that the film form seemed to have at the time that *Napoleon* was made. This was the era when Gance and his friend, the critic Ricciotto Canudo, and many others were celebrating film as the art toward which all other arts had been tending through history, as the art of renewed and yet unimagined possibilities. The fabric and fire of *Napoleon* say as much about that faith as they do about the content of the picture. And that faith is very moving, in a poignant way, to people today who care about film. Fine films get made in our day—finer ones than *Napoleon*, in my view—but that kind of faith is not their dynamics. Not everything is known, can ever be known, about the technique and esthetics of film, but the explorations now take place in a seemingly delimited territory.

That insufficiently read American critic, Harry Alan Potamkin, who died in 1933, admired much of Gance greatly but said that he "was Hugo without Hugo's vision. That makes him the counterpart in cinema to Eugene Sue." My own vote for his counterpart is Edmond Rostand. If the author of *Cyrano de Bergerac* and *L'Aiglon* had written and directed a film about Napoleon, it might conceivably have been this one. The neglect of Gance stands high on the long list of the film world's shames. Everyone must be happy that his biggest film is now tolerably restored and available, must hope that all his work will soon follow. Gance should have had his rightful important place long ago. Restitution tends to exaggerate.

Postscript. Abel Gance died in Paris on November 10, 1981.

The Last Metro

(February 28, 1981)

What's going to happen in film? The question recurs—and not only in this column—for assorted reasons, economic and cultural. It's not arbitrarily a gloomy question: possibly, in the long run, we're going to have to ask it under different aspects, toward different ends. But in a shorter view, we ask it in terms of directors. Just as the question about the state of the theater usually means: "What important new playwrights are there?" so the question about film implies: "What important new directors are there?" Perhaps the strangulating economy, the alterations in political-social continuities throughout the world, the very changes in film technology (video tape, cassettes, and home viewing, for example) will alter our needs and expectations in ways not yet decipherable.

At the moment, however, that opening question—if it means anything more than "What immortal classic will open next week and justify my seeing it?"—centers on directors. What new directors are there about whose careers we can hope? And the hard fact, in my view, is that we're still hoping about the old-timers, we're still hoping that Bergman or Kurosawa or Antonioni or Fellini or Buñuel or Bresson will come along with a new film to buck us up. All these men, in effect, burst on the world in the 1960s. There has been no post-1960s crop to succeed them, or others of their contemporaries, at anything like their level. Abroad, the last twenty years brought forth Fassbinder and Wenders and Syberberg, Jancsó, Troell, Bellocchio, Olmi, and Teshigahara, of whom the first three still kindle hope. In the U.S., Peckinpah and Penn, Bogdanovich, Altman, Schrader, Allen, Scorsese, and Coppola, the last three of whom still kindle hope. Only certain film journals or film scholars (teachers and doctoral candidates), desperate for subjects, would maintain that the last twenty years have produced directors, internationally, on a level with their predecessors.

In which case, a film from one of the old-timers is more than a work in itself, it is or is not inspiriting generally. *The Last Metro* is not. This latest film from an "old master," François Truffaut, now a ripe forty-eight—has, in a limited sense, a resemblance to Bergman's *The Serpent's Egg*: it's the film about the Nazi era that he's been promising himself for years, and it's one of his weaklings.

The first shot is of a Paris street in September 1942 hung with huge swastika flags. The first movement in the film is (as it often is) a tip-off to the quality of what follows. The camera zooms in on the flags. *Zooms in on them*—to say "See? Get it?" The hamminess of that camera strophe is quite unlike anything I can remember in even the feeblest Truffaut films; it was a kick in the hope—for the film in front of me and for the film world around me.

The Last Metro does not get much better. The direction never sinks to that banality again, but neither does it reveal anything of the celebrated Truffaut style, either in surprises of perception or in lyrical movement. It shows a sharper sense of editing rhythm than the merely competent, but it is directing without notable texture or reward.

Truffaut's new indistinction affected two of his longtime collaborators. The music by Georges Delerue, who did lovely scores for many Truffaut films including *Jules and Jim* as well as for Godard, De Broca, and Resnais, is here coarse, whooping things up when danger threatens, etc. The cinematography by Nestor Almendros, a master whose films for Truffaut include *Two English Girls* and *The Story of Adèle H.*, is done with the palette of a marzipan factory—exactly the edible colors of those fake fruits and vegetables.

A quasi-melodramatic, flimsily clever script is what Truffaut has written, with his collaborators Suzanne Schiffman and Jean-Claude Grumberg. Truffaut says they wrote it to express "our aversion to all forms of racism and intolerance." Stanley Kramer could have said no more. There are only two "forms" of intolerance in the film. The first is not dramatized, the Nazi proscription of homosexuality. The male and female homosexuals in the film never run the slightest risk of discovery. If you didn't know that such individuals ran a risk with the occupying government, the film would not tell you. The second is anti-Semitism, and how could he have made a film about the German occupation without being against anti-Semitism? How does Truffaut explore the subject—in thematic or experiential or any other terms—to deepen our understanding or even, minimally, to move us? This film's statements on anti-Semitism are about as daring and enlightening as the abuse of Mussolini's corpse by the Milanese mob after he was executed.

In no way does Truffaut extend our comprehension of the Occupation, not even through the specialized spectrum of the theater where most of the film takes place. Of course he was too young for adult experience of the period, but this wouldn't in itself disqualify him any more than the fact that he wasn't around in 1912 disqualified him for *Jules and Jim*. Some of the details in *The Last Metro* contradict things I've read. (For instance the theater in the film is always crowded, yet Jean-Paul Sartre, who was writing plays then, said: "Under the Occupation people seldom went out in the evening; the theater was virtually moribund.") But details aside, empathically or imaginatively Truffaut adds nothing and, I'd say, subtracts something. He makes the sole offense of Nazism its anti-Semitism. I'm not exactly forgetting the Vel d'Hiver and Dachau when I say that there was a great deal more danger to the world in Nazi Germany than in its hatred and murder of Jews. Truffaut's view is reductive of the danger then—and of possible future fascist threats. (Anything not anti-Semitic is O.K.?)

The title refers to the last subway train at 11 p.m. by which Parisians had to get home under the German curfew. Its only relevance to the story is that every theater had to plan its shows so that patrons could catch that train. The director of an off-Boulevard theater, played by Heinz Bennent, is German-Jewish and has disappeared, alleged to have fled France. His wife, Catherine Deneuve, the leading actress of the theater, takes over as manager with an old friend as director. A young actor, Gerard Depardieu, is engaged for a new play. Soon, and with complete non-surprise, we learn that Bennent has not fled: he is hidden in the cellar of the theater, listening to rehearsals through a ventilator, offering suggestions to and through his wife who visits him nightly. The fourth prominent character is a leading critic, the editor of the strongly pro-German *Je suis partout*, played by Jean-Louis Richard and apparently modeled, in some degree, on the theater critic and film historian Robert Brasillach. (If it is Brasillach, then, as he did in *The Story of Adèle H.*, Truffaut monkeys with historical facts to suit his emotional prejudices. Brasillach did not, as Truffaut's critic does, according to a voice-over, skulk away after the Liberation to die in Spain of cancer 20 years later. He turned himself in—courageously, one must say—to join his mother and brother-in-law, defended himself calmly, was condemned and shot.)

Out of these ingredients could have been built a black comedy (romance between Depardieu and Deneuve in a grim context) or a symbolist drama (the Jewish artist gone literally underground but still inspiring the operation; the theater as mask for truth-telling before tyrants, which, in the case of Sartre's

The Flies and Anouilh's *Antigone*, it was). But this script doesn't use either of those approaches or any effective one: it doesn't even fall between stools—it lacks the weight. It just sets its situation, implicitly promises development of some kind, delivers none, utilizes a few conventional narrow escapes, then ends. The finish is a replay of an earlier Truffaut device. In *Day for Night* the street where the film opens is soon revealed as a film set; in *The Last Metro* the hospital scene that closes the film turns out to be a theater set.

The film doesn't bore, it simply never grips. The chief reason for its interest is its performers. Heinz Bennent, father of the child David Bennent who was in *The Tin Drum*,* plays the hidden Jew with quietly stated substance; he has a neat lined face that speaks of much experience well understood. Gerard Depardieu acts with his usual vigor and more shading than usual, which gives him more the feeling of a man, less of a sex salesman. In rehearsals he sometimes has to do a scene two different ways; this would have been impossible for Deneuve on whom Truffaut's demands are carefully restricted. But she is so beautiful—more beautiful than she was in her twenties—and she uses her beauty so much more subtly than whatever acting talent she has that the "space" allotted to her in the film is filled. The loathsome critic is well and genuinely performed by Jean-Louis Richard, out of the knowledge that many Parisian artists and intellectuals, far from feeling conquered, welcomed the German victory as a fresh start for France. An elderly dresser is played by Paulette Dubost, whose charming face kept teasing me for recognition. A look at a reference book later and I knew why: Dubost was the flirtatious maid who makes much of the trouble in Renoir's *Rules of the Game* (1939). Truffaut likes these private linkages: the ingenue of the company is Sabine Haudepin who was Jeanne Moreau's child in *Jules and Jim* (1962). And—another link—Richard was once Moreau's real-life husband.

Given the domain of the story and the validity of the cast, the clinkers in the script are especially troubling. Depardieu is seen stealing a record-player from the theater, and shortly afterward a German officer is killed by a bomb in a record-player; why does no one connect the two events? When Depardieu says he's leaving to join the Resistance (whose presence hovers on the edges of the film), why does Deneuve slap his face? After Depardieu assaults the politically powerful critic in a restaurant for his vile anti-Semitic review of the theater's new play, why is his acting career undisturbed? Why indeed did the critic savage the play after we see him at the opening night standing and applauding? And since Bennent knows that his wife is in love with Depardieu, does our final post-Liberation view of the three of them on stage, bowing to applause, signify a *ménage à trois*?

The mind that let all these points pass is also the mind that failed to probe the theme of the film, that went for a sort of free ride on anti-Nazism and anti-Semitism, that was unable, despite the choice of setting, to make much use of

*See p. 39.

theater resources as an enrichment of filmmaking. (Compare Bergman's *The Magic Flute*.) And it's the mind that settled for the look of the film and the sound of its score.

So, no help from Truffaut in the matter of hope. Maybe the new Fellini?*

The Woman Next Door

(November 11, 1981)

It's one of the oddities of film history that a filmmaker so lyrically subscribed to the adoration of women as is François Truffaut, whose feeling for them so deftly blends wide-eyed wonder with sexual heat, should also so often link those feelings with the killing of men by women. If it isn't death, it's disaster, as in *Such A Gorgeous Kid Like Me*, but often it's death, as in *The Bride Wore Black*, *The Soft Skin*, and, of course, that beautifully decorated account of a raging psychopath, *Jules and Jim*. As I've noted before, we musn't overlook the fact that Truffaut's autobiographical first feature, *The 400 Blows*, is about a boy whose mother betrays his father and has ambivalent feelings toward her son.

Truffaut's latest film, *The Woman Next Door*, is once again about loving that ends with killing by the woman. Poor Gerard Depardieu. I can't think that it's male-chauvinist to sympathize with this latest victim of a woman. He is pleasantly married; he and his wife have a child and a home in the country outside Grenoble; he has a job he likes. Another couple rent the empty house across the way, and the wife turns out to be Fanny Ardant, with whom Depardieu had a passionate affair some eight years before, which ended with a wrench. She (we learn later) attempted suicide, married quickly and divorced quickly. Now she is married a second time, placidly.

The move next door is completely accidental. Depardieu is ill at ease; Ardant is stimulated. Neither says anything to the respective spouse. Depardieu makes no overtures to Ardant—quite the reverse—but he responds when the clandestine opportunities present themselves. Both lovers go through considerable stress because of their passion, which is quickly rekindled and is much more consuming than what they feel maritally. Ardant eventually has a nervous breakdown, and when her husband learns the reason, they move away—to an apartment in Grenoble. But one night she comes back to the empty house. Depardieu hears the door banging across the way and goes over to investigate. They make love on the floor. Then she reaches into her pocketbook which is next to her, takes out a pistol, puts a bullet in his head as he lies on her, and puts another in her own head.

As in *Jules and Jim*, the woman kills herself along with the man she can't have, but I couldn't help feeling sorrier for Depardieu. Certainly he was her more-than-willing partner, but it wasn't he who restarted the affair or who,

---

*See p. 240.

after all the travail, insisted on coming back that night. He certainly didn't know he would be asked to pay for this encounter with his life. That was entirely Ardant's decision, and just a bit one-sided, I thought.

But the film does create an atmosphere of fate, of the consequences of actions, no matter how long the consequences are delayed. I certainly did not feel that Depardieu had wronged Ardant, either in Part One or Part Two of their affair, but she believed he had, and it was his fate, having become involved with her, eventually to suffer from her belief. She decided that her life was not worth living without him; that may not be, in the wholest sense, rational, but it's a point of personal privilege. However, she also decided that he was not to live without her; and that's Truffaut. He quite clearly thinks that a woman believes that her passion for a man gives her the right to determine whether or not the man may live without her.

The best quality in the picture—written by Truffaut, Suzanne Schiffman, a previous collaborator, and Jean Aurel, a new name—is its atmosphere of the inescapable, of an Appointment in Samarra. This is another way of saying the picture is well done. Just when I'm afraid I'm getting tired of Depardieu, because I see so much of him, vigorously eating and lovemaking and kissing children, bursting the screen frame with his vigor, he reappears doing all those things all over again but in a role that does more than exploit his vigor; and by fulfilling all the emotional demands of the role with ease, he refreshes the very vigor on which he often coasts. Depardieu hasn't shown astonishing range since his U. S. debut in *Going Places* (1974): most of his characters are modulations of a few basic chords. But he never makes a false move, and the truth of the moves he does make, within a relatively narrow perimeter, compels.

Fanny Ardant, whom I've not seen before, has a strong-jawed, heavy-browed beauty—of a sort one could expect to see in life, unlike (say) Catherine Deneuve, and none the less beautiful for that! She is very affecting, both as lover and sufferer. Possibly the novelty of her first appearance helped her performance. Exactly the opposite case from Depardieu, she has no burden of familiarity to overcome. I'm eager for her next film, to see whether she wears well and grows. (That's almost redundant.)

The script has a few moments that stretch credibility. For instance, Depardieu slaps Ardant around at a party in her house in front of her husband, and apparently the husband is not particularly upset; the move out of the neighborhood doesn't occur until after further developments. And Truffaut's directing can't quite shake a clinging cuteness or two. He begins well, with a helicopter shot of a police car speeding through the countryside—to color everything that we see in flashback thereafter—and returns to that shot at the end. But right after the opening, we get a close-up lof a lovely middle-aged woman addressing us in front of a tennis court. She tells us we mustn't assume that she's a player. She asks the camera to move back, which it does, revealing that she has a brace on one leg and carries a cane. (She's the tennis club manager.) The idea of a one-woman chorus for this film, lame because of an attempted suicide-for-love twenty years earlier, is apt, but the talk to us and the camera, resumed at the end, is pointless, tricksy. As is the one iris-out that Truffaut feels he must include in each film.

But, overall, he directs with strict attention to business—*his* business, of fluent film narration, unstrained emotional emphases, and speed. *Speed*, more than the less specific terms "pace" or "rhythm," is a big factor in Truffaut. *The Woman Next Door* is the work of a born filmmaker, born a long time ago (as the film world figures), who has spent the intervening years learning a lot, of course, but being particularly careful, while learning, not to lose his innate *brio*.

François Truffaut

(November 26, 1984)

I had dinner once with François Truffaut—in Brooklyn, of all places. It was in early 1964, I think, when he was in New York to organize the filming of Ray Bradbury's *Fahrenheit 451*. He and his translator were invited to the Brooklyn Heights home of Bradbury's literary agent who invited me, too, both because of my keen interest in Truffaut and because, in my book-publishing days, I had been Bradbury's editor on *Fahrenheit 451*. After dinner, without announcement, our host put on a record of "Singin' in the Rain." Truffaut leaned back in his chair, then started to hum and to make his hands do a little dance as he remembered Gene Kelly. I thought of that moment when I heard the shocking news of his death on October 21 at the age of fifty-two.

During that Brooklyn evening I asked a question or two, to our host's wry amusement, about why Truffaut wanted to film a book that was so far out of his vein. The questions made him impatient, but in the course of time the film made many of his admirers impatient. (By mordant coincidence, Oskar Werner, the star of the film, died three days after Truffaut.) What his admirers wanted from him—which the Bradbury book, whatever its merits, could not permit him—was his unique quality: the lyric lift with which he treated joy and poignancy, savagery and death.

Two chief subjects are visible in his body of work, children and women. No director has ever dealt better with children, and not many have dealt comparably well. Truffaut seemed to become one of the children, not an adult looking down on them fondly, whether it was the Antoine of *The Four Hundred Blows* or the Wild Child himself or the youngsters in *Small Change*.

Closely connected with his feelings for children (as *The Four Hundred Blows* demonstrates) were his more complex feelings about women. He adored them, and he quite literally feared them. To him, women were objects of romance, in an old-style, balcony-serenade way, and were also killers of men, in the most steely-eyed, post-Freudian way. After the man in *The Soft Skin* fixes a rendezvous by telephone, he walks around his darkened hotel room unconsciously turning on all the lights until the room looks as bright as he feels. When the man in *The Woman Next Door* is lying on his lover, she takes a pistol from her handbag and blows out his brains. The marvel of Truffaut was that all these matters, and more, were touched by the same unique, vaulting imagination. In 1964 I made a three-month trip around Europe, east and west, talking to film people, and I asked directors everywhere the same question: Among working directors, who are the ones who mean the most to you? Almost always the answers were: Ford, Godard, and Truffaut—and with the name Truffaut, they almost always smiled.

The received wisdom about lyric poets is that, like mathematicians, they do their best work when young. This is pretty cool compensation for Truffaut's relatively early death, even if almost all his best work was done before he was forty. More of Truffaut's lesser work would be stratospheres above what we usually see, would very likely have continued to evoke that smile, which is fundamentally one of gratitude. In a backward look at *Jules and Jim* four years after it appeared, I said: "Whatever its shortcomings, *Jules and Jim* is one of the moments when the history of film suddenly glows." The comment applies to Truffaut's whole career.

Nine Months

(March 28, 1981)

A memorable "first." In a new Hungarian film the heroine becomes pregnant, and the picture ends with the birth: we see the actress of the role actually giving birth to a baby. Childbirth scenes as such are not novel; they've been used in documentaries ever since Vertov's *Man with a Movie Camera* (1929) and occasionally in fiction films, such as Le Chanois's *Case of Dr. Laurent* (1957). In the latter, shots of a birth by another woman were intercut with shots of the actress's face. Not here. In *Nine Months* we see Lili Monori naked with swollen belly, then we see her on a bed in labor, and the camera pans down her body to her son's appearance in the world.

The director, Márta Mészáros who wrote the script with Gyula Hernádi and Ildiko Koródy, says that the birth sequence was shot first; later, they did the bulk of the picture, the (fictional) material leading up to the birth. Mészáros doesn't say whether the idea for the heroine's pregnancy came from the fact that Monori became pregnant while they were writing, but if that was so, why not? Many an artwork has its form because of circumstances around it.

The difficulty with the birth sequence is not a feeling of exploitation, no trace of it, but that the birth is a different order of reality from the rest of the film's reality. Until then we've had the lovely double truth of Monori's acting: the truth of the actress plus the truth of the woman she is playing. In the birth sequence, the second truth disappears and we have Monori alone. It disrupts the texture of the film—but only for a time. Afterward, it becomes supportive:

retrospect makes us consider that if Monori was willing to have the birth photographed, it was as an act of confidence in the film, the director, the theme; that her decision to let it be photographed – not the birth itself – was one of the many decisions she made about her performance.

Monori and the man who plays her lover, Jan Nowicki, are in the Mészáros film *Women* which has already played here but was made a year after *Nine Months*, which has just arrived. Since then the pair have made a third film with Mészáros, with whom they clearly work congenially. Nowicki is a Pole – in *Nine Months* he spoke Polish which was then dubbed in Hungarian – and is the kind of actor who delivers more or less what he promises in the first minute or so. In that first minute Nowicki, with lean grim face and manner, promises quiet complexity, bitterness, contained force, nothing like as engulfing as Jean Gabin but along those lines. When the role calls on him to "give," he does it, credibly, but never with blinding flashes of emotional power. He is certainly not dully predictable, neither is he an actor of surprises or enlargements.

Monori is the opposite of him. Her first minutes promise little: a pudgy, round face with the tablature neither of beauty nor of a strong actor's "mask," with only the cautious confidence of a cat who has learned to look out for herself. Then she starts to grow, and she keeps growing. When she breaks into a smile, the face changes more than most faces change with a smile: wholly different prospects of self appear. Her instinct for oddness, which is really an instinct for verity under acting cliché, gives that doughnut face a range of color – of sexiness, too – that is moving, even a little shaming of us because we expected less. Monori has an inner self that marries with the inner self of the woman she is playing, and that marriage triumphs through her unpromising face. Some beautiful actresses also have that talent, of course, but to see the tradition of beauty in film actresses flouted so justifiably is like seeing a blow for authenticity as against protocol.

Monori has a scene near the end in a new apartment, just before she has her child, just after she has left her lover and the job and town where she lived. She has been shown the new place where she will work after she gives birth, has been shown her new flat. She likes both. Now she is left alone in the empty place, and she sits on the window sill. Everything in her that has been struggling against the strength of her suppression, everything she hasn't wanted to admit feeling because admission isn't going to help her – the hurt and fear and increased loneliness – all these things flood through her as she sits there. It's like a separate small film contained within the larger one, shown only on her face. I haven't seen anything like it – a kind of silent solo drama – since some of the work that Liv Ullmann did for Ingmar Bergman. I'll remember the childbirth in *Nine Months* for reasons stated, but what I'll treasure from the picture is that window sill sequence.

Mészáros, to judge by the two films shown here, wants to explore womanhood, the reaches and possibilities for a contemporary human being who is female. What's especially interesting about her is that her views on women don't appear to be doctrinaire and the society in which she works *is* doctrinaire, one of its doctrines being egalitarianism. *Nine Months* is binary, interwoven. We get the life of industrial workers, dramatized through the encounter of a foreman and a new woman worker. As he woos her, with much discouragement from her at the start, in the plant and in the nearby restaurant, as they move around the neighborhood and encounter his mother and his friends, the rhythms and aspects of the small city's life are made manifest. In this sense, the story is a libretto for the score of the environment.

But also, by following the story, we get an anatomy of the moral climate in the new social order, a mixture of puritanism and license. Nowicki trails Monori one Sunday and discovers that this independent, free-thinking woman has a small son (an earlier child) who lives with Monori's mother; later he learns that the father is a former teacher of Monori's, a married man. This shocks Nowicki, but eventually he's able to accept it as long as she keeps it a secret until they are married and have moved into the house he is still finishing. When one day she visits the unfinished house and finds five of his friends there, she is invited to make a sixth for an orgy, but gets away. When she is studying for her final exams in agriculture, Nowicki nags at her for attention and questions the worth of her studying if she's going to be his wife and keep their house for them. (She passes, well.) When he and she and his mother and relatives are putting final touches on the house, a remark is made that forces Monori to tell them about her child. His mother and relatives call her a whore. She, though pregnant, leaves Nowicki and this town—to live her life as she chooses. The one note of hope is that he is sufficiently shaken so that he may in time see her value, her honor. The picture combines the survival of bourgeois liberalism and its pathetic attempts at depravity along with the survival of a bourgeois puritanism that the new order apparently encourages.

The combination of themes makes clear that a life for women equally free with men's life still lies ahead in communist states as well as elsewhere. Mészáros has realized her film without didactics, with fluency and vividness, and with Monori's performance. The title has the right neatness: it describes the story, and it suggests a truth under it—birth of a different sort of womanhood.

Raiders of the Lost Ark

(July 4 & 11, 1981)

Even before you see *Raiders of the Lost Ark*, after you've read the ads and got some sense of the reviews, you know that the picture is offering you a pact: you agree to be a kid again, in return for which *Raiders* will give you old-time movie thrills expressed in modern cinematic terms.

No, thanks.

I won't pretend that I got no thrills or tingly laughs out of *Raiders*, but the more it happened, the more it irritated me. (Bernard Shaw said it happened to him when he found himself laughing at certain comedies.) *Raiders*, as bruited, *is* the Saturday-afternoon serial in excelsis. It was directed by Steven Spielberg (*Close Encounters of the Third Kind*), and one of the executive producers and authors was George Lucas (*Star Wars*)—two of the brightest young successes in Hollywood. But the more spectacular the sweep, the more stunning the special effects, the more ingenious the editing, the more my irritation grew until it toppled into depression.

Raiders is set in 1936. The hero is an American archaeology professor, Harrison Ford, whom we first meet in a South American jungle, pillaging a temple full of booby traps and blowguns, just escaping with his life. Then, after an unconsciously droll academic interlude back home, he is commissioned by U.S. secret agents to keep the Germans from recovering the Lost Ark. This ark, said to contain the original fragmented tablets of the Ten Commandments, is buried in Egypt where Germans are now digging under the guidance of a ratty French archaeologist. (One of several dozen rational questions that it's idle to ask: why did Egypt admit detachments of German troops and armored vehicles?) The U.S. must keep the ark out of Hitler's hands, for prestige reasons and because Hitler believes in the power of the occult. Our hero sets off, and en route—in one of the coincidences that are the film's best features, that keep it on the edge of spoof—he meets an old girl friend, Karen Allen, in Nepal. We first see her drinking a Nepalese giant under the table in the tavern that she owns. Germans are tailing our hero, and as Allen joins Ford, the bad guys chase the two of them to Egypt.

The action in Egypt is so febrile that, if some gags were not included, the pace itself would be funny. In the sequence just before the finish, the bad guys seize the ark, which arouses the ire of Jehovah in ways that only His prophets Spielberg and Lucas could envision. At the end, when the Lord's ark is in the right hands—ours, of course—the U.S. government assures Ford that the contents will be carefully investigated; then we see the crate being wheeled away into the anonymity of an immense warehouse. This last high shot is presumably meant to suggest the last shot of *Citizen Kane* except that this "Rosebud" is not being destroyed: it's available for sequels, which will doubtless be forthcoming. (And fifthcoming, sixthcoming. . . .)

Raiders is totally different in intent from *Close Encounters*, a film that in its original—and, I hope, preserved—version was moving and important. From its start, the earlier film, despite some strained domestic sitcom sequences, built the credibility of an approaching cosmic mystery. The last forty minutes were, I think, an event in the history of faith, not so much faith in the creatures of outer space as in the means by which they were presented. Spielberg, then thirty, a product of what some call the post-literate age, was demonstrating (to quote myself) that "the way to faith seems to be through the transsubstantiation of the twelve-track Panavision film." We made the technology that was making the answers to our questions.

Spielberg is still an immersed film zealot, but now he is using his zeal on the *subjects* of old films in which he was immersed. (I'm omitting discussion of *1941*, his intervening film, which was just an arrogant joke that went wrong and long.) Here are some of the points that depress me, ultimately, about this change:

Implied limitations. Spielberg seems to imply that to be at ease in film Zion, to love film, one must be a film buff, a movie fan. Ingmar Bergman once said that he makes a film with full consciousness that it will be shown on a screen that showed a Western the week before and will show a romance the week following, and that he likes this situation. But that isn't a matter of worship, it's a recognition of lexical community and common humanity: it's not to *make* Westerns and romances. Spielberg heads straight for the bottom of the film pyramid, as if that were where the truest cinema lies, rather than in applying cinematic post-literacy to contemporary society and using the new language for the new world.

Nostalgia. The future is the past — spiffed up with the latest technology. I've commented often on the nostalgia of the film world, its worship of the high Hollywood days, its belief that the best has already been. If that studio work had strict limitations, it also had securities. (Truffaut once said that he would like to have been a studio contract director in the old days, to be handed three or four scripts a year with nothing to worry about but the making of the films.) *Raiders* is an eloquent testimony of faith in pastness. The fact that it's set in 1936, that the hero can wear corny 1930s fedoras, that we can see 1936 automobiles and airplanes and old-fashioned unpsychologized villanies — all this underscores a feeling that Spielberg is one more Miniver Cheevy, born (he believes) too late. His ideal, I suppose, is to have been born around 1905 but to have had his present cameras and film stock and Dolby stereo. None of this is regard for the past as much as it is refuge from the present. Nostalgia used to be characteristic of older people; now there are probably more youthful nostalgia addicts than ever before in history.

Innocence. The nostalgia in *Raiders* is coupled with innocence. This, I'd guess, is the influence of George Lucas. One of the most distasteful aspects of *Star Wars* was its assumption that life is better before sex intrudes. Remember how Carrie Fisher looked? She helped to keep *Star Wars* sexless, back in that part of our lives when we could really have good clean fun, ray guns, killing without consequences, and so on. One of John Updike's characters says that in America a man is a failed boy. The only significant error in that remark is that, to judge by the international success of *Star Wars*, it's no longer an American monopoly. What's wanted is, not all that nasty growing up but physical-yet-sexless games in which only bad people die.

What's depressing me most in all this is the future. I mourn no lost paradise of film. I know that, in a good year, ninety-five percent of the world's films were trash, four percent plus were good entertainment, and there was a small fraction of seriously good films. In a good year. But that small fraction seems to be shrinking. Economic and cultural conditions all conduce to shrink it. What's grim in the film world, as *Raiders* attests, certainly in the U.S. and gradually becoming so elsewhere, is that the stringency of filmmaking conditions is making the talents with the best possibilities *want* to revel in the movie-ness of the past. Yeats worried that "The best lack all conviction, while the worst/Are full of passionate intensity." But Spielberg and Lucas, as far as ability goes, are among our best, and they are full of passionate intensity.

I don't want to be a child again, not even for two hours. I reject the *Raiders* pact.

E.T.

(July 5, 1982)

Fervently, seductively, Steven Spielberg evangelizes on. *Close Encounters of the Third Kind* seemed to me "not so much a film as an event in the history of faith," and that faith, I thought, was less in beings Out There than in the film medium's ability to convince. Technology, at the behest of the culture that created it, had been called on to satisfy the culture's deeper needs, to soothe its fears. If you discount the revised version of *Close Encounters*, which I hope has been withdrawn, then Spielberg's next work in this line is *E.T., The Extra-Terrestrial*, which too manifests the thaumaturgy of film, but on a quite different scale and with quite different colors.

In a sense *E.T.* begins where *Close Encounters* ends: we're not awaiting Their arrival, They are here. A spaceship from Somewhere has landed in a California forest at night, and one of the extraterrestrials has left the ship to explore. Suddenly men burst into the forest, searching for the ship. (Through most of the picture these men are photographed from the chest down; the emphasis is on their heavy belts with keys and guns. Or they are photographed from the back. They are impersonal forces.) The spaceship takes off hurriedly, leaving the one adventurous E.T. stranded. He—we are told later that the creature is a "boy"—is vaguely human in appearance, with eyes and arms and elongated hands and fingers, with very short legs, an enormous head, and an extensible neck. His skin is a sort of greenish hide. His chest glows when he is frightened; his fingertips glow when he is exercising his special powers. From the start he is shown to be very far from a threat or a monster: he is vulnerable, unaggressive, and frightened.

The E.T. is discovered by a boy of about ten who lives in a town nearby, a boy of the same height as the creature. He befriends the E.T. and hides him in the closet of his room in the new house where he lives with his older brother and younger sister and their mother. (The father of the family has decamped with another woman.) All three children keep the secret as long as possible from their mother, as if they had taken in a stray animal whose presence she might dislike. The children know very well that this creature is an E.T. They are fascinated and friendly; the E.T. responds with at least equal affection, and he demonstrates the quickness of his mind by picking up words of their language.

All the while that this warmth grows between him and the family—eventually the mother discovers him, too—the U.S. government is tracking him down with electronic devices. The E.T., fond though he is of his new friends, is homesick. The ten-year-old scrapes together some materials for him, including a computer game that's in the house, and the keen-minded E.T. fashions a device to send signals to his compatriots Out There. The climax of the picture is a contest between officialdom's fight to capture the E.T., in the course of which they nearly kill him, and the family's fight to let him return. Which, after a chase whose banality is leavened with neat fantasy, he does.

One old plague plagued me again. This California family is hip to everything in pop culture, so I couldn't help wondering why they hadn't seen *Close Encounters*, why they never referred to it in their dealings with the E.T. The modern characters in film, no matter how detailed their lives are in other minutiae, are usually shorn of the film knowledge they would otherwise have, if that knowledge would damage the film they are in.

A basic difference between *Close Encounters* and *E.T.* is that the former is epic—certainly in its forty-minute conclusion—and the new one is domestic, enclosed in one town, almost in one home. The tone of the first film is heroic, of the new one, intimate and cozy. But we can now see some constants, so far, in the Spielberg space credo.

1) Children are our best communicators with Them. Children are open, unafraid, curious. The small boy in *Close Encounters* goes willingly with the visitors. The somewhat older boy here, who is really the protagonist, has the same openness, with some added intelligence and some sense of the dignity of every living being.

2) The boy's mother is alone. For whatever reason, her husband doesn't live in the house. This removes a too-authoritative male presence from the design and keeps the household sex-free. The mother in E.T. certainly misses her husband and the children refer to him feelingly, but his presence would add a jarring note of dominance. And the relations with Them in Spielberg films have no sexual suggestion on either side. Sex, of any kind, is no part of the promise Out There.

3) The extraterrestrials make their contacts in the U.S. They may cause ructions elsewhere, as in *Close Encounters*, but when they communicate, it's in Wyoming or California, not Swaziland or Burma. Certainly not the U.S.S.R.

4) The American stratum with which they are juxtaposed is gadgety middle-

class—TV, computer games, kitchen appliances, kids' closets overflowing with toys, refrigerators jammed with supermarket stuff. The extraterrestrials don't come in contact with sharecroppers' cabins or millionaires' mansions or the Institute for Advanced Study. Achievement in intergalactic exploration is contrasted with achievement in household doodads.

5) Adults are profession-hardened—allowing for exceptions like Truffaut in the first film and one doctor here—to the point of obtuseness and inhumanity. This is the Mark Twain-Salinger syndrome carried into sci-fi.

6) Hope for communication between our planet and other places—thus, by extension, hope for continuance and maturing of the human race—lies more in feeling (the openness of the child) than in intellect (the grim efficiencies of the adult). The visitors from Out There are assumed to have higher intelligence, if only because they got here and we didn't get There; but we are happy to be their inferiors. In a way, it's a relief to relegate adulthood to them, to keep ourselves children, free for fuller feeling.

7) All of this is made apprehensible, credible, by film. None of it would be so powerfully *presentable* without film. Finally, that fact seems more important than what is presented. Film does not facilitate the god from the machine: it's the machine as god.

I once read a short story—by Ben Hecht, I think—in which Jesus looks down on Hollywood from on high and sees that a film is being made about him. For whatever reason, Jesus secretly takes the place of the actor portraying him and brings off the miracles without the help of special-effects men. The only way that Spielberg's religious films (as I'd call them) could move from centering on worship of film to centering on the film's subject would be if the equivalent happened here—if, for instance, an actual E.T. had substituted for the ingenious puppet that represents him. But if that had happened, we'd probably have had word of it by now. So the weight remains with Spielberg's faith in film—and film's reciprocity.

And an appealing film this new one is, with some charm, some glee in the childrens' triumphs, some share in their friendship with the E.T. There are few of the great surges of *Close Encounters*, but with the cleverness of the E.T. creation designed by Carlo Rambaldi (who did the creatures in *Close Encounters*), the swooping music of John Williams (who did the *Close Encounters* score), and the serviceable dialogue by Melissa Mathison, Spielberg makes the picture hold and grow. And, of course, with the authentic feeling he gets from the three youngsters, Henry Thomas, the ten-year-old, Robert Macnaughton, his older brother, and Drew Barrymore (sweet granddaughter of the illustrious John), their little sister.

At the last parting between the ten-year-old and the E.T., with the spaceship waiting, they are both in tears. The E.T. puts his finger next to the boy's temple—the fingertip glows—and says, "I'll be right here." Then he boards the ship, which blasts off and streaks across the sky, leaving—even though it is night—a rainbow.

Well, maybe some day, over *that* rainbow. . . .

Stevie

(July 25, 1981)

It's twenty-five years anyway since I first saw the title of a poem that seems to me the best poetic title since *The Divine Comedy*. The poem is called "Not Waving But Drowning." The poet was an Englishwoman named Stevie Smith, and, yes, the poem itself is good, too. The last two of its twelve lines:

> I was much too far out all my life
> And not waving but drowning.

Of course I read more Smith—her collected poems are published by Oxford University Press—and got the sense of an English Emily Dickinson: lesser, certainly, but certainly comparable.

In 1977 I read London reviews of a play called *Stevie* (she had died in 1971), arranged from her life and writings by Hugh Whitemore, and I restrained a youthful impulse to fly the Atlantic at once. Later I read that the play had been filmed with two of the London principals, but the film didn't come here. Then, in 1979, the Manhattan Theater Club, off Broadway, presented the play in a good production directed by Brian Murray with a cast headed by Roberta Maxwell. It was lackadaisically received and soon disappeared. I do not slight this sensitive production when I say I'm glad that the film has at last arrived.

The film is the play minimally embellished, so I must make the shape of the play clear. Four characters only: Stevie, her aunt, a boyfriend who appears in one flashback scene, and a character called The Man. The last is chorus as well as character: he often speaks to us, introducing people and explaining transitions, and he also occasionally steps "into" the play. (I surmise that he is based on James MacGibbon, an English publishing figure, who wrote the introduction to the collected edition.) Stevie, too, often speaks directly to us, just as easily as she speaks to others on stage, simply by looking at us. (The aunt and the boyfriend remain "within" the play.) In the film, the "us" is of course the camera. This is hardly a new device, but in serious work, it's always a bit risky. It can smell of false naiveté, treating the technology of production and the pastness of the film as if they didn't exist—a risk that doesn't apply in the relatively untechnological, present-tense theater.

But that risk never bothers *Stevie*, and not just because the writing is limber and the address to the audience uncoy. It's because the presence of the audience is taken absolutely for granted. That acceptance is no mere dramaturgic device:

it involves metaphysical truth about Stevie herself. It's as if our presence had always been part of the woman's life. What the audience was in the theater, what the camera is here, is the witness that every artist needs to perceive all his secrets whole, secrets that even his nearest and dearest cannot wholly see. His art is the externalizing of only some of those secrets: but all of them need witness. (Somewhere Auden said that, when he arrives in Heaven, God will walk toward him speaking lines of the poems he never wrote.) Stevie says firmly that she is an agnostic. This is relevant to the method of the play and the film. A devout believer wouldn't need to address us so much, she would *have* a witness of all her secrets.

None of this to say that *Stevie* is grand. It's a small film about a small-scale poet who, by temperamental choice, led a suburban life outside London. Born in 1902 as Florence Margaret Smith, called Peggy by her aunt, she was nicknamed Stevie because, when riding, someone thought she looked like the jockey Steve Donahue. She commuted most of her life to a job in a magazine publishing firm in central London and lived in a row house with her adored aunt from the Midlands. (The aunt's name is never given: Stevie refers to her as "the lion of Hull" or "the lion aunt.") There were only a few variants between Stevie and the other inhabitants of Avondale Road. First, she was physically very exhaustible. She had spent three years in a tuberculosis sanitorium as a child, and all her life she fluctuated between exhaustion and ebullience. (Once, depressed, she slashed her wrists.) Another difference from her neighbors: she wrote. In fact her first book was a novel, *Novel on Yellow Paper*, and she wrote two more; but it was her poetry that quietly achieved some quiet fame; brought her broadcasts on the BBC (George Orwell, whom she distrusted, was her producer); won her the Queen's Medal in 1969. (Her account of her visit to Buckingham Palace is perfect: awed but witty.) On the whole, however, the suburban ambience, with the tea waiting in the cozy living room, the Tio Pepe shared with the lion aunt before dinner, the confined and understood Avondale Road life, was Stevie's clear preference over the metropolitan literary life she could easily have chosen.

That suburban environment, loved, is one part of the drama: because it contrasts with the immensity of spirit in this particular commuter. Within the overdecorated little house, with its fake Burne-Jones drawings, great wings are beating in one suburbanite bosom. Avodale Road is, after all, not so far from Keats's Hampstead, and if there had been a camera and recorder on hand at the time, we might have heard *him* wavering between mint sauce and red currant jelly for his roast lamb. The film, even more than the play, gives us the godlike sense of looking down into one tiny mortal dwelling to discern the immortality within it.

Whitemore's method is pastiche: of chronicle, dialogue, soliloquy, and many seamlessly spliced bits of Stevie's poetry. We follow her from early middle age through her aunt's death to her own disintegration via brain tumor. The drama is chiefly in the fact that *a drama is being shown*: the contrast between the quiet living of a life and the fact of its presentation to us.

So far as we are told, there was only one amour in Stevie's life, one engagement, and she broke that off because she couldn't brook the idea of a married Stevie. (Also, during the night of love with her gent, played by Alec McCowen, he asked her—as she reminds him the next day—whether she was enjoying it. Not only that, she says: he actually asked, "Are you enjoying it, *dear?*") She tells us later that she's a friendship girl, not the marrying kind: "I love people, but I love the thought and memory of them just as much."

Possibly the subtlest aspect of the piece is its language, which mirrors the double suburban-cosmic perspective of the shape. It combines the platitudinous with the piercing. Some unmemorable observations, such as life being like a railway station, and insights like "We've all got to go sometime" are mixed with lines like the above and fragments of her poetry. ("Unique and cheerfully gruesome," Robert Lowell thought it.) When she talks about Anglicanism, there's more two-fold structure: she likes the hymns but doesn't like the faith. And Glenda Jackson, who plays Stevie, always give the word "Christian" three syllables—Christ-i-an. This makes the source of the term stand clear.

About Jackson's acting, I have little to add to what I've said many times: she is one of the best actresses alive. When she enters a room, the room then exists. Her intelligence, her concealment and revelation of feeling, her musicality . . . but I wasn't going to talk about her. I'll just note that I was glad to see her with her 1978 "normal" hair instead of the shingle cut she subsequently adopted for Shakespeare's Cleopatra in London and her Broadway appearance in *Rose*.

Jackson did Stevie on the London stage, and with her as the lion aunt was Mona Washbourne, who is with her again in the film. In all the shouting, so well deserved, about Jackson, please, please let us not overlook Washbourne. This is fine character acting by a fine character actress at the apex of a long career: exquisitely controlled, beautifully selected, timed impeccably, utterly inhabited. See her in the doorway when Stevie is helped out of a taxi after her suicide attempt. See her—after her earlier scenes of marcelled hair and perfect composure—as illness encroaches, in her dressing gown, with one loose tendril of hair, making her way fearfully to her easy chair. It's an actor's poem about the passage of time.

Trevor Howard is The Man. Howard has become mostly a hearty old blunderbuss of an actor, but here he has a chance to recapture some of the range and color he used to have. It is he, walking by a pond one day, who speaks the "Not Waving But Drowning" poem. I wish I had a recording of it.

The director is the American-born Robert Enders who has been writing and producing in England since 1972. With Jackson he co-produced the excellent film of Genet's *The Maids*, and has since made several other pictures. *Stevie* is Enders's directing debut, and he does well. The only cinematic contrivances come when he "breaks out" of the house into outdoor sequences—like the mimed sequences of Stevie's childhood—to avoid theater contrivance. And I wish he had omitted the drawing of the curtain on the lighted window of the aunt's bedroom to signify her death. Other than that, high marks for fluency.

The music by Patrick Gowers, played by the Gabrieli String Quartet and the guitarist John Williams, gives the right reticent richness to this *multum in parvo* film. Babs Grey's costumes have the precise touches of English propriety (the aunt) and ignoring of chic (Stevie) – though I confess I missed the gray wool ankle socks and open-toed bright green sandals that Roberta Maxwell wore in the New York production. The film was shot by Freddie Young, who was a mere 76 when he did it but still managed precociously to lay lovely sepia on the past and to make the modern suburban interiors both crinkum-crankum and endearing.

The French Lieutenant's Woman

(September 23, 1981)

Harold Pinter is in love with time – not the neat unceasing sequence of the clock but the time in our minds, the time in which we live and remember and fantasize, time expansible and contractile, infinitely contrapuntal, time tyrannical and elusive. It has always seemed to him a prime locus for drama, as witness *Old Times*, a perfect double-meaning title, and *No Man's Land*, an attempt at a cubist play. And his *Proust Screenplay* has been recognized by many on both sides of the Atlantic as a small masterpiece derived from the greatest artwork about time.

That screenplay is still unproduced, and I'd conjecture that Pinter has used the chance to write the screenplay of John Fowles's *The French Lieutenant's Woman* as a way to work off his frustrations – in the film medium – about time exploration. The Fowles novel is set in the England of the late 1860s, but the narrator is our contemporary, who keeps making comparisons with today, supplying references, adding footnotes. However one reacts to this device – my enthusiasm is mixed – it's clumsy for a film. Narrators have sometimes been used to wonderful effect in films (*Diary of a Country Priest, Jules and Jim*, etc.), but there was always a recognizable *cinematic* need for them. That need can't be felt with the Fowles book. Yet merely to have extracted the period story and told it straight would have been to misrepresent it.

The solution, says Pinter, was suggested by the director, Karel Reisz, but Reisz knew the man to whom he was speaking: Pinter quite evidently leaped at the idea, possessed it, and flew. To make the screenplay at least equally as binary as the novel, Pinter has interwoven a present-day story strand about the actors who are making the film. Where Fowles commented today on the book he was writing, the actors comment today on the film they are making – comment, not in a direct way like Bergman's cast in *The Passion of Anna*, but by living through a story in their own lives between the shooting of scenes.

The intent is made immediately clear and is immediately arresting. The very first shot is of Meryl Streep's face in a mirror. (Mirrors recur throughout.) She is in period costume and is having her hair and face touched up. Then we see a film clapboard and slate, the camera pulls back, and Streep sweeps into the first long bravura motion of the film, striding down the long breakwater of Lyme Bay in 1867. It's a subtle, concise, provocative method at once. The film grows organically from that opening microcosm—although it doesn't grow to fulfillment.

First, however, let's look at what is splendid in it—which is a great deal. The production designer, Assheton Gorton, and his associates have provided a nineteenth-century milieu at the high level of *Tess* and *The Story of Adèle H.*; and their details in the contemporary strand wryly complement and contrast. The cinematographer, Freddie Francis, showed in *The Elephant Man* an insight into grimy Victorian England; he extends it here to some of the grander aspects of the era. Many of the period scenes are shot under a gray sky that gives them a unique, almost pastel palette; many of the modern sequences are shown in a spanking fresh light. The music by Carl Davis aptly embraces and supports.

Reisz, the director, is home again. With his last picture, *Who'll Stop the Rain?*, made in the U. S., I lamented his unease, his purportedly brave statement of those commonplace American heterodoxies to which the tourist is susceptible. Now he is on familiar territory, literally and otherwise. This has been no guarantee of success for him in the past, but here it has brought out the best in him. He seems absolutely sure of how he wants every scene to look and move, and his confidence breeds conviction. He skillfully alternates between two kinds of dynamics, dramatic and pictorial. That opening shot of Streep, for instance, as she strides along the sea wall with the sea lashing at her, is a strophe of romantic drama. In a later scene, she sits leaning against a tree, one arm arched over her head, gazing out at the quiet sea, and one feels that the Pre-Raphaelite brotherhood, who obviously inspired the shot, would have approved it.

The editing is superb. Reisz has, in fact, written *the* book on the subject, *The Technique of Film Editing*, and here his work with the credited editor, John Bloom (brother of Claire, incidentally), makes us feel the intelligence, the vitality, of the rhythms and combinations. One instance: in 1867, Streep's character, a woman of tainted reputation, is being interviewed for the post of companion to a rich elderly puritanical woman. The camera lets Streep make her entrance into the old woman's drawing room as a Victorian actress might have done—except that, for a sliver of a second, Reisz flashes in a close-up of the beady-eyed old woman watching her. Thus to the Victorian theater, Reisz adds the film's power to include the "audience."

Meryl Streep plays two roles: the 1860s woman and the actress of that woman. Jeremy Irons plays two roles: the 1860s man and the performer of the part. In 1867 Streep is called the French lieutenant's woman because she has the reputation of having dallied with a visiting French officer, and she abets the repute. Irons is a London gentleman engaged to a rich tradesman's daughter who lives in the neighborhood—played by Lynsey Baxter, a paradigmatic English rose. He sees Streep while visiting Lyme, becomes infatuated, and eventually breaks off his engagement to devote himself to the tarnished woman. Fowles's novel has been read by many; still, because surprise is part of the structure, I'll say only that the surprise, the very structure of the period strand, is essentially romantic. "What was the Romantic movement?" asked Bernard Shaw in 1897, and continued:

> I don't know, though I was under its spell in my youth. All I can say is that it was a freak of the human imagination, which created an imaginary past, an imaginary heroism, an imaginary poetry . . . Romance is always, I think, a product of *ennui*, an attempt to escape from a condition in which real life appears empty, prosaic, boresome . . . . For all that, the land of dreams is a wonderful place; and the great Romancers were . . . pure enchanters . . . .

Fowles is not a great anything, but the movement of his story holds like a dream. Unfortunately it also punishes like a dream: it leaves us frustrated and bewildered. I don't understand the behavior of the French lieutenant's woman except as an example of self-poisoning by dream values. Possibly it was boredom with her reality that drove her to create her own romantic character.

The contemporary story, about the actors who play the two lovers, is less romantic, in the literary sense, and though full of feeling, more sexually pragmatic. He has a wife, back home near London; the actress has a lover back in London. Together every day, the two performers have a passionate affair, which she ends when the last day's shooting is done. The modern story is no perceptibly applicable comment on the Victorian one; it has only the pathos of an affair begun, pursued, and necessarily finished, which is no more than the pathos of mortality. That's quite a lot, of course, but it's not specific in any sense to the patterns of the period story, in balance or contrast. When the film is over, we are left with a lot of lovely atmospherics, past and present, but no clear reason for the being of the work, particularly in its twinned form. It shows us how people behaved and behave in compacts of sexual passion, but the period story is so eccentric and the modern one so common that their juxtaposition is unenlightening.

But the doing of it all is beautiful. (One nit: Reisz sometimes permits the pronunciation "lootenant" which is exclusively American, instead of the British "leftenant" which is used at other times.) Reisz has cast his picture perfectly, and he has got performances that reflect his cast's belief in him. Jeremy Irons is a young actor of sex and force and ease, with a sense of line and with sufficient brutality to make his gentleness truer. He has had extensive experience in British theater and TV, but this is only his second film role—the first being his vivid Fokine in *Nijinsky*. He has just finished the leading role in the British TV version of Waugh's *Brideshead Revisited*. With a little wisdom and a lot of luck, Irons can have a large career.

Streep is having one. After she finished shooting this lavish film last year, she did *Alice* in Elizabeth Swados's quirky musical based on Lewis Carroll at the Public Theater in New York. Clad in T-shirt and overalls, Streep sang and tumbled about, with no tinge of slumming but—I imagined—enjoying the difference from what she knew and what we didn't yet know about this film.

I cite two moments from her performance here. When the 1867 woman decides to give herself to Irons, he carries her into the bedroom, and she lies on the bed waiting for him to get out of his complicated Victorian clothes as quickly as he can. Reisz wisely keeps the camera on her the whole time. Her face is like an elixir of fate and fascination. And there is a scene—the best use in the film of its double structure—in which Streep and Irons, as the two modern actors, rehearse a scene, in casual modern dress, in a modern room. She is moving toward him, she tells us from her script, when her dress catches in a bramble, she stumbles, and he helps her. First, they merely "walk it," speaking the words and timing the movements. Then, they start over, and Streep, still in mod clothes, *does* it: with sheer, sharp imagination, steps into Tennyson and Millais; and the character, not the actress, walks toward us and stumbles. Reisz cuts instantly to the same scene in the period strand as Irons, now in costume, steps forward in the woods to help her. It's good directing and editing; but the effect is as if Streep's power had forced the scene out of the informal modern into its true period and place.

My only stricture about Streep is that, while she easily sustains the vocal flourish of the period role, she sometimes lets her voice go dry in the modern role, something I thought she had overcome. It's as if she needs strong vocal demands in order to come up with sufficient voice.

Lynsey Baxter gives more than saccharine simper to the forsaken fiancée: we believe that Irons once wanted to marry her, which is not always true in "jilted" roles. Milton McRae, as Irons's servant, a sort of surly Figaro, and Leo McKern, as a friendly local doctor, get a special note, though every actor deserves one.

How I wish they would film Pinter's Proust script. Then perhaps he would not need to work off his "Proust frustration" on lesser material. This script is far above average from moment to moment, but it leaves us with more mystification than mystery.

But I have to add one more but. What a lovely two hours to watch and hear.

True Confessions

(September 30, 1981)

The career of Ulu Grosbard, director of films and plays, has been a nineteen-year tease. He has long seemed to be on the edge of major stature. Everything he has touched has shown at least some evidence of high directorial quality, but almost every script he has touched—either through bad luck or bad judgment—has not been good enough for him. If inside every fat man there's a thin man struggling to get out, then inside Grosbard's succession of flabby scripts there's a strong director similarly struggling.

I first saw his work in 1962, an Off Broadway production of William Snyder's *Days and Nights of Beebee Fenstermaker*, a commonplace play which was handled with unmistakable delicacy. Since then, Grosbard has done a number of other things, including the play and film of Gilroy's *The Subject Was Roses*, in which Grosbard struggled imaginatively against mundane odds, and two films, *Who Is Harry Kellerman. . . ?* and *Straight Time*, neither of which became the exceptionally incisive work it patently wanted to be.

Now here's Grosbard's new film, *True Confessions*, and again he is stuck with a script that isn't good enough for him. What extraordinary acting he gets from his cast!—lavished on a script that is all pedestrian smartness and stale shock.

It was written by John Gregory Dunne and Joan Didion from Dunne's novel. This pair are professional insiders: they make their living by knowing the frauds and corruptions and anguishes under the surfaces that deceive us innocents; and once in a while they deign to pull the scales from our eyes. This time they're telling us that the priesthood of the Roman Catholic church is made up of mortal men with mortal faults, that the wealthy communicants of that church sometimes influence and manipulate it, and that policemen—are you ready for this *again?*—sometimes sin, even in Los Angeles.

Recovering from the impact of these revelations, we can see that Grosbard has constructed his film figuratively between, around, and above the wisenheimer banalities of the script. For example, there's a quarrel scene between Charles Durning, a rich and crooked contractor who is being given a testimonial banquet as an outstanding Catholic layman, and Robert Duvall, an L. A. detective who knows the greasy truth about Durning and who tells it at the banquet. As writing, it's stagy stuff, including the strophes in which onlookers intervene to keep the pair from fighting. I recognized the scene because, minimally, I've seen it once a year for every year I've been filmgoing, but I've never been convinced before by the familiar hold-me-back-or-I'll-murder-him ballet. Under Grosbard's direction, I felt that one man might really have killed the other except for the forcible restraint. Under Grosbard's direction, the movie platitude becomes truth.

Or take the opening sequence between Duvall and his brother, a priest, played by Robert De Niro. The picture begins and ends in the "present," with a graying De Niro as a parish priest of a lonely little church in the California desert. (The body of the film, in the "past," explains how De Niro, who had been a monsignor on his way to auxiliary bishop, ends up in clerical Nowheresville.) In that opening, Duvall arrives at the empty church, is greeted by his brother, and is taken inside where the priest tells him that he, De Niro, has just been informed by doctors that he hasn't long to live. Another trite scene, the not-long-to-live bit, particularly at the start. But these two greatly gifted men are working with a director who helps them to weave the texture of silences around the lines. As is often the case in this film, what's important is what is not said.

It's true again in the closing sequence, back at the little church. De Niro takes his brother out into the scrubby churchyard in the desert and shows him the small fenced plot he has saved for himself and for Duvall when his time comes. "So this is it," says Duvall (the best line in the picture). And Grosbard's camera lifts above the two brothers standing on either side of the tiny patch in the middle of vastness where they will lie side by side.

The bulk of the script, under its slickness, is another version of those old-time movies about two brothers, usually from New York's Lower East Side, one of whom goes right while the other goes wrong. The difference here is that one, Duvall, goes worldly, and the other, De Niro, goes not quite unworldly enough, develops political ambitions within the church. And Duvall's detective work, pursued with a certain viciousness, finally spoils De Niro's ecclesiastical chances. Because Dunne and Didion are so insistently knowing about "real" life, we get a priest who dies of a heart attack in a brothel; a brothel madam who was once a lover of Duvall's; a girl who was apparently murdered in the making of a "snuff" porno film; and other harsh facts to bring us all to our senses. Somewhere buried in the script is an interesting theme of the many shapes of basic power drive, but Dunne and Didion are too proud of their hipness to dramatize it freshly and adequately.

Two points baffled me. I couldn't understand why Georges Delerue, composer of so many lovely film scores in his native France, put an angelic chorus under the sequence in which Duvall explores the blood-soaked porno-film studio. Second, I didn't understand the plot crux. Why was De Niro's churchly career ruined because, quite accidentally, he was a passenger in Durning's car on the day Durning decided to give a lift to a strange girl? The girl later became a tart and the "snuff" victim, but De Niro had absolutely nothing to do with it, not even any knowledge of it until long after the event. If he had been a fellow-passenger on a bus with a drug dealer, would that have tarnished him, too? No one would have believed that De Niro had anything to do with the drugs; why should anyone have found anything defamatory in the accidental encounter with the girl?

De Niro's performance is almost one of his best. I think he relies a bit too much on his difference from Duvall's push and bite to help delineate his own character, supposedly a man with more of the wheeler-dealer in him than he cares to acknowledge. At the end De Niro tells his brother that he's grateful because the result of Duvall's investigations was to get the monsignor off the ambition track and back into his vocation; this comment would ring a tone truer if we could sniff the ambition in him a bit more strongly when he's on the way up. But, as usual, De Niro has begun his performance with an idea about his body. This was overwhelmingly clear in *Raging Bull*, more subtly pervasive in *The Last Tycoon*. The way De Niro bears himself, walks, and gestures as the priest is his primary act of transformation.

Duvall is again slow-fused dynamite, with his little smiles of anger or disgust, his hesitations, his half-glances away. But a well-based character is counter-pointed throughout: Grosbard has helped Duvall build the anger from a buried agony. These two men worked together in the theater twice: in the celebrated 1965 revival of Miller's *View from the Bridge* with Jon Voight and with Dustin Hoffman as understudy; and in what is Grosbard's best script-choice to date, the Broadway production in 1977 of Mamet's *American Buffalo*. (Incidentally, Hoffman, star of *Harry Kellerman* and *Straight Time*, got Grosbard to direct both those pictures. Apparently Grosbard's actors are his biggest fans.)

Durning gives the rich crook a sharp contradictory combination of piggish egomania and resentful fear of the church. Kenneth McMillan, another *American Buffalo* alumnus, is Duvall's detective "partner" and is again a mobile knockwurst; at least Grosbard deploys him usefully. Burgess Meredith has the right odor as a nagging failed priest, a nuisance to his cardinal. That cardinal is Cyril Cusack, and I feel that Grosbard had little more to do with Cusack than appreciate him. Rose Gregorio (Mrs. Grosbard), who was Beebee Fenstermaker long ago, gives the madam more than Warner Brothers world-weary snarl—we get a forecast of her tired fate.

True Confessions leaves me a Grosbard admirer, still eager for the chance to admire a whole Grosbard work.

Chariots of Fire

(October 7, 1981)

Most films are much more producers' enterprises than the public is made aware of or than criticism acknowledges. The driving figure behind *Chariots of Fire* was a man of whom I wouldn't have expected much, an Englishman named David Puttnam who previously produced the deplorable *Midnight Express*, the ludicrous *Bugsy Malone*, and *The Duellists*, a painfully precious Conrad adaptation. To these meager expectations of Puttnam, add the fact that, after he got his film idea, he engaged a screenwriter named Colin Welland whose past labors include *Straw Dogs* and *Yanks*. Then, as Puttnam has done before, he engaged a director whose principal experience had been in TV commericals, Hugh Hudson. At the least *Chariots of Fire* shows that unforeseen chemical combinations can explode prophecy.

"I was looking for a story not unlike *A Man for All Seasons*," said Puttnam in the (London) *Observer* last August 16, "about a man who does an unexpedient thing. I looked for it in the sporting world because sport is a clean simple metaphor." He found a story of *two* such men—a true story, at that, about the 1924 Olympics. Puttnam went on his unpredictable way by engaging David Watkin, who is a masterly cinematographer but not the one would would first come to mind in connection with sport. (*How I Won the War, The Charge of the*

Light Brigade, Catch-22 are some of Watkin's films.) Clearly Puttnam and colleagues had a view from the start of how they wanted this sport film to look—and that look is not much like a conventional sport film.

Neither is Welland's script structure. To link from the beginning the stories of two men who didn't meet until far into the chronological sequence of events, Welland begins with a flashback, not from the 1924 Olympics but from a 1978 funeral service for one of the men. And within the body of the film, there are more flashings forward and back. They are never confusing: on the contrary, they add to the sense that this film is about something more than its double story.

Here I'll just lay out the two main lines. One of the two young men is Eric Liddell, the son of Scottish missionaries, born in China, who himself has a religious vocation and wants to return to China, who is urged to do so by his sister. It's an anguish for her, and—differently—for him, too, that he must do the unexpedient thing: he feels his talent for running is a gift from God that he must not spurn. He will be able to go on with his missionary work only if, at whatever pain to his family, he first serves God in his own way, by running in the Olympics.

The other young man is Harold Abrahams, the son of an immigrant Lithuanian Jew who prospered in England and who worships the country, who has raised Harold as a thoroughly English, thoroughly gentle, English gentleman. Young Abrahams, too, has a talent for running, and he, too, faces the rigorous way—not of God's will, like Liddell, but of proving social mettle. One night Abrahams is having dinner with the Gilbert and Sullivan soprano whom he loves and who loves him, and she asks him why he runs. He replies, "Because I'm Jewish." When she says she doesn't understand, he says, "You're not Jewish."

The climax—in the plot sense, anyway—occurs at the Olympic meet in Paris. Liddell refuses to run in his 100-meter event because the first heat is scheduled for a Sunday. (Remember when Hank Greenberg of the Detroit Tigers refused to play on Yom Kippur?) This causes consternation among bigwigs, including the Prince of Wales and assorted peers. I won't go into details of how a solution is found, but I can't possibly be accused of giving away twists when I note that on page 801 of the 1981 *World Almanac*, you can read that, at the 1924 Olympics, the 100-meter run was won by Harold Abrahams, the 400-meter run by Eric Liddell.

Even in this sketch, you can see that the film involves much more than the usual sport picture. History has considerably provided Puttnam with two stimulatingly contrasted heroes, and each of the stories carries with it a fascinating context of social colors, prides, vanities, virtues, and emotion. Also, through the earlier section, 1919 and thereabouts, there's a grim background of the war's aftermath. When Abrahams's class enters Cambridge, the master of his college, standing before a wall covered with the names of college men lost in 1914-18, tells the newcomers in a well-written speech about their predecessors and responsibilities. And (something Stroheim did in *Foolish Wives*) we see bad-ly maimed veterans in the background of various scenes.

Hudson's direction is utterly understanding. The editing, done with Terry Rawlings, seems to me flawless. We look always at what we need to see, whether we know it immediately or not, and we see it without camera maneuver—except in the slow-motion sequences which of course are meant to draw attention to themselves and which justify it either with helpful lyricism or emphasis. There and throughout, Watkin's camera work is lovely.

Two other aspects support the film strongly. First, the clothes—Scottish tweeds, Cambridge gentlemen's gear, London ladies' chic—authenticate the visual texture of every scene. Second, the music, which seems aerated out of school songs and old hymns, gives the film continual lift. These ultra-British contributions are by a designer named Milena Canonero and a composer named Vangelis Papathanassiou.

Welland's dialogue is brisk, funny, sometimes pithy. When Abrahams, already a celebrated runner, dines with the soprano for the first time, she says, "My brother would envy me," to which he answers, "So would mine." When Abrahams is given dinner by the masters of two Cambridge colleges, is asked to give up the professional trainer he has engaged, and firmly declines, one of the Cambridge masters says, after Abrahams leaves, "There goes your Semite." (Pronounced "Seemite.") "A different god, a different mountain-top." To categorize that line as sheer Jew-hatred is to simplify anti-Semitism and Euro-pean social history.

Writing about the acting is like remembering a feast. Ben Cross, the Abrahams, is making his film debut, I believe, after considerable experience with the Prospect and Royal Shakespeare companies. His face is bony, tight, a perfect field for mercurial, half-suppressed flashes. His very ears seem hyper-sensitively tuned for whispered comment. Yet there's witty temperament in him. Cross's performance is a highly engaging compound of glints and knots.

Ian Charleson plays Liddell, thus giving me my second fine Charleson ex-perience within a few months. The first—and the first time I ever saw him—was as Bertram in the BBC production of *All's Well That Ends Well* on PBS, not on-ly the best production in that bumpy series but one of the best Shakespeare productions of my lifetime. Charleson, merely by understanding Bertram, blew to smithereens some centuries of critical quandary about that "problem" character. After that cool, proud, aristocratic performance, Charleson gives us this quiet, charming, thoroughly religious man, who lives in a purposeful cosmos without any tinge of hosanna or smugness. He truly knows who he is and—which modern "identity" discourse often omits—he also knows why he is who he is.

Then there is Ian Holm, of whom there are not enough statues in the English-speaking world. If you saw him in *The Homecoming* and *A Severed Head* and *Robin and Marian*, you know that he is extraordinarily strong and almost frighteningly versatile, but you'll still be unprepared for his gruff, uncanny portrayal of Abrahams's half-Italian, half-Arab trainer. The scene in which he watches the crucial race from a distant room is one of the picture's joys.

I tick only three more names: Nigel Havers, as a very rich and very endearing young lord, also a Cambridge runner; Lindsay Anderson, better known as a director, and the blessed John Gielgud, as pillars of Cambridge elitism.

The making of any film is something of a lottery. It entails a prodigious amount of planning, yet the outcome depends very considerably on chance. (A famous director once said to me after he had finished shooting and was about to start work with his editor, "Now I've got to find out whether I made the film.") Various kinds of luck are involved, not only happenstance but the luck of learning that the careful plans one made were the right careful plans. Everything went well in *Chariots of Fire*, which is why I began with the producer, Puttnam, and why I end with a salute to his command. His film is no towering masterwork, but it is gripping, intelligent, rewarding.

The title is the plural of a phrase from Blake's preface to his *Milton*. That preface, if you recall, addresses "Young Men of the New Age" and exhorts Blake's countrymen to be "just & true to our own imaginations." The famous poem with which the preface ends contains this stanza:

Bring me my Bow of burning gold;
Bring me my Arrows of desire:
Bring me my Spear: O clouds unfold!
Bring me my Chariot of fire.

The film never refers to Blake's poem in any way. I call that irony and class.

(January 27, 1982)

"Why was I born with such contemporaries?" sighed Bernard Shaw at one sorely beset moment. If a comparative mite can presume to commiserate, I understand how he felt; but I wonder why he thought he would have been better off in any other period. The trees change in the surrounding forest of stereotypes; the forest remains. In his day Shaw contended mostly with yea-sayers, knee-jerk affirmers of the status quo. In our day—for quite a number of our days—we've had a forest of knee-jerk nay-sayers. Lately they are being joined by, or are metamorphosing into, the New Slick.

The New Slick can't be fooled. The magazines published specifically for them assure them of it. They can read signs, are wised up, are proof against hype. What they don't know is that their state of mind is the result of an ultra-clever "inside" hype: they have been hyped into thinking that everything is hype. Their knowingness is impervious to the event: it's a form of defense against the event, against the possible testing of their sensibilities and perceptions.

I thought about the New Slick when I saw *Chariots of Fire* again a few days ago. They had all sniffed it out as a "Masterpiece Theater" film even before they had seen it; and those who bothered to see it had their smartness confirmed. After all, it is British, a period piece, relies on social distinctions and socially colored motives, and contains nothing remotely heterodox socially, politically, or esthetically. Since these points are also true of most "Masterpiece Theater" series on PBS, the New Slick felt it could afford to smirk.

But that smart-cat smirk extended to, protected them from, the theme of the film, which is belief: religious conviction, social/national conviction, ethical conviction, convictions about excellence. The New Slick knew, in advance and in proof, that any film which takes such propositions seriously must be "inspirational" in the cheapest platform-pulpit way.

Pathetic, it seems to me. Because self-aggrandized, self-anesthetized. A second viewing of *Chariots* underscored for me that the quality of the writing and the acting made the characters' convictions genuine—susceptible of my complete empathy even when I couldn't share them. It's far from a flawless film; a second viewing made *that* clearer, too. Some of the slow-motion passages seem intrusive prettiness; some of the structure is slightly fuzzy. (Example: the memorial service that frames the film is—apparently—for Abrahams, but it's in an Anglican church. Why?) Still the several story strands are held in good balance; the film tightens as it goes, through the suspense of its characters rather than through whooped-up editing; and the beliefs they live by are moving. They're additionally moving because we see this film some sixty years after its date. We see those beliefs through the perspective of subsequent grimness, though the beliefs were believed and are still believed. That's why the film evokes irony, not cynicism.

But the mere surface is enough to deflect the New Slick.

One final word, about the title. I said in my review that the film made no reference to the Blake poem from which the title is drawn. Numerous readers wrote to state that Parry's setting of that poem is sung at the end. But only those who recognize the music from having sung it in school—or who recognize the title beforehand for the same reason—would get the reference. For anyone else, the film still makes no reference to Blake because, though the hymn is sung at the end, *not one word* of it is comprehensible.

My Dinner With André

(November 25, 1981)

Since the Industrial Revolution, the development of Western civilization has been accompanied by resistance to that development. From Luddites to the communes of California, the line of resistance twists and turns but is unbroken. Each of us has met the carpenter or market gardener who gave up university teaching or advertising because he hated the values and pressures in his former environment. As forces of scientific and social progress have striven to make life less brutalizing and more pleasurable, a dissenting group has continually struggled against the progress, its members feeling that the price of the advantages was too high in loss of self-defined freedom.

One recent testimony of this struggle is *My Dinner With André*, a two-hour film directed by Louis Malle which consists entirely of conversation at a restaurant table between two men: Wallace Shawn, a New York playwright in his thirties, and André Gregory, somewhat older, a director in the avant-garde theater who made a considerable reputation in the 1960s and early 1970s in New York and elsewhere but who has not lately been active. We go to the dinner with Shawn; he talks with Gregory—who does most of the talking—while they have their meal; then they part and we travel back downtown with Shawn.

Gregory had directed a play of Shawn's called *Our Late Night* (a poor play, I thought) at the Public Theater early in 1975, and they had not seen each other in the five years since. Gregory fills Shawn in on his activities since then, which are extraordinary. Gregory has been in Poland, participating in extra-theatrical group experimentation with Jerzy Grotowski. (Just last summer in New York, Gregory introduced Grotowski at a large meeting I attended, then served as translator, from the French.) He has also been in Tibet and the Sahara and elsewhere. His stories are fascinating, not least because he is a magnetic speaker, with a face like an affable hawk. All his travelings, burrowings, flights, and returns grew out of a search for what he calls "reality"—as good a word as any other to define what he feels is missing in modern Western life. I couldn't help thinking of Bunyan's hero who left his wife and children (Gregory has a wife and family) and "ran on, crying, 'Life! life! eternal life!' " I also couldn't help thinking that, unlike Bunyan's hero, Gregory could afford it; apparently lack of money never hampered his traveling and, at the end, he pays the bill in this *luxe* restaurant without a tremor.

Shawn, when he finally gets the chance, tells us that his reaction to much the same stimulus has been quite the reverse (possibly because he has no money): he has pulled in his horns and lives through each day for the good he can get out of it. He loves trying to write every day, trying to pay his bills, sitting at home every night with his female companion, reading Charlton Heston's autobiography, which happens to be his book at the moment; and out of these actions, he has, apparently, built a stockade.

Two hours of this talk, and yet it's rarely dull. First, Malle has directed with no trickery. He has simply shot it all in adequate color, cutting from face to face as necessary. I assume that several cameras were used simultaneously: it's hard to credit that many scenes were repeated for reverse angles. Malle's reticence here is not customary, and it implies a conviction that is not constant in him.

Much of what Gregory has to say is stuff we all have, in one form or another, heard or overheard, perhaps spoken ourselves; but his stories are good as stories, and he always sounds as if he is being translated—that is, even when the material verges on the banal, we feel that there is a richness in the man that is being lost in translation.

Shawn looks like a balding *putto* in an Italian Renaissance painting. His "method" is the exact opposite of Gregory's: he self-deprecates, he doesn't theatricalize. He uses a lot of unfinished gestures, and his statements, even when they are not apologetic, sound so. I call it a "method," but I don't mean that it is fake. Readers who happen to be human beings will understand.

What's astonishing is how fluently and continuously the two men converse. Of course, any gaps and sags have been edited out, but, though a script is credited, I think the term is retroactive. The publicity says that Shawn wrote the script after the two men had taped lengthy previous conversations, nevertheless I can't feel that, in the film, they spoke memorized lines: they seem to extemporize on previously selected topics.

Memorized or extemporized, the two performances, which is what they are, are extraordinary. The men are performing themselves; this is hard if it's not to look like performing, which would then not be one's self. The presence of camera and lights makes it enormously different from sitting in the same place with the same companion and saying perhaps exactly the same things. Anyone who has ever been on a symposium panel or a radio or TV interview knows this. The difference is not only that one is performing but that what one is saying is being recorded, one way or another; and thus it's being given a permanence, an importance, that ordinary conversations would not have.

And this leads to a basic contradiction. The "My" of the title refers to Shawn. Interesting though this film turned out to be, why should anyone have wanted to make a film of his dinner conversation? It's somewhat ridiculous to hear him say, as he goes uptown to meet Gregory, that he's an obscure playwright trying to pay his bills, when he's doing this confession of obscurity as one of the two principals in a film being made by a famous director.

Shawn, the son of the editor of the *New Yorker*, is becoming a New York phenomenon of sorts, whatever his playwriting gifts. A few years ago he did a version of Machiavelli's *Mandragola*, which I left after twenty minutes; then last year he wrote a play called *Marie and Bruce*, produced (like *Mandragola*) at the Public, in which vile language was set early as the norm and within which norm a contemporary marital agony was pretty well dramatized. A few months ago, *The Hotel Play*, a long work of his with a large cast, was produced at LaMama. The play was utterly uninteresting; the cast was astonishing. (And they turned up for a number of performances.) Small parts were played by well-known actors; smaller parts and walk-ons were done by other playwrights, a celebrated young novelist, a *New Yorker* cartoonist-writer, and one of the most successful book editors in New York. And now someone produces a two-hour film about this "obscure" man of relatively small accomplishment. Phenomenal.

What I liked last about *My Dinner With André* is that this account of the flight of two men from the horrors of a deadeningly technologized world is available through the technology of film.

(December 23, 1981)

When I reviewed *My Dinner With André*, which I had enjoyed, I indulged in some guesses about the way it had been made. Wallace Shawn, one of the two conversationalists, informs me that my guesses were all wrong. There *was* a script; they didn't (as I said) "extemporize on previously selected topics." He and André Gregory, the other participant, had met two or three times a week for about three months and had taped long conversations; then Shawn worked for a year to make a script out of those tapes; then both men memorized the script, rehearsed with the director, Louis Malle, and even performed the piece at the Royal Court in London. My guess about several cameras being used simultaneously was also wrong: only one camera was used, and there were many takes of each section from several angles.

I'm glad to correct my errors, but I can't stop there. This film is now transformed, by the data above, from a super TV talk show to an art work in a rarely used vein: the re-created documentary, "life" reenacted after some sharpening and distillation. One antecedent is Georges Rouquier's *Farrebique* (1947), in which Rouquier, watching a French farm family for a year, asked them to reenact key events in each of the four seasons. This method is not *cinéma-vérité*, in which non-actors perform fictional stories or in which the camera records some lives while they are being lived. This method is the re-creation of reality, selectively, by the people to whom it was once spontaneously real.

I don't know how Rouquier handled his French farmers, but it's irrelevant here: because Shawn and Gregory are artists, quite conscious of the process they were invoking, and it was they who took the script to Malle. They knew that they were after an intensification of the superficially nondramatic, and Malle responded. The core seems to lie in one exchange in the (now published) script. The two men—or the two characters, as they must now be considered—are discussing experiences in strange places, and Shawn says:

> Why do we require a trip to Mount Everest in order to be able to perceive one moment of reality? Is Mount Everest more real than New York? Isn't New York real? I mean, I think if you could become fully aware of what existed in the cigar store next door to this restaurant, it would blow your brains out. . . .

And Gregory replies: "Well, I agree with you, Wally, but the problem is that people *can't see* the cigar store now."

In the light of the true facts about the film, it can now be taken as an attempt to make people see the cigar store. But this effort is partly blunted if the viewer doesn't have all the facts that Shawn gave me. I don't know of many films where off-screen data are essential to the work—and make it quite different and more interesting. *My Dinner With André* is one such.

Ragtime

(December 2, 1981)

Six years after the novel's publication, $32 million after the film transformation began, here is *Ragtime*. A mistake.

Not utterly without good points, still a mistake. This is announced at the very start. The first shot is of a 1906 couple waltzing, and, as the waltz continues, the title is superimposed on them. The sensibility that could put that word and that waltz rhythm together is defective. I braced myself against confirmation of my fears, but, despite a few good performances, the fight was hopeless: the fears were confirmed.

I *went* there with fear—because the novel had been filmed at all. The success of E. L. Doctorow's book had made it one of those "Because It Is There" projects: a novel that had to be filmed, according to film-mogul thinking, just because it had been a best-seller. How easy it would be to draw up a long list of poor films made from best-sellers, some of them good novels, which just could not be satisfactorily transformed into film.

That's not precisely the case with *Ragtime*. The odds against filming it well were huge but not insuperable; it was just unlikely that anyone in Hollywood would see those odds or, seeing them, want to buck them. What was needed to make that book a good picture was complete disregard for the conventions of success, of film-industry worriments. The only way the film could have been good was to forget the presumed need to "lick" the book, as Hollywood lingo puts it, and to try to recreate its essentials in cinematic terms. Of this there is no trace.

So, for my argument, I have to start with the book itself. I was one of those who admired it very much (and reviewed it elsewhere). I watched carefully the adverse comment that followed the book's success and noted that it mostly fell into one of two categories. First, there were those critics who suspect any highly praised book of being merely chic, especially if it sells well. (I recall samples of this reaction with *Herzog* and *Doctor Zhivago*.) I'm convinced that, if *Ragtime* had been panned or largely ignored by the press and had sold 900 copies, the quarterlies of the last five years would have been studded with articles drawing attention to an overlooked gem and bemoaning American critical blindness. Second, there were the red-white-and-blue bloodhounds, who are hunting ever more strongly in the arts these days, sniffing out traces of radicalism or even discontent, any hint that the U.S. is less than paradise, present or potential. Their apparent belief is that, since inarguably the U.S. is the most free and liberal country in the world, any artist who dares find fault with it, especially in terms of historical and deep-rooted conflicts, must be sniffed out and his work judged principally on their self-designated primary grounds. In *The Book of Daniel*, Doctorow's previous novel, he had depicted the ideological climate of mid-century, showing how political radicalism had been brought from Europe and had flourished in the Depression;* in *Ragtime* he went back to the turn of the century to show how the gently meliorist qualities of nineteenth-century America began to change, were fated to change because of powerful selfishnesses. The bloodhounds frothed at Doctorow. The subtext of their hatred was an updated version of an old taunt: "If you don't like this country, why don't you go back where you came from?"

Recently I've reread much of *Ragtime* and still admire it. I quote from my review of the novel as ground for comment on the film. I thought the book a

> work of art about American destiny, built of fact and logical fantasy, governed by music heard and sensed, responsive to cinema as method and historical datum . . . . Film infuses the conception of the book. *Ragtime* almost apotheosizes the fact that the very existence of the film form has changed the ways in which fiction is written. Over and over again, for instance, the narrative follows a character until he meets, in person or in reference, a second character: the narration then flows off with the second person, very much as Renoir's or Kurosawa's camera might have done.

The screenplay—written by one of the inflated mediocrities of the American theater, Michael Weller—ignores every one of these, to me, quintessential characteristics. The logical fantasy about historical characters is almost completely omitted. The musical governance of scene and episode and organism does not exist. Doctorow's carefully reticulated surface—virtually made to order for the best cinematic imagination—has been jettisoned so that the film can wallow, in old-fashioned movie style, within a few story elements. No, they haven't even had the courage to do that completely: some of the book's other elements have been retained—without explanation: like a series of shots of Houdini, who was a figure of mysterious suggestion in the novel and who recurs in the film without integration or point.

I'm of course not arguing that every detail of the novel ought to have been kept. (I'll admit, though, that I'd like to have seen some of the real/fantastical episodes: for instance, J. P. Morgan snubbing John McGraw, the manager of

---

*See p. 204.

the New York Giants, when they meet at the Sphinx.) But the shape and the method of the original were essential, and they have been discarded. The film is the slow, sentimental tale of a New Rochelle family—principally Father, Mother, and Mother's Younger Brother—who, through generosity to an unmarried young black woman and her baby, become involved in an armed insurrection led by the young woman's lover after he has been insulted in New Rochelle; and how Younger Brother, after an affair with Evelyn Nesbit Thaw following her husband's murder of Stanford White, rebounds into the insurrection as a blacked-up participant. Everything that the book interlaced to give us the fabric of an America at the height of its optimism—the layers of power and opposition beginning to stratify and collide, the counterpoint of energy and bounce, of *ragtime*—all this is lost. So the climactic sequence, when the rebellious blacks take over the Morgan Library, makes almost no sense. In the novel we had seen Morgan and Henry Ford conversing there, as older and younger monarchs disposing of the world, and the seizure of the library by the blacks was a symbolic shout against that ordination and sovereignty. In the film the Morgan Library is just a place with some valuables that can be held as hostages.

And the important story of Tateh, the immigrant Jew whose wanderings with his small daughter gave us a bird's eye view of sprawling northeast America, is slashed almost to incomprehensibility. One of the delicacies of the book was that Tateh's story, an abstract representation of how Russian-Jewish immigrants entered and led the new motion-picture industry, mirrored from the inside the cinematic motions of the whole book. All muddled here. Yet the ultimate union of Tateh and the New Rochelle Mother is retained, without motivation or credibility.

The only kind of filmmakers who could have succeeded with *Ragtime* are those who understand the tactics of Renoir and Kurosawa and the strategy of early Eisenstein and early Jansco. The last two knew how to film *history*, how to make history itself the protagonist, rather than try to wring tears and laughter out of individual stories selected from history. The producer of *Ragtime*, Dino De Laurentiis, might once have been the right man for this job—years ago he did *The Nights of Cabiria* and *La Grande Guerra* and *Tutti a Casa*—but not lately: his most recent film was *Flash Gordon*. The director, Milos Forman, born and trained and first experienced in Czechoslovakia, was ridiculously overrated before he ever got to this country; here is only work of distinction has been *One Flew Over the Cuckoo's Nest*. (And I'm not sure how much Jack Nicholson had to do with that.) His work in *Ragtime*, far from the impasted pyrotechnics of his last film, *Hair*, is as conventional as the script. With Miroslav Ondricek, the cinematographer who has worked with him abroad and here, Forman has got too much out of every color, has kept people too consistently in closeup, and has shot too much from below eye-level. Sometimes the film gave me the feeling of walking past a head-high fruit stand or a series of costume displays in a museum.

Forman's worst work with actors is his use of extras in the street scenes on the Lower East Side in Manhattan. I've rarely seen people so clearly, if invisibly, labeled "Extras." The best performance in the large cast, and the least ostentatious, is by James Olson as the New Rochelle Father. Olson is an actor of little charisma but of considerable truthful dignity. The dreary-voiced Mary Steenburgen, as Mother, at least seems a little less dopey than usual, a little more human and humane. As her Younger Brother, Brad Dourif plays with that bitten-off neurotic reticence that has by now become his trademark. The proud young black man, Howard E. Rollins, is strong and handsome and forceful: his performance suffers only from numerous antecedents very much like it in tension and tonality, work by Sidney Poitier, Brock Peters, Albert Hall, Al Freeman, Jr., and others. Elizabeth McGovern as Evelyn Nesbit is a dead loss. Neither physically nor temperamentally does she convince as a celebrated beauty. But her husband, Harry K. Thaw, is very sharply and frighteningly played by Robert Joy — a maniac whose mania is heightened by his wealth.

Quite the worst piece of casting is Norman Mailer as Stanford White. Apart from his arrant amateurism, Mailer's speech and manner don't exactly suggest the beau monde at the turn of the century. The most interesting piece of casting is James Cagney as the New York police commissioner. Cagney, who is among the very best American screen actors, always danced his roles, like Astaire, even when there was no music. He's too old and heavy to dance now, but he's not too old for what he's asked to do — to look solid and stolid and to time his lines perfectly.

One bit in his part baffled me. In the novel the commander of the police forces surrounding the Moran Library is the district attorney, and I assume that, since the film people wanted Cagney, they altered that matter to put the police commissioner in charge on the assumption that Cagney would be more comfortable as a cop. All right: but why, when the black leader comes out of the library with arms upraised, does Cagney order the sharpshooter by his side to fire? In the novel the black man is mowed down by two troops of policemen who reportedly thought he was trying to escape. The screenplay converts the commissioner from a trustworthy leader to a louse. There isn't even any hint that he thinks he may be doing the black rebel a harsh favor by cutting short his sufferings.

The film finishes with another shot of the opening couple waltzing. "You see?" they seem to be saying. "We warned you it was going to be all wrong."

Amadeus

(October 22, 1984)

Lucky are those who see the film of *Amadeus* without having seen the play. Peter Shaffer's original was markedly different in the London and New York productions that I saw, but both of them used theatrical conceits as if they were virtuosity, when in fact they were padding for a thin body—tricks like an address to the audience and a stylized chorus. Shorn of this spurious décor, the film fares somewhat better.

Shaffer's screenplay, which was worked out with the director, Milos Forman, is a more straightforward narrative; it goes on too long and heaves toward a dreadfully contrived climax, but in the main it's a lively piece that tells a story about Mozart and Salieri. Not *the* story: those familiar with Mozart's life may die the death of a thousand cuts unless they agree from the start to a romance. Still, that romance is presented here with much less of Shaffer's undergraduate playwriting cleverness, less tinselly rhetoric, and a lot of nice things to look at. With, of course, a great many bits of Mozart's music—bits only, yet ravishing, more than in the play and played more sonorously. (Those who complain that the music is overrecorded might remember that Mozart liked large orchestras, was happy when he could get them.)

The story takes off from the myth that Salieri, the Viennese court *Kapellmeister* more successful than Mozart yet jealous of him, poisoned the younger man. (The material was used at least once before in the theater. Rimsky-Korsakoff wrote an opera, *Mozart and Salieri*, based on Pushkin's dramatic poem, and Chaliapin was successful as Salieri.) Shaffer's notion is neither to prove nor disprove the poisoning but to assume that Salieri believes himself responsible for the death, principally because he is so jealous of Mozart. Thirty-four years later, plagued by his obsession, Salieri attempts suicide, and soon afterward dies. In the play the old man recounts the story to us, with flashbacks, as he tries to redeem himself with future generations. This abominable idea is shucked in the film: Salieri recounts the story, with flashbacks, to a priest who visits him in the hospital after the suicide attempt. The wiping off of greasepaint metaphysics—by making the narrative a straight confession—helps immensely.

It would take too much time to dwell on all the liberties with fact. Just a few samples: Where is Aloysia, Mozart's sister-in-law, so important in his life? Where is the trip to Prague for the premiere of *Don Giovanni*? (The omission is all the more odd since the film was largely made in Prague.) Why would the Commendatore in that opera, slain father of a violated daughter, be linked in Mozart's mind with his own father? And—wildest of all—why would Mozart on his deathbed dictate some of his Requiem Mass to Salieri? First, what remains of the score is in Mozart's firm hand; second, the one composer at the deathbed was, apparently, Süssmayr. But let's generously allow factual license to Shaffer as we do to Schiller for *Mary Stuart* and Brecht for *Galileo*, and see what we get in return for our generosity.

Forman cast the three leading roles with actors relatively unknown in films, but he showed more courage than sense. F. Murray Abraham, long familiar in the theater, plays Salieri and does especially well as the older man. Younger, he tends to make too much of hiding his true feelings; older, he is affectingly resigned to his hell. Still, all through the role, he gives us a man with enough honesty to recognize Mozart's superiority and to be bitter about his own bitterness.

Tom Hulce comes halfway toward realizing Mozart. The casting idea, as in both theater productions, was to use a young man with a non-ethereal face (supported by several portraits), capable of vulgarity (supported by many Mozart letters), and credible as a genius. Simon Callow, who plays Schikaneder in the film, was Mozart in London and caught it all. Hulce has the energy, gives us Mozart's complete confidence in his powers even when he is broke, but his face is *too* doughy—and his voice is insufficiently modulated. He can't give the role the fineness of inflection and color that it needs.

As his wife, Elizabeth Berridge is disastrous. Constanze was a rough diamond, at least in her young years, but Berridge is a rough rhinestone. Presumably Berridge was supposed to bring the audience close to a just-plain-folks girl. If that's what she really is, then she can't even be herself on screen.

Forman has never directed so well. This is a relative statement. Most Czech writers about Forman say that he was better in Czechoslovakia and became ill at ease with American producers; but some of us who saw his Czech films, such as *The Firemen's Ball* and *Loves of a Blonde*, think those earlier works were more clever than good, that his American films were more clever and less good.

Amadeus is not free of middle-European artiness: closeups of repellent guffawing faces, stark shadows, grotesque angles, many masks. (If only some higher power would inspire the U.N. to ban the use of masks in films everywhere and forever.) Still, except for such impossible sequences as the parodic performance of *Don Giovanni* and the whooped-up climax, Forman shows much more control, more intent to serve his story and actors, than ever before. He balances the picture nicely much of the time between historical appreciation and a view that is touched with a present day satirical edge.

Forman, along with his cinematographer Miroslav Ondricek, was working in Prague as a visiting emigré. Together they have resisted and divulged: they have resisted any temptation to show off their intimate knowledge of the place, while they have divulged some of the secrets of that captivating rococo city. The opera sets in the film were done by the Czech artist Josef Svoboda, widely considered the best scene designer alive, but Svoboda is wasted here because he has little chance to do more than follow neoclassical models.

The fundamental question in the film, as in the play, is the justice of God. Was it just of God to make the scatological, arrogant Mozart a supreme genius, thinks Salieri, while his own decent behavior and hard work are rewarded only with serviceable talent? The justice of God is an old question in drama but, more often than not, is taken as unfathomable in mortal life, to be explained hereafter. (In fact, a whole genre was devised—melodrama—to compress the dilemma and make God's justice clearly visible at the end of the play.) The muzziness of Shaffer's exploration is exposed by one question. Would Salieri have been any less jealous of Mozart's genius if the other man had been conventionally well spoken and modest? The implication is that Salieri is more incensed by bad manners than jealous of genius.

The very close of the film, however, has a power that the play lacked. In the play, the last lines were addressed by Salieri to the audience: "Mediocrities everywhere—now and to come—I absolve you all! Amen!" He raised his arms and we heard a beautiful bit of Mozart. It seemed both presumptuous and self-exculpatory for Shaffer. In the film we, the future, are left out of it. Salieri is being wheeled down the corridor of the hospital through a crowd of lunatics chained to the walls, and it's to these lunatics that he speaks those lines. This gives irony, not impertinence, to his act of absolution. And the final sound is not Mozart's music but Mozart's high-pitched, irritating giggle. That's good.

Reds

(December 16, 1981)

Reds is both an accurate and a possibly misleading title. It's accurate because the two leading characters devote much of what we see of their lives to Communist activities. It's possibly misleading because the focus is on the people, not the activities. This is not, in essence or intent, a political work; it is biographical. Solanas's *Hour of the Furnaces*, Pontecorvo's *Battle of Algiers*, Wajda's *Man of Marble* are political films, which posit and explore political questions, then strongly support particular action about them: *Reds* is a patently different order of work. The people in it are politically inspired, but their convictions are.explored only sufficiently to validate them. The film concentrates on the beings who gave themselves to certain issues, rather than the issues themselves. A somewhat large analogy: *Reds* is to communism and the Bolshevik revolution what *Hamlet* is to Danish foreign policy: the work is inconceivable without its political context, but context is what the politics remains.

All this by way of explanation, not indictment. What *Reds* sets out to do, it does—in a number of ways—with power. Warren Beatty is the name with which comment must begin. Beatty produced *Reds*, collaborated on the screenplay (with the English playwright Trevor Griffiths), directed, and plays the leading male role. If *Reds* were not as good as it is, those facts about a three-and-a-half-hour film would still be impressive in terms of energy. But *Reds* surges past statistical praise—and past the defects that I'll note. This film about John Reed and Louise Bryant is extraordinarily stirring.

When I reviewed a biography of Reed in *The New Republic* (November 4, 1967), I began with a summary of his life and said, "The story might have been contrived by a clever popular novelist." *Reds* proves that my term was wrong: as Beatty presents it, the story might have been written by F. Scott Fitzgerald if Fitzgerald had ever developed the political sense that Edmund Wilson tried to inculcate in him. Not just the period but the flavor, the hurts and mendings, the golden yearning are fundamental Fitzgerald. *Reds* begins in 1915 when Reed is twenty-eight, five years out of Harvard, has already been a war correspondent in Mexico and Europe, has written a book of poems in Greenwich Village, has been the lover and companion of Mabel Dodge. He visits his native city of Portland, Oregon, where he meets Louise Bryant, then twenty-one and married to a dentist. The events of his life before their meeting are barely sketched: but to deal with only Reed's last five years, the picture needs every moment of the time it takes. It splashes through the roaring social and political currents of the day; it treats radical clashes as the hero's personal challenge; and (a true Fitzgerald theme) it shows the American hero's face turned often toward Europe—in Reed's case, toward European intellectual and ideological tradition, with even a hint of envy for the European miseries that had ultimately produced revolution.

To situate the film historically, Beatty has interwoven bits from interviews with Witnesses (his term), people who were contemporaries of Reed and Bryant, some of whom knew one or both. Always the Witnesses are shown against a black background, so that they seem revenants, suspended in time. None of these speakers is identified, which was a mistake, I think: each could have been tagged on first appearance. I recognized some: Dora Russell, Rebecca West, Scott Nearing and—deceased since the filming—Roger Baldwin, Arthur Mayer, Henry Miller, George Jessel. (He comments on popular music.) But I'd like to have known who all of them were.

Still the device helps: the Reed-Bryant story, private and political, is so wildly dramatic that these occasional comments act both as ballast and support. Louise and Jack become lovers in Portland: she follows him to New York, into his radical political and journalistic life—which featured antiwar activity—and she pursues a journalistic career of her own. They go to Provincetown where, though she loves Jack and marries him, she has an affair with the infatuated Eugene O'Neill. She and Jack quarrel; in June of 1917 she goes to France as a war correspondent. Jack finds her in France, persuades her to come with him to the "real story" in Russia; they witness the "ten days that shook the world"; they come home where he writes an eyewitness account. (No book ever had a truer title.) Then, after a split within the U. S. Communist ranks, Jack returns to Russia—with great difficulty—in 1919 to represent his group's interests in the plans for world revolution. He deals particularly with Grigory Zinoviev; accompanies Zinoviev and other functionaries on a railway trip through White-held territory to a conference in Baku; is caught in battle with the Whites on his return trip; is reunited with Louise who has followed him to Russia; and he dies there of typhus in 1920. The film omits his interment under the Kremlin wall, though this is mentioned earlier by one of the Witnesses.

There's some material about Reed's possible disillusion with the Soviets before his death, or at least some fluctuation. Fourteen years ago, my review of the Reed biography brought me a letter from a ninety-two-year-old Portland woman named Elizabeth Olsen who had known Louise well and wrote: "It is very difficult for me to believe that Jack recanted . . . [Louise and Jack] were romanticists but surely shrewd enough to realize there had to be a practical side to this world-shaking venture." I take this to mean that Olsen thought the Reeds would have foreseen some tempering of pure principle by the hard facts of governing. But according to Max Eastman and others, Louise said that Jack had become disheartened by Soviet behavior, that she had "to bolster up his morale." Because her words don't come to us through impartial people, the question of Jack's last beliefs will probably remain open. The film, rightly, leaves it that way.

The first, longer section of *Reds* (before intermission), ending with the ten days in Petrograd, is about two lovers whose personal life is stormy and whose public life is increasingly bound up with radical politics. The second section is about two people in political life—especially the man—who are lovers. This transition is conveyed by the finish of the first section. Magnificent shots of the Petrograd masses marching up a wide street, carrying banners and singing the "Internationale," are intercut with shots of Jack and Louise making love in their Petrograd apartment while the march is going on. This juxtaposition seemed to me quite the opposite of cheap or sensational: it was emotionally and dramatically just, and it prepared for the shift of emphasis in Part Two.

I want to praise so much of *Reds* that I must get my objections out of the way. Chief is the choice of cinematographer. Vittorio Storaro, possibly selected for his work on Bertolucci's *The Spider's Strategem*, *The Conformist*, and *1900*, helped to make those political pictures look like confectionery. Perhaps Beatty wanted to underscore that his two leading characters were "romanticists," but the romantic colorings don't stop with them. *Everything* looks a bit too lush, and this hampers the historicity that Beatty achieves so well in other ways.

Jack Nicholson, as Eugene O'Neill, is Jack Nicholson. His role is written blandly, without individuation, and Nicholson does nothing to supply colors—he just floats through. He's too healthy-looking, anyway, for the gaunt O'Neill.

Maureen Stapleton is Emma Goldman—which is a difficult sentence to type. No screenplay could do real justice to Goldman without centering on her, but, in proportion, she's moderately well drawn in this script. Then the role of this Lithuanian-Jewish anarchist, this glowing battleship of a woman, was given to an Irish-American sentimentalist who seems to have trouble with long words.

Some characters have been snipped to near anonymity, presumably in the film editing. Gene Hackman's role as a labor editor is so reduced that it's now overinhabited by this good actor. Max Eastman and Floyd Dell are just names pinned on some actors who pass through. Paul Sorvino is arresting as Louis Fraina, the Italian-born leader of the splinter U.S. Communist group, but the editing leaves unexplained how he, too, got to Moscow in 1919 and was reconciled with Reed. And the success of Reed's book in the U.S., which stood him in good stead in Russia, is not even mentioned.

Beatty commits cutenesses. The Reeds have a dog that keeps trying to get into their bedroom when they make love. In their Petrograd apartment, Jack keeps hitting his head on the low chandelier. When Jack and Louise embrace on the train platform after his return from Baku, marshmallow music—by Stephen Sondheim—bloats the soundtrack. Near the end, when Louise goes down the hospital hall to get water for her sick husband, the tin cup accidentally drops from her hand with a clatter—a pat signal to us that, when she gets back to the room, Jack will be dead.

But much of this immense film is so fine that all these flaws, and others that could be noted, cannot spoil it: they just seem inexplicable, which they would not be in a lesser picture. Begin the praise with Diane Keaton, a special pleasure because unexpected. "Louise was a very beautiful woman," Elizabeth Olsen wrote me. There's a certain style in which photographs show that to be true, and in that style, Keaton is beautiful, too—as she is dressed and lighted here. Her look and manner, sexual and mercurial, imperious yet tender, are the ground of Keaton's performance as the New Woman, a figurative sister of Isadora Duncan, entering the twentieth century with an appetite for every freedom, with an air of a released prisoner's vengeance for wrongful past confinement. Nothing in Keaton's previous work prepared me for the fire and determination and *fullness* with which she lifts this woman into being. Allow for Beatty's perception of her possibilities, for the help he apparently gave her in direction; it's Keaton who did it, even triumphing over some bits of mouthy rhetoric that come her way. She is the legendary Louise whom Jack needed. (Evidently Louise needed Jack even more. After a subsequent marriage that failed, she ended with a wretched, drugged, drunken death sixteen years after he died.)

Another acute stroke was the casting of the novelist, Jerzy Kosinski, as Zinoviev. That Kosinski is a resourceful performer is no news to those who have known him in private life. I don't know that he has ever before done conventional acting, but he does it here, with razor sharpness and an authority that comes from precise knowledge of Soviet atmospherics. Beatty directs all the Soviet political meetings well, but Kosinski's presence in many of them contributes a wiry dynamics; and he contrasts provocatively with the openness of Reed.

In Reed, Beatty has found himself as an actor—has perhaps found areas of himself that surprised him. Beatty has sometimes done good work in the past, but this performance is on a new plane. He very clearly loves Reed, the entire gifted, egocentric, passionate, foolish, large-spirited, aspiring man. It's as uncommon as it is wonderful to sense such love in an actor for a character, to see it result in such completeness of creation. Sherwood Anderson said of Reed: "I have never met a man who awakened so much quick affection in me." I believed this, and a great deal more, of Beatty's Reed. I wouldn't equate Beatty as artist with Laurence Olivier; still, Beatty gives here the best self-directed film performance since Olivier's Henry V.

As director, Beatty has inevitably had models, especially because of his subject. (There's even a sly reference to Eisenstein's October—Kerensky on the staircase of the Winter Palace—when Reed goes up those stairs to meet Kerensky.) If Beatty's directing has the lapses described, if it never shows a marked individual style, it has clarity and control almost all the time. And the large scenes—the political rallies in America, the ten days in Petrograd, the Soviet conclaves, the battle on the Baku line—are swirled out before us with the sweep of a generous dramatic imagination. No doubt Beatty is grateful to his two exceptional editors, Dede Allen and Craig McKay, and he certainly was blessed by the art direction of Richard Sylbert, but warts and all, Beatty made this picture: and it's a big achievement.

Reds, as noted at the start, is not a revolutionary film. (Anyway, the very term "revolutionary film" is almost an oxymoron. Film is an expensive art; private capital or government subsidy is not often forthcoming for work intended to upset the status quo. With a few exceptions, the famous so-called revolutionary films are not insurrectional, they celebrate revolutions already made: e.g., the work of Eisenstein, Pudovkin, Vertov, Riefenstahl, Jancsó.) Reds is not politically revolutionary, it's about two people caught up in revolutionary politics. It doesn't even ask, let alone answer, basic radical political questions.

But if no one will learn much about politics from this film, Beatty has nonetheless put the fire of two burning lives in it. There is plenty in it about the risks that commitment entails, but it is about commitment. Under the closing credits, one of the Witnesses says: " 'Grand things are ahead, worth living and dying for'—he always said that." It's not necessary to believe those words completely in order to be moved by them, to want to be moved by them. That's something.

Sisters, or The Balance of Happiness

(February 10, 1982)

"Dido's Lament" from Purcell's *Dido and Aeneas* is heard several times in Margarethe von Trotta's new film and is doubly apt. The heartbroken queen, about to end her life, sings (in English in this German film): "When I am laid in earth . . . remember me," which becomes part of von Trotta's theme; and the style of the music itself—gravely simple, mutedly intense—could be the paradigm that she followed in her directing. *Sisters, or The Balance of Happiness* is a delicate, lovely work, ultimately just out of reach but all the more fascinating for that. And, from von Trotta, it surprised me; nothing that I had seen of her past work prepared me for it.

She has acted and co-written and co-directed with her husband, Volker Schlöndorff. Her acting, of the leading roles in *A Free Woman* and *Coup de Grâce*, has been unexcitingly passable; the Schlöndorff films on which collaborated—those two and others—all strained to soar. Von Trotta has since written and directed a film of her own that I haven't seen. *Sisters* is her second independent work (with "additions" to the script by three other women), and it's not just an advance in her career, it's a transfiguration.

First and fundamentally, merely watching it is wonderful. It was photographed by Franz Rath, and the wonder is in the way he sees apartments and offices in modern Hamburg, not in gorgeous scenery. It is edited with almost ESP acuteness by Annette Dorn. Both Rath and Dorn are obviously in closest ensemble with von Trotta, fulfilling her vision, and the cast continues that sense of ensemble, of unity, of utter belief in the director's intent and power to fulfill it. The three leading performers are women. Jutta Lampe, who plays the older of two sisters, was one of the original members of Peter Stein's Schaubühne, along with Bruno Ganz and Edith Clever. She moves through this film like an ivory woman, with emphasis on both words—shining and fallible. Her younger sister is Gudrun Gabriel, who has one of those beautiful faces that are private disclosures. The young Jessica Früh, who plays a friend, is pert and pushy and, as such young people often do, surprises us with eventual contradictory revelations. The décor by Winifred Henning is modern, nearly but not quite astringent, with an economy on the human side of spareness—which is the general tone of von Trotta's method throughout. There is not one split second of waste or of haste in this film. The making of it is perfect.

In the opening shot the camera moves forward through a dim forest of tall trees while a girl's voice tells a story about the place. Then we see the girl, about thirteen, reading this story to her little sister as they lie huddled together in bed. Easily we slip from childhood to the present. The older sister, Maria (played by Lampe), is now executive secretary to a big business chief; Anna (Gabriel) is a university science student. They live together, supported by Maria; their widowed mother lives in a suburb. Maria, who had to abandon her education when their father died, enjoys her competence in her job and is devoted to Anna, eager for her success. Anna confesses that she has lost interest in her work, wants to quit: Maria says that this would be mad so close to the finish, and urges Anna to take her exams before deciding.

Three other characters figure importantly: a young man—the son of her boss—who loves Maria and with whom she has a brief affair; a typist in the office (played by Früh) who is looking for fun and advancement; a youngish executive who spends his evenings singing his own songs in a small cabaret and who soon gives up his job for his music. The typist, Miriam, who once had her eye on the boss's son, takes up with the singer, whose songs—written by the actor of the role, Konstantin Wecker—sound like latter-day Brecht-Weill.

When we are alone with Anna, which we often are, we learn the real cause of her disaffection. It has to do with herself, not the work. (It's Anna who plays the Purcell recording.) She is haunted by terrors that seem generated by the pressure of incestuous love for her sister. No overt move is ever made. So far is it from Maria's awareness that at one point she cradles the exhausted Anna against her naked body in nothing other than sisterly compassion. But Anna spends most of the time, when she should be studying, writing in her notebook fragments of thoughts and poems, pasting in pictures of gargoyles and grotesques or Polaroid photos of herself which she takes because she says she can now see only the back of her head in the mirror.

Maria continues in her role as she honestly sees it, working hard, expending affection on her sister, urging her on in her work. The inevitable happens. Maria comes home one evening and finds that Anna has cut her wrists, has bled to death. (Maria tells someone later that she cleaned it all up herself.) It's impossible to overpraise the reticence, the unheard but deafening explosion, of this scene. Some days later, looking through her sister's notebook, Maria finds a poem addressed to her, begging her to beware. Anna isn't through with her. ("When I am laid in earth . . . remember me.")

All this, I emphasize, is dealt with in the physical and atmospheric setting of a modern, moving city. It's not anything like a ghost story. Anna's presence recurs (as we see) in the apartment; Maria is grieving for her and remembering the poem, that's all. It's not eeriness; it's duration past death.

To reestablish the shape of her former life, Maria invites Miriam to move in with her; encourages her to take English lessons and pays for them. But in time Miriam, who adores Maria in a way but is not tied to her by sisterly or other bonds, packs and leaves to go off with the singer, abandoning the lessons and Maria's plans for her. Left alone, Maria thinks that, from now on, she must be Maria *and* Anna.

My description of the film is risky because it could suggest that Maria is a hard-driving young woman, working out her frustrations first through her sister, then through Miriam: that also she has an unwitting incestuous-lesbian component. Both of these statements are clinical reductions of what is presented as a tangle of relationships and chemistries between people. All relationships involve tangles: if they are to be treated in art, they have to be bodied forth in one form or another so as to be visible. Every color, every agony in *Sisters* rings true, but less with the truth of specificity than of existence itself. That is, von Trotta has not made a film pointedly about the imposition of one person's ideas of success on another person or about the latency of lesbianism between sisters or even about "haunting." She seems to be saying, "These are the emotional-psychological elements of this complex, but if there hadn't been these elements, there would have been others. Beings pay penalties for being."

This generality of insight works for and against the film. It gives the picture a finely pitched modernist approach—or perhaps I should say postmodernist: von Trotta is more interested in exploring shadowy domains than in shaping her film to a regularized thematic shape. On the other hand, this quintessentially abstract method does leave the picture just out of reach, as I noted. We know that Maria is most certainly not a villain, witting or unwitting; she is just trying to live her life in order and benevolence as she understands them, making her way through experience as she meets it and creates it; yet our relation to her at the end is more observant than empathic.

But I must take a further step because the film is so splendidly made. The usual questions of narrativity can be suspended here, along with questions of detailed character explication, under the force of the film's beauty as such. At the last, I don't really care that *Sisters* leaves me with some questions: it substantiates yet again Flaubert's view that the subject of subjects is secondary if the making of the art is good enough.

However, I don't assume that von Trotta would agree with my remarks. I know, from her career, that she is working as a woman on material about women and may think she is being much more concrete than I have allowed in treating of experience among women through a woman's view and talent. At any rate what's inarguable is that she brings into focus the conflict of two and then three differing appetites for life—for lives possible to women: Maria's, which is conscientiously making the best of things; Anna's, which is waning because of impossibilities; Miriam's, which is hedonist without being stupid. It is Anna's view, because it is the most harrowing, that overarches the picture and that will, at least in tempering by grief, live on in Maria. By coincidence, I had just read Robert Bly's lucid new translations of Rilke when I saw *Sisters*, and Anna made me think of "The Song the Suicide Sings." Some lines about life itself:

> It heals others, it makes me sick.
> Grasp that some can't stand it.
> For at least a thousand years now
> I'll have to fast.

It's these differing appetites—in women, seen by a woman—that *Sisters* puts before us.

Marianne and Juliane

(June 2, 1982)

Statements by artists about their work are not always sound, but what Margarethe von Trotta says about her third film puts it in helpful relation to her first two independent works. From *Kino* (April 1981):

> In this film I try to draw a synthesis between my first and my second films. *The Second Awakening of Christa Klages* was a stock-taking of external conditions in Federal Germany; the second film, *Sisters*, brings into focus the inner life of its characters. . . . My latest film . . . acts on both levels, it looks inside as well as outside.

Simplified though the comment is, it's not misleading. *Sisters* was made in 1979; when I reviewed it,* I had not seen the earlier film. I've since had a chance to see *Christa Klages* (1977), which is only one more competent piece of New German Cinema, full of self-consciously dramatized radicalism. Beginning with its title, it's more like the cinematic maneuverings of von Trotta's husband, Volker Schlöndorff, than like the artist she has since become. (Christa Klages is a worker in a day-care center who resorts to armed robbery to get funds for her center when other sources fail.) *Sisters* moved out of membership in a "school" of film to uniqueness, a dark and disturbing poem about a loving, strong, somewhat blundering older sister and a younger adoring one who kills herself. *Marianne and Juliane* (1981) is also about two sisters, the younger of whom dies, but as von Trotta said in her interview, here the outer world is integrated with the inner one; the forces of politics and social action are now part of the tensions between the two women.

The German title of this third film translates as *Leaden Times*—from a line in Hölderlin, "I almost feel as if in leaden times." Von Trotta's screenplay comes from a true story of the 1970s concerning two daughters of a Protestant pastor. (The film is dedicated to the survivor.) The younger one, here called Marianne, becomes a political activist-terrorist; the older one, here called Juliane, devotes herself to "above-ground" social work, particularly on a woman's magazine. Strife grows between the sisters though love never dwindles. Marianne is eventually imprisoned—Juliane's prison visits are among the most masterly scenes—and one day is found hanging in her cell. The announcement says that she committed suicide. Juliane then becomes obsessed with proving that her sister was in fact murdered.

In the film Marianne has been married, had a son, then abandoned husband and child for activism. After his mother's death, this boy is horribly abused—literally set on fire—by his schoolmates. When he recovers, he comes

---

*See preceding review.

to live with his aunt. On the wall is a photograph of his mother, which he takes down and tears up. Juliane tells him that he is wrong to be angry with his mother, that she was a wonderful woman. Juliane then sets out to tell him the truth about his mother; and that truth is the film which we have just seen.

The above sketch, though not inaccurate, could hardly be more brutal. It makes linear what is, in experience, a work of time-texture—not of flashbacks but of inseparable time planes. This method was used to some extent, very affectingly, in *Sisters*; but here one doesn't feel that it's "used," it *is* the film. "If I were to sum up the essential theme of the picture," said von Trotta, "I would say it is the confrontation of remembering and forgetting." This confrontation runs all through the film, mostly in the mind and memory of Juliane—played by Jutta Lampe, who also played the older sister in the previous film.

Sights, glints, deliberate recall hold the various levels of the past on the frontier of the present. The museum of Baroque statuary, which is where the sisters must meet secretly at the beginning of the "present" story, epitomizes the unshakable presence of the past. The sternly religious home of their parents, with its immense sanguine painting of a crucified Jesus, contrasts with the casual quarters of Juliane and her lover. The films of Nazi atrocities that their father showed his parishioners in the church hall, which made Juliane so sick that she had to run out, underlie present states of mind. The fact that, when they were seventeen and sixteen it was Juliane who was the troublemaking rebel and Marianne her father's silky-haired, lap-snuggling pet, links with Juliane's work on a feminist magazine now and Marianne's much more intense rebellion, surging past her sister into terrorism. When Juliane vists her sister's prison, the color of a brick wall reminds her of a wall opposite their childhood home where she and Mariane used to practice handstands; yet they quarrel as much as they love during those prison visits. And this presence of the past culminates in Juliane's reaction after her sister's death. "There'll never be another face like that," she sobs hysterically in the ambulance that has to be summoned to take her to a hospital from the prison morgue.

It certainly is an extraordinary face, Marianne's. Barbara Sukowa, who plays the role, is experienced in German theater, principally in Hamburg and Munich, and has made two films for Fassbinder, not yet shown here. Her face is so lean as almost to be gaunt, but it is beautiful; she burns and commands. A special bow, too, to Ina Robinski and Julia Biedermann who play the two sisters at seventeen and sixteen, very acutely. The one member of the cast who seems to me more a fixture of New German Cinema than an impressive actor is Rüdiger Vogler—here Julianne's lover—who has been seen in many Wenders films, as well as others. Vogler doesn't resemble Bruno Ganz in the least, but I always feel that he's a vapid substitute for Ganz.

Franz Rath is again von Trotta's cinematographer, again using precise, reticent, apt colors. The very first shot is of the gray wall of an apartment house, seen through bare trees. Silence. The camera pulls back, inside the apartment overlooking the courtyard. We hear steps as someone walks slowly back and forth; the low notes of a solo clarinet wind in; and colors begin to enter the gray shot as Juliane, in silhouette, moves past the camera. Thus we know a good deal about the tone of the film, the imagination and control of the director, within a minute.

Cinematically, the film is built with lightness and strength. Example: Juliane and her lover are in southern Italy (Sicily?) when they see a photo of Marianne on the TV news. Juliane telephones home and gets word of the hanging. Her lover embraces her. Then there's a cut to a brief shot of the outside of the sun-drenched hotel before we go back to the pair inside. What we see for a second is so lovely that it underscores the disharmony in their lives, in our world.

But I must note two sequences that are much more Schlöndorff than von Trotta. When Juliane gets a sedative injection in the ambulance after seeing her sister's body, we're shown her nightmare—in red light—involving the bloody crucifixion picture in her parents' home and a stern father looking down from a Himalayan pulpit. After we hear of the near-murder of Marianne's son, we see the horror in flashback. (The term is justified in this case.) Both of these sequences are heavy-handed and superfluous.

Traditional religion, including the duty that honest German clergymen feel to face the German past; the rivalries of two sisters for their father's love, as a possible psychological base for the younger one's later extremism and violence; the perplexities of a generation in Germany that must face what the members of their generation must face everywhere but who also have the burden of that German past—all these course dynamically through *Marianne and Juliane*. Yet, because von Trotta is so fine an artist, almost nothing is handled clinically or polemically. We see these two sisters, as children and as young women, carrying within them the fundamental humanity that would make trouble even if the world around them were more kindly and sensible than it is.

Missing

(February 17, 1982)

Missing is set in the middle of bloody civil struggle. It's an American film based on the true story of a young American named Charles Horman who disappeared in Santiago, Chile, during the turbulent days of Allende's overthrow in 1973. Witnesses told his wife several versions of a story which came down to the fact that, while she was out, a group of men had taken him away in a car, then made a mess of their home. Horman, a writer and filmmaker, was alleged to have "known too much," though all he knows in the film version is some general stuff about *American* activities in Chile, ostentatiously planted on him by an American stranger in a bar. Horman's father, a New York businessman, flew down to press the investigation. After some initial abrasion between them, he and his daughter-in-law worked together, plagued the American Embassy, and finally found out that Charles was one of the very many who had been executed. We're told, as the father and widow return to New York, that he sued the U.S. government for various defaults in duty and lost his case.

Missing was directed by Costa-Gavras who collaborated on the script with Donald Stewart. Eight years ago Costa-Gavras made a comparable film, *State of Siege*, about the abduction of an American AID official in Uruguay, his "trial" by revolutionaries, and his execution—a film whose attempted objectivity did not cover its anti-U.S. animus and which had plenty of the excitement and political flavor that Costa-Gavras had put into such pictures as *Z* and *The Confession*. *State of Siege* was a foreign production, made in French.

But *Missing* is an American film, so Chile isn't even named. It takes place in an anonymous Latin-American country. Inferably, Costa-Gavras wanted to make a film attacking U.S. interference in Chile, using the Horman story as his locus, but that intent got very watered down on the way to the forum. In one scene the American ambassador tells the father that there are 3000 American businesses in "this country," and that he must guard their interests: that's as close as the film comes to any kind of indictment. It never comes close to excitement. Whatever your views on the anti-Allende coup, it's boring to watch a film obviously on that subject in which Allende is never named and which carefully avoids having *any* view. We just see the father trudge from hotel to office to hospital to detention center, and so on. Costa-Gavras says that "filmmakers dream of going to Hollywood. This is my pilgrimage." It's also his castration.

The script is not only politically pallid, it's badly written. The structure is repetitious, the roles are unrewarding. John Shea, the son, seen early in the film, is given one of those highly compressed displays of characteristics which are a tip-off that this character is going to disappear soon. Sissy Spacek, his wife, is mostly sullen, not overwhelmed with anxiety about her husband, though they are said to have been happy, and has little belief in the inquiry. The spats between her and her father-in-law are tedious, put in to zing up the drama, which they don't, and to fill screen time, which they prolong. Jack Lemmon is the father and is less overblown than he has become in farce, like the recent *Buddy Buddy*, but not nearly as affecting as he was in *The China Syndrome* because he just doesn't have good material to work with.

(March 10, 1982)

Because of the brouhaha about *Missing*, reviewed three weeks ago, further comment seems needed. This new film by Costa-Gavras, his first American production, deals with a true story: the murder of a young American named Charles Horman in Santiago, Chile, during the anti-Allende coup in September 1973—though neither Allende nor the country is named—and the investigation by Horman's father, Edmund, which convinced him that the U.S. Embassy was implicated in his son's death. *Missing* has so exercised the State Department that, even before it opened, they issued a statement "objecting to the impression left by the film that the United States had contrived in the death, or had at least covered up events surrounding the case" (*The New York Times*, February 10). Flora Lewis wrote a long article for the Arts and Leisure section of *The New York Times* (February 7) investigating the materials, and she concluded that Costa-Gavras "winds up distorting fact without even noticing." Alexander Cockburn (*Village Voice*, February 10-16) sniffed suspiciously at Lewis's article and reported that Seymour Hersh, whom Lewis had quoted, is writing a book about Kissinger with new information about the rightist coup. More debate will doubtless follow. As prelude to their arguments, Lewis and Cockburn praised the film cinematically. Lewis: "Tautly well-made and convincing"; Cockburn: "Powerful." I disagree vehemently with these opinions of *Missing*, and my disagreement is not abstractly esthetic: it's tied to what this film is supposed to be convincing and powerful *about*.

I have no "new information." I'm talking only about what's in the script written by Costa-Gavras and Donald Stewart, based on a book by Thomas Hauser. I've seen the film again: I not only disagree about its conviction and power, I think it's the weakest of Costa-Gavras's political films, a very Hollywood work of daring, and that the outcry about it, to different ends from different sources, says more about the sources than about the film.

Two issues are involved. First, was the U.S. involved militarily in the coup? About American involvement before the 1973 coup, the public record is plain: President Nixon and friends tried to provoke a coup to prevent Allende's election in 1970 and, failing this, funneled funds to anti-Allende parties and their media. About American military involvement in the 1973 overthrow, there is—as yet—no official evidence. But the Costa-Gavras film *shows* such involvement. Young Horman and a friend were in a coastal resort in September 1973 when the coup began, and, according to his notes, he saw and heard evidence of U.S. military presence. A film called *The Battle of Chile*, a documentary made by Allende partisans during the last ten months of his regime, showed much of the bloody fighting and, on its soundtrack, made allegations about CIA infiltration. *Missing* doesn't allege: it uses Horman's notes, which have not been challenged and whose materials his friend also witnessed, to show us a U.S. Army officer walking around the crowded seaside hotel in full uniform and confiding in Horman just because he was a fellow American: to show a plainclothes Navy operative volunteering information to Horman in the hotel bar, bragging that he had come there to do a job, had done it, and was now moving on to Bolivia. Dozens of people were nearby all through these scenes. If this was supposed to be a secret U.S. military operation, it was done at the Marx Brothers level.

The second and, for the film, the more important issue: did the U.S. have a hand, or did it withhold a deterring hand, in the arrest and execution of Horman? To speak only of what's in *Missing*, absolutely no credible motive for such drastic action, or inaction, is given. What Horman saw and heard at the coastal hotel was also seen and heard by his friend, who was unharmed and was allowed to return to the U. S. some days later. What Horman saw and heard was also seen and heard by dozens of others who were presumably not molested. Horman's only difference was that he was connected with a Santiago magazine that is said to be about as leftist as the *New York Post*. But his friend, who was allowed to leave, was a member of that magazine "circle." (We are shown the arrest and the dead body of another American member of that magazine staff, but he had not been at the coastal hotel! The film contains nothing much about this man's activities and no investigation into his killing.) To one viewer, it seems entirely possible that Horman was arrested and executed during the coup in one of those jittery accidents that occur in frenzied times. It seems entirely possible that the new junta tried to conceal his death to prevent embarrassment. (To repeat: the other American's body is *displayed* in the huge morgue, but—in the film—this causes no American protest or inquiry.)

How does Costa-Gavras imply U.S. involvement in Horman's death? The embassy staff is shown to be smooth and cool. (Easy laughs from a hip audience here.) The top military attaché is shown to be lecherous. (Therefore a conspirator in murder?) Absolutely nothing is shown to explain why the staff should have wanted Horman's death (out of all the witnesses at that silly coastal hotel exhibition) or why they should have concealed the fact of his death from his father if they had known it. It takes several weeks for Edmund Horman to hear that his son had been killed earlier in the month, before the father had even arrived in Santiago. He hears about it from a Ford Foundation economist who heard it from a friend in "an English-speaking embassy." The U.S. Embassy investigates (the method is undisclosed) and confirms the death. The father then says angrily that the killing couldn't have been done without a "kill order" from our embassy, but his grief and rage hardly constitute proof.

The one thread of "proof" is the statement by an ex-policeman of the new regime, who quit the junta after two weeks and is now a refugee in the Italian Embassy. He says that he served as interpreter at a meeting in the office of the general who was the Chilean equivalent of CIA chief when it was decided to kill Horman, and that an American official took part in the decision. (To step outside the film for a moment: Lewis reports that this policeman later said he knew the official was American by his shoes.)

My purpose here is not to exculpate the U.S.: it's to indict Costa-Gavras. His picture is a mixture of caution and irresponsibility. He cautiously names nothing and no one precisely; he glibly implies deep guilt, making empty heroic gestures of protest without foundation and without risk. It's thus a perfect Hollywood liberal picture, playing to a gallery of trained seals and to another gallery of the gullible, for the happiest kind of Hollywood profit—big returns plus big ego-satisfactions. The glib implications of black guilt are especially ex-asperating to those like myself who, not innocent about the need for secret operations by every big power, would like to see such guilt confirmed and punished. And since this uproar about *Missing* has started, Costa-Gavras's statements have paralleled his film: they've been paradigms of caution-cum-irresponsibility.

For me, those qualities are integrated with, the cause of, the surprising soft-ness of the picture itself. (Shootings and corpses don't automatically make a pic-ture grim and hard.) When Costa-Gavras was working with fervor and with facts—as in *Z* and *The Confession*, which were set in Greece and Czecho-slovakia, not Fredonia—his films were made with an almost religious sense of vocation, with a hatred of sentimentality, with blaze. (Think, for instance, of the system of montage he worked out for Yves Montand's imprisonment in *The Confession*, which provided the film both with dynamics and with a counter-point to the prisoner's refusal to change.) In *Missing* we get cute stuff (a little boy coming up to Horman's house to ask his wife about a pet duck); we get puffed-up quarrels between her and her father-in-law in an attempt to give the picture moment-to-moment edge; and we get that nadir of cinematic imagery, the riderless white horse galloping across the screen. (Inconceivable in *Z*.) *Missing* is the roar of a well-fed tame tiger who once really attacked the system that is now feeding him.

None of his previous, stronger films aroused comparable controversy because they weren't widely distributed here: they weren't in English and they had no American stars. In 1973 *State of Siege*, about the murder of a U.S. official in Uruguay, was eliminated from a program at the Kennedy Center, but that's about all the trouble it caused. Wry note: the location shots of that film were done in Chile, under Allende. (The location shots of *Missing* were done in Mex-ico.) This new film will be seen widely. It's tickling the gleeful assumptions of some and the choleric nervousness of others; and both groups, eager to get on to their glee or their choler, overpraise the picture as such, unwilling or unable to see how its defects fail to justify either of their views.

Victor/Victoria

(March 24, 1982)

Allow for a mediocre opening, ten minutes or so. Forgive some splatters of banality throughout. *Victor/Victoria* is the best American film farce I've seen since *Some Like It Hot* (1959).

Blake Edwards, the author-director, has had a career ranging from cold to tepid: of his last two pictures, *10* was unbearable, *S. O. B.* was bearable. Julie Andrews, the star of the new film (who is Mrs. Edwards), has been more consis-tent: her career has been generally tepid, although one could see her struggling with the *Zeitgeist*. She moved from *Mary Poppins* in 1964 to button poppin's in 1981, when she bared her breasts in *S. O. B.* Her co-stars, Robert Preston and James Garner, are solid, likable actors, ebullient and understated respectively, but not unfailing harbingers of joy. Putting them all together, with the foreknowledge that *Victor/Victoria* is a farce involving homosexuality and transvestism, I hoped for the passable.

And passably it begins. Paris, 1934. Preston, an aging American queen who performs in a nightclub, goes to the club one day and by chance hears the audition of an English soprano, Andrews. She sings a corny old recital piece, "Cherry Ripe," so we know at once that (a) she is going to flunk the audition, and (b) later on she will sing differently. Preston gets fired that night because of a fight during a performance involving a young male lover of his (the first of several tedious brawls). In a restaurant he runs into Andrews, eating voraciously though broke, and they become friends by beating the restaurant bill together. (Another brawl.) After that, the film picks up considerably, and, for the most part, stays up. The only real sags are those occasional brawls, allegedly comic, which occur mostly so that Preston and, later, Garner, can prove they are not cowards though gay or suspected of it. Fights as fun have always bored me, since long before Victor McLaglen. In one fight here, Edwards even includes the chestnut of having someone knocked onto a piano and collapsing it.

But there's paradoxical virtue in this boredom: these *Victor/Victoria* fights are especially wearying because they are so out of key with the rest of the script, which, like all the acting, is clever. Preston hatches a scheme to make Andrews a success. He cuts her hair, dresses her in men's clothes, and "sells" her to a club manager as a Polish count who does female impersonations—a woman playing a man playing a woman. (*Rosenkavalier* fans, remember Octavian.)

Andrews is a hit, performing as a woman (and singing better than she has done in some time), then, for her curtain call, pulling off her wig to reveal her "real" male self. Garner, a Chicago gangster visiting Paris, is smitten with Andrews when she sings, then is disturbed at the finish to discover that he has been attracted by, as he thinks, a man. (*Twelfth Night* fans, remember Orsino's liking for Cesario who is Viola in disguise.) Really funny complications follow, ingeniously convoluted.

The actors, under Edwards's direction, keep the ninepins twirling. I've never been an Andrews devotee, but there's less suburban-night-out giddiness here, more genuine verve and sex, than I've seen in her. Preston plays the bewigged old gay with comic verism, not cartoon; he makes his gayness his being, an amusing being. If you've seen Garner in the Polaroid commercials, let alone his many films and TV shows, you've seen him, and that's not a dig: he knows how to play quiet, quizzical comedy. Edwards even takes the stalest cliché in twentieth-century farce, the sexy dumb blonde with a nasal voice, and gets some vital use out of her because Lesley Ann Warren plays her—Garner's moll at the start—as if the character had just been invented.

The musical numbers, and there are at least half a dozen, are staged with that cinematic luxe that only the Folies-Bergère could have afforded, but they're well-designed by Rodger Maus and Patricia Norris, rightly choreographed by Paddy Stone, and well lighted by Dick Bush. The songs by Leslie Bricusse and Henry Mancini strike the right balance; they seem both "period" and fresh.

I began think of *Some Like It Hot* about halfway through *Victor/Victoria* because, first, I was laughing so much; because of the period (a few years later than Billy Wilder's film); because of the transvestism (though Wilder had no homosexuality); because of the Chicago-gangster element; because of the musical numbers used to advance the story. Afterward, when I read the credits, the relation between the two films was italicized. Wilder's film was based on a German film of the early 1930s. *Victor/Victoria* was based on a German film of 1933 called *Viktor und Viktoria*, subject by Hans Hoemburg, written and directed by Reinhold Schünzel. (It was also made in French as *Georges et Georgette* and was remade in Germany in 1957. Schunzel himself acted and directed in Hollywood during the Hitler years.) The cynical naughtiness, the easy acceptance of behavior that would startle the bourgeoisie, the flowering of elegant comic complications out of poverty, all give a "continental" base to both Wilder's and Edwards's film, mixed with American technical polish. (The combination doesn't *always* work: Wilder's latest, the dismal *Buddy Buddy*, came from a French farce.) For at least a hundred years, a lot of European dramaturgic ingenuity has gone into the fabrication of sophisticated, clever comedy, and some American filmmakers—or filmmakers in America—like Wilder and Lubitsch and now Edwards have harvested bits of it.

Not knowing Schünzel's film, I don't know how much of the plotting here is Edwards's, how much of the daring on the subject of gayness, or whether he devised the good running gags, like the suspicious waiter, the stolid private detective, and the man repeatedly trying to leave his shoes outside his hotel-room door. But the neat dialogue is surely Edwards's—as are the anachronisms: nobody said "Have a nice day" or "I'll buy that" (meaning "I'll accept that") in 1934.

That raises one other possible anachronism. *Victor/Victoria* is set in 1934, and I'm wondering whether some of the things said about gays in this film aren't out of synch. (Only Garner and his Chicago friends are disturbed by gayness.) Not knowing Schünzel's film, I wonder whether some *Cage aux Folles* ambience hasn't been imposed retroactively.

But even if that's the case, it doesn't hurt the fun. And Edwards, like Wilder before him, at least chose a good antecedent, then adapted it well. What's more, he has directed it with fine farce timing—which does not mean frantic rush. (Note the handling of the finger caught in the closet door, for instance.) Edwards's experience with farce, especially the *Pink Panther* series, is the ground for a lot of what he does here; but in *Victor/Victoria* he zooms far above that ground.

Postscript. The German original was also remade in Britain in 1935, as *First a Girl*, directed by Victor Saville from a screenplay by Marjorie Gaffney, starring Jessie Matthews. I subsequently saw this version and, again baffled by the adulation once heaped on Matthews, was chiefly aware that sexual innuendo had been carefully censored. Of the two versions I've seen, *Victor/Victoria* is easily victorious, although it has the advantage of being made in a more permissive time.

Passione d'Amore

(March 31, 1982)

Once in a while a corny title becomes, after seeing the film, the only one possible; it rises from corn to exactness. *Passione d'Amore* could be the title of ten thousand trashy pictures; here it fits so precisely that the phrase seems fresh. The film is about a transformation effected by the passion of love—a change much more in the beloved than in the lover. And the residual truth of that change is disturbing, haunting.

Insofar as I expected anything at all from the director, Ettore Scola, who is co-author of the screenplay, *Passione d'Amore* isn't it. Out of his prolific career, the two Scola films best known here are probably *We All Loved Each Other So Much*, a bittersweet study of modern male bonding, and *A Special Day*, about a one-day affair between a housewife (Sophia Loren) and a homosexual (Marcello Mastroianni) on a Fascist holiday in the 1930s. Scola always seemed to be feeling along the outer edges of the acceptable in a tamely daring way. This time, with a script based on a nineteenth-century story called "Fosca" by Iginio Ugo Tarchetti, he has gone further.

In 1862 an Italian cavalry captain is having an affair with a beautiful married woman in Milan. (A narrator's opening comments imply that the whole film is a flashback.) It's a period when romanticism, which was dominating all European art, was also, as Marvin Carlson reminds us, interwoven with politics in Italy—therefore with military life. The beginning suggests Visconti and *Senso*, but the picture soon moves into the shadowy outer edges of romanticism, into Brontë and E. T. A. Hoffmann country. The young captain is transferred to a military station in the mountains where he takes his meals in the colonel's house with a few other selected officers and where he soon learns about the colonel's cousin who lives upstairs, a highly neurotic woman who rarely appears though a place is always set for her. Her screams from upstairs are often heard, and servants rush up to care for her; but neither the colonel nor the other officers pay great attention. The fits are expected.

The captain visits his beautiful mistress on occasional leaves. Then at last he and the sequestered cousin meet. We see her feet coming down the stairs, and the atmosphere, the suspense, even the very period of the story, lead us to ex-

pect some sort of pale Lucia di Lammermoor figure. Fosca, the cousin, is home-
ly, even ugly: with a big beaked nose, a wide toothy mouth, and a sickly aura.
This reversal of conventional expectation is first of all a narrative shock. We
wonder immediately what kind of *story* this is going to be. Where will it lead?
How can it end?

What happens thereafter can hardly be called reversals: they are consequences – psychological, emotional, humane. Fosca falls in love with the captain, besieges him, behaves as if he were betraying a professed love for her
(when he has only been trying to offend her as little as possible), begs for a
touch, a caress. Her health, never good, worsens; the regimental doctor
believes that she will die unless, as he tells the captain, the young man pays her
a nocturnal visit. The captain refuses, then is persuaded. In the fact that he is
finally persuaded, reluctant though he is, lies the core of the story.

Eventually, this visit and further encounters alter his relation with his
beautiful Milanese mistress and with the unbeautiful Fosca. The latter's very
passion alters him, compelled as he is by circumstances to stay within reach of
its heat. She begins to stir feelings in him other than the initial repulsion, more
than the compassion that touches the repulsion, more than the contradictory
blend of the two. The film ends with the narrator whom we heard at the start:
it's the captain himself, older, now out of uniform, seedy, finishing his tale of
the change in his life wrought by that unlovely woman's passion.

"Even if we are often led to desire through the sense of beauty, can you say
that the beautiful is what we desire?" So asks Richard Rowan in Joyce's play *Ex-
iles*, and his friend Robert Hand begs off replying for fear of a headache. No
begging off in Scola's film: the question persists. We prattle about love as more
than skin-deep, as being ultimately unconnected with beauty, or else why
would we not love every and any beautiful person? We talk about love as af-
fined with the soul, as surpassing time and distance and (some believe) death.
What have any of these beliefs to do with that hypothetical extra inch at the
end of Cleopatra's nose that would have changed the course of history? The
captain in this film is "imprisoned" with a woman to whom he does not immediately respond, to whom very few males could conceivably respond. If he
could flee, he would, but confined with that woman and her passion for him,
he is forced to see and feel differently. His "sense of beauty" led him to desire his
Milanese mistress, but is the beautiful all that can be desired? The passion of
Fosca's love is transformative for him, becomes almost a kind of spiritual
epiphany. It is not so superficial a matter as redefining beauty, as seeing "worth"
beneath the surface; the drama becomes a metamorphosis of all values, a
redeployment of self. In a way, the transformation disaffiliates him from the
world by disconnecting him with its values that he used to share.

I don't know Tarchetti's story, but presumably he was an explorer, not a
moralist, and that's how Scola handles the material: not as a tract against the
vanity of physical beauty but as an exploration of sensibility in the protagonist.

A few points in the filmmaking raise questions. Sequence by sequence the film is composed fluently, but between sequences there are frequent bumps: as if reels were being changed. And three French actors were used for important roles in this Italian film. International casting is hardly new: it usually has something to do with international financing and tax regulations, but it's not always helpful to the film. Bernard Giraudeau (the captain), Jean-Louis Trintignant (the doctor), and Bernard Blier (a gourmand fellow-officer) are all good actors but are all obviously dubbed. The married beauty is Laura Antonelli. Massimo Girotti, whom I saw again just the other day as Valli's cousin in *Senso* and whom I would welcome in almost every Italian film, is solid as the colonel. The fact that the colonel is so handsome—Girotti is maturing well—helps the contrast with his cousin. She is played by Valeria D'Obici, an actress new to me, who has (I've read) a puttied nose in the film. Hers is of course the key performance. The best tribute one can pay her—and she deserves much tribute—is highly subjective, much more subjective than usual: without mitigation, she creates a woman whose affection is at first frightening to a male viewer, whose approach makes the skin sweat, and whose persistence—in its pain and humility and self-humiliation—finally begins to shame and discomfort. For one male viewer at least, D'Obici's performance had something of the same effect as it had on the captain.

Mephisto

(April 7, 1982)

Anyone who has seen Fritz Lang's *M* (1931) has seen Gustaf Gründgens: he plays the leader of the criminals, in bowler hat and leather coat. *Mephisto* is a Hungarian film (1981) derived from a novel of that name (1936) by Klaus Mann which is a *roman à clef* about Gründgens. Ariane Mnouchkine, the French theater director, dramatized the novel several years ago, and a translation of her play was produced in London last October.

Gründgens (1899-1963) was thought by many to be the greatest German actor, director, and theater intendant (general manager and artistic director) of his time. That of course would not in itself explain the novel/play/film. Look again at "his time": it encompasses the Hitler era. Gründgen's career began before Hitler, prospered during Hitler's rule, and continued after it. His life, outside of his artistic achievements, is a marvel of navigation. Politically he began as a leftist. Before Hitler's ascent, he married Erika Mann, daughter of Thomas (and sister of Klaus). He became head of prominent German theaters, and he swayed with the Nazi whirlwind in order to retain his eminence. His wife emigrated and they divorced; his second wife was a very Aryan actress. He became a friend and protégé of Goering. He managed the Berlin Schauspielhaus from 1934 to 1944. He also directed and acted in films under the

Nazis. He was imprisoned after the war but was "de-nazified" on the ground that he helped keep German culture alive in a barbaric time—also he had done all he could do to help people who were being harried by the Nazis. After release by the Allies, he worked in the Deutsches Theater in East Berlin for a year or so, then went to West Germany to take over the major theater in Düsseldorf. He ended his career as intendant of the Hamburg Schauspielhaus where he was also leading actor and director. When Bertolt Brecht came back to Berlin—East Berlin—after the war, he offered his play *Saint Joan of the Stockyards* to Gründgens, over in the other Germany, and Gründgens did the first production in Hamburg in 1959. In 1960 a filmed record was made of one of Gründgen's most famous productions, *Faust*, with himself as Mephistopheles. Three years later he died while on holiday in the Far East, possibly a suicide, possibly because of a love affair.

I haven't read Klaus Mann's novel, which has only recently been published in Europe after delay by legal obstacles. (Added irony: Mann committed suicide in 1949, supposedly depressed because of those obstacles.) The film, like the novel, ends before the war. It claims to be based "on motifs" drawn from the book, and it implies the pattern of its protagonist's future by what we see.

Mephisto was made in Hungary, but the soundtrack here is in German. Only a few of the actors are German or Austrian; most are Hungarian, a few of other nationalities—all dubbed into German with extraordinary skill. The Austrian actor Klaus Maria Brandauer plays Höfgen, the name here given to Gründgens. The roles is so juicy—it *begins* with a tantrum—that only a desperately inadequate actor could fail in it, and Brandauer is better than adequate. He has more force than fire, more energy than magnetism, but he does well.

Rolf Hoppe, presumably German, is excellent as the Nazi prime minister. It's Goering, naturally, complete with blonde Valkyrie consort, but somewhat altered. I can't remember any newsreels of Goering moving quickly; Hoppe, who is stout, always strides rapidly, making his retinue scurry, as if to show that corpulence can't slow this leader down, that party zeal lends him wings. In repose, in close-up, Hoppe uses his fat face with an eloquence I haven't seen since Sydney Greenstreet. His quivery jowls seem themselves to cajole or threaten. It's a lithe maniacal performance within a gross body.

Krystyna Janda, the Polish actress familiar from several Wajda films, plays Höfgen's first wife with the most focused acting of hers that I've seen, confident and restrained; perhaps the dubbing into German holds it together. And Karin Boyd, a German black actress well-known, I'm told, in the theater there, is superb as Höfgen's movement teacher and also his lover. (The character had a German father; mother unspecified.) Their passionate meetings are seen first in Hamburg in his leftist days; then in Berlin, secretly, after his nazification; then in Paris after he has maneuvered an exit visa for her and he visits her for the last time. In these scenes Boyd gives us both a tiger and an intelligent, dignified woman; and, through her, we see Höfgen at both his truest and his most pathetic. Their affair brings out the deepest feeling of which he is capable and also the deepest cowardice, because he dare not acknowledge that feeling publicly.

Most of the other actors are Hungarian, and the assemblage of faces gives the film a marvelous texture. Together the faces compose a map of the heartland of Europe. Among the characters are a super-Nazi sculptor named Leni, shown as lesbian and an intimate of Höfgen's wives (you can draw your own inferences about Riefenstahl and other matters); a leftist actor whom Höfgen is able to protect for a while; another actor who is a fervent early Nazi but who, after Hitler takes office, loses both his faith and his life.

The screenplay was written by the director, István Szabó, and Peter Dobai. Szabó, now 44 and accounted one of Hungary's top directors, was last represented here by *Confidence*, the story of a Budapest man and woman during the German Occupation, forced by circumstance to pose as man and wife. (Both of the actors are also in *Mephisto*.) The script left me with questions, but the making of the film was extraordinary, a nice balance of melancholy and menace.

With the same cinematographer, Lajos Koltai, Szabó has given *Mephisto* an equally appropriate, therefore utterly different, look. The subject of the film is seen as *performance*; the lighting and composition and movement are as theatrical as realism will bear. An instance: in one of Höfgen's apartments, all we see through the windows is thick white—no other buildings—as if the sky were fleecy and low. This renders the absolutely veristic room into a stage setting.

Light, sheerly theatrical light, is what ends the film. After Höfgen has triumphed in a Nordic, "positive" production of *Hamlet*, he is whisked off in the middle of the night by the adoring prime minister to an immense empty stadium. The minister orders the puzzled actor into the middle of the great field where intense spotlights catch him. Apparently he is to be recruited into staging huge political rallies here. The camera closes in on him in the white and whitening light, suggesting the white makeup he has worn as Mephisto. Now, a bit frightened by what his cunning has brought him to, he gasps: "What do you people want of me? I'm only an actor." The light on his face continues to intensify until the screen goes white, and the film finishes.

Obviously, *Mephisto* wants to fix a moral dilemma. An actor cannot do what any other sort of artist, even a writer, can do: practice his art at its best in a foreign country. No mature actor can hope to become as good in a second language as he is in his own, though of course (which is a different subject) many actors have been successful in second, even third languages. Quite apart from whether or not we approve of Höfgen's choice, it's easy to understand, especially since *Mephisto* ends before the war, how he can rationalize himself into acceptance of the new regime because his life is his acting—his greatness as an actor—and he can't imagine acting in another language. He declines to join a female star who emigrates early. When he journeys to Budapest to play in a film for a famous Berlin theater director, patently modeled on Max Reinhardt, the director tells him that one reason he was engaged was so that he could flee Germany with the director. Höfgen returns to Berlin.

Höfgen's dilemma is the very reason why, at the last, the film falls short. It never becomes more than the dilemma of an actor; it never enlarges sufficiently to become a representative moral agony, to make Höfgen a protagonist for millions. That agony was great in Germany, is great today in totalitarian countries. Under such a government, all people—except those who are lucky enough to escape—fall into one of three groups: the proscribed and hopeless, which in Germany chiefly meant Jews, Communists, homosexuals and gypsies; the heroic antagonists, who could get by if they chose but who resist, risking imprisonment and death; and the majority. Many of the majority in Germany, I'm quite willing to believe, disliked the Nazi movement but were not sufficiently heroic to resist once it took power. Are they therefore villains? All grief to the victims, all honor to the heroes, but are the others villains? I'm uneasy about judging them because I'm not so nobly certain that if I had been an "Aryan" German, nominally acceptable to the regime, I'd have resisted. I know that I'd have been anti-Nazi; I'm not so sure that I'd have been willing to be tortured and/or killed for my belief. So I'm reluctant to judge those who did not resist.

Mephisto doesn't grow to embrace "my" dilemma. Höfgen never becomes more than a professional with a particular professional problem. The film is vivid, well performed, sharp; but it never quite leaves the parish of the theater.

A Week's Vacation

(April 14, 1982)

Bertrand Tavernier has a sense of lineage. *A Week's Vacation* is set in his native city of Lyons. It's about a schoolteacher, Nathalie Baye, who withdraws from work for a week because of difficulties with her students and who, among other things she does in that week, goes to the country to visit her parents. Her beloved father, now ill and immobile, is played by Jean Dasté, who was the new schoolteacher in Vigo's *Zéro de Conduite* (1933), the frisky young man who wins the boys' confidence.

At one point in the week Baye has dinner with a local innkeeper who is the father of one of her students: another guest is the title character of Tavernier's film *The Clockmaker* (made five years earlier), played by the same actor, Philippe Noiret.

And Tavernier dedicates his new film to Jean Aurenche, now seventy-seven, who collaborated with him on the scripts of several films and has been writing films since 1936.

Busy though he was with affectionate remembrance, Tavernier has not neglected to make a good film, which reestablishes him on the American scene. He's had a peculiar career here. His first two films, *The Clockmaker* and *Let Joy Reign Supreme*, were revelations. His next has not yet been shown here. His fourth, *Spoiled Children*, was shown briefly in a special series and was, I thought, a dud. His fifth, a sci-fi film with Harvey Keitel, has not been shown here. I was sadly prepared to write him off as another Alain Tanner, a director who started strong and who quickly ran down into polished vacuities, when along comes, with pleasant surprise, this small, quiet, firm film.

Tavernier's script, written with his wife, Colo Tavernier, and with Marie-Françoise Hans, tackles a difficult subject—difficult both because it's hard to dramatize and because many have tried. A cloud of futility and pointlessness afflicts the thirty-one-year-old woman who has loved the work of teaching and who, in her private life, has a pretty happy time with a young man. The immediate straw is the recurrence of discipline problems with her early teenage students, a conviction of inutility because she has to spend so much of her class time *not* teaching. (Not exactly news to grade school and high school teachers everywhere.) She's on the edge of physical collapse when her doctor orders her to take a week off.

No magic reaffirmation occurs. The week itself, plus the visit to her parents; plus the support of her lover, plus a friendship with the innkeeper (the man develops a crush on her that embarrasses him); plus some time with a troubled student; these restore her strength and give her some belief that she is, to a degree at least, needed. Nothing is cured. If the film has a lesson, a term for which I apologize, it's not that a sane person can get rid of doubt, it's that doubt is now a condition of ongoing life—especially for people whose work consists of affecting other people. Midnight weariness is no more *the* condition of life than is morning vigor. Baye is reconciled: to the fact that perception of doubt is now a concomitant to the possibility of action; that, when one understands this, one can function. A kind of peace comes with that perception. The last line of Camus's essay, "The Myth of Sisyphus" is: "One must imagine Sisyphus happy."

What holds this film together are the characterizations and Tavernier's skill. The people are not startlingly original or profoundly drawn; they are completely credible, therefore interesting. Baye, who has been seen here mostly in Truffaut films, is addicted to smiling—someone apparently did her the disservice early in her career of commenting on her winning smile—but, in between smiles, she summons up the being of the teacher. Her lover is warmly done by Gerald Lanvin, and in the small pivotal role of the innkeeper, Michel Galabru gives a taking performance. Galabru has been, as I've seen him, a fair to foul *farceur*, in the *Cage aux Folles* films and elsewhere. I can't remember him in anything serious and I don't know whether Tavernier is responsible for his "conversion"; anyway, their collaboration here results in a human portrait.

I could have done without a few of the mood touches: when Baye is depressed, an old man shuffles by, so weak that he drops his cane; an old woman sits in the same chair in the room across the way every day, until one day the shutters are closed. But Tavernier's film has a fabric of reality. Into it, I felt, was stitched another Camus passage, from the essay on Kafka: "The human heart has a tiresome tendency to label as fate only what crushes it. But happiness likewise, in its way, is without reason, since it is inevitable."

The Judge and the Assassin

(September 6, 1982)

The film world *is* mad. Any lingering doubt about it is wiped away by the belated arrival of a superb French film made in 1975 that hasn't even yet had a full-fledged release in the U.S. It's been shown only a few times in a few places while lesser foreign films get plastered around. For years I've been reading and hearing about Bertrand Tavernier's *The Judge and the Assassin*. Now, thanks to the Film Forum in New York – may it live and prosper – I've had a chance to see this fine work.

Tavernier's previous films shown here, *The Clockmaker, Let Joy Reign Supreme, A Week's Vacation** established him as a director of seriousness and range. *Let Joy Reign Supreme* was set in Regency France of the early eighteenth century and authentically lived there. *The Clockmaker* and *A Week's Vacation* were set in present-day Lyons, Tavernier's birthplace. (*Spoiled Children*, the one disappointing Tavernier film I've seen, is set in Paris today.) *The Judge and the Assassin*, which was made just after *Let Joy Reign Supreme*, begins in 1893 and is set mainly in a town in the mountains of the Ardeche, not far from Lyons. The two main characters are the judge in this town, who is virtually the law incarnate, and a murderer, a homicidal sexual-religious maniac. The judge, played by Philippe Noiret, is a quintessential bourgeois, conservative, self-approving, proper; he lives with his mother and has a working-class mistress whom he visits occasionally and pays. The assassin, played by Michel Galabru, is a former army sergeant, working-class, about the judge's age, fiercely and rhetorically Catholic; he shot the woman he wanted to marry when she absolutely declined him – she had never encouraged him – then put two bullets in his own head. Both he and the young woman survived. He fled, to wander the roads of France. (Along with, we're told, 400,000 other vagabonds. This and some other societal notes are small editorial intrusions.) From time to time, as his aching head and his sexual-religious delusions command him, he ravishes and murders girls and boys out in the countryside. The judge keeps track of these murders on a map; in time he manages to have the madman arrested and

---

*See preceding review.

held for trial in his court.

Most of the film takes place between the arrest and the trial. The confrontations between judge and assassin are usually amicable, even with the madman's ravings. One of the film's subtleties is that, in some ways, the assassin insinuates an influence on the judge. (Once, after an interview, the judge hurries to his mistress and insists on sodomizing her, at her worktable, as the assassin had done to his victims.) But chiefly the judge is trying to prove that the assassin is not truly insane, is an anarchist pretending to be crazed. (Loathing for anarchists—apparently a collective term for all radicals— runs through the picture.) A friend of Noiret's, another judge who has just returned from Cochin-China (the old name for Vietnam!), reassures him: Galabru is poor, therefore will not be found insane. This proves to be true. We see neither the trial itself nor the execution—these are not Tavernier's interest—but the ranting madman is held responsible for his acts.

By the intensity of its focus, much less than through polemical comment, the film presses into the questions of privilege before the law; of anti-Semitism, virulent because of the Dreyfus case which arises during this period; of class structure and political turbulence as dramatized in this town by the occasion of the assassin's trial. The screenplay is by Jean Aurenche and Tavernier. Aurenche, who was also Tavernier's collaborator on *Let Joy Reign Supreme*, is thirty-seven years older than the director, which fact is a lovely *hommage* to the idea of continuity, besides being fruitful in itself. The writers selected a historical case, then worked it open the way cryptographers can find detailed information hidden under a period at the end of a sentence. Under the microscope of their sensitivities, Aurenche and Tavernier found in this case, or credibly inferred, large quarrels and antagonisms, ancient prides and fears.

Then Tavernier and his other colleagues took over. What fixes all the script's elements in place is, to begin with, the breathtaking re-creation of the period. Tavernier showed splendid ability to do this in his eighteenth-century picture; here he has the same cinematographer, Pierre William Glenn, the same costume designer, Jacqueline Moreau, and an exceptional production designer, Antoine Roman. With them, Tavernier has again made a film of a historical texture that compares favorably with Feyder's *Carnival in Flanders* and Carné's *Children of Paradise*. Lives are maintained, clothes and streets are inhabited, customs are followed through imaginative art. A street singer and his harpist do a ballad about news of the day, not as a quaint folk rite but as the era's answer to hungers that are fed nowadays by electronic media. Institutions are laid bare as underpinnings of the surface prettinesses; grim though they look to us, prisons, hospitals, examining boards are seen as they are accepted by the people of the time, which is exactly the way similar institutions are viewed today—unsatisfactory, perhaps, but the best that is possible.

Tavernier works with no nostalgia for old Europe that Americans still hope to find when they visit and with no smug superiority about past brutalities of many kinds. Yet, humanitarian that he unquestionably is, he knows that something existed then—a community of the rich, a community of the poor—that has since been greatly diluted. He does not long for the return of heaven-ordained luxe for the privileged nor for the sympathetic fraternity of huddled peasants; but, like a true artist, he recognizes what all these people did for themselves within the limits of their time, conditioning, possibilities.

As for the acting, I feel that I do and don't owe apologies to Michel Galabru. I've disliked him in a number of farces and have admired him only once, as the love-smitten innkeeper in A Week's Vacation. All the while, his achievement as the assassin here has been waiting, finished, hidden from us by our mad film world. Galabru gives an absolutely shattering performance as the murdering, maniacally transfigured murderer, a performance that comes straight from the heart of Dostoevskian torment. Rasputin, it is said, sinned so that he could hate his sin and repent; this assassin sees his sin, when he can recognize it as such, as holy violence, which seems to bring him, through physical agony and wild exultation, closer to the Virgin Mary whom he adores. Perhaps I risk profanity, but I have seen little in film acting closer to the ecstasy that frequently bursts from Galabru other than some moments of Falconetti's ecstasy in Dreyer's film about Joan of Arc. (Unsurprisingly, at one moment, the madman compares himself to Joan.) Since, in my experience of his work, Galabru has done his best in Tavernier films, I conclude that this director sees this actor's possibilities better than other directors do and can help him more than others do.

It is no slight to that excellent actor, Noiret, who is a Tavernier regular, to say that his performance contains no surprises like Galabru's. In the happiest sense, Noiret does what I expected: he deepens an already well-written role with technical perfection, understanding, and compelling presence. The other principal character, the magistrate returned from Cochin-China, is played by Jean-Claude Brialy with an ethics of elegance, class prejudice, and expectation of sympathy from his equals. The details of his troubles in the East are not explored, but he has brought back with him a young manservant who is probably a clue. Those troubles lead, near the end, to Brialy's suicide, which Tavernier handles with gentle irony. The camera moves slowly across his sumptuously furnished living room, to reveal him lying gracefully on a divan, a discreet red round spot on his temple, a small revolver lying near his hand, while, all through this camera glide, Brialy's gramophone plays Offenbach—music by a Jew, and German-born at that.

That near-casual camera movement is typical of the way the whole film seems to flow—with differing speeds—through crowded streets or following a steam-plumed locomotive around a turn or drawing back from a place on a mountainside to acknowledge the green universe. Only once is this feeling of flow drastically altered. Near the end, the red-headed woman whom Galabru loved and nearly killed meets the judge's mistress, another red-headed peasant woman. (The latter is played by Isabelle Huppert, since celebrated.) As their talk intensifies, the film cuts more and more sharply from one face to the other. The editing method stands out because it is used only here; and it underscores, through the meeting of these women, the mysterious bond of like and dislike between the assassin and the judge. I should note, too, that Tavernier has used Panavision for this film, which he handles as comfortably for intimate scenes as for vastness.

He also uses selective sound. For example, at one point Noiret and Huppert converse in the street while behind them a sort of carnival is going on. We barely hear the music and the people in the background. The device suggests the novelist's power of selection, whatever the environment.

The Judge and the Assassin is not a murder mystery: there is no mystery and we see very little violence. What we see, under the burning glass of epitome, is the result of centuries of egotism and hatred—in France, in Europe, therefore in that portion of the world that inherits from Europe. Even the insanity of the murderer is made a battleground for enmities and ambitions. The future is foreshadowed by the violence of attack—from clergy and others—on such creatures as Zola and anarchists. In the last sequence, after the assassin has been executed and the judge expects to advance politically thereby, we see Noiret on the platform at a meeting of a royalist association—the slogan "Everything national is ours" on a banner behind him—listening to himself being praised. Anarchists burst in, red flag and all. Noiret and his mother flee into the street and hide in a nook in front of a poster advertising a newspaper that claims to be the most anti-Semitic of all. Which is where we leave the film. But the film does not leave us.

Postscript. The Judge and the Assassin has since been shown with the inclusion of a final scene (which is in the screenplay published by *l'Avant-Scène*). Huppert and a group of workers face soldiers at the gates of a factory and sing a revolutionary song. The scene helps little.

A Sunday in the Country

(December 17, 1984)

Right from the start of his directing career, Bertrand Tavernier has had a singular relation with old men. His first feature, *The Clockmaker*, made in 1973 when Tavernier was thirty-two, had a screenplay by Jean Aurenche and Pierre Bost, both then in their seventies. Bost died in 1975. Tavenier's next two screenplays, *Let Joy Reign Supreme* and *The Judge and the Assassin*, were collaborations by himself and Aurenche. Later came *A Week's Vacation*, which had a pivotal scene played by Jean Dasté, an actor fixed in the firmament by Jean Vigo in *Zero for Conduct* and *L'Atalante* in the early 1930s. Aurenche was again Tavernier's collaborator on *Coup de Torchon*, and now Tavernier salutes the memory of Pierre Bost by filming a Bost novel called here *A Sunday in the Country*. (Tavernier and his wife adapted the book.) The main figure, a painter, is played by Louis Ducreux, well known in the French theater as actor-playwright-director, who has worked very little in films and now plays his first major film role at seventy-three.

This exceptional partiality for older collaborators quite possibly derives from Tavernier's interest in history (*Let Joy Reign Supreme* and *The Judge and the Assassin* are masterly explorations of the French past) and especially in film history (he has written much on the subject). His partiality is capped in this latest film because its very subject is age. The Sunday is spent with the painter, early in this century and late in his own life, who looks back at his own history with acceptance, then feels some impulse to question that acceptance.

But the sad report is that *A Sunday in the Country* falls into Group Two of Tavernier's works. Group One includes the excellent films named above (except *Coup de Torchon*), which show Tavernier's understanding of oppressions in the world and in the self, of communion with other human beings as the only verities. The films in Group Two, *Spoiled Children*, *Coup de Torchon*, and this new work, seem to start, not with impulse, but with attitudes. In *Sunday*, for instance, it's as if Tavernier had begun with an image of himself as the maker of *Sunday*, rather than with a close concern about the material—as if he had begun with a vision of the film finished and himself hailed as the creator of a gentle film about a gentle old man.

This sense of what Tavernier wanted to be said about the film, rather than of what he had to say in it, strikes us from the start and continues throughout. *Sunday* is loaded with recognizable enticements of lyric film. It begins with a woman's voice speaking out of the dark, as in *Jules and Jim*. Then we get *belle epoque* décor and costumes, used with abject dependence on their accepted "meaning"—the innocence of the days before the First World War. The cinematography, by Bruno de Keyzer, clings closely to the memory mode, the suggestion of sepia to evoke the feeling of old photographs. The screenplay has reminders of *Wild Strawberries*: scenes with the old man's long-dead wife are spliced in, not as flashbacks but as presences in his mind. And two dream children, little girls whom no one sees except the old man, play about his garden in their summery frocks as if shipped over from the nearest Symbol Shop.

The script has a shape—a life in a day—that has nothing wrong with it if something right is done with it. This Sunday, out of endless Sundays, is meant to be a moment of anagnorisis for the old man. On Sundays his son and daughter-in-law and their three children come down by train from Paris for lunch; this day they are joined by Ducreux's daughter, an attractive young Parisienne (she seems more like his granddaughter) who motors down, bustles around the place, has imperiously affectionate moments with her father and her niece and nephews, upsets the fixed routine of the day with her freshness, gets a telephone call from her lover, and drives hurriedly back to town. She has had time, however, to have a meal and several snacks—I lost count of how often this group took various refreshments during the day—to give her father some gently piercing comments about his career, and to serve the film both as contrast to his esthetic complacency and her brother's philistine complacency.

Every characterization, every contrast is familiar. More, Tavernier's use of them has a patness, a consciousness of design, that further vitiates them. And the distance between us and the patterns is frozen by the character of the painter. Not much self-discovery or shedding of illusions is possible here because the old man has few illusions about himself. He doesn't think he is more than he apparently is, a minor painter who has had moderate success. (Apparently he has always had some money.) He exhibits neither false grandeur nor keen bitterness: he just lives quietly and well, and paints conservatory pictures of flowers and landscapes and rooms. When he is left alone at the end of the day, facing a blank canvas, tears well in his eyes—but not in ours. No painful vision of futility of life and the waste of possibility has come to this man. His tears are themselves conventional, age's regret about time irretrievably gone. The penetration of character, the revelations of this detailed day, are as superficial as the making of the film itself.

This thinness is underscored by Ducreux's performance. The publicity told us of a long, active life in the French theater and prepared us for an actor of importance belatedly revealed to the world, perhaps a Victor Francen or Sacha Guitry or Louis Jouvet who had been foolishly ignored by film. But Ducreux proves, in a sense, too mimetically apt for his role: he plays the competent minor painter like a competent minor actor. He has no depth or force of personality; he seems nothing more than a quite acceptable stock company Old Man.

The other adult performances—the faithful old servant who worries about her master, the pompous son, his proper wife, the headstrong daughter—are complete after the first thirty seconds with each: we can fill in the rest ourselves but are not allowed to. Tavernier puts them in place like puppets he has taken from a box, then keeps manipulating.

A Sunday in the Country is worrisome because Tavernier is worth worrying about. He is one of the very few directors to emerge since 1970 anywhere in the world—at least as we are enabled to see what's happening in the film world—who have a claim on the first rank. The best comfort in his new film is that he has made clinkers before and has followed them with good work. He is in love with film and runs the risks of that love, of making a film like this one that does nothing but display his love. His better work shows him *using* that love, not coldly but austerely.

Diner

(April 28, 1982)

American men hate to grow up. I don't know any other national literature that has produced national epitomes comparable to *Huckleberry Finn* and *The Catcher in the Rye*, novels that are not only about the condition of being young but about its superiority. Our best dramatist wrote one of his most durable plays, *Ah, Wilderness!*, about lost innocence. It's hardly a surprise that this state of mind has marked American films: a few examples are *Summer of '42*, *September 30, 1955*, *Breaking Away*, and, my favorite to date, *American Graffiti*. The last is especially interesting because its director, George Lucas, subsequently made *Star Wars*, which is a projection onto the future of the *American Graffiti* ethos, the ideals and tastes of boyhood and adolescence in the past impasted on the space age to come.

Underneath this American male hatred of maturity—and what sets it apart from, for instance, Peter Pan's refusal to grow up—is the American male's hatred/fear of women, which translates readily into the deer-park mentality: women as the hunting preserve of men; manhood proved by expedition *and return*. Clear signs of contemporary change in these attitudes are growing, but those attitudes in their earlier, pure state are the locus of *Diner*, written and directed by Barry Levinson. It takes place in 1959. The setting is Baltimore, presumably because Levinson grew up there, but it could have been virtually any American city or sizable town in 1959.

Diner has been loudly acclaimed—for two reasons, I think. The first is extrinsic: the picture was finished over a year ago, and for a year its owners and distributors have fiddled with it. Levinson and some loyal supporters fought for an appropriate release, and at last they won. They deserve congratulations on their courage, especially since *Diner* turns out to be a good picture, funny and observant, hardly earthshaking but well worth seeing. (In the last few years most of the completed pictures that had trouble in getting release have proved, when seen at last, that the distributors were right.)

The second reason for the cheers is that *Diner* is one of the youth celebrations described above, and there's nothing that brings a greater reaction of relief-plus-joy from American critics and public than a good film in that genre. How pleasant it is (the tone of the reception implies) to have a good new American film that rolls right down the middle of the alley, a film that is simultaneously enjoyable and reaffirming. We can admire it without being disturbed in any way, without having our imaginations stretched or our experiences enlarged. No good film gets as rousing a welcome as one that doesn't "cost" us anything. A good youth film is a bull's eye.

Here they are again, the young pals—six of them this time, in their early twenties this time—complete with their "headquarters"—a diner this time—kidding one another, chasing and comparing girls, reveling in popular culture.

They delineate themselves, just as a painter would use oils and canvas for a self-portrait, by their use of girltalk and pop-cult talk. Their language comes to them less from parents and schools than from pop music, sports, and films. (Hollywood films, naturally. Two of the youths go to an Ingmar Bergman festival—though 1959 seems a bit early for that in Baltimore—and the predictable gibes get gibed.)

The six principals are a mixed lot, of course, but not so ostentatiously mixed that we can see the hand of a movie chef selecting ingredients. All are middle-class, though some are on the wealthier side. Some are Jews, some not. One of them is already married and already regrets it because he can't talk to his wife the way he can talk to his pals with whom he hangs out almost as much as if he were single. (What this says about his parents and about what's going to happen to his sons or daughters is scary.)

Some of the film's sequences, much praised by now, are apparently destined to become points of reference, less because of their novelty than because of the non-novel verity under the fresh approach. One fellow, engaged, refuses to go through with the marriage unless his fiancée can pass an exam on the history of professional football (to which his father contributes questions!). The already married fellow quarrels hotly with his wife because she misfiled his record albums and because she doesn't understand how important it is to know what's on the flip side of hit records. For me, there was an even more memorable sequence in which another fellow takes out that album-muffing wife, with whom he used to sleep before she was married, both to restore her dimmed feeling of sexual allure and—which she doesn't know—to win a bet. She's willing to visit his apartment, but at the last moment he can't go through with it.

The script has sequences that burden its general ease with movie guff: a faked car accident as a practical joke; a scene in a strip bar; one fellow's tight fix with a tough professional gambler and his miraculous rescue; that same fellow's encounter with a society girl galloping around her estate outside Baltimore. (The blonde equestrienne has something of the same allegorical function as the elusive blonde in the white T-bird in *American Graffiti*.) These "scripted" moments stick out because the rest is so casually credible.

All the leading actors are relative newcomers, all are attractive. Possibly the best known are Mickey Rourke, who was the professional arsonist in the otherwise deplorable *Body Heat*, here a reticently strong, secret idealist; Kevin Bacon, as a hard-drinking, secretly intellectual daredevil; and Steve Guttenberg as the affianced football nut. These three and their friends play together like an ace basketball team. (All right, so it's a six-man team.)

Levinson's previous writing has been collaborative: on Carol Burnett shows, Mel Brooks pictures, and the Pacino film, *And Justice for All*. His dialogue, when it's written dialogue and nothing else—like some sequences between one young man and a pregnant young woman—can get a bit starchy; but when he throws the ball to the team and lets them *go*, when the dialogue overlaps and undercuts and gushes in sidewise repetitive vernacular—in short, when Levinson has been shrewd enough (apparently) to let his actors improvise on given materials—the talk has vitality and shape. This is the kind of dialogue that American realistic actors do best; still it can be done badly, and here it's done well. This is Levinson's first directorial job; he handles it as if it were his tenth. I could have done without the ritual obeisance to Edward Hopper in a shot of a nighttime diner, but on the whole, the film is smoothly made, precisely pitched.

Diner is knowingly dated in more than its date; its tone is unremittingly sexist. What men want and how they want it is the basic law of the society shown. The engaged girl agrees to the football examination and studies for it. The young bride's hurt ego is restored when her former boyfriend assures her that she was a good lay and that she is still sexy. I don't begin to believe that these attitudes—in young men and in the response of young women—are now obsolete in the U.S., but it's patent that, since 1959, great changes have shaken the basic law cited above, largely through social, educative process and partly, I think, for physiological reasons. The Pill, added to those cultural causes, has changed young women's attitudes toward sex. The combination of causes has inevitably altered the old deer-park, hunting preserve sexual attitudes of young men. Sexual behavior is much more egalitarian now—in some social groups, anyway, in some parts of the country. By 1992 *Diner* may have become an historical document.

Several commentators have compared *Diner* with Fellini's *I Vitelloni*. This is obtuse. Fellini's masterpiece (1953) deals with the economic-spiritual paralysis of a nation, as manifested in a group of young men who drift around their hometown simply and only because they can't find work—at least, work that holds any promise or interest. *Diner* is about a group of very comfortable middle-class young men busily creating memories of freedom to take with them into the involvement, advancement, probable success that lie ahead of them. They know that this is the happiest time of their lives; Fellini's youths know it is the unhappiest.

Levinson himself, looking back at Baltimore in 1959, apparently thinks it was the best time of his life. Engaging and enjoyable as *Diner* mostly is, it's still one more case of an American disease.

Some Kind of Hero/Richard Pryor—Live on the Sunset Strip
(May 5, 1982)

The likable outlaw and the hooker with the heart of gold ride off together to possible happiness. So ends *Stagecoach* with John Wayne and Claire Trevor. So, too, ends *Some Kind of Hero* with Richard Pryor and Margot Kidder. Both films share the feeling that two people on the wrong side of society will try to make their own right society. There's a further resemblance: like Wayne, Pryor is a Good Guy whom the unjust world has turned into a Bad Guy.

Otherwise, *Stagecoach* and *Some Kind of Hero* are widely dissimilar films; but what's interesting is that these dissimilar films end with identical resolutions. If we work backward it's revealing to see how two disparate eras—1939 and 1982—reached that same resolution. One difference, hardly minor: Pryor is black and Kidder is not.

Pryor's film, adapted from James Kirkwood's novel of the same name by Kirkwood and Robert Boris, tots up a series of contemporary injustices that press him to his own system of justice. In *Stagecoach* Wayne breaks out of prison to avenge his brother's murder. In *Some Kind of Hero* Pryor is released from prison and then is himself legalistically "murdered." He spends some years as a P.O.W. in North Vietnam. After release, he is brought home and glad-handed. Then he finds out that: his mother has had a stroke and is about to be evicted from a rest home for non-payment of bills; his wife has left him for another man, taking Pryor's daughter whom he has never seen; he must undergo harsh military inquiry because in prison he signed a confession of American guilt, though we have seen him frequently refuse to sign—complying at the last only as a means of getting medical aid for a dying cellmate. But the fact of the inquiry delays the back pay that he very badly needs for his mother and to set himself right. Wayne has one focus of revenge, the Plummer gang; he has broken out of prison to kill them. Pryor has no one focus: he's fighting fog, the System. Times have changed, not only since 1939 but since the Western. There are no more villains; there are only soft-voiced people with furry answers to drive you crazy.

While Pryor is bouncing around Los Angeles, waiting and hoping—hoping for a while, anyway—he meets Kidder, a high-priced bar girl, who likes him and takes him home for the night as a friend. She tries to discourage further visits, but she likes him too much to refuse him her phone number. Pryor, harassed and angry, concocts a scheme to steal a lot of money without hurting anyone other than some killer types. He gets himself into serious trouble but gets himself out—the equivalent of his "shootout"—and finds Kidder waiting. They drive off, not in Wayne's buckboard but her sports car.

This is a comedy. That's not all that's amazing about *Some Kind of Hero*: what's more amazing is the interaction between Pryor and the script. That script is only stitched together and is uncertain in tone. Pryor, by sheer force of talent, affects the script the way a great tenor acts on a rackety opera libretto to give it wholeness.

It's been said that in this film Pryor shows he's more than a comedian, he's a serious actor. For me, that statement coarsens the truth: he never stops being funny when he's serious, or vice versa. For instance, when he's a P.O.W., there's no *Stalag 17* buffoonery, no cartooning of the captors (under Michael Pressman's direction); Pryor is in a harsh prison and there's no question about it. Yet a counterpoint of "What the hell am I doing here?" a tacit yet urgent sense of the idiocy of the world, gives the sequences a nonrisible cosmic comedy. And the risible comedy, like a holdup in a men's room, is made funnier by the desperation behind it.

It isn't enough to say that Pryor is better than his material: he *is* his material. I don't want to excuse previous execrable scripts like *Stir Crazy* or *Bustin' Loose* or even this one, which is better though thready. But all he needs is a series of scenes that he can use—with some sort of rising graph, if possible—and if that material is congenial, he will fulfill it scene by scene. He doesn't need, possibly would be hampered by, thoroughly developed material. I hope that no one will go mining novels and drama—*The Confessions of Nat Turner*, Gawd 'elp us, or *The Emperor Jones*—for the Big Vehicle that Pryor has been awaiting. He isn't waiting for anything; he's doing very well with whatever comes along. Some great comic actors, like Chaplin and Keaton, are at their best in developed work; some, like W. C. Fields, make silk purses out of whatever sows' ears come along. Fields would only have been burdened by as integrated a work as *City Lights* or *The General*.

But this doesn't mean that Pryor is at his best in filmed records of his staged appearances. The latest, *Richard Pryor—Live on the Sunset Strip*, has a sprinkling of high spots—the animal imitations, a scene with the Mafia—but the direct confrontation of Pryor and audience encourages sentimentalities in him, both of heart-tug and profanity. Also, it puts a double load on him, of performing and being the whole show as well. I don't mean that he improvises everything in these shows; he uses some of his standard bits. But the selections, the relative lengths of bits, the pacing, all make demands on him that he has to keep in mind while he's also performing, with no help from anyone else.

Many cultures have developed genius clowns who do much more than make their audiences laugh, they remind and chide and reassure and rive—Karl Valentin in Brecht's Bavaria, for instance, Dario Fo in terrorized Italy today. In his own style, vastly empowered by film, Pryor is becoming our culture's prime clown and actor and (as particularized above) screenwriter. I know that I've come a long way from the *Stagecoach* comparison at the beginning, but that's less my discursiveness, I think, than Pryor's range. Partly because he is black and uses his blackness as he does, largely through his powerful talents, he is making his films into some of the best political art we now have, whatever the scripts may be.

Gregory's Girl

(June 23, 1982)

A conventional film of early love comes from Scotland, written and directed by Bill Forsyth, whose second feature it is. *Gregory's Girl* is about high-school love in a Lowlands "new town" about halfway between Glasgow and Edinburgh, and technically the picture is crudely made. The editing is obtrusively bumpy, the use of the camera is pedestrian, and from beginning to end the soundtrack is freighted with studio deadness: the voices sound like after-thoughts.

The story could hardly be more commonplace. A zooming boy, five inches taller than he was last year, falls dreamily in love with a hearty girl who tries out for the football (soccer) team and who can't be denied a place because she is so good. She is a humdinger—her photo sells like hotcakes in the boys' toilet—and Gregory finally summons the nerve to ask her for a date. He gets it, and by the end of the evening, after several prearranged transfers, he finds himself with a different pretty girl, dreamy again.

But the picture has charm, for two reasons. Forsyth's dialogue is fresh, true, and funny. (Gregory's ten-year-old sister, according to a ten-year-old boy who admires her, "has the body of a woman of thirteen.") And all the youngsters, helped by their Lallans accent—mistakenly thought abroad to be *the* Scottish accent—are captivating. Dee Hepburn, the girl footballer, is the picture of every kind of health. Allison Forster, Gregory's kid sister, is prematurely sober and concerned; her scenes of love-counsel to her brother were my favorites. And Gordon John Sinclair, the Gregory, is gulping, humorous, unaggressive, but eager. Seeing *Gregory's Girl* is like spending ninety minutes in the company of youngsters who are going clumsily through a lot of familiar throes and thrills but who are doing it with such unsentimental commitment that it would be im-pertinent to patronize them.

Local Hero

(March 21, 1983)

Bill Forsyth, the Scottish filmmaker, is getting better. On the other hand, he is also getting cleverer. *Gregory's Girl*, which he wrote and directed, was a homespun film in two ways: it had some knots in it, but it came freshly from some lives. Forsyth told a conventional yet taking story about high school boys and girls in a Lowlands town near Glasgow. Now Forsyth has moved to the Highlands. He has written and directed *Local Hero*, which, though it's set in a much smaller, less modernized place, is not homespun. The producer was David Puttnam, who did *Chariots of Fire*, and who has provided Forsyth with a budget and with colleagues that—not to discount Forsyth's learning by ex-perience—have helped him over his earlier bumps. Once again Forsyth has made a film of considerable charm, but this time it's not of lives observed with sympathetic verity but of Movieland toured skillfully.

The affections of reality have been forsaken for the comforts of romance. The nub of the story is Scotland's offshore oil—transposed, apparently, from the northeast to the northwest coast. This offshore oil is coveted by a huge

American oil company, headquartered in Houston. High in a Houston skyscraper is the ruler of the oil empire who, like all film tycoons, is a boy at heart. From the Acquisitions Department he sends to Scotland a young man named MacIntyre, on the assumption that a Scot can deal with Scots. Mac confides to a friend that he is really of Hungarian descent: his immigrant father changed the family name. I was surprised that Forsyth made nothing of this fact later, but I was thunderstruck that he thought a giant oil company would send one young man to acquire a potentially rich oil field—in which they had already invested millions for exploration and planning.

Well, at least Forsyth doubles the number. Mac picks up another young employee of the company, a true Scot, in Aberdeen, and the two young men drive up to the village of Ferness on its bay. Why the village isn't called Briga-doon, a place where two young men first arrived in 1947, is probably a matter of copyright, but barring the music and the magic, Ferness comes pretty close. It's a picture-postcard fishing village. That aspect is realistic enough: I once spent a blessed week in such a place. But in Ferness, everyone is lovable, nobody quarrels, nobody falls down drunk, and *it never rains*! More: the one hotel is run by an attractive educated young couple who set a haute cuisine table—true enough in Britain these days but not where there are no tourists. A punk girl is one of the inhabitants. A baby, presumably hers, could have been fathered by numerous men who all apparently look after it. The skipper of a Soviet fishing trawler visits often, is loved by all—amorously by the woman who runs the general store—sings Western songs at a dance and is resented by no one although his boat is taking fish from Scottish nets. There's an old recluse in a hut on the beach who is dignified and philosophical, and the wee village kirk has a black African minister.

What dull literalist would disturb one atom of all this? Forsyth virtually tells us that this is going to be Getaway Time and that he'll do his best not to let us down. It is, and he doesn't. From the start in Houston, where the tycoon needs the help of a therapy-by-insult psychoanalyst, where Mac encounters nothing but unpleasant girlfriends, we know we are in for contrast, for an idyll of the ideal. The skyscraper is set against the whitewashed cottage, the imperial grab against ecological ethics, even the canny money sense of the Scot against an-cient ways of living. To quarrel with any of this, or the resolution, would be like quarreling with *L'Elisir d'Amore* because Donizetti doesn't accurately portray life in a nineteenth-century Italian village.

If we grant all this, which Forsyth amiably persuades us to do, then *Local Hero* joins the company of such cozy British-made film romances set in Scotland as *I Know Where I'm Going* (1945) and *Tight Little Island* 1949). (*Briga-doon*, Scottish setting though it has, is a somewhat different kettle of kippers.) In Forsyth's persuasion, there's only one partial flaw: the casting of Peter Riegert as Mac. He isn't quite credible as a rising oil-company hotshot, and he isn't sufficiently responsive to his Highland experiences. Compared with our own reactions, merely watching the the village and villagers, the reactions of Riegert, who is "there," seem a bit stodgy. Burt Lancaster is the old tycoon and the old Lancaster. Denis Lawson does trimly as the smart young innkeeper, and Fulton MacKay radiates the right friendly self-reliance as the beach recluse.

On the whole, *Local Hero* is a pleasing bit of—I almost said Scottish pastry, but it's tastier than that. And there's a very last moment with a small, sharp stab. Wild haggis couldn't drag it out of me.

That Sinking Feeling

(March 5, 1984)

This is the first film by a gifted filmmaker, Bill Forsyth, whose second and third we've already seen. Forsyth's first appearance here was with his second film, *Gregory's Girl*, a nubbly bit of homespun about Scottish Lowlands adolescents. His next, *Local Hero*, was more luxuriously made: David Puttnam, the producer of *Chariots of Fire*, was behind it. Its narrative was clever rather than revelatory, still there was charm in its Scottish fishing village. Now we get Forsyth's first, *That Sinking Feeling*. It's the least smooth of the three, naturally, but a picture that shows where a man of talent and good feeling came from.

This first picture was made in 1979, was shot in 16mm on that ubiquitous shoestring, and used members of the Glasgow Youth Theater. (Some of the cast were later in Forsyth's second film, including Gordon John Sinclair, Gregory himself.) Forsyth, who is now thirty-eight, had graduated from the British National Film School in 1970 and had been working at various film jobs for five years even before that schooling. After graduation, he formed his own outfit in Glasgow and made three or four short films a year. Then he got the backing for this first feature.

In a way, what's best about *That Sinking Feeling* is the fact that it doesn't reflect all his film education and experience. Partly, of course, this is because he didn't have enough money to do everything he knew how to do. But the shortage was a disguised blessing because it gives the picture a comradely feeling, like a home movie made with friends by one of them who has some equipment, knows the craft, and gets fun from both film and his fellows, the teenage Glaswegians of whom he had recently been one. I've seen a number of American student films through the years that were more polished than *That Sinking Feeling*, but few of them had this vicarial sense—that it was made by the one of the group who was a filmmaker.

It's a slight piece of work, and ought to be. It's about a robbery planned and executed by some bored and frustrated adolescents. (Or are the adjectives superfluous?) They think they can get money to help them with their boredom and frustration through a heist of stainless steel sinks from a warehouse. They manage to get away with a van load, but the only money they realize comes from an art dealer. One of the youths hopes to sell five or six of the sinks to a gallery owner; a dealer comes in and sees the pile in the middle of the gallery floor and buys them as sculpture. That's the total, as one of them says, of their "ill-gotten drains."

It would be ponderous to view this as a story of juvenile crime. It's a juvenile crime fantasy, a comedy acted out by the fantasists and filmed by someone who isn't long past that kind of fantasizing himself. The film's chief residual interest is that it fills a gap in our knowledge of a man on his way to being a considerable regional filmmaker. (Forsyth has already finished his fourth film, also set in Glasgow.) Still, on a bleak winter night you could get some warmth from this agreeable eighty-two-minute hand-knitted film.

Comfort and Joy

(November 12, 1984)

Bill Forsyth is the Dr. Feelgood of film. He doesn't shoot us full of Movieland happy dust: he tells the truth, but it's about what he loves in people—surely as true as what he and we dislike in our species. This Scotsman makes his films about a Glasgow (and environs) where sanity consists in seeing how ridiculous even hopelessness is; once that's realized, considerable pleasure and manageable pain can be had out of daily life.

The great merit of his latest, *Comfort and Joy*, is that it's a big-budget picture, by Forsyth standards, and it's just as casual as the first two. He's been knocked for this by some commentators. For me, the pleasure in *Comfort and Joy* is precisely its nonchalance about plot: some things happen to the hero, and he proceeds through them, that's all. The two major events are only abstractly connected. But the man himself is seen so affectionately that all I wanted was to spend more time with him. Ultimately, that's what the picture comes to, spending time with this fellow, with just enough story to show Forsyth winking at story requirements. And what makes it even neater is that he directs the same way he writes—with all the skill that he needs and no compulsion to prove that he has it.

His hero is a thirtyish Glasgow disc jockey, chatty, well-liked in the city. He is played by Bill Paterson, impeccably. Paterson looks like a reticent Scottish cousin of Christopher Plummer, and he earns the corniest critical comment: he doesn't seem to be acting. Forsyth may have shaped the part to fit the actor (whom I've never seen before): if so, this was a good idea for both of them because together they give the role cautious vigor, accessible tenderness, reluctant anger.

The film opens in a Glasgow department store on Christmas Eve, with a surprise that's a perfect opening chord for what follows. It prepares us for the next development: Paterson's girlfriend, the lovely Eleanor David, to whom he's devoted, suddenly moves out. She tells him this just after they have made love, adding that she had meant to tell him ages ago but that the occasion never arose. (One of the "travelogue" bonuses of the film is that David, like all the attractive and stylish young women in the film, speaks broad Glaswegian. This continually surprises and delights.)

So here is Paterson, at the beginning of the season of comfort and joy, bereft of the girl he loves, having to go to the radio station every morning and be cheery for a couple of hours. Lonely, he is attracted to a pretty young saleswoman in a passing ice cream van. (No explanation of why there are ice cream vans on the Glasgow streets in late December.) In his red sports car Paterson follows the van until it parks in a lonely spot, then buys a cone. He's about to eat it when two men in ski masks drive up and beat in the windows of the van with iron bars. (One of the van vandals recognizes the petrified Paterson as the disc jokey and asks for an autograph before he speeds away.) It turns out there is an ice cream war in Glasgow between two factions, that all the participants are Italian, and that behind it all is a *capo* who is, to plunder Wallace Stevens, "the emperor of ice cream."

The story is too simple to be explained. I note only two elements. The rival gangs want Paterson to serve as peace emissary between them. He demurs, and they force him into it. How? They leave a dozen ice cream cones upside down on the front seat of his car. That's Forsyth's idea of mob violence. And his Italians, who speak Italian among themselves, speak broad Glaswegian to Paterson. I couldn't help remembering the way Woody Allen treated Italians in *Broadway Danny Rose*. Allen mocked, expecting to be forgiven because he also mocked himself. Forsyth chuckles. Forgiveness doesn't enter into it.

A couple of glitches. A comic scene with a psychiatrist is just one more comic scene with a psychiatrist. A radio executive, speaking of a contract, uses the phrase "sanity clause," which, especially at Christmastime, is misunderstood. Isn't this a lift from Chico in *A Night at the Opera*? ("There ain't no sanity clause.")

But then there are the squabbles among the hulking sons of the *capo* about choice bits of cake when they stop for coffee. And there is Paterson walking across the huge garage floor of an ice cream company, passing two men who are recording a jingle to be played over the vans' speakers. One man tinkles the chimes, and the man next to him purses up his mouth and says, "Helloo, folks!"—just as Paterson passes en route to a gang meeting. I could watch moments like that for a long time.

I hope Forsyth keeps his word about never making films outside his home territory. I hope he keeps on being casual. The Scots have a word, "pawky," which the Concise Oxford defines as "drily humorous." I hope Forsyth keeps on being pawky.

Rainer Werner Fassbinder

(July 12, 1982)

The death of Rainer Werner Fassbinder on June 10, at the age of thirty-six, was of course shocking; and soon it brought a second shock. The first one doesn't need explaining. (It was heightened by the suggestion of suicide. As I write, the autopsy result isn't known.*) The second shock is the realization—really comprehending the fact—that his career is over.

Not all of Fassbinder's forty-one feature-length films have been shown here. Approximately thirty have had American release, of which I've seen about half. But a key element in seeing them was that, up to now, each new Fassbinder film was a sort of installment, a message from someone who sent messages continually. No modern director except the Godard of the 1960s has given us an equivalent "diary" feeling; the cascade of Fassbinder films kept us informed of his emotional-political-social-esthetic whereabouts as he kept moving. The quality of a new Fassbinder film was something like the latest stockmarket quotation on his talent, not to be engraved in marble any more than today's Stock Exchange listings, but to be "read" against the last quotation and the future possibilities of the enterprise. Part of the excitement or pleasure or anger or tedium with any of his films was the knowledge that we were already out of date on Fassbinder as we watched it. No new work by a living artist is taken as the last word on him, but with Fassbinder the sense of "To Be Continued" was exceptionally pertinent: what was running through the projector was less a finished work than a strophe of ebulliently unfinished activity.

Now that feeling is gone. An end exists; the career is shaped. Now each Fassbinder film—those we haven't yet seen, those we see again—will lack that extraordinary ingredient. They may seem better or worse or much the same, still it will be something of a shock to see them as works by a dead man.

I offer no obituary accounting of his career. At least one reason to refrain is that several of his most recent films are yet to arrive here, including *Berlin Alexanderplatz*, from the famous Döblin novel, and *Lola*, derived from *The Blue Angel*. But it's possible now to see more objectively the Fassbinder aura, the heat rays of an odd, odd-looking, obsessed, variously tormented man, ripping through the theater into film, where he continued to rip. He once denied that sequence, by the way: he said that he had gone from film into the theater, because he had made two short films (in 1965 and 1966) before he joined a theater group. But this is no more relevant, substantively, than the fact that Eisenstein and Welles did some film work early in their theater careers; all three men went through theater into film. In 1967 Fassbinder entered the Action-Theater, performing in a Munich basement, and worked as actor, director, and playwright. (I first saw his name in 1969, when he was twenty-four and listed by

---

*On June 18th, the Munich prosecutor's office said that Fassbinder "had probably died of an overdose of sleeping pills and cocaine."

the [London] *Times Literary Supplement* as one of Germany's promising dramatists.) He was rarely interested in anything but attacking the givens of the form in which he worked; his theater group was devoted to "anti-theater." Presumably he moved into film in 1969—though he continued to do some theater work—because he could shape more elements there with more expedient idiosyncrasy.

In a film about filming, *Beware of a Holy Whore* (1970), Fassbinder himself played the production manager of the film-within-the-film, and at one point he said, "The one thing I acknowledge is despair." Later he made a film out of Nabokov, called *Despair*. Oddly, both these facts flashed into my head while I was reading the sickening news.

Lola

(August 2, 1982)

The past tense now, for Rainer Werner Fassbinder. He had developed several distinct styles in his work, which he never mixed; there was no overlap of methods among, say, *The Bitter Tears of Petra von Kant* and *Jail Bait* and *Effi Briest*. Still another Fassbinder style was his homage to Douglas Sirk in the latter's *hoch* Hollywood vein. Sirk may have appealed to Fassbinder because, under Hitler's rise, he worked in Germany—his real name was Detlef Sierck—as a theater director of serious plays, many of them classics, and a maker of films that included Ibsen's *Pillars of Society*; and after Hitler he returned to work of this kind in Germany. While Sirk was in Hollywood, he mastered the "magazine" film—*All I Desire*, *Magnificent Obsession*, *Written on the Wind*—and it's possible that Fassbinder, eager for heterodoxy, was drawn by the fact that a classical director could take on the work of lesser Hollywood craftsmen and beat them at their game. Without ever going to Hollywood, Fassbinder, too, apparently wanted to enjoy working in the "magazine" vein, to share the admired Sirk's experience, to delight some of his own devotees and horrify others, and simply to practice another kind of filmmaking.

Lili Marleen, made last year, was done à la Sirk—lush look, *schmerz*-packed twisty plot, and all. This year Fassbinder made *Lola*, just arrived, which is an odd mixture. Stylistically, it, too, is made à la Sirk, full of blue and red overlays on scenes, with the camera often gazing "open-mouthed" at big emotional scenes, as between bites of popcorn. But the source of *Lola* is no novelette, it's *The Blue Angel*, Josef von Sternberg's 1930 film whose script was derived by Sternberg—or by Carl Zuckmayer, says Zuckmayer—from Heinrich Mann's novel *Professor Unrat*. So the homage to Sirkian Hollywood is complicated this time, as if a good composer decided to write a score à la Sigmund Romberg with themes from Ravel.

Fassbinder's *Lola* is set in Coburg (in his native Bavaria) in the 1950s. The principals are an energetic, rich, and crooked building contractor; his mistress, who is also a singer and prostitute in the plush local cabaret; and a newcomer, a solid honest man about fifty who is the new building commissioner. Two analogies with *The Blue Angel*: the honest commissioner falls in love with a woman—before he knows her profession—who causes a moral declension in his life; the woman is not designedly vicious, she is simply true to her nature.

Stylistically, *Lola* has no relation to Sternberg, and there is only one echo of his symbolism. When Lola and the commissioner are walking in the country one day, he proposes and she accepts. It rains, and they take shelter in a barn; she climbs to the hayloft, stretches out, and says she has a present for him. Later, when the commissioner is walking in the country with Lola's little girl (child of the crooked contractor), they go into the same barn. The child climbs to the loft and, quite innocently, stretches out in the same place. We know, though the commissioner does not, that the contractor has bought the cabaret and has given it to Lola with the provision that it go to the child when she reaches twenty-one. Sternberg might have used that idea, though he certainly would have photographed it differently.

Lola doesn't opt for the character complexity of *The Blue Angel* any more than for its style. It opens and closes with a still of Adenauer; a black American soldier (a Fassbinder icon of that era) lives in the commissioner's boarding-house but this film is no anatomy of the years of the *Wirtschaftswunder*. It could have been set in the 1920s or 1970s. It's a deliberately superficial, easy-flowing narrative—generally predictable, whether or not one knows the source—asking you to be a movie-watcher, getting fun from a movie. What keeps it from being a Sirk imitation or a mere parade of Movieland figures is the quality of the acting. Barbara Sukowa, of *Marianne and Juliane,** is Lola. She can sing well and ought to have been dubbed; she doesn't have allure comparable to Marlene Dietrich's. (Who has? Not even Liv Ullmann in comparable scenes in *The Serpent's Egg*). But she is a vivid actress, with flamboyance and reserve, and she has a "transparent" face with which the actress can reveal what the character is concealing. Mario Adorf, the Swiss actor who has been a burly blast of energy in German films since 1954, is excellent as the contractor, a man with confidence in both his shrewdness and his immorality, who laughs a good deal, especially when opposed, because he can foresee victorious maneuver. He never hits anyone in the film, but we feel that he knows he could and doesn't need to. And Armin Mueller-Stahl plays the commissioner with relaxed yet forceful presence, with a modest sense of his own maturity. Mueller-Stahl made over sixty films in East Germany and moved to West Germany in 1980.

So . . . here's the first Fassbinder film I've seen since his death, and the experience is much as I expected it to be—a feeling of historical inquiry rather than contemporary report.

---

*See p. 148.

Berlin Alexanderplatz

(August 8, 1983)

Rainer Werner Fassbinder made *Berlin Alexanderplatz* in 1980, backed by the West German and Italian television networks. It runs fifteen hours and twenty-one minutes: thirteen parts of about an hour each with an epilogue of almost two hours. Each part begins and ends with credits, as for a TV series, but Fassbinder thought of the work as a film; it was shown at the Venice Film Festival (after its German TV première); it will be shown as a five-part film in New York, Los Angeles, and San Francisco, with series tickets available for five three-hour visits to the theater. Arrangements for other cities are to follow. (I and others sat in a screening room for two days from 9:30 a.m. until about 6:00 p.m. with a half-hour lunch break.) Obviously a work of this unique length raises unique critical questions, about which more later.

Berlin Alexanderplatz is based on the well-known novel by Alfred Döblin, published in 1929, translated into English by Eugene Jolas in 1931, and available in paperback from Ungar. (For some reason, the two words of the title were reversed in English. As with many foreign novels, this book needs a new translation which it is not likely to get.) Döblin (1878-1957) was a Berlin physician and psychiatrist who practiced in the Alexanderplatz vicinity and who wrote copiously all his life. He was born a Jew and became a Catholic; he was politically radical and eventually altered his views. Until that alteration, Bertolt Brecht considered Döblin a teacher and friend. In the mid-1920s when Brecht was evolving his ideas of epic theater, he wrote to Döblin, "It is really only a question of finding a form that will make possible on the stage whatever it is that differentiates your novels from those of Mann!" Yet it was Mann who helped the refugee Döblin to get some screenwriting work at M-G-M in 1940. After the war Döblin returned to Europe and continued to write, but with diminished stature.

The title *Berlin Alexanderplatz* is hint enough of the book's intent: it depicts the teeming life in and around the square (now in East Berlin). The common observation is that the novel shows the influence of *Ulysses*, but, in translation at any rate, this is not perceptible. It is a book of wide embrace in style as well as material, using realistic narrative, naturalistic probe, "choric" interlude, lyric surge, interweavings of contemporary statistics and news stories, and more—to create a universe. The part titles and frequent aphoristic subheadings suggest Brecht, as do some presentational sections; the use of factual material—sometimes contextually relevant, sometimes grotesquely juxtaposed—suggests Dos Passos. Walter Benjamin, no wholehearted admirer of Döblin, called the novel a "thieves' *Education Sentimentale*."

Fassbinder had long been enamored of the novel. Many leading characters in his other films are named Franz, like Döblin's protagonist; the role that Fassbinder himself played in *Fox and His Friends* bears the protagonist's full name, Franz Biberkopf. Fassbinder of course wrote his own screen adaptation of Döblin's book and strove to suggest the complex prose texture while centering on a flow of images. Very often in the film, at least three things are going on: the scene as we see and hear it, a voice (Fassbinder's) commenting like a divine observer of the scene between the bits of dialogue, and the interpolation of aphorisms—further complicated by the English subtitles for the German dialogue. And, of course, music. (The extremely helpful score by Peer Raben combines his own work and contemporary songs.) The result may sound messy, but it's rich. Only when the English translations of the aphorisms are flashed on the white backgrounds used for those inserts is there difficulty. Fassbinder has done his best to transmute Döblin into film. His best is modified only by the nature of the second medium and by the nature of Fassbinder's temperament.

The story begins in 1927. Franz Biberkopf, a laborer, is released from Tegel prison where he has served four years for the unpremeditated killing of a woman named Ida who had lived with him. When the prison gates open, the roar of Berlin blasts in and frightens him. (Döblin's line, flashed on the screen: "The punishment begins.") A guard calms Franz and helps him through the gate, but it takes some time for panic and phantasmagoria to subside. They never quite leave him.

Berlin is full of poverty and politics, vice and crime. We move with Franz through the next year or so as he settles into his old lodgings, rejoins his old circle of friends, most of whom are unemployed and some of whom are on the shady side, has some love affairs including three (serial) live-in companions, tries various pathetic peddling jobs, then joins occasionally in the ventures of a gang of warehouse thieves. Through it all, he is rather placid and tolerant, his prevailing amiability splotched from time to time by fits of torpor or fierce rage that seem more connected with mental instability than with spiritual canker.

In the course of one robbery, he is thrown out of a speeding van by a fellow-thief named Reinhold as a means of stopping what they think is a pursuing car. The accident costs Franz his right arm. But he is markedly unvindictive: he feels that hatred won't bring his arm back, and he has the unintellectualized conviction that Reinhold is as much a pawn of social circumstance as himself. Franz continues his generally pacific way, scraping by financially, is adored by his landlady (a character added by Fassbinder) even though she had witnessed the murder of Ida, is subject to dreams and fits, and floats through the political turmoil between Nazis and Communists, dabbling on both sides without understanding either, just as chance or employment dictates. Only two factors are constant: his fondness for drink and his attraction for women.

Döblin, not for the first or last time in art, shows how a society can affect the moral spectrum, then depicts his hero behaving by the best standards available within the revised spectrum. Franz, though in fact a murderer and a thief, thinks of himself as a good man, as do his friends.

The intricate story builds to two chief elements: his affair with Mieze, a young woman who adores him, who becomes a prostitute in order to support him and whose love, within the work's moral spectrum, must be called joyfully innocent; and his relation with Reinhold, the man who cost him his arm. The moral relativism of the work is taken further with events between Mieze and a woman named Eva, then between Mieze and Reinhold.

Mieze loves Franz so much that she wants them to have a child. She is barren, so she asks Eva, a high-class whore who has long loved Franz, to bear his child for them. Eva agrees, as does Franz—to Mieze's exultation. (Much later, Eva miscarries.)

Reinhold, who had previously handed on a couple of women to Franz, eventually meets Mieze; determines to seduce her; contrives to get her to the woods outside Berlin. In a long scene that is one of the best in both book and film, the pair go through a kaleidoscopic emotional struggle that ends with his strangling her. To escape, Reinhold gets himself arrested under a false name for a minor crime. Franz, when he hears of Mieze's death, is mentally stricken and is hospitalized. In time, the killing is tracked to Reinhold and he is tried; Franz, released from the hospital, is present at the trial, somewhat numbed, but free of hate. Within the story's aberrant moral scale, Franz and Reinhold can be seen as the Chosen Good and the Chosen Evil. Other views of their relationship are also inherent in the work, and Fassbinder, as we'll see, explores them.

Franz, in both book and film, carries, I think, an extra cultural charge. One might assume from all the above that he is some sort of conventionally good-looking man. In fact he weighs two hundred pounds, is paunchy and plain. As I watched Günter Lamprecht in the role, I got a sense of reciprocity between a nation's life and its art. Lamprecht kept reminding me of Emil Jannings, the idol of German stage and film. In the Germany of that day, Jannings was an actor of considerable sexual appeal because, as usual when that happens, he embodied various idealizations for both sexes. I think it quite possible that Jannings, just as much as the Berliners of the Alexanderplatz, served as partial model for Franz in Döblin's mind. Films figure in the book; Döblin must have known Jannings well. And, as with many another twentieth-century novelist, a film figure may have helped to crystallize what Döblin was trying to "assemble" from observed life—especially since that figure was a popular vicar for much of that life. For us to be reminded of Jannings by Lamprecht may thus be the fulfillment of a circle. (An earlier film of Döblin's novel, directed by Piel Jutzi in 1931—a normal length film—had Heinrich George as Franz, an actor of Jannings's size but not his power or appeal.) The Franz whom we see, uniting (I believe) a bygone film figure, a novelist's view of that figure against a metropolitan tapestry, and a modern filmmaker's appreciation of all these qualities, is a particularly striking cultural avatar.

Excepting most of the epilogue, the film contains little that is not in the novel or is not patently derived from it. Fidelity sometimes even takes the film to the edge of the tedious, as in a Salvation Army sequence. But Fassbinder, while keeping extraordinary faith with the book, has nonetheless shifted tones and colors, sometimes risking the ludicrous.

That shift is from the novelist's general objectivity to subjectivity much of the time. Döblin shows Franz as one figure, the figure on whom he happens to be concentrating, in a whirling world; Fassbinder shows us Franz, preeminently, with the world whirling around him. In Part Eleven, for instance, there's a quarrel between Franz and Mieze which ends with both of them screaming and with his beating of her. In the novel the scene occurs in a couple of pages of prose, in different styles with differing immediacies, all intended to "contain" the scene within the book's tone. Fassbinder gives us the quarrel straight on and hot, with two actors on all fours screaming at each other, followed by Franz's savage beating of Mieze. The worst instances of intrusive subjectivity are the many reprises, including frequent flashbacks to Ida's murder, scenes that are superfluous to the film's dynamics and, oddly enough, are unfair to its peculiar morality. If Franz is truly haunted by that killing, then the morality of the film is out of kilter. My argument is not that a novel may not be adapted for cinematic purposes but that Fassbinder often strays from his implicit intent to be faithful to the book's very essences.

But whatever his choices in tone—and again excepting most of the epilogue—Fassbinder directs with mastery. Three qualities shine in his directing: composition, traversal, apt distance. Often he composes frames with an object large in the foreground and with details in progressive planes to give the screen depth—an approach he learned from one of his idols, Josef von Sternberg. (No coincidence: a few times the near object is a birdcage, as in the first sequence of *The Blue Angel*.) Fassbinder makes his camera traverse—circling, tracking characters, closing in to intensify—as if to suggest that each moment is important but that each moment is also a step on a long journey. And he has an acute feeling for distance, when to keep away and let the scene reach us. The long scene in the forest between Reinhold and Mieze, the scene that ends in her death, is done mostly in long shots. This doesn't quite reproduce the effect of Döblin's prose—if it did, the whole film should be in long shots—but, seen at that distance, the grim sequence becomes an event in the history of the world.

Even when I was not completely held—and what film could grip continuously for fifteen hours?—I was aware that the film and I were in good hands. (One odd point, however: perhaps it was a concession to TV, but the sex in the film is always consummated by people who keep their clothes on.) Obviously connected with Fassbinder's mastery is the quality of the acting. Not one of the many actors is anything but good, and some of them are marvelous. The role of Franz is prodigious, and Günter Lamprecht fulfills it with no hint of strain. His face doesn't have the ambiguities, the explorability of Jannings's, but he has the same gigantic presence, conveys the same sense that the huge frame itself contains a theater within which a drama is playing.

Gottfried John, more "conventionally" large, is the stuttering, crafty

Reinhold, craftily creating the nether, complementary territory of this moral world.

Mieze was Barbara Sukowa's second film role. She had made her screen debut in a Hungarian film (not shown in the United States) after nine years in the theater. Then came *Berlin Alexanderplatz*, which she followed with her fiery revolutionary in von Trotta's *Marianne and Juliane** and her excellent neo-Dietrich in Fassbinder's version of *The Blue Angel* called *Lola*. Sukowa is a wonderful Mieze, all the more wonderful if you have seen the subsequent pictures first. The outbursts of girlish happiness, the gratitude, the happy female subservience (a strong theme in the film) are all very moving. Few film acting careers anywhere promise more for us than Sukowa's.

Hanna Schygulla, the best known of Fassbinder's regular acting group because of *Effi Briest* and *The Marriage of Maria Braun* and *Lili Marleen*, plays Eva, and I regret that I haven't given more space to this important role. As the luxe tart who lives with a lover, rents herself elegantly, but is nonpossessively devoted to Franz, Schygulla is not just completely credible, she is lovely.

At least a few other excellent actors must, in decency, be specified: Elisabeth Trissenaar, as Polish Lina (not as plump as Lina is in the book), the first of Franz's "steadies" after prison; Hark Böhm, as her treacherous "uncle"; Franz Buchrieser, as the taciturn, loyal Meck, a workman corrupted by unemployment into crime; Claus Wirt, as the wing-collared barman of Franz's *lokal*, who has avuncular truth that grows quietly through the film.

The art direction by Harry Baer, who often acted for Fassbinder (he was the boy in *Jail Bait*), catches what Fassbinder apparently wanted: a combination of Sternberg and Lang. He provides a Sternberg décor so detailed, no matter how impoverished the dwelling, that it's almost like a journey into the interior of a life. (But I didn't understand the clump of machinery—a printing press?—in a corner of Franz's lodgings. Why?) And he gives us Berlin streets with Lang's combination of the real and the theatrical, along with numerous odd lodgings and hideaways located downstairs—we descend to them.

Xaver Schwarzenberger, the cinematographer, worked on 16mm film with contradictory results. Sometimes the color is syrupy (it's never first-rate) and the figures slightly soft; but the subtlety of the lighting and the large compositions—amusement halls, for instance—are extraordinary for 16mm and also imply the technical superiority of European television, a matter of finer screen lines.

The major flaw of the film is the epilogue. (Imagine—a film so long that a section of about an hour can be discussed as a flaw.) Fassbinder called it "My Dream of Franz Biberkopf's Dream": it's a fantasia on Franz's fantasies during his stay in the asylum after Mieze's death. Fassbinder devises variations on many of the scenes and themes of the film, as a cadenza in a concerto offers

---

*See p. 148.

variations on themes in the preceding movement. (And the cadenza used to be improvised by the performer.) But the results are as rank and lurid and vacuously symbolic as the worst of latter-day Pasolini, as precious as Fassbinder's own last film *Querelle*. Fassbinder believed of Franz and Reinhold that they were "two men whose little lives on this earth are destroyed because they never get the opportunity to muster up the courage even to recognize, much less to be able to admit to themselves, that they desire one another in an unusual way." Certainly a basis for this view exists as one component of the work, particularly in the way that Reinhold passes on women to Franz—a common enough index of suppressed homosexuality—in the way that Franz forgives Reinhold for the loss of his arm and that Reinhold is stupefied into helpfulness, in the way that at the last Reinhold must have and destroy the woman who loves Franz the most.

But the very fact that Fassbinder had to invent and insert the epilogue to underscore this theme is a proof of lopsidedness. The body of the work itself would not permit this skewing: Fassbinder had to create a quite separate commentary, intended to throw a retrospective light on the (nearly) finished film. Döblin's careful calibration of a moral scale, his juxtaposition of circumstances with causes ("We all lie under the same ax," says Döblin), are shouldered aside by emphasis on *one* of the elements between the two men.

Among the many dream episodes, psychosexual and *religioso*, in the epilogue, are a boxing match between Franz and Reinhold that ends with their kissing each other; a closeup of Reinhold, bleeding, with a crown of thorns; a long shot of Reinhold crucified with the Mushroom Cloud billowing behind him as we hear jazz, followed by a crooner singing "Silent Night." I don't want to give more details because I don't want the epilogue, abysmal as it is, to seem to outweigh the value of the huge work that precedes it.

At any event, just as a cadenza journeys to the conclusion already written by the composer, this epilogue ends with the novel's finish, Franz working as a watchman in a factory. His life is now continent and dull. Society has punished him into blandness and rewarded him with a job.

We come at last to the questions raised at the outset, one question really: How long is a film? Put aside short films as quite a different subject. Put aside Syberberg's seven-hour *Our Hitler*, my previous longest experience, because it was a "documentary" rhapsody on historical motifs. Fassbinder is working in fiction, and we are all conditioned by the fiction-film conventions of our time. All our present ideas of narrative structure, character development, pace, and completion are bound up with films of 90 and 120 minutes. A few of them run an hour or so longer. (Sixty years ago they usually ran only one hour or so in entirety.) Our conscious and unconscious instruments of appreciation are tuned to experience in the 90 to 120 minute range. Kenneth Burke says somewhere that form is the arousal and satisfaction of expectation; and our arousal of expectation with a film is connected to satisfaction within a time-frame that had its origins in the theater.

Fassbinder attacks that theatrical expectation and invites us to replace it with the expectation we have for the novel. If you call *Berlin Alexanderplatz* only a TV mini-series shown in a clump, you merely dodge the esthetic problem. A mini-series shown in a clump (I've sampled one) looks exactly like that. Fassbinder had a different goal. It's not merely that his directing is better than most TV direction. Most TV direction seems to reach the tiny screen gasping at its good luck in getting that far and finishing its job. Fassbinder's direction is only utilizing TV, as a means of getting this giant job done, as a means of making a giant *film*. The head of West German TV programming, Günter Rohrbach, one of the film's backers and a Fassbinder champion, insists on the future of what he calls the "amphibious" film, one equally suited to showing on the little and on the large screen. Europe has given us a number of such good works in the last decade or so. *Berlin Alexanderplatz* is only (only!) the longest of them. But by its daring, it attacks the very bases of our film expectations. True, so true that it's a truism, the intrinsics of film structure often resemble the novel much more than the drama, but the exterior has still had theatrical "shape." That, and all that grows from it, is what Fassbinder has attacked.

To see *Berlin Alexanderplatz* is to experience, right from the start, a sensation of danger, of venture. A film is going to take time (the phrase acquires a new meaning): take time to explore character, evoke themes, delineate architecture. I felt both excitement and the sense of settling in for a long haul, heightened by the fact that the frame-by-frame skills are those that would be used for a good picture of conventional length. (The opposite of the journeyman knitting needles of Masterpiece Theater.) The sense of launching into new "space" was greater than any space picture has given me.

"Immensity," said Gaston Bachelard, "is a philosophical category of daydream. Daydream undoubtedly feeds on all kinds of sights, but through a sort of natural inclination, it contemplates grandeur." The daydream of film has been extending its ideas of immensity since the turn of the century. Fassbinder has pushed the boundaries further. I am scarcely eager for a flood of fifteen-hour films — not unless the span of healthy, active life can be trebled to accommodate them. But Fassbinder committed an act of mind-opening, esthetic imperialism, claiming the same time-territory for a film that we would give Döblin's 635-page novel. For thirty years or so, it has often been said, truly, of good directors that they were taking on the work of novelists. Antonioni and Bresson and Bergman and Ozu did that work within time precincts set by the theater. The real value of Fassbinder's imperialism may lie in this: *whether or not* most films grow to be much longer, his action may affect the ways that the best filmmakers and the best audiences come to consider all films.

Blade Runner

(July 19 & 26, 1982)

It's always been staggering to think of the sheer quantity of talent, craft, brains and ingenuity in Hollywood. From the beginnings, some seventy years ago, the film colony has had as high a concentration of those qualities as, proportionately, any center on earth. The level of abilities, allowing for one exception, has been Olympian. That exception is, obviously, the core matter, the *raison d'être*. But, aside from the purpose of it all—the usual level of the films themselves—Hollywood has been almost unremittingly marvelous in technique and in art. The scene and costume design, the photography, the photographic devices and effects, the sound recording and mixing have set a mark for the world.

Blade Runner, though all its achievements are used for a dull and silly film, is crammed with wonderful achievement. It's set in Los Angeles, 2019. The streets are extremely crowded, with people, vehicles, and mountainous buildings crowding in. The light is always heavy, as if the whole city were under a dome; fierce rain is frequent. The air is thick with floating electric billboards that sail by with gigantic "TV commercials," most of them featuring smiling Japanese women. Police cars are Hovercraft that land and take off vertically. The atmosphere is claustrophobic, the environment technologically saturated.

My first reaction was that privacy was virtually gone. Privacy has already become, in our time, the most expensive commodity in urban life, and by 2019, the streets are choking; even apartments, except for one tycoon's residence, are cluttered, as if people feel uneasy with roominess. The Space Age has brought, in personal reaction, an aversion to space.

In older sci-fi films, such as *Things to Come* (1936), cities of the future were airy and ennobling, with the feeling of the East Building of the National Gallery of Art in Washington. Not in *Blade Runner*.

It's all superbly done. The director, Ridley Scott, maker of *The Duellists* and *Alien*, is better known for his visual interests than for anything else; here he has outdone himself. No posings, no imitations of paintings, but the creation of a new "fabric." His chief associates were the industrial designer, Syd Mead, the production designer, Lawrence G. Paull, the art director, David Snyder, and Douglas Trumbull, the magician of special effects for *Close Encounters of the Third Kind* and many other films. The cinematographer was Jordan Croneweth, who has lighted to emphasize intrusion and encroachment: peering searchlights or creeping crepuscular tones that seem to struggle against the dark. That lighting emphasizes the honeycomb surface of many of the walls, so that we sometimes feel trapped inside a gargantuan Louise Nevelson sculpture.

To enjoy *Blade Runner*, you need only disregard, as far as possible, the actors and dialogue. (And the score. Vangelis, who did the sensationally successful music for *Chariots of Fire*, here contributes mostly wind and goo.) The script is another reworking of a threat to humans by humanoids—one more variation on the *Invasion of the Body Snatchers* theme. A blade runner—an unexplained phrase and a clumsy title—is a secret policeman assigned to detect and kill these humanoids. The chief BR here is Harrison Ford, which is confusing because he always strikes me as a humanoid himself. But except for its reason for being, *Blade Runner* is splendid, a strong argument for the Style is All thesis.

Fitzcarraldo

(October 18, 1982)

What are films *for?* Every interesting director has found an answer to that question. In fact, one distinction between interesting directors and others is the awareness of that question, the need to answer it. Hundreds of directors have made enjoyable films, as relatively unquestioning competent journeymen. But film swerves out of the mainstream, out of its several mainstreams, when a director wants to answer that question. The attempt doesn't always exalt him: Robert Altman kept trying to answer it and, mostly, failed pretentiously. The reverse is truer: no first-class film is not the result of that inquiry.

The German director Werner Herzog, now forty, has made films of fluctuating quality, but he has never done anything other than ask that question. His reply is unique. Film, to him, means danger. Not danger as a subject necessarily, but physical risk for himself and for at least some of his collaborators in the making of the film. A few examples: *Fata Morgana* was shot in the Sahara where, says John Sandford in *The New German Cinema*, "he and his crew encountered floods and sand-storms and were repeatedly thrown into crowded, rat-infested jails on suspicion of being mercenaries." *La Soufrière* was made on the slopes of that Guadeloupe volcano when Herzog had learned it might erupt and had hurried there. *Heart of Glass* was made, after a trip in open boats, to some small and rocky islands in the Atlantic off Ireland. For *Aguirre, Wrath of God*, Herzog took some five hundred people deep into the mountainous jungles of Peru. Compared with Herzog's career, previously celebrated difficulties, like John Huston's problems on location with *The African Queen* or Stroheim's problems with the Death Valley sequence of *Greed*, seem nursery tales.

Around such a figure as Herzog, stories are bound to accrue: threats of murder (by him) when others threatened to quit, threats of self-maiming or suicide as proof of earnestness. I don't know how many of the stories are true; perhaps all of them. The key point about the stories, about the career, is that Herzog is not remotely concerned with adventure in the old-fashioned, swashbuckling, open-shirted sense. His answer to the question of purpose goes deeper. Almost impatiently, he ingests all the acceptances about the film form: its additions to the vocabulary of realism, its flexibility of place, its playfulness with time, its transmutation of inanimate objects into performers. All these mysteries, still mysterious to many of us, are to Herzog only initial matters, known territory beyond which he must explore. For him, film has become a means of going to the edge of mortality itself, a physical test of the metaphysical, a way of looking past existence and perhaps coming back. Film being what it is, he can't venture alone, but he has obviously found some who will follow, some of them more than once, some who share his basic drive. Filmmaking is generally too easy, too easily powerful, he seems to say; he wants his films to look as if they had been wrested from death.

He wants, in short, to be a saint—if necessary, a martyr. He wants to prove that his life means less to him than film; film is the place left to him in our world where he can put the risk of his life at the service of others.

If he is mad, nothing is clarified by saying so. Is Thomas Mauch, his wonderful cinematographer, mad as well? And the other gifted Herzog colleagues? The test is not whether we, or anyone else, would do what they do but that they do it and, having done it, show why they thought it must be done. Herzog's films bring us images we cannot have seen before (like the opening and closing sequences of *Aguirre*): not travelogues of the remote but visions of the remote in us. Rilke's most famous line is the end of his poem about the archaic torso of Apollo: its beauty says: "You must change your life." Herzog's films, uneven and inconclusive as they sometimes are, ultimately say: "Open. Life is not knowing and controlling. Life is trembling."

His latest film is *Fitzcarraldo*, and much has been bruited about the making of it. PBS has already shown, twice, a condensed version of a documentary about the making of *Fitzcarraldo*. Here are just a few of the pertinent facts. Like *Aguirre*, the picture was made mostly in the remote mountains of Peru, took almost five years to complete, and ran into all the logistic and health and technical problems that could be foreseen, plus many that were unforeseen, plus many other difficulties. Not far from the base camp, Peru and Ecuador were engaged in border strife. The local Indians made trouble; eventually an armed band surrounded the camp, forced the film people out, and burned the camp to the ground. A new base camp had to be built 1,500 miles to the south, amongst different Indians with whom friendly relations were first established.

There were sheerly filmic troubles. From the start Jack Nicholson had been in mind for the leading role; after two-and-a-half years of preproduction work, he bowed out. Warren Oates was tapped but never actually signed a contract; four weeks before shooting was to begin, Oates decided against it. After a two-month delay, shooting started with Jason Robards in the lead and with Mick Jagger in an important supporting role. After almost half the film had been shot, Robards contracted amoebic dysentery, flew back to America, and sent word that his doctors forbade him to return. The delays caused Mick Jagger to drop out because of previous commitments. Herzog called Jagger's departure "the biggest loss I've had in my career" and didn't even try to replace him: he eliminated the Jagger role. After a further two months, Herzog signed Klaus

Kinski for the title part. Kinski had been the protagonist of three previous Herzog films, including *Aguirre*, so he was familiar with Herzog terrain, figuratively and literally. The picture was then made. The one major player who was in it from start to finish was Claudia Cardinale. (The final version is in German; Cardinale, like all the Hispanic Peruvians and most of the Indians, is dubbed in German.)

The story is simple but wild. Early in this century an Irish adventurer named Brian Sweeney Fitzgerald — called Fitzcarraldo for Hispanic ease — is active in Peru, making and losing money. His specialty is attempting the impossible: his biggest previous venture was an (aborted) TransAndean Railway. Fitzcarraldo is passionate about Italian opera. His current dream is to build an opera house in Iquitos, a river port 1,600 miles up the Amazon, and open it with an appearance by Caruso, whom he adores and whose records accompany him everywhere. To raise money for his theater, Fitzcarraldo has an idea that is appositely extreme: he will collect rubber from a large area that is untouched because inaccessible. To get that rubber, for reasons I won't detail, means portaging a 350-ton steamboat over a wooded hill from one river to a parallel river. Fitzcarraldo borrows the initial capital from his lover, Cardinale, who is the prosperous madam of an Iquitos brothel. The steamboat is acquired, the trip upriver is made, the apprehensive Indians are enlisted (five hundred of them). They clear a road over the hill for the boat, build winches, and, helped by the boat's engine, drag it up and over into the other river. This is the main physical action of the film, and its baroque quality is underscored by our knowledge that it's being done in order, eventually, to bring Caruso to Iquitos.

The opera house is not built and Caruso is not engaged because the rubber is not gathered, for a reason that suggests the lurking triumph of the primitive over the civilized; but out of his failure, Fitzcarraldo rescues the means to make one grand closing gesture, a gesture that is in every sense operatic. The last scene confirms that three bizarre characters have joined forces for this exhilarating film: Fitzcarraldo; Kinski, who plays him; and Herzog himself.

How much does our knowledge of the facts about the making of the film affect our response to it? If Herzog had made the film in (say) Colorado with American Indians as extras, with a mock-up steamboat instead of the real thing, with Holiday Inns just out of camera range? (Articles tell us that the steamboat was actually pulled by a tractor.) It's difficult to answer that question after one knows the details, but two points are clear. Knowing the facts enhances the film; and the film would not exist, Herzog would not have made it, if he could not have done it as he did.

The result, *Fitzcarraldo* itself, is more a jagged, fascinating, beautiful, grotesque, dramatic, and hyperdramatic collection of images than an organic, consistently powerful work. I suppose that, given the circumstances, it's miraculous that it's as smooth as it is. Some of it is inexplicable. For instance, Herzog wants Sarah Bernhardt to appear in Verdi's *Ernani* with Caruso at the Manaus Opera in the opening, with a soprano in the orchestra pit singing the role while the actress mimes; why does he have a man play Bernhardt?

But despite the rough seams and emphases on lesser moments (presumably caused by lack of footage that would have helped spacing and rhythm), the film never loses its grip. Picture after picture, moving pictures, underscore the idea of difficulty, of near-impossibility, as ethics—within the film and around it.

And I'm very glad, obviously excepting Robards's illness, that the previous leading actors gave way to Kinski. Robards could have supplied Irishness in the role, on the assumption that he played in English, but he has in him these days not much more than the ability to burst into anger from time to time, unlike Kinski who carries caged and quarreling demons within him even in his happiest moments. Kinski's shock-headed haircut, his soiled but dignified white clothes, a necktie almost always (like Chaplin), his immense Panama hat, contribute to a physical icon, the figure of an emperor on the wrong planet. And Kinski has here something I've never seen in him before—motion. He is full of energy, always pressing forward, urgent, impatient. Sensitive actor that he is, he has imagined this character as dreading that bubbles will burst, that dreams will evanesce, if he doesn't hurry on. Kinski's performance, more than any other element, gives the film its kinetics.

I'd grant that on balance, if such a balance really exists, *Fitzcarraldo* can't be said to be "worth" the terrible agonies, let alone money, that it cost. Besides, as art, the work is uneasy and unfulfilled. But it's a privilege, a rare one, to see a film that, from beginning to end, shivers with passion.

Céleste

(October 25, 1982)

One of my favorite memoirs about a great artist is *Monsieur Proust* by Céleste Albaret, who was Proust's housekeeper from 1913 until his death in 1922. She was a country girl who married Proust's chauffeur, moved to Paris, and was brought into Proust's home for a few odd jobs. He responded to her with such affection that she eventually became his most trusted servant, even—as far as possible—his confidante. Céleste worshipped the ailing man and understood his consecration to his work without necessarily understanding the work itself (though Proust never patronized her). In 1972, when she was eighty-two, she dictated her memoirs of Proust to a French editor and translator named Georges Belmont because she thought it needful that the facts about Proust be known in order to explode myths and theories. Her book is no substitute for George D. Painter's masterly biography, but it's an endearing supplement.

Now from Germany—from Germany, if you please—comes a lovely film, called *Céleste*, derived from her book. Percy Adlon, a maker of documentaries for German TV, has written a script that concentrates on the last few years, and he has directed it with a sense of stillness that is gripping. Two rooms necessarily are the scene of most of the action: the kitchen, where Céleste sits waiting for Monsieur to ring for his coffee (once she has to wait so long that she dozes and falls off her chair); and the dark bedroom where she serves him, tidies his bed, helps with his asthma inhalations and responds to his gratitude with affectionate simplicity.

In a practical way, she also helps him with his writing. As we know, Proust kept adding bits to manuscripts, scribbling addenda on odd pieces of paper. Céleste devised what she called the "concertina"—she pasted the bits to the edge of the manuscript in the right places, in sections that sometimes unfolded for three feet. Principally, what's established in the film is that she knows and he knows that she is fulfilling a double role, mother and child. In manner, he always treats her as a friend who graciously assists him. When the string quartet comes to play for him (would the cellist have been a woman?), Proust sees Céleste at the door of the drawing room and invites her to come listen with him.

Adlon has directed with a vitalizing respect. Outside of a few fancy touches he has kept to a well-sustained adagio feeling, made dynamic by a conviction that he is dealing with an important moment in Western civilization. He is much helped by Jürgen Martin's exquisite lighting—for example, the very first shot in which Céleste, arms folded, sits next to the kitchen table just outside the lamplight, as if to signify that she is attending a brighter presence.

The two central performances are flawless. Jürgen Arndt plays Proust. It's the first time I've seen him except for a few small stage roles—he was in the Bavarian State Theater company that visited New York in 1966—and he is plainly an actor of inner resource and imagination. He counterpoints the two elements of physical weakness and secret strength; and we understand from Arndt that Proust is "writing" his bodily life as he is writing his novel about it, designing both to end simultaneously. Mysteries and excellencies resound from the recumbent, gently demanding figure.

Céleste is played by the wonderful young German actress, Eva Mattes, previously seen in Fassbinder's *Jail Bait*, Herzog's *Woyzeck*, and several other films. With crystal understanding, Mattes has gone straight to the core of Céleste, settled there, and has let every manifestation, vocal and physical, follow from that residence. This Céleste knows that she may not understand the complexities of Monsieur's greatness, but she understands the fact of his greatness and the honor of her place. After Monsieur's death she snips off a lock of his hair and gives it to his brother, Robert; then she snips off a lock for herself. In the last shot she looks at the wisp of hair in her hand, and her face is not in the least sorrowful. She is happy: she knows that she has been privileged and that everything has ended as it was meant to end.

Time Stands Still

(November 22, 1982)

The filmmakers in Soviet-swayed countries have long been concerned with the disaffection of young people. In the Poland of the early 1960s, Andrzej Wajda made *Innocent Sorcerers*, which got him in trouble with Gomulka; since then, the theme has recurred in East European film. Recurrently, too, these films have dealt with more than political doubt: they explore the faltering of the private hopes that public policy was intended to support. Of course Western countries know something about disaffection of their own young, but in Communist countries such disaffection was theoretically meant to be impossible. And Eastern disaffection has an added, particularly wrenching quality. Eastern European countries suffered agonies in World War II: the struggle against the Germans in several of those countries was monumentally heroic. But the sons and daughters of those heroes are not much interested in the subject. It is obtuse on their part to believe (if they do) that a Hitler victory wouldn't have made much difference in their lives, especially in the light of Nazi belief in Slavic inferiority; but apparently—to judge by films—some Eastern European young people feel, not only the universal tedium of young people about the exploits of their elders: they also feel that the bright world promised by Communism after the victory of the Germans has turned into a grim, hypocritical joke.

Time Stands Still, a Hungarian film, is the latest in this line of pictures about the unhappy young. The irony of the title, which is also the title of a song done by an aging cocktail pianist, is there before the film begins. That beginning is in 1956; then it moves to 1963, which is when most of it takes place; then it concludes in 1967; so for the young director Péter Gothár, the story has autobiographical implications. Gothár is a theater director who founded and still runs his own group outside Budapest. This is his second film (his first won the Golden Lion at Venice in 1980); his co-author on the script was Géza Bereményi.

We've seen a lot of Hungarian films that are set in 1956, or soon after, in order to criticize the present by indirection. *Time Stands Still*, even if there were no current censorship, would still take place when it does. It deals with the effect of 1956 on the children who lived through it and with their elders who fought on both sides. The opening black-and-white newsreel shots of the 1956 Budapest fighting are intercut with black-and-white sequences about some of Gothár's main characters. A resistance fighter has just ten minutes to escape after the resistance crumbles. He begs his wife and two small sons to accompany him; they refuse. Mother and sons watch from the window as he leaves. Freeze. Color and time seep into the shot; it's now 1963, and the boys are teenagers. The credits roll past, and the main story begins.

Through the amnesty of 1963 a fellow-partisan of the escaped father comes out of prison, gets a job, and lives with the boys' mother in their apartment. (This disturbs the boys not at all, as long as the newcomer doesn't interfere with their lives.) The younger son's high school teacher, an old man who is a relic of "prehistoric" humanist days, is replaced by a buxom woman in her thirties whose husband had fought on the victorious side. The tensions of 1956 persist at least to the degree that virtually everyone we meet is identified primarily by the side he or she was on during the struggle.

The center of the film is the younger son, Dini, played with sensitive dignity by Istvan Znamenák, a sort of gentler Jean-Pierre Léaud. And the center of his life, naturally, is not politics but sex and romance. It's one of Gothár's best touches that, right after the bloody opening and the credits, the next sequence is a class in social dancing for teenagers. The prettiest girl in the school, Magda (Anikó Iván), is desperate for Dini, but he doesn't really respond until she revenges herself on his coolness by sleeping with his older brother. Possibly because of his anger at her—and at his own reticence—Dini develops a crush on his new teacher. Later, at a drunken party in her apartment, drenched in the American pop music that persists throughout, with some of the students apparently high just on the excitement of drinking smuggled Coca-Cola, the teacher either does or does not give herself to Dini. It's deliberately ambiguous: she makes a move, but we don't know what actually happened, and his later accounts of it are contradictory.

Right after the party, Dini and the insistent Magda and a rebellious friend named Pierre (bitterly acted by Sándor Söth) steal a car. They mean to crash the border, but they dally at Lake Balaton for a swim, and, after other dallying, Pierre goes on alone to try his luck. Dini and Magda, reconciled, return to Budapest to see what, if anything, they can make of their lives there.

Much of the material is, on the surface, conventional rites-of-passage stuff; but close under that surface is political clutch. Very little is mere student prank or schoolroom drama. When some of the boys burst into the school after hours to vandalize it, one of the pictures thrown on the floor is a portrait of Lenin. The vice-headmaster, with shaven head, inspects students' belongings like a commissar. When Pierre interrupts the headmaster's speech over the school's p.a. system and shouts American song titles into the microphone—an action that gets him expelled—the headmaster has been speaking, not of school matters but of the seventeenth anniversary of the victory over the Axis and the consequent liberation of the workers. When Dini's mother goes to visit her boy's teacher, as any mother might when her son is troubled in school, she offers a money bribe (declined) and learns that the teacher's husband is almost mad with guilt about his role in 1956.

The script has four or five endings. The first is the parting of Pierre and the young lovers in 1963. Then we skip to New Year's Day in 1967 for a series of brief scenes to tell us what has happened to the chief characters, each of whom has settled down or settled in. The very last shot of Dini, now doing his military service but home on leave, peeing drunkenly against a wall. These scenes, like a checklist being ticked off, are supposed to support the title, I assume, to show us that, after all the hubbub, the status is still quo. For that reason those closing vignettes are in the black-and-white of 1956.

Gothár's direction has sympathy, heat, vigor. He keeps close to people without dousing us in close-ups; he integrates emotional movement with camera movement. But he's not yet secure or individual enough to avoid some strain or imitation. Blue mistiness hangs over the main (1963) portion of the film. It's related, he says, to the arrival of neon in Budapest, but that's *his* secret: the effect on the film is visually subversive, tending to soften its edges. Gothár gives us some heavy hints: when we see the buxom teacher talking to Dini in school with a tendril of her hair loose, we get the signal that something intimate is forthcoming. And Gothár has been an assiduous filmgoer. He has seen Welles (the floor-level tracking shots in the corridor); and Lester (the boys running through the streets in high-hearted Beatles fashion en route to vandalize the school); and Truffaut (the *Jules and Jim* bits of the girl driving the car crazily, the profiles of the three fugitives in the sunlight).

Yet, despite Gothár's occasional over-anxious lapses, *Time Stands Still* stands up. If we feel that we've been through some of these matters before, there is nevertheless a difference. Our rebels without a cause are precisely that; these rebels were supposed to have a cause so the picture holds a good deal more than conventional adolescent turmoil.

Gandhi

(December 13, 1982)

Bernard Shaw's *Androcles and the Lion*, his play about early Christians under the Romans, has his customary extensive preface, the first section of which is headed "Why Not Give Christianity a Trial?" In that section he says: "I am ready to admit that after contemplating the world and human nature for nearly sixty years, I see no way out of the world's misery but the way which would have been found by Christ's will if he had undertaken the work of modern practical statesman." It's unlikely that Shaw had heard of Mohandas Gandhi at the time he wrote the preface, 1915, and it was another sixteen years before the two men met in London, but I've often wondered whether, in the intervening years or after, Shaw ever thought of Gandhi in connection with that line.

Richard Attenborough has now made a film about Gandhi, the one man in world history often compared with Christ who undertook much of the work of a statesman. From before the film's opening, it ran a peculiar risk. The moment I read about the project—and I'm sure this was true for many others—I knew more or less what the film would be. The only question was whether it would be more or less. "Less" is the pleasant answer: that is, *Gandhi* is somewhat less predictable than expected. Attenborough has done virtually all that sincerity, dedication, and professional competence could do. He is not a first-class director, but no first-class director would touch the subject of Gandhi. Good art filters experience, which includes historical knowledge, through the persona of the artist, and no such filtering is wanted, is likely to be tolerable, with the Gandhi story. All that's wanted is the chronicle, done as faithfully and compactly as possible. I wouldn't want to see Bergman's or Bresson's film about Gandhi, not even Satyajit Ray's. Attenborough was the man for the job, especially since he has striven to realize the project for twenty years.

He gives us a prefatory note, warning us that his chronicle is, had to be, incomplete—and this for a film that runs three hours and twenty minutes including intermission. It begins with the assassination in 1948, then goes back to South Africa in 1893 with Gandhi's arrival there, as a London-educated barrister, to fight discriminatory legislation against Indians. He spent twenty-one years there. (The film is oddly nebulous about time lapses.) We see his humiliation in the first-class carriage of a train and the start of his long struggle, first, for the rights of Indians in South Africa, then, after 1914, for the independence of Indians in India, a struggle that did not end until 1947. Then came the spilling of the blood between Indians, Hindu and Moslem, and Gandhi, who had previously used fasting as a plea, announced that he would fast once again, until death took him or the fighting stopped. The fighting stopped, temporarily at least; but death came anyway. He was murdered by one of his own Hindu faith for his efforts to bring peace. Not for the first time, a religion had killed one of its communicants for taking its precepts seriously.

I see no point in checking the film script, item by item, against the biography. Attenborough admits omissions and selected emphases, which were of course unavoidable; there are also condensations and a few minor changes. Sticklers will surely find details to quibble about (for instance, Gandhi's remains were in fact dropped into the Ganges from a military amphibious craft, not from Attenborough's flower-laden boat), but the film epitomizes the life. The stages of Gandhi's pilgrimage are generally clear; and the sunsets over Indian rivers, the great fields fringed with far mountains, the crowded cities, the street battles, the train journeys, the government palaces, the immense funeral procession, all glide by as we expect them to. The dialogue by John Briley is limber enough and often pithy; some of it is quotation. The apt music by Ravi Shankar is aptly used. Attenborough and his editor John Bloom have done their best to fight foreknowledge and the lulling rhythm of historical procession by means of incisive cutting: for instance, by abruptly slicing off a dissident Anglican minister's sermon in defense of Gandhi or by exploding the one word "Salt!" in sudden close-up of the British viceroy as he hears of Gandhi's campaign to break the government's salt monopoly.

But none of these elements would have mattered, would have had the chance to matter, without the element that saves the film (and "saves" is the word I have to use): the acting. Almost all of the large cast are excellent. Gandhi is played by Ben Kingsley, a member of the Royal Shakespeare Company who is in fact half Indian: his real name is Krishna Rhanji. To put it exactly, he is simply fine. How consciously brave and "historical" and pious and coyly twinkle-eyed the performance might have been. How easily Kingsley avoids all these snares by grasping the central truth of the character's dynamics: Gandhi could not lose. He knew he might be killed, he knew he would certainly be hurt and jailed, he knew his political causes might fail, but he could not lose: because he had invested all his being in his beliefs. This understanding is the rock on which Kingsley's portrayal stands. George Orwell said in his review of Gandhi's autobiography (1949): "Saints should always be judged guilty until proved innocent. . . ." So should actors who portray saints. Kingsley passes the test in his first few minutes: we realize very quickly that he is not standing outside the character admiring him, he is journeying with him, visibly and invisibly. Even one technical fault seems a refracted virtue: in Gandhi's last years, Kingsley doesn't look quite old enough, but I'd guess that a decision was made not to use a lot of makeup or a rubber mask because this would obtrude artifice into a performance clarified with truth. In an extra-cinematic sense, it could be sheer respect for both Gandhi and Kingsley's performance that keeps him from complete physical verisimilitude at the end.

A few of the other good actors: Ian Charleson, taciturn yet firm as an Anglican priest drawn to Gandhi; Saeed Jaffrey, humorous and humane as Gandhi's colleague, Patel; John Gielgud, commanding as the viceroy in whose imperial wounds Gandhi rubs his salt campaign; Trevor Howard, subtle as a British judge obliged to sentence Gandhi yet well aware of the quality of his prisoner; and—a tacit irony—Athol Fugard, the South African actor-playwright who has fought all his life against apartheid, wiry and wily as General Smuts. Two actors who are less successful: Martin Sheen, as a "composite" American reporter, over-lolling in contrast to the disciplined people around him; Candice Bergen, as Margaret Bourke-White, once again professionally inept.

One curious aspect of Gandhi is that we can view the picture as a possible act of contrition. It was Britain against which Gandhi struggled and which made the struggle hard; but British incentive and talent and, in some part, financing, produced the film. In penitential terms, the result makes considerable amends: Gandhi is a whole-souled tribute to a monumentally consecrated life. Few will remember the film as a work of art; but, especially because of Kingsley, many will be strongly reminded of—or will learn about—this singular man. A very humbling and a very bitter story.

Why bitter? Because Gandhi believed that history shows how love and nonviolence always eventually triumph. I can't see that history shows anything of the kind. Inarguably it was because of his willingness to die for his beliefs, not to kill for them, that Gandhi won; but his political victories were not inevitable, only his personal victory – the knowledge that, through dedication, *he* could not lose even if his causes did. George Woodcock points out, at the finish of his acute little book on Gandhi:

> Where Gandhi was extravagantly wrong, it was usually from ignorance of the facts rather than from bad judgment. And the most important fact, of which he was almost willfully ignorant, was the extent and reality of evil.

For substantiation, look no further than India's history after the independence to which Gandhi led his country.

Further, it's bitter because Gandhi's life is not, in any illustrative sense, exemplary: the world can't become saintly, and for worldly improvement, it doesn't really need the exceptions we call saints. Shaw didn't say that Christ's holiness would help the world's misery but Christ's will applied to a modern statesman's work. Orwell rejected the ideal of sainthood (while stipulating that Gandhi never made any such claim); "but regarded simply as a politician," said Orwell, "and compared with the other leading political figures of our time, how clean a smell he has managed to leave behind!"

Not saints but statesmen with Christ's or some comparable will, not saints but politicians who will leave a clean smell behind – that is wan-enough hope for the world without the burden of hopes for saintliness. The last proof is what happened after Gandhi's assassination. Says Woodcock: "His murderer was hanged under a law inherited from the British, and none of Gandhi's old comrades in the government was moved to protest that denial of his beliefs." The last bitterness for us in his story is that his example was immediately forgotten: that, for change of the world's misery, we need better "old comrades" more than we need saints.

Postscript. I was mistaken to say that *Gandhi* would evoke only quibbles about details. There were strenuous objections to major points and omissions, and there were strenuous replies. After the dust has (partially) settled, I stand by my view of *Gandhi*. It is not remotely a first-class film: it is a vehicle for a first-class performance that dramatizes a spiritual view of political action. It is thus a film with an inevitable implication of bitterness.

The Verdict

(December 20, 1982)

Paul Newman has long been linked with Common Man themes (though one of his best performances was as a hard-shell conservative in *Sometimes a Great Notion*, which he also directed), so it's no surprise to find him starring in this film. Similarly, it's no surprise to find Sidney Lumet directing it. In fact there are few surprises in the whole enterprise on the thematic-atmospheric level, only in the plot twists, which are agreeable if not shattering. *The Verdict* is one more David and Goliath story except that it's modernized—David is no spotless hero, and Goliath, though not admirable, has at least a plausible case.

Boston. Boston Irish—that's the real "territory." All the action is pretty much confined to Boston Irish inter-fighting. Newman is a middle-aged B.I. lawyer, seedy and sodden, whom we first see trying to hustle business from new widows in funeral parlors. We learn later from his older pal and former law teacher, Jack Warden, that Newman is a Man of Sorrows. Naturally. No film hero can be seedy and sodden congenitally: he has to have suffered unjustly and in manly silence.

But he has been running out his string, with drink and general disorder. Warden has obtained one last case for him—last, because if Newman doesn't come through on this one it's the end of his nearly finished legal career. The case is one of gross negligence against a hospital run by the archdiocese: a young woman in childbirth has been turned into a vegetable for the rest of her life through medical blunders on the delivery table. The bishop, with whom the defense decision finally rests, wants to settle the case quickly out of court—with a hefty settlement—because it's important that the hospital's reputation not be sullied in public: the hospital must keep the public's confidence because it serves the community generally well. Any hospital could conceivably have such a ghastly accident: therefore compensation, quietly and amply, and continuance.

But Newman has seen the victim and has heard the opinion of a medical expert: and, further, resents the smugness with which they expect him to snap up the check of which (they know) he is to get a third. He declines and chooses to go to trial. The archdiocese then engages the best B.I. trial lawyer, James Mason, who has an army of assistants and the glamour of success. Up against him goes Newman, with bloodshot eyes into which he keeps squirting drops, with whiskey breath into which he keeps squirting other drops, trying to pull up his socks and his life, aided only by Warden.

The story is mostly well built and briskly paced, the characters drawn with that sharp quick-sketch quality of good entertainment where a little counts for a lot. None of these people would be considered profoundly drawn in a serious film, but here they have just enough depth to assure us that the filmmakers didn't want them to be puppets. The very last sequence is one of those *Maltese Falcon-Third Man* endings that leave an agreeably tart, "mature" aftertaste.

David Mamet, an occasionally interesting playwright, adapted the screenplay from a novel by Barry Reed, which I haven't read. The script has a nice pop-cynical tone, and it comes through when it absolutely must deliver: Newman's summation to the jury. This speech is terse and pungent: the powerful have the power to convert all the rest of us into victims and that condition probably cannot be changed, but must it *always* prevail?

The script has its fissures. Would Newman have turned down a hefty settlement offer without consulting his clients, the woman's sister and brother-in-law? Would he have opted for trial without a deposition in hand from his key witness? Would his new lady-friend have carried telltale evidence in her pocket-book? And would the bishop be willing to blink, as he does, at the fact that a surprise witness has shown the hospital to be truly criminal? Would he have been willing to shield the guilty behind a legal technicality?

The film's firm qualities themselves make these flaws stand out. Good visual texture comes from the production designs by Edward Pisoni (Newman's entresol office in particular), and considerably more comes from the cinematography by Andrzej Bartkowiak, who did *Prince of the City* for Lumet. Bartkowiak tones down colors all along the spectrum in a way that sobers them aptly without making them drab.

Lumet handles much of the film theatrically. Many scenes are shot from the fifth-row-center angle, and he uses the theater's simultaneous two-room composition a few times. For instance, in a fairly long shot, we see Newman bring his lady-friend home to his apartment. He switches on the light in the kitchen where they come in; the light has been left on in the bedroom where they will end up. Between the two lighted areas is the living room, which is dark. The composition is V-shaped with the camera at the point of the V and with blackness in between the two lighted places. The V fixes depth and destination.

As he often is, Lumet is adroit with his actors. His key achievement is with Charlotte Rampling, Newman's amour: Lumet almost manages to make her tolerable, a Herculean job. He holds down Milo O'Shea, as the judge, which O'Shea always needs, and he keeps Mason, the star lawyer, from being a star actor. From Warden he gets a generous slice off the enjoyable Warden loaf; and Lumet gets Newman back to acting again.

In the past several years Newman has shown that he has one of the rare faces: it doesn't age, it purifies. The youthful prettiness is replaced by a moving clarity. (Think of Gary Cooper, Celia Johnson, Victor Sjöström, Wendy Hiller.) But his acting can get lethargic and facile, as it was in *Fort Apache, the Bronx*. He was better in *Absence of Malice*, if only because there he couldn't coast on clichés: he had to supply the reality missing in the role. In *The Verdict* he has a reliable traditional role, the Man Who Came Back; it's always been juicy, he knows its perimeter, knows its possibilities, knows what he can assume and what he must supply. But he has gone further. With Lumet's aid or insistence, he has apparently chosen a real-life model or models and has shaped his performance on what he has observed. He seems to be working on a short axis, holding his performance close to his vest, doing no more and not a damned bit less than he can verify; yet it's all affectingly colored by—that lovely counterpoint of acting—his own feelings about the character and his own personality. This is realistic American film acting at its veristic/imaginative best.

Daniel

(September 12, 1983)

At one point in E. L. Doctorow's novel, *The Book of Daniel*, Daniel says of his father, "He wrestled society for my soul." The model for the 1971 book was the Rosenberg case, but it is not about the Rosenbergs. It could not be viewed then as a roman à clef, and it cannot be reassessed now in the light of new data. It is a work of imagination: what it would be like to be a son (and brother of the daughter) of people like the Rosenbergs, a son living in the late 1960s with various planes of the past constantly intersecting the present. I thought, and think, that Doctorow wrote the American political novel of the age.

Lately he wrote a screenplay of the novel. Now the film itself makes it necessary to tell the screenwriter that he hasn't served the novelist well. Any argument about the changes needed for the film medium won't begin to wash: why didn't those needs hamper Peter Handke and André Malraux, among others, in writing screenplays of their novels? Doctorow's screenplay is severely reductive of his novel, and no one can possibly know this better than himself.

Begin with the title. Apparently some unwritten law says that you can't call a film *The Book of . . .* , so the title becomes mere *Daniel*. This is a significant stricture. The man who chose the original title, who chose everything carefully in his novel, presumably had two reasons for it. First, the Old Testament resonance, the suggestion of prophetic mission and of the Jewishness specific to the material. Second, the essence of the novel. That essence is the writing of a book within the novel. Daniel's attempt to write his book is the dynamics of what goes on in Doctorow's book, an attempt that summons up Daniel's "present" actions, his memories, his imaginings. But the film, from the title on, has no hint of this propellant interior action, no hint that it is Daniel's venture into creation, his act of imaginative summoning, that spills history into the "present," and vice versa.

This omission leads to the second fault. The omission of imaginative texture strips Doctorow's work to the narrative, which is substantively retained, and that narrative can't bear the emphasis. The novel has no new insights into the Rosenbergs as such, not even any useful guesses. It doesn't even have a fixed finish: there are three optional endings. The novel is an expedition into response: what it means to live inside the body and mind of a "Rosenberg" son, as recorded on an acute literary seismograph. Without that texture, we look for the wrong kind of revelation and are, of course, disappointed. The new stripped structure turns the work into a relatively conventional "quest" novel, with flashbacks, a quest for a buried secret. That quest was an armature of Doctorow's book, not its purpose. And since the quest is doomed to discover nothing, the film is doomed to fizzle.

All that Doctorow did in his screenplay was to extract. From his novel, he took scenes, patches of dialogue, glimpses, and wove them into a relatively linear script. He shunned the very element that gave his book its quality. The film *Daniel* courses along as if it had been made from an American cousin of John Le Carré, but without a satisfactory conclusion.

Sidney Lumet directed and, for the most part, shows again that he is excellent with actors. The excellence is the film's strength; the qualification is its major weakness. For Daniel, Lumet chose Timothy Hutton, and despite all that Hutton and Lumet try, the actor cannot rise to the role. No matter how Hutton flashes his eyes and pumps up feeling, he remains pallid, two-dimensional. A Daniel who convinced us that he had caverns within him, that the past echoed in them, would have helped to compensate for the synoptic script. Hutton does not deliver.

His sister, driven to madness and suicide by her parents' executions twenty years after the event, is played by Amanda Plummer, who is making a specialty of psychotics on stage and screen. Plummer has a lean, sinewy intensity, but so far her most successful performance was as the young mute in *The World According to Garp*. Her voice couldn't intervene. Her voice is so tinny and grating that it almost obscures her image: it makes me want to avert my eyes. All the inflections of feeling that her face and body suggest are virtually nullified by her peanut-whistle voice. The children who play the brother and sister at the time of the trial, Ilan M. Michael-Smith and Jena Greco, are much better than Hutton and Plummer. Those sequences in the past are a great deal more than fill-in flashbacks: the child actors are thoughtful and affecting.

Those young people are part of what is best in the film: the good acting. Further testament to Lumet's (generally) extraordinary ability with actors is Lindsay Crouse's performance as the children's mother. Crouse, whose theater work has left me tepid, did fairly well for Lumet as the runaway Irish nurse in *The Verdict*. Here, as a Bronx Jewish Communist, she is strong, a pillar of fire. It's not a matter of accent and intonation only, though both are flawless: it's a matter of passionate *being*, right to her last utterance outside the death chamber. (She tells the prison rabbi to leave. "Let my son be bar mitzvahed today. Let our death be his bar mitzvah.")

Mandy Patinkin, as her husband, is equally good but less surprising: his role is less of a reach for him, and he has been impressive before. As the affectionate, impulsive, humorous, apostolic father, Patinkin is complete.

The script contains two risky set pieces. The children are brought to see their parents in prison. The authorities won't let the parents be in the room together so there must be two scenes of reunion, children with the mother, then children with the father. We know, while we're watching the first scene and admiring the way that Lumet and his actors vitalize it, that we're going to go through a parallel scene right after it. Lumet faces this challenge and, with his actors, meets it well.

Ed Asner, as the parents' lawyer, has a relatively easy role, but he doesn't coast on it: he underplays it beautifully. Ellen Barkin is rapidly becoming one of the most important young women in American films. She caught attention as the pathetic young wife in *Diner*; in *Tender Mercies*, as Duvall's daughter, she created a full and memorable character in a few scenes; and here, as Hutton's wife, she is immediately arresting and true. Lee Richardson, a veteran, is superb in one brief but meaty scene as *The New York Times* investigative reporter consulted by Hutton when the reporter writes a follow-up story, twenty years after the executions, for the paper. Virtually every word of the scene in the novel is retained in the film—it's a key scene—and Richardson gives it the rich savor of experience, the reporter's and his own.

Andrzej Bartkowiak (trained at the Lodz film school) photographed Lumet's two previous films with distinction, *Prince of the City* and *The Verdict*. His work here is good but somewhat patly labeled: past scenes are in sepia, present scenes are in full color dominated by different shades of blue. The differentiation is a bit heavy, also a bit superfluous. Lumet apparently invested most of his directorial energy in his actors; because visually the film is only occasionally striking (the children being passed over the heads of the crowd to the platform at a protest meeting for their parents.) Mostly, it's merely competent. And it ends with a regrettable cliché. The camera pulls back from a 1960s protest meeting in Central Park to a very long shot; then the camera tilts up into the sky. The only fresh touch is that the sky is gray.

In Doctorow's novel, his theme is much less the Rosenberg case as such, indirectly or otherwise, than the history and fate of nineteenth-century European radicalism in twentieth-century America: the fervor with which it was brought, the occasions that fed it, the reactions it evoked, the way it was tempered and metamorphosed by American fact as our century went on. (In his subsequent novel *Ragtime*, he treated the theme at an earlier date, turn of the century.) A huge subject; and it evoked in him, not a fictionalized treatise but a varicolored prose poem. His screenplay loses almost all the poetic quality of the book, and we are given an inconclusive story, trimmed with utterances.

Sophie's Choice

(January 10 & 17, 1983)

Stingo comes back to his newly rented room in the Brooklyn boarding house bearing a carton of Spam packages on his shoulder, looking apprehensively at the ceiling of his room. The sounds of what is presumably a torrid sexual encounter are coming from above. The carton totters on Stingo's shoulder as he totters into his room. I hoped—in vain. The sounds so unnerve Stingo that he stumbles into cinematic cliché: he spills the packages. I'd hoped he wouldn't. The chandelier in his ceiling is shaking. Again I hoped—in vain—that the camera wouldn't go in for a close-up. In it went, close, so that we couldn't miss the shaking chandelier. Thus, from the start, platitude flecks the direction of the film that Alan J. Pakula has made from William Styron's novel *Sophie's Choice*.

In some ways, however, the film is better than the book. Primary benefit: we are spared almost all of Styron's grandiose prose. It is only when the unseen Josef Sommer, as the older Stingo, reads brief sections on the soundtrack, for commentary or transition, that we realize how lucky we are: whatever there is of merit in the book has been freed by the film from its prison of gummy rhetoric. Also, though the script necessarily condenses, it does not significantly reduce. It's a sorry comment on any novel that a film can improve its realization of character and place; but it's true here. Sophie is more vivid than she was in the book; and a glance of the camera can eliminate pages and pages of detail that Styron laid in, stratum after stratum, in language blended of Dreiser and Warren and Wolfe, then pumped full of sophomoric exaltation. Those glances of the camera further indicate how the film medium in general has liberated the novel in general from the drudgeries that Styron still piles on it—a liberation exploited by the best of contemporary novelists here and abroad. Pakula's film demonstrates (unintentionally) that Styron's whole view of novel-writing is tediously antiquated.

But in other ways the film is just as unsatisfactory as the book, because it's inseparably strapped to basic flaws. The story has no center, no protagonist. To whom does the action of the novel happen? What *does* happen in the book, other than the gradual revelation of action that has already happened? Sophie has long ago made her choice; all that is left for her in dramatic action is to reveal it. Her lover Nathan is not a character, he's a pathological case; he evokes little more than, at best, pathos and a wish that someone would phone for an ambulance. Stingo is in very nearly the same position as Christopher in *I Am a Camera*. He watches, consoles, and grows wiser through watching. But, despite the fights that he witnesses and the picnics and games that he joins, what does he actually *do* in the story? In the novel he could function as our eyes and could filter what he saw through the perspectives of the intervening decades. In front of the camera, Stingo merely occupies space without dramatic justification; he's a confidant posing as a protagonist. When he arrived in Brooklyn (Styron tells us in his priceless prose) Stingo's spirit was

> unacquainted with love and all but a stranger to death. [This means that he had not yet made love; does it also mean that he had not yet died?] I could not realize then [O venerable phrase! Often it's rendered as "Little did I know at the time . . . ."] how soon I would encounter both of these things [*things?*] embodied in the human passion and human flesh [as distinct from horse passion and horse flesh?] from which I had absented myself in my smug and airless self-deprivation.

Or, less smugly and airlessly, he had not yet got laid or seen a corpse. But almost all that Stingo does, in both film and book, is to "encounter" these "things" as an observer.

Inevitably the film was bound to be more interesting in its flashbacks than in its "present" action. But in those flashbacks, the film underscores a grossness in the book.

All through his career, Styron has been in search of evil—not mere villainy but evil that would be credible for the contemporary reader. I won't trace that career here; but it seems reasonable to assume that he felt he had reached the Unholy Grail when he lit upon the Holocaust as a subject. One of the novel's epigraphs is from Malraux: " . . . I seek that essential region of the soul where absolute evil confronts brotherhood." What more absolute evil than the Holocaust, what starker confrontation with brotherhood? But the facts of Auschwitz were not enough for Styron: he had to contrive a Big Moment to cap them. (I don't remotely contend that such horrors did not happen: I'm speaking only of Styron's contrivance.) He had to devise a theatrical zinger to top the Holocaust. In Auschwitz a diabolical German Army doctor forces Sophie to choose between her two children: one is to live, one to die. If she doesn't choose, both will die. With one flip of his masterly hand, Styron turns the Holocaust and Malraux's absolute evil into melodrama. How easily we can envision a nineteenth-century poster of the scene, the distraught Sophie hugging her two children, the evil doctor leering at her, the background streaked with red, the title coursing along the bottom. In the film as in the book, the long-delayed revelation of her choice is what, I infer, frees Sophie to die. But the film provides even less explanation than the book as to why she chose the son over the daughter; and the film provides nothing of the doctor's reason for forcing the choice on her. (In the book Styron carpenters some mechanics that allow Sophie to overhear conversation about the doctor's background. He was in fact a very religious man. Stingo deduces that the doctor committed a great sin so that he could repent greatly. Pallid Dostoevsky is used to aggrandize old-fashioned hokum.)

I have been treating the novel as inseparable from the film because *Sophie's Choice* has been read by many people who may see the film; for the same reason, I haven't sketched the story. Pakula wrote his own screenplay. The condensations were inevitable, of course (even so, the film runs over two and a half hours); but, though one cannot blame him for the defects in the book, once can still deplore Pakula's Choice. Cinematically speaking, he has chosen tough nuts before, notably *All the Presiden't Men* where, essentially, he had to make a film about typing—two reporters typing away. But this time his penchant for the cinematically difficult has led him into the flaccid. And, though he showed in *President's Men* some touches of style, here he shows only a weakness for calendar art.

The cinematographer, Nestor Almendros, has previously done much wonderful work, but collaborating with Pakula, he frequently sinks into imitation. The shot in which we discover Nathan "conducting" Beethoven's Ninth in his room, with four or five reflections of him in the panels of his bay window, is pseudo Welles. The misty twilight window-seat shot with Sophie and Stingo, which is where the flashback narrative begins and ends, is sheer Maxfield Parrish. And the tilted-camera views of Brooklyn Bridge are like hand-me-down Joseph Stella.

But Almendros photographs Meryl Streep excellently, which is hardly an incidental matter since her performance as Sophie is the film's sole achievement. To begin with, she looks more translucently beautiful than ever, and she has the Polish accent right. (I know; some of my best friends are Polish.) What Streep has wrought, possibly with Pakula's help, is a psychological verity for Sophie that she reveals through patterns of motion: she seems often to be moving sideways to avoid confrontation, she seems to be shunning the close scrutiny of others. Yes, of course, she often faces people, often embraces, kisses, converses with them, but the overall impression of her movement is sidling, gently attempting to hide herself in open space. Through this kinetic concept, Streep gives Sophie an aura of concealment. We know, without any grimaces or meaningful sighs, that she is not revealing her whole self to anyone, including her lover. When the truth about her father arrives, when we learn of her "choice," they seem like resolutions of suspended chords.

Sometimes Pakula hands the picture over to Streep: the camera fixes on her in medium close-up and, virtually without any change of shot, she tells a long story. It's what Bergman has done a number of times with Ullmann, and it's been done before with Streep. (It's done even in her recent abysmal thriller *Still of the Night*.) She handles these moments like a virtuoso—a compliment that contains a hint of worry. Virtuosos like John Wood or George C. Scott can grow to consume their roles rather than portray them. Streep is nowhere near that solipsism yet, but she is at the point where her knowledge of her excellence has begun to accompany the excellence itself.

This is not a quibble: it's a concern for a major talent. Here are two moments that are wonderful but in which we are aware that she knows it. When she first talks about her father, she sits on a piano bench, playing with a feather boa that hangs about her neck. She plays "off" the boa adroitly, but cleverly. Later she recalls a moment when, after she had reached Sweden following her rescue, she felt that Christ had turned away from her. Listen to what she does with the one word "Christ": the tiny pause just before it, the slow formation of the first consonants, the suspension of the middle, the almost reluctant close of the word. She makes the monosyllable an utterance. It's wonderful. Very, very few American actors could do it, and it's something worth being able to do. Still, it's noticeable.

None of which is to deny that the value of the film is in Streep's richness. Pakula even closes the picture, as Stingo trudges back across the Brooklyn Bridge to Manhattan with a Botticellian image of the now-dead Sophie hanging over him in the sky. (Just so you'll know he'll never forget her, folks.)

Kevin Kline, as Nathan, works feverishly. He has great energy and some fire, but he cannot fuse the fragments of this character into—if the phrase is possible—a schizoid whole. We get a series of ecstatic and furious bits. Peter MacNicol, the Stingo, is a pleasant youth. It's hard to believe that he has served a hitch in the Marines; it's harder still to believe that Sophie would have wanted him as even a one-night lover. MacNicol does nothing wrong; but he is less like a young man trembling on the edge of a life in art than a sensitive high school poet who wishes he could make the basketball team and attract girls.

Tootsie

(January 24, 1983)

Sophie's Choice struggles to be profound but, except for Meryl Streep's performance, collapses. Then *Tootsie*, which could be called an industry comedy, with Dustin Hoffman playing a man who plays a woman, turns out to be better than the alleged serious film.

All the portents for *Tootsie* were dire. First, there were reports in the trade press about script troubles. The final credits say that the screenplay is by Larry Gelbart and Murray Schisgal from a story by Don McGuire and Larry Gelbart, but it's rumored that others whittled at it, especially Elaine May. Then there were almost weekly war bulletins about battles between Hoffman and the director, Sydney Pollack. *Tootsie* acquired the pre-natal atmosphere of a rapid-transit diaster. But it turns out to be a delight.

Does all this say something about the nature of American filmmaking, the chaos of multiple "input" and front-office pressure and star temperament and director conflicts and agent harassments? Of course it does. It says that chaos doesn't make bad work any more inevitable than virtual one-man control makes good work inevitable. I've always been amazed, given the integral conditions of filmmaking, that Ingmar Bergman can get a film together; and when a good one comes out of the high-power conglomerate West Coast, I feel the same amazement, extended. Chance plays a large part in the making of every film. More so in some films than in others, of course—least of all in the work of a director like Hitchcock who had absolute contol and every smallest move blueprinted in his mind before he started. But filming is not just the million-monkeys-typing-until-they-produce-*Hamlet* thesis. Structures can be built, lost, and recovered, if some sort of governing idea exists in the mind or minds of the governing figures. Not always, not even with the same people. Robert Redford and Sydney Pollack gave us the memorable *Jeremiah Johnson*. Redford and Pollack, plus a woman named Streisand, gave us the forgettable *The Way We Were*. There is no way to know: there is much reason never to believe. All one can do is, on the basis of the past, hope. On the one hand, ludicrously defying reason and spirit, are the conditions of filmmaking. On the other, there is a large treasury of films ranging from the good up to, at the peak, some of the best works of the century in any art.

Tootsie is somewhere in that treasury, nowhere near the top, but better than merely good. First of all, *Tootsie* is surprising—and not just because it's successful after all the prior hooha. It's considerably more than the laugh-getter that it seems to be at the start and continues to be. Hoffman is a New York actor named Michael Dorsey who also teaches acting because he can't get enough acting work. (This was once true of Pollack.) Chances for acting jobs are scarce enough, but Michael has extra troubles because he has a mind of his own. (For instance, he loses a job as a tomato in a TV commercial because he's told to sit and he doesn't believe that vegetables sit.) Thus he has troubles with his agent, played by Pollack. Dorsey dresses as a woman to get a part in a soap opera, calls himself Dorothy Michaels, gets the role, and makes a hit—particularly because Dorothy insists on discarding the pasteboard dialogue of her role and speaking as the woman that she is!

Two main complications follow from the impersonation. Michael falls in love with Jessica Lange, who is a leading woman of the soap and of course knows Michael only as Dorothy. Lange's father, Charles Durning, a widower living in the country, falls in love with Dorothy and gives her an engagement ring, asking her to think it over. So a young man dressed as a woman loves a young woman whose father falls in love with the impersonated woman. It's further complicated because Lange loves Dorothy as a friend but declines to see her privately anymore because, after a gaffe by Michael in the heat of passion, she thinks that Dorothy has lesbian feelings which Lange can't reciprocate.

It's a well-machined farcical setup, buttressed with tributary subplots which I won't detail. And some of it is played excellently by Hoffman sheerly as farce. For instance, after Dorothy is hired for her role, the woman producer takes her to her dressing room. The door opens, and there is a gorgeous girl in skimpy bra and panties, an actress also using that dressing room, who greets Dorothy with outstretched hand. Hoffman does no Bob Hope "takes": in a splinter of a second, you can see him leave the laughs to us, as Michael senses immediately that he must play Dorothy even more strenuously. Michael's split-second summoning of determination is funnier than any "take" could have been.

This and other sequences work variations on some of the situations in that farce masterpiece, *Some Like It Hot*, but *Tootsie* goes beyond farce. It moves much closer to social comedy. The subject is sexuality, not homosexuality, which it was in Blake Edwards' polished farce, *Victor/Victoria*, where the old queen played by Robert Preston was the Rosetta stone of the tangle.* No, *Tootsie* grows to Michael's realization, through his female impersonation, of at least some of what it's like to be a woman. As soon as he "becomes" Dorothy, he can't stand the male-inspired dialogue that Dorothy is given; he resents the fact that the macho director calls all the male actors by name but calls the women

*See p. 154.

Honey or Tootsie. In short, by playing Dorothy in order to get work, Michael learns what it is to be Dorothy, working.

And in short, out of all this, *Tootsie*, turbulently born, is healthy, organic, funny first and last, moving, and disturbing. Pollack has directed briskly, without any of the occasional intrusive touches that marred even his best work (*Jeremiah Johnson*, for instance), and he plays the actor's agent with hairy-knuckled, smoothed-out, third-generation, push-cart push. Lange is competent, as is Durning. Bill Murray is at last tolerable, as Michael's playwright roommate who is in on the ruse from the beginning. (But how do that pair afford a loft as large as the one they're in? In Manhattan today?)

Sometimes Hoffman's work, as Michael, is deceptive; he makes it look easy, loafing, leaning against cars and bars. But everything is finely tuned, planned to a needlepoint spark. As Dorothy, his ease is different: not in apparent loafing but in the seeming facility with which he completes the transformation – of movement, voice, and sensibility – without any trace of swishing. Michael, the actor, wants to understand Dorothy, the woman; and Hoffman understands both of them. Hoffman's powers of transformation have been startling since 1966 when, at twenty-eight, he played a fortyish nineteenth-century Russian office drudge in the Off-Broadway *Journey of the Fifth Horse*; and his gift for bright farce performance came clear soon after, in the Off-Broadway production of *Eh?* Since his smashing film debut in *The Graduate*, he has done his share of bad films and has ambled though some better ones, like *Papillon*. But there's never been any reason to doubt that Hoffman carried great gifts within him no matter what he was doing, and in *Tootsie* he uses them well. Endearingly.

To see within a few weeks Paul Newman in *The Verdict*, Meryl Streep in *Sophie's Choice*, and Dustin Hoffman in *Tootsie* is to be permitted some pride in American acting: and in its ability to triumph over American filmmaking conditions.

Betrayal

(February 28, 1983)

The film of Harold Pinter's *Betrayal* is graceful, economical, and strong. It's a civilized entertainment, by which I mean that it's consistently engrossing and that it takes its being with exceptional directness from the civilization around it.

As usual, Pinter made the screen adaptation of his play, and, as usual, he found new possibilities for the play in its film form. This is a matter of distinction, not hierarchy. The play has qualities that the film could not have. For example, in the London-New York production directed by Peter Hall and designed (scenery, lighting, and costumes) by John Bury, every scene began with the actors immobile in dim silhouette, city sounds behind them, and were brought to motion by the coming of the light. Each of the London settings was done in spare line and color; the one Venice scene was done in curves. These theatrical devices helped to distill the realism poetically. Film could not accommodate those devices: they would have worked against both realism and poetry. The film needs rooms that are rooms, with life going on in them before and after the bits of that life that we see. In the theater, plaques of action were placed before us as in a three-dimensional mosaic; on screen, the camera just seems to arrive at opportune moments in these people's ongoing lives—opportune for us. And, growing out of that approach, Pinter fills in material around the edges that eases the play into this second form and, without fuss, corroborates it as film. We glimpse Emma's daughter at different ages, which makes her a kind of calendar; we see Emma getting into her car after the breakup of the affair and sitting there for a moment crying; we see the husband in his office, verified; we see the landlady who rents the lovers their rendezvous and, without rudeness, disbelieves everything they tell her. Pinter handles these additions so that they don't flatten suggestions into explicitness: they certify and expand.

However, the film doesn't "deepen" the play (though it does deepen a tone that I'll discuss). Exquisitely wrought though most of the dialogue and most of the scene structure are, *Betrayal* still asks for support from its performers in disproportionate measure. Every good script relies for fulfillment on its production, but Pinter over-relies here. After appreciating the dexterities and insights, one must still note that Pinter's performing collaborators have to give *Betrayal* more of its texture than in other plays of his.

But the film, because of its flexibility, does make the overall pattern seem less of a stunt. The story begins at its conclusion and moves backward to its beginning. Pinter doesn't use the method slavishly: three of the play/film's nine scenes occur *after* the scene immediately preceding; but the story goes from 1977 to 1968. (Titles are flashed on screen to keep us straight.)

Betrayal concerns three people: Jerry, a London literary agent who is married and a father; Emma, his lover for seven years, an art dealer who is married and a mother; Robert, Emma's husband and Jerry's best friend, who is a publisher. In 1977 Jerry and Emma meet for a drink, the first time they have seen each other in the two years since their affair ended. She tells him that she and Robert are separating, that they had a long talk the night before, that Robert confessed to a number of affairs and she told him about the long-finished affair with Jerry. (Thus her affair could have no real bearing on the breakup.)

As the story "progresses" backward, Jerry learns, to his astonishment, that Emma actually had told Robert about the affair four years ago. Robert had known about it while continuing his friendship and publishing business with Jerry and while he had also been busy with his own dalliance (apparently much more casual than his wife's). Then, moving further backward, we see that, though we may indeed weave a tangled web when first we practice to deceive, the management of tangled webs is part of our society's order: that part of the fabric of marriage—of valuable and lasting marriage—is the management of tangled webs, which usually means bringing the beauty and importance of marriage into alignment with actualities.

For me, the chief interest of both play and film is in imagining a question mark after the title. Jerry and Emma use the term "betray" in the first scene, but as I wrote in reviewing the play, *Betrayal* may be a spinoff from some lines in Pinter's previous play, *No Man's Land*. Hirst tells Spoooner that, years before, he seduced Spooner's wife:

> Proposed that she betray you. Admitted you were a fine chap, but pointed out that I would be taking nothing that belonged to you, simply that portion of herself that all women keep in reserve for a rainy day.

Couldn't these lines, in essence, be spoken as well by a woman to another woman about the latter's husband? In *Betrayal* Pinter seems to be dramatizing the idea that, in our society, the rewards and the duration of marriage come less from ceremonial promises than from mutual respect; that, in the married person, there is an honor that is more private and more sacred than public vows; that, in marriage, sometimes the hypocrisies can transmute a marriage—which one wants to maintain or one wouldn't bother with the hypocrisies—into gamesmanship.

That gamesmanship leads to the matter of dramatic tone mentioned earlier. This film underscores an element that was in the play, as in *No Man's Land*, and is in many of the plays of lesser English writers such as Tom Stoppard and Simon Gray. They delineate a radical change in the locus of English high comedy. From the Elizabethan age until well into this century, high comedy was virtually the exclusive preserve of aristocratic and/or rich characters. One reason was that the plots of high comedy were possible only to people with time on their hands, people who didn't have to work for a living. Another reason was that these people—I mean these people in the real world, not the characters based on them by Congreve and Sheridan and Wilde—developed comedic skills *in their lives*, qualities of arch and elegance, of tease and brusque politeness, of rapier skill in the drawing-room duel.

Increasingly through the twentieth century, as those upper classes dwindled proportionately against an educated, reasonably affluent middle class, the talent for high comedy in life has been acquired by that middle class. The action now has to be worked around office hours and carefully planned vacations and nannies for the children, but many of the English middle class now conduct their lives and conversations with a style as smoothly cruel and tacitly affectionate and wittily articulate as they can make it, based on upper-class paradigms—perhaps impelled by a quite English imperative to maintain elegance, to keep the social backbone arched. Pinter, preeminently among his colleagues, has perceived this social shift and writes high comedy about these middle-class people who, as far as their dailiness will permit, try to live their lives with high-comedy panache. The tonal change in *Betrayal* from stage to screen has much less to do with the "breaking open" of stage work than with intensification of this high-comic style in middle-class London life.

This would be impossible, of course, without the right execution. Pinter's film, excepting only the snatches of strident and unhelpful music, is splendidly done.

The direction by David Jones is a heartening surprise. My first acquaintance with his work, a production of Gorky's *Enemies* at the Royal Shakespeare Company in 1971, made me respect him, but that respect withered through his tenure at the BAM Theater Company in Brooklyn, 1979-1981. I had never seen any of Jones's extensive TV work for the BBC, but his first feature film makes it plain that he understands how to use a camera, how to look and choose and move. The opening sequence, possibly planned by Pinter but perfectly done by Jones, is outside Robert's and Emma's house as they bid goodnight to departing guests. The pair shut their front door; the camera comes closer to the house, then moves along to the kitchen window through which we see the couple conversing, not calmly. They slap each other. All this in one long camera take. I felt confidence suffuse me.

Then, in the next scene, Jerry and Emma in the pub the following day, Jones begins the cat-and-mouse technique that fills the rest of the picture, and is greatly aided by the editing of John Bloom, who did such good work on *Gandhi*. Jones and Bloom craft the film like jewelers, right to the finish where Jerry persuades Emma to start the affair whose end we have already witnessed. Her hand slides down his arm to his hand. The two clasped hands, a pretty wryness, are what we last see.

Jeremy Irons, back from his false fiddling as a Polish workman in *Moonlighting*, is Jerry and shows thoroughbred mettle and sensibility. Not a nuance is lost or overdone. In that last scene, which is the affair's beginning, Jerry's passion must win Emma. Irons is right in the fire. Ben Kingsley—Kingsley, who was impeccable as Gandhi!—is impeccable as Robert, corrupt, vulnerable, tart. To see Kingsley in these two roles is to realize again that the future of imaginative acting is far from dim.

Patricia Hodge, well experienced in British theater and TV but new to me in films, is initially a somewhat unsettling choice for Emma. She is not instantly appealing. She almost seems a composite made from a national survey as to how a middle-class Englishwoman should look and sound. But she very soon shows fine skill at dealing with implications of feeling, with tenderness on guard; and very soon she becomes an argument for womanliness, as against immediately apparent beauty. In a quite subtle way, then, middle-class Hodge assists the shift in this film—from acting about life to acting about people who act in life.

The Return of Martin Guerre

(May 2, 1983)

The basic aim of historical films is mystery. The best of them—such as Carné's *Children of Paradise*, Bergman's *Virgin Spring*, Kurosawa's *Seven Samurai*, Tavernier's *Let Joy Reign Supreme*—burrow through their stories, characterizations, complexities of every kind, to a fundamentally naive question, nonetheless awesome: How could the camera have been present at this moment in the past? If the question never rises in our minds, to be ridiculed and to rise again, the film in some way lacks fullness. The question never rises with contemporary films because the world around us, next door or next hemisphere, exists to be photographed, is certified by photography. When a historical film is good, it begins to take on a verity that is an anachronism: it enters a world of data communication to which it doesn't belong. In the theater, no matter how good historical re-creation may be, this mystery never rises because the theater is not, as the camera is, an instrument of reportage as well as art.

The mystery occurs in *The Return of Martin Guerre*, which means of course that the film has other virtues, or the mystery would never be manifest. The film puts us in a sixteenth-century French farming commune as casually as it might put us in a twentieth-century French village. Only after the picture has been running a while do we perceive the absence of re-creation, of strain, to fabricate the past. Then the pleasantly naive question surfaces: How can we possibly be seeing these things? And the question teases even though (as in many good period films) we know some of the actors from contemporary work. The actors' transformative imaginations are, of course, part of the time miracle.

Historical films that make the miracle are to some degree rewarding whatever else they may or may not provide. *The Return of Martin Guerre* makes the miracle and something more; so, though it's not in a class with those that I've mentioned above, it's engrossing. The screenplay, by the director Daniel Vigne and Jean-Claude Carrière, collaborator with Buñuel and others, is based on a true incident. This can be an obstacle because it sometimes leads to justification by accuracy rather than by art, but Vigne and Carrière have constructed a script that, through incisiveness and a small convolution of chronology, limbers a chronicle into a drama.

That drama rests on one question: Is Martin Guerre, who returns to his wife and small son after an absence of eight years, really Martin Guerre? (Lovers of Pirandello will immediately scent the breeze.) Martin was a stripling when he left: he comes back a solid young man, a veteran soldier. All the people in the commune, including his wife, recognize him, and he certainly knows all of them by name and in personal history. Doubts about his identity come later, as does resolution.

One question raised by the film, a question you have probably heard before, is: What is truth? Everything is fine in the Guerre family, in the commune. The returnee *is* Martin Guerre, until doubt is raised: quashed: raised again. In between the doubts, the man is Martin Guerre. What difference does it make if, in "reality," he is not? Does the "reality" change, in between the doubts?

Finally the question is settled. Even though the story is historical, I won't reveal the settlement because the pleasure is in the succession of doubts more than in the conclusion. Unlike Pirandello (*As You Desire Me*, for instance), that conclusion is unambiguous. This of course makes the story less resonant than Pirandello, but life, that bumbler, is not an artist. On the other hand, *Martin Guerre* has the gloss of really having happened.

The returned Martin is played by Gérard Depardieu, whose career is continually surprising. He does so many films, so many of them reliant on his macho energy, that we can begin to think he is more a made-to-film-order star than an actor. Occasionally, as in *Mon Oncle d'Amérique*, he reminds us that he can range from that persona, can do more than fill screen space characteristically, more than bustle his magnetic self around. In *Martin Guerre*, he seems to have changed the location of his neck. Instead of the strapping Depardieu whose physicality endorses his personality and vice versa, an Olympic weightlifter who can act, here he seems reshaped by labor. His neck seems to grow out of his upper chest. He is no less strong, but here he is a man who needs his strength in order to eat, a peasant.

His wife is played by Nathalie Baye with many secrets and, thank heaven, few smiles. As long as Baye has a part that keeps her from smiling a lot, she convinces and appeals. The whole cast is exemplary, the most notable being Roger Planchon as a judge/examiner. I can't recall seeing Planchon on screen before. He is of course a famous name in the theater, one of the outstanding French Brechtians, a playwright, and the director of over fifty productions. (One of the most famous, by the way, was Pirandello's *Henry IV*.) His composure, his grave and well-modulated voice give dimension to his role.

Certainly a word must be said about the cinematographer, André Neau, particularly for his interiors. The lighting inside looks like the light that would be available by day through small windows and by night from candles, yet Neau doesn't use the old device of trying to reproduce effects derived from paintings of the period. The costumes by Anne-Marie Marchand look homespun, worn to the shapes of people who don't have many clothes. The overall historical accuracy is guaranteed by a Princeton professor of history, Natalie Z. Davis, who served as consultant, but is made by the director.

Daniel Vigne is forty-three; this is only his second theatrical feature. (His first was not shown here.) This puts him with such other late debutants as Antonioni and Tanner. After he graduated from a French film school, he worked as assistant director on twelve films, then did considerable work in television, including a six-hour series about the French countryside. His work here is marked by lucidity; his editing, with Denise de Casabianca, is invisible, therefore right. But what most distinguishes his work is his sense of the multifarious life he is treating. No actor is in costume, no actor has actor's "business." Anyone who has driven through France has seen, besides the towns and villages, clusters of old farmhouses that have grown through the centuries on common holdings. If you have ever wondered what life there was like in the sixteenth century—and without such questions, why bother to look at those places?—this picture will fascinate on that ground alone. The picture's story is good; the picture's raising of that old question—of the camera's anachronistic presence—is even better.

(May 23, 1983)

Postscript. Several readers have written, apropos of my review of *The Return of Martin Guerre* three weeks ago, to note that Janet Lewis used the same historical material for her novel *The Wife of Martin Guerre*, as did William Bergsma for his opera of the same name.

The Draughtsman's Contract

(May 9, 1983)

The Draughtsman's Contract is unique. I know of no other original screenplay in English set in late seventeenth-century England and written in the manner of Restoration comedy; I can't even recall a screen adaptation of a Restoration play. Evidently the brocaded language and the masking of action by etiquette have been reasons for avoiding the period; but they are precisely the reasons that Peter Greenaway chose it. The result doesn't prove that others were wrong to avoid it—probably they weren't—only that Greenaway was right.

His film is a diabolical delight. The prime term for the dramatic writing of the period is artifice; Greenaway has written and directed his film as an overarching artifice, cantilevered by interlocking smaller artifices. Since artifice cannot be unconscious, this film (figuratively speaking) takes care not to reveal everything about itself, not even when it is finished. But we accept this as its prerogative, thus admitting that its quality earned the prerogative. The whole work is so assured, so elegantly vicious, that the small secrets it retains seem its due.

Greenaway, now in his early forties, is English, was educated at an art school, and worked for a time as a painter and illustrator. In 1966 he began to make films, most of them short (I've seen none), that earned him an avant-garde reputation. Nothing about *The Draughtsman's Contract* is avant-garde except its daring to use Restoration forms and diction, which is certainly avant of the film garde. But Greenaway's past is shown in his painterly eye, not oppressively picturesque but sharply selective.

He has plumbed the Restoration far deeper than its locutions and finery: in Restoration style itself, he has found the moral dynamics of his story. Just after I first saw *The Draughtsman's Contract* last September at the New York Film Festival, I met a poet I know and I told him that the picture is like Congreve, only cruel. He said, "But Congreve is cruel." He was quintessentially right, of course. Under the Congreve glitter is, often, steely egoistic drive—sometimes, as in *The Double Dealer*, not so deeply buried. (This film could be called *The Double Dealers*.) On second viewing, I saw how Greenaway had accomplished two aims. First, he ferreted out the cruelty under the polish, after perceiving that the polish was essential *because* of the cruelties under them. Second, he dramatized that perception by putting a murder story in that period; the blunt brutalities show the underside of the politesse.

The protagonist—even that term turns out to be an artifice—is Mr. Neville, a young draughtsman whose specialty is drawings of country estates. The time is the summer of 1694, the place a great country house in southern England which belongs to a Mr. Herbert. The film begins at a dinner where Mr. Herbert informs wife, daughter, son-in-law, and guests, including Mr. Neville, that he leaves in the morning for Southampton where, we learn, he plans to do a bit of whoring. Mrs. Herbert, a maturely attractive woman, invites Mr. Neville to remain during her husband's absence and to make twelve drawings of the house and grounds. Without alacrity, he accepts the commission, but he insists that a contract be drawn up specifying that Mrs. Herbert shall provide him with the use of her body when and how he asks. Thus it seems that the haughty Mr. Neville is as much in the command of the situation here as he is of his art. (The drawings we eventually see were in fact done by Greenaway.)

But the careful observer is curious. Why does Mrs. Herbert, who is clearly not enamored of the artist, consent to make her body part of the bargain? Further, though Mr. Neville gives a written schedule of the prospects he intends to draw at what times, and though he orders that each prospect be clear at that time, still in each prospect one item is out of order. A shirt is on a bush, a ladder is against a wall, a pair of boots is in a field. These objects contradict his instructions, yet the artist doesn't object, he merely includes them in the drawings. It's almost as if he were punishing Mrs. Herbert for her carelessness by putting the extraneous object in the drawing. Ultimately this vindictiveness bites the biter. Those objects are connected with crime—and more crime.

Janet Suzman, the South African actress known here through TV appearances and several films (e.g., *Nicholas and Alexandra*), doesn't seem the ideal Mrs. Herbert. She gives the role everything but what she ought not to need to give it—the casual assurance that she is to the manor and manner born. On the other hand, Anthony Higgins, known more in English theater than in films, easily infuses Mr. Neville with self-confidence—an arrogance that derives from his skills in art and sex but that blinds him to other occurrences around him. Anna Louise Lambert, the Herberts' daughter, captures the cunning innocence of the gentlewoman-as-shepherdess, and Hugh Fraser, her high-bred boor of a German husband, sniffs superciliously at everything English and everyone inferior that come his way, while his eyes watch narrowly the property that will one day be his.

Much of the film was shot at a Stately Home in Kent, and the cinematographer, Curtis Clark, appreciates—affectionately and humorously—the petted gardens and the homey mansion. He lights interiors dexterously, using fat candles that seem to provide the color and that also balance the compositions. Sue Blane's costumes are splendid in two senses, though those formidable male periwigs batter us into submission from the start. Michael Nyman has written an exceptionally helpful score which, like much in the picture, combines authenticity with an edge of parody—the vigor and song of Locke and Blow and Purcell used with overview.

A sort of parallel exists between Mr. Neville and his author Greenaway. Mr. Neville is making drawings that are ostensibly symmetrical but are a bit disturbed by intrusions. Greenaway has made a film that looks symmetrical but is subtly and increasingly out of moral balance. For instance, the opening and closing shots are seemingly symmetrical: both are close-ups of a person eating fruit, the first of Mr. Herbert tasting a plum, the latter of a bronze-green naked figure gorging on a pineapple. (This figure is almost mystical: a kind of court jester on the grounds who sometimes climbs porticos or sits on a statuary horse or stands peeing into a fountain and who is not invisible or mistaken for bronze because at one point a guest swats him away with a hat.) The seeming symmetry of opening and close is really a contradiction between Mr. Herbert, who has left the film, and this nonspiritual spirit.

Contradictions are integral to Greenaway's system here: contradictions between the punctilio and the serpentine lusts and deceits: between the harmony of the setting and the disharmony of murder: between the extravagant courtesies and the barely covered Catholic-Protestant hatreds (1694 is only five years after the Glorious Revolution): between the Neville who is a coolly perfect draughtsman and the Neville who is a coolly ravishing satyr.

All these contradictions are, as noted, mined by Greenaway out of the style that he has chosen. Evidently he has understood that the very name of the style, Baroque, is itself a contradiction, a word that means both grotesque and intricately ornamented. Those exquisitely contradictory meanings suit this exquisitely wrought film.

The Grey Fox

(August 1, 1983)

In the mid-1860s, when he was sixteen, Bill Miner began to rob stagecoaches in the far West. Eventually, after he had earned the sobriquet Gentleman Bandit, he was captured and sent to prison. He spent thirty-three years in San

Quentin. When he got out, in 1901, he stayed with his married sister in Washington State; after a try at an oystering job, he went back to robbery. The railroad had completely eliminated the stagecoach, so he became a train robber in the Northwest and in British Columbia. His first attempt failed, and one of his partners was killed. His second attempt succeeded, but he and a sidekick had to lie low for a while in a remote town in western Canada. The hotel owner, who knew Bill from prison, provided the hideout but blackmailed him into more theft—horse rustling. In time Bill, his sidekick, and a new partner broke loose with another train robbery. They were caught. All three were sentenced, Bill for thirty-five years.

The facts suggest a film. But how do you make a winning film about an incorrigible thief, unreformed after thirty-three years in prison, a man long past any youthful impulse to adventure who just can't endure honest work? Simple. You make *The Grey Fox*.

First, you get the right actor for the leading role. The filmmakers, all Canadian, hit the jackpot. They chose Richard Farnsworth, who has been in American films for over forty years. In recent years he has come to some prominence, as Jane Fonda's one ranch hand in *Comes a Horseman*, the grizzled filling station man in *Resurrection*, and in a few other visible roles, but he spent most of those decades in stunt work and bit parts. Sometimes bit players move up. (It's fun to catch glimpses of them in their earlier days. Try to spot Norma Shearer in the barn-dance scene in *Way Down East*.) But I can't remember a precedent for the rise of a bit player at Farnsworth's age.

He is excellent. He plays as if he had been a star for years and is counting on your remembrance. It's a performance of complete repose, charming honesty, and strength. An old star knows he has it made; an old Farnsworth, instead of bucking to succeed as a young Farnsworth might have done, doesn't give a damn about all that. He doesn't strain, he just does what he has to do—well. (In the film Bill says, "To a man my age, the future don't mean much unless you're talking about next week.") Perhaps it's a stretch to suggest an analogy between Bill Miner's release from prison after thirty-three years and Richard Farnsworth's relatively recent release from decades of film obscurity; but Farnsworth convinces us that he knows what Bill is talking about, and he plays the part with the ease of recognized mortality.

Next, the screenwriter, John Hunter, made the most of the gentlemanly legends attaching to Bill, all of which fit Farnsworth snugly. Bill says "sir" quite a lot, even to victims, apologizes for disturbances, and so on. But, more centrally, Hunter has made the most of the cultural change in the story's era. Not only had stagecoaches gone and railroads conquered while Bill was in prison but film had arrived. It's at a showing of (naturally) *The Great Train Robbery* that Bill's future comes into view, that he sees how to utilize his specialty of vehicle-robbery. The film atmosphere is established early: clips from stagecoach robberies in old Westerns are spliced between the titles that give the data of Bill's youth. And the film presence continues: during one of Bill's chases near the end, clips from the 1903 film are interwoven—in fact, there's one quick shot of Bill himself in old-style black-and-white. *The Great Train Robbery* didn't make a criminal of Bill; the film sparked his imagination in his long-practiced profession. Bill is thus used as an early, if eccentric, example of the effect of film on the secret life.

He was no Robin Hood; he stole from the rich and gave to himself. But it was the railroad that he robbed, and the railroad is shown as such a tyrannical institution that, even if Bill kept the proceeds, people applauded. That leads to the next element in the filmmaking, the director's vision. Phillip Borsos was educated at Canadian film schools and has made a number of shorts and documentaries. *The Grey Fox* is his first feature, but one would never know. For prime instance, take his use of the railroad throughout. Admittedly, it's impossible for a moving railroad train to be unexciting, unromantic, but Borsos finds angles, prominences, a process of iconography that make the railroad all the more dangerous for being so seductive and overwhelming.

Borsos has a feeling for faces. With one exception, he has cast the whole film very well, using what Eisenstein would have called typage—defined by Jay Leyda as "presenting each new figure in our first glimpse of him so sharply and completely that further use of this element may be as a known element." The principle is not mere typecasting, it makes us feel that, out of all the faces in the world, this surely is the right one—for Bill's brother-in-law or sidekick or the local policeman or whatever. And having chosen faces well, Borsos then works in close, though not with enormities, to get their richness.

With an acute editor, Frank Irvine, Borsos has cut and phrased skillfully. Lots of the elisions between major sequences are abrupt, thus flattering: they assume our impatience with trudging details, our ability to make leaps. And one sequence uses a device which, if not new, is amusingly handled. It starts with Bill in the hotel bathtub, scrubbing, singing "Sweet Betsy from Pike." His voice continues as we watch a montage of his growing acquaintance with a lady in the town. By the time he finishes his bath, he is ready to leave for his date.

Principally, what Borsos has done is what the best directors have always done: before he began, he envisioned a tone and rhythm that, whatever else might change or be invented, he wanted to maintain. He maintains it. *The Grey Fox* is not a jaunty ballad of Billy the Kid or the romance of two young buckos like Butch Cassidy and the Sundance Kid: it's the faintly melancholy but determined story of a man whose life may almost be over but who means to redeem his past by *not changing*. To reform would be to trash his youth and his long years in prison. So, despite the robberies and fights, the film's tone is resolutely quiet, a tone that tests every moment by (whatever we may think of them) tested values.

The last major contributor to the film's quality is the cinematographer, Frank Tidy. He has helped to realize Borsos's intent with a palette of slanting golden light and the deep blue between sunset and dark. Occasionally Tidy's work edges toward *Days of Heaven* gorgeousness, lushly distracting, but mostly his colors fit what's going on inside Bill. And, excepting Kurosawa, I've never seen better photography of pelting rain. The scene in which the three robbers are brought back in an open wagon through a downpour is chilling.

My only strong reservation about the film is the performance of Jackie Burroughs as the woman photographer who becomes Bill's lover. Burroughs is a celebrated Canadian theater and TV star and wants us to be aware of it. Her acting is self-consciously thoroughbred.

But, overwhelmingly, *The Grey Fox* triumphs over the difficulties I cited at the outset. It's a highly enjoyable film. At the end, as Bill leaves for prison on a train (!), a small boy hands him an orange. (He had given that boy an orange earlier in the picture.) As the train pulls out, townsfolk come onto the track to wave goodbye. The sound fades under the picture, then the picture fades—and the closing titles give us some surprises. But before those heart-tuggers and those surprises, *The Grey Fox* has succeeded. The lovely making of the film in itself makes us care about its gentle, unregenerate protagonist.

Ways in the Night

(August 29, 1983)

"Zanussi is a moralist," said a Polish book called *Polish Cinema* in 1972. Well, that's a fairly safe statement about any filmmaker (or playwright or novelist, any artist who deals with the representation of behavior): It's difficult to make a film that doesn't embody some sort of values and some attitude toward them. But that statement has been even safer about Krzysztof Zanussi. I've seen five of his ten or so features, and, in each of them, principles were expounded, sometimes ironically but nonetheless expounded. Zanussi, born in 1939, was educated as a physicist, then went to the celebrated film school at Łódź. It's easy but not therefore necessarily wrong to discern those two educations in his work: his films have been like laboratory demonstations at the same time that, cinematically, they have had considerable fluency.

But Zanussi has moved up. Several years ago he made a film for West German television (WDR) that is just released here in theaters. WDR was chief sponsor of Fassbinder's *Berlin Alexanderplatz*;* in discussing that giant work, I mentioned that the WDR production head is promoting the idea of "amphibious" films, which can live on both little and large screens. For the same sponsor, Zanussi has made the best film of his that I've seen, one that presumably succeeded on TV and that certainly succeeds on a theater screen. (Will WDR turn out to be the Medici family of contemporary European film?)

Ways in the Night is unmistakably concerned with morality. But this time

*See p. 183.

Zanussi treats the subject obliquely, evocatively; and he has taken a considerable cue from the fact that he was making this film for Germany. (Possibly, after Fassbinder, I ought to mention that it runs only two hours.) *Ways in the Night* deals with the German occupation of Poland in World War II and has a mixed cast of Germans and Poles. Zanussi pulls no punches about the harshness that is typical of wartime occupying forces nor about the special religious and racial strictures of this occupation. This is the soil that feeds his moral inquiry.

He uses a familiar dramatic situation, and proves again that only *reliance* on familiarity breeds contempt. Intent and conviction are all. What could be a more familiar situation than a soldier's attraction to a woman on the other side in a war? But Zanussi is so concentrated on the truth of their characters, of their interactions, that the story quickly becomes just a means of our getting closer to these people. The young German officer, played by Mathieu Carrière, is that well-known cultivated European military man: he does his military duty, and he knows his Chopin and Plato. The Polish woman, played by one of Zanussi's favorites, Maja Komorowska, is a baroness, owner of the estate where the German officers are quartered, who has moved to a smaller house across the way. She helps the Polish partisans, and she plays the Chopin.

Carrière makes all the moves that, in a conventional story, would lead to a consummated affair, which in turn would lead to poignancy. He apologizes to the baroness for the inconvenience of occupation, he eavesdrops on her piano playing and comments knowledgeably, he compliments her on the pictures in her house—in short, he displays his "true" self, under the uniform, in the sensitivity mating-dance. He's not faking. It really is his self, part of it anyway, and he is really smitten by her. But his overture has none of the stock fictional effect.

Far from being won or even weakened, Komorowska is strengthened in antipathy, although she deploys her dislike skillfully. She views his proofs of sensitivity as perverse proofs of German brutality, all the worse for being carried out by people of cultivation. Further she seems armored by some sense of being caught in a situation, almost a "script," and she refuses to obey it. Carrière, too, shows signs of recognizing his situation objectively, but he is so besotted with love that he can't reject his role. This is pointed out to him by an older, sardonic brother-officer, played by Horst Frank. He was once Carrière's professor of esthetics, and if that fact is the one neat coincidence in the story, at least it's well used by Zanussi. It underscores Komorowska's refusal to distinguish between iron fists and velvet gloves.

Carrière doesn't take Frank's advice to forget the woman or to have her as quickly as possible. The younger man struggles, insists on living through his drama, tries to reach Komorowska. She uses his feelings to deceive him in ways that help her family and that help partisans. When he confronts her with her duplicity, she is more than unashamed. She is an enemy, using what weapons she can; he has given her weapons. (She declines the figurative script; he accepts it.)

Zanussi wants to cut open the idea of public versus private morality. Carrière kills a partisan with a knife, pays no heed to the dangling corpses of two hanged partisans, accepting that these matters are part of his obligated public self. His private self is his important self, which validates him. One reason that he needs to be in love with the baroness, hopeless though his case may be, is that his love gives him a chance, in the midst of his public obligations, to show that he is privately otherwise. Komorowska is obviously the stronger: because her being as a Pole is inseparable from her playing of Chopin—and vice versa.

Zanussi, attacking the consolations of schizoid morality, gets in his last blow with an epilogue twenty-five years later. Carrière's daughter by his German wife, now a young woman, is not at all interested in her father's experiences. She refuses the one chance she is given, a posthumous letter, to distinguish between what she knows of her father through his public actions and what the letter might reveal of his private self. (I couldn't help wondering what her reaction would be to this film if she could see it.)

Zanussi's move from dexterous laboratory constructs to vital film is tremendously aided by his two leading actors. The role of the baroness was presumably written for Komorowska, for whom he has written before but not as well. Here he shows, as Shaw once said of himself, that he is a good ladies' tailor. He brings out the best in the blonde, poised, mature Komorowska with a role in which her very reserve underscores her eroticism and in which her perceptions seem only part of a larger understanding.

Zanussi has also done well by Carrière, and vice versa. Carrière is less immediately promising, thus more pleasantly surprising when he deepens. I had seen him in Rohmer's *The Aviator's Wife* (I think he's bilingual, not dubbed in either film) where he did not impress. Here he gets it all, the smoldering torment, the hopelessness, the almost purified acceptance of it.

As the former professor, Frank has a simpler role, but he repeats his two or three chords musically. Zbigniew Zapasiewicz, whom I've seen in earlier Zanussi and in Wajda films, is the librarian-tutor on the estate and is, as before, extremely heavy.

The film looks grainy—I assume that it's been blown up to wide-screen size from its TV original—but the color and compositions and flow are good, harmonized. Chopin is frequently present on the soundtrack, and the look of the film, aside from its scenes of violence, has a matching hush and loneliness.

For some time I've been reading that Zanussi is the best of the post-Wajda generation, but to me, that's not much of a milestone. Besides, *Ways in the Night* is more subtle than any Wajda film that I know. I hope it marks Zanussi's passage into full artistry.

The Big Chill

(October 31, 1983)

This year's Paul Mazursky picture is by Lawrence Kasdan. A Mazursky picture (e.g., *Alex in Wonderland, Blume in Love, An Unmarried Woman, Tempest*) is one that bravely faces social or psychological problems of our time—and that's it. The picture faces them; then, after a while, it stops facing them, and that's the end. Mazursky didn't originate this line of honestly spurious films, but he has become the pre-eminent practitioner, and now he has a scion.

Kasdan made his directing debut with *Body Heat* after working as a script-writer. Perhaps throwing scraps to future authors of critical tomes about him, he goes from *Body Heat* to *The Big Chill*. The first film was a tepid try for styliz-ed sensuality in Florida. The second is a differently but equally tepid try for a societal microcosm in South Carolina.

Of course the film has actors and a cinematographer and settings and editing, but all of them are less important—and would be, whatever their quality—than the script. Some films triumph over their scripts: John Ford made many such. Some, however, are fundamentally writers' films. This is not necessarily deroga-tion: I think it true of most of Bergman and Rohmer. And when it is true, the film depends very heavily on what the author has to say, in the most specific sense of the word. Kasdan has, in sum, nothing to say.

The vacuity is even more oppressive in this particular sort of writer's film. It's the sort in which the author gathers a group of contemporaries, and, through their interactions at that gathering, attempts to lay bare their society's soul. Kasdan, with his script collaborator, Barbara Benedek, had at least two kinds of antecedents. First: the last decade's lot of European pictures about groups: for examples, *Vincent François Paul and the Others* and *We All Loved Each Other So Much*. Such films often start with scenes involving small children, to show that the adults whose taints will be revealed are good at heart. Second and more especially, John Sayles's *Return of the Secaucus Seven*, which is a group pic-ture about a reunion, some years later, of 1960s political activists. This is the locus of Kasdan's group film.

Obvious as is his film's derivation, I had some expectation. It arose out of my persistent belief in rationality. It's difficult to assume from the start that a writer is *not* rational, that he would launch still another film in this form with not much more than the form itself in mind, that he would choose to treat a group of refugees from the 1960s with virtually nothing to add to the subject, with no greater intent than one more use of the lozenge-shaped script: the quiet begin-ning, the swelling as characters and problems accrete, the diminution to a quiet ending. But my faith in Kasdan's rationality was disappointed (though I know it will persist, to be disappointed again). Kasdan does no more than haul forth yet once more a collection of sellouts and compromisers—doggedly defiant or cynically craven, all with their college-years glow now greatly dimmed—put them through their generically typical paces, then shove them away to wait until the next writer-ringmaster hauls them forth to put them through their paces once again. And, again, the ostensible point will be that their paces are a comment on our times.

This is Mazurskyism in essence: the belief that to raise problems is to deal with them. At first view, Mazurskyism may look like Hollywood tailoring: a grandstand play for serious regard by tackling serious subjects, then avoiding the serious consequences of those subjects by neat platitudes and neat finishes. In The Big Chill campus idealism and Vietnam and sexual liberality are the core subjects. (A wife consents to her husband's impregnating a friend who wants a child.) Love gets mentioned a good deal—agape, not eros—because this group has gathered for the funeral of one of their number who killed himself for causes unknown. And all these big subjects, plus others, prove to be merely a species of chic, of décor, not the source of any new insights in Kasdan.

Possibly this insufficiency may look like trimming, like a pullback from ideational consequences—assuming Kasdan to be capable of them—because of big-budget nervousness. Of course Hollywood, with its current average budget of $12 million, isn't eager for intellectual or social risks in its scripts. But Mazurskyism is not a film monopoly: it has long been operative in our theater, not least in off-Broadway, sometimes far off, where budget considerations are much less strangulating. The vacuous group play has an extensive history in our theater: Philip Barry's Hotel Universe dates from 1930. And we have lately had a number of vacuous group plays about 1960s refugees: for instance, Lanford Wilson's The Fifth of July.

The lineage of the group play goes back to Chekhov (although a case can be made for Turgenev's A Month in the Country). To some degree, many great artists leave curses as well as blessings. The Chekhov curse has been the seeming ease of his form, which has resulted in the imitation of that form by lesser writers, all the way from Gorky (whose plays are down the slope from Chekhov) to Kasdan. I don't impute insincerity to the American playwrights and screenwriters in that long line. Quite the reverse: I indict them for sincerity, for believing that sincerity is enough, especially in a drama-film world riddled with insincerities. They are sincerely moved by the dilemmas and agonies they see around them: and are moved to write about those matters sincerely, without pausing to consider whether they have anything to add to what has already been perceived. This charge, the inadequacy of sincerity, applies as much to Mazursky and Kasdan, writing for the screen, as to Wilson, writing for off-Broadway.

The result with such films is just what it is with comparable plays: not enough. There's no reason on earth why any intelligent person, moderately sensible of the Zeitgeist, should see The Big Chill. It does no more than chew over what is already familiar. Kasdan and his fellows are not obligated to solve our problems; Chekhov didn't solve anything. But we have the right to expect perceptions at least equivalent to our own, and Kasdan provides none.

His direction, in purely cinematic terms, is only modestly competent, except for a witty series of dissolves that link some breakfast scenes. His actors are, as noted, more than usually limited by the script in this case, but Kasdan hasn't helped the film with his casting. William Hurt, who was in *Body Heat*, is once again supposed to be charismatic—this time as a pop psychologist who pops pills—and once again he suggests the surreal image of a side of beef from which Muzak gushes. Tom Berenger, as an unhappy TV star, is a fuzzy carbon copy of Burt Reynolds. Glenn Close, afflicted with a hairdo that makes her look like a bewigged hen, is pale as the housewife-hostess who, possibly because the character needed depth, suddenly turns out to be a practicing physician. Her husband, a proudly successful businessman, is Kevin Kline, who proves that his superficial work in *Sophie's Choice* was not a lapse. Some items on the credit side: Jobeth Williams, who has an astonishing resemblance to the late Natalie Wood, is good as an unhappy wife who has long loved Berenger, and Mary Kay Place is all right as the woman who wants a baby. Jeff Goldblum's sardonic urban Jew would be amusing if it hadn't already become his shtick.

All of them, and a few others, discuss the condition and prospects of Hope in Our Time, and when they are finished discussing it, they and we go home. They and we should have stayed there.

Passion

(November 7, 1983)

If there were no Godard, it would be necessary to invent him. This would be difficult because he invented himself, and he is the only one equipped for the job. He has a unique position in the film world, and the more exceptional that position becomes, the more the film world needs him. Since he first became visible some twenty-five years ago, he has fashioned an idiosyncratic career, making films for one reason only: personal need. Some of those films, especially in the 1960s, seemed to me exhibitionistic or silly; some were fascinating, even beautiful; a few were fully achieved works of art. But increasingly, as the years rolled on, as Godard metamorphosed, I've become convinced that judgment of individual works is less relevant to Godard than to almost any other practicing filmmaker. What matters is his existence, his persistence, his imaginative anarchism within the film domain.

Other filmmakers have worked as long, as courageously, as freely, but none that I can think of has so consistently stirred up helpful insurrection at his level. (Miklós Jancsó tries but becomes increasingly hermetic.) Godard has purged himself of avant-gardism for its own sake and is now rather like an eccentric poet or painter living off on a hillside in a cabin somewhere, sending down works once in a while that cannot make the mainstream but are professionally valuable to some good people in that mainstream.

The paradox of this eccentric career is that, disruptive of the esthetic status quo as it means to be, it is nevertheless adequately financed much of the time. If we're not talking about *Star Wars* budgets, neither are we talking about scratchy "underground" expedience. Godard's new film *Passion* is a co-production of French and Swiss companies; the chief cinematographer is the illustrious Raoul Coutard (a Godard colleague of the past); the cast includes three big European stars, Isabelle Huppert, Hanna Schygulla, and Michel Piccoli, as well as the now-noted Polish actor Jerzy Radziwilowicz, who was in recent Wajda films. *Passion* could not have been done on an "underground" budget, yet Godard has made not the slightest concession to success. His new film is as completely concerned with what concerns him as any he as ever made. His financial road can't be smooth, but obviously he can, much of the time, enlist producers and eminent colleagues primarily because of their respect for him.

I suppose there's some hope of eventual profit from subsidiary uses of the film — among them, 16mm and cassettes — but no one could have signed on for *Passion* because he thought it was going to be an immediate theatrical hit. First, if Godard was running true to form, no complete script existed before shooting started, from which to make a judgment about success. Second, if there had been a script of the picture as it finally turned out, no one would have been commercially reassured by it. Now that the film *is* made, it's still hard to describe. It seems to center on the making of a TV film in Switzerland; and the TV film involves living-picture reproductions of some famous paintings. The TV film is being co-directed by two East Europeans, Jerzy and Laszlo. The latter is played by Laszlo Szabo: every character is called by the actor's first name. Also involved are Hanna, who owns the motel where Jerzy is staying and who is having an affair with him; Michel, her husband, a factory owner; and Isabelle, who works on an assembly line in that factory. What the precise intent of the film is, what thematic or other shape these characters and incidents inscribe, I cannot say, and I disbelieve those who do say. Although everything in the film is sternly representational, I think the intent is abstract. To attempt analysis of this film is something like trying to treat a Picasso collage as if it were a Goya. I choose Goya because he is one of the artists whose paintings are made into tableaux, all of which are highly representational. The contrast between their intrinsic storytelling methods and Godard's method seems part of the film's point. But "point" itself is an inappropriate term: Godard explains nothing, ties up very little, merely moves around, watching his people, observing them at this moment or that, prizing this or that view of them or their environment. *Passion* is not a narrative about these people, it is a cinematic essay on them and the places they are in.

Thus, for many of us conditioned by traditional films, eighty-seven minutes of *Passion* are not continuously gripping: they don't contain anything like

eighty-seven minutes of passion. But the film is never dull-witted, always visually pleasurable, often comic, and occasionally startling in its juxtaposition of
shots or its heterodox composition. An oddity about Godard's career for me is
that the further he departs from conventional narrative, the more completely
he ignores convention, the more interesting he becomes.

During a press conference at the recent New York Film Festival where *Passion*
was shown, Godard was asked to comment on someone's statement that his
latter-day films had become his "thinking out loud." Godard, takingly gentle,
replied, "Perhaps they are thinking in silence." This seems more than a fast
answer. His recent films can be seen as attempts to make interiority visible and
audible, in ways that try the borders of cinematic acceptance.

First Name: Carmen

(September 10, 1984)

Carmen continues. Last year we had Carlos Saura's (largely) danced version;*
early in the fall we'll get Francesco Rosi's film treatment of Bizet's opera.**
At the moment here is Jean-Luc Godard's *First Name: Carmen* which is adapted
from Mérimée's novella and which—unlike the recent Peter Brook theater production that also touched Mérimée—shucks Bizet completely. Godard's film
comes quite close to shucking Mérimée, too: there's not a great deal of reason
why it couldn't be called *First Name: Manon*.

The script, credited in France to Godard, is here ascribed to Anne-Marie
Mieville. Set in France today, the film deals with a security guard, Joseph, who
falls to the ground in a tussle with a terrorist-robber named Carmen and, while
tussling, falls for her in other ways. He runs off with her. The comic element in
this episode, typical of a Godard who sees the quirks in a quirky cosmos, runs
throughout: seriousness is continuously mocked. But so much else runs
throughout that even Godard's sidewise skeeter off the universe gets fuzzy,
more dogged than delightful. Aside from his usual practice of presenting only
samples of scenes, to keep himself and us from being bored with the scenes
enacted from beginning to end, there are recurrent shots of a quartet rehearsing Beethoven; Métro trains passing each other; the sea. Exegetes are
already busy revealing the significance of these strands, of the whole concoction. Offhand lines of dialogue—about good and evil, about sunrise—are getting intense analysis. Add that this film—once again in Godard's
career—encloses the making of a film "inside" it and that Godard himself plays
a somewhat loony film director who is Carmen's uncle, and it's clear that *First
Name: Carmen* is manna from hermeneutic heaven.

---

*See review following.
**See p. 259.

My own view is that Godard's procedure, here as in most of his work, is more a matter of temperament than design, that to analyze him is almost like looking for representation in abstract painting. His profligacy and disorder have often caused explosions along the borders of filmmaking, blasting apertures for advance. His last two films, *Every Man for Himself* and *Passion*, hardly textbook exercises, were often interrupted by flashes of cinematic vision that gave a thrill of purpose, of accomplishment, to the whole. That's much less true with *First Name: Carmen*. A few moments jolt us about the way our eyes have been viewing the world. For instance, the close-up silhouette of a hand behind a curtain turns out to be an outstretched hand on a "snowing" TV screen—which is witty. But these moments are rare.

Something else is becoming bothersome in Godard's recent work: he's getting dirty. I don't, need I add, mean sexy. He has gone from one extreme in sexual matters to the other. His films of the 1960s were famously chaste, even when they dealt with prostitution. Recently I saw again *The Married Woman* (1965), a lovely film with insights into the condition of woman in the bourgeois world far deeper than in many subsequent films on the subject. *The Married Woman* begins and ends in bed, but there is no heat: it has much nudity but always as exploration of unrealized beauties, not as excitant. I don't argue that this treatment of bed and nudity was "better," I note how far it is from what Godard is doing now and that his career contains little between the extremes, little that could be called erotic. He seems to have swung directly from the marmoreal to the mucky.

This was notable in *Passion*, where naked women were used as props, almost with an air of male ownership. The utilization of nakedness is much increased in *First Name: Carmen* with more strip-show atmosphere than with the humid heat of Mérimée's marvelous novella. This peering quality, plus some of the action, plus some of the dialogue that Godard himself speaks, gives the film much less unleashed animality than middle-aged drool.

A Dutch actress named Maruschka Detmers is Carmen, is naked quite a lot, and is neither strikingly talented nor appealing. Nor is anyone in the cast.

Carmen

(December 5, 1983)

Carmen is Carlos Saura's fantasia on Mérimée's novel, with generous helpings of Bizet on the soundtrack and even more music by the flamenco guitarist Paco de Lucia, all built toward the film's principal element, the dancing and choreography of the celebrated Antonio Gades. In the film Gades is creating a dance production of *Carmen*, searches for a young woman to dance the leading role opposite his Don José, finds her, falls in love with her, and begins to live the *Carmen* story with her while creating the dance version.

The girl's name is Carmen, and the film's first virtue is that it survives this neatness. The second, greater, is that it runs almost a hundred minutes, is composed largely of Spanish dancing, and is continuously gripping. For me, Spanish dancing—at any rate, the kind most commonly dubbed so, with arched backs and castanets and stamping feet—is the most quickly wearisome of all dance. Ten minutes is about all I can usually take, not just because the vocabulary of this dance is restricted but because its thematic range is narrow. Spanish dance is about sexual intercourse. All dance has some connection with sexuality, I suppose, but no other serious dancing that I know concentrates so narrowly on the arousal of sexual excitement. This is not a dull subject in life, as readers may have discovered, but in art, it has its limits. For the first time in my experience, Gades and his colleagues keep long segments of this highly repetitive dance alive and stinging.

Thus, though Saura directed, it's Gades's film in the most substantive way. He dances excellently, unfailingly electric, moving like a whip. And the dancing he evokes from others comes close to matching his own. His assistant in the film, Cristina Hoyos, is also a fine dancer, but, as he tells her, she's just not Carmen. The young woman he finds for the role is Laura del Sol, and she's an explosion of beauty and risk. To an amateur eye, del Sol's dancing seems not to have the snap and flash of Gades and Hoyos, but she's good—utterly believable as Gades's choice for his production and seduction.

Saura gets credit as co-choreographer with Gades. What is unquestionably to his credit is the choreography of the camera. Almost all the film takes place in Gades's huge studio, with his apartment attached, and within that locus, Saura leads the film back and forth from the *Carmen* being created to the *Carmen* being lived during that creation, with no cuteness and with just enough ambiguity to blur slightly (which is what he wishes) the line between the dance and the dancers' lives. Much of Saura's previous work has seemed sententious: here, with Gades, he has created a unique, sensual organism.

Yentl

(December 19, 1983)

At last Barbra Streisand has found the right director, one who has perfect sympathy with her talent, personality, and ambition. Herself, of course. She directed herself in *Yentl*, and, certainly as far as her performance is concerned (but in other ways, too), she has done a good job of it. Consider *Yentl* as a Streisand display piece, and it's a knockout.

I've long been in the adverse minority about her films, and, to judge by what I've read so far, I'm still in the minority by responding warmly to this film. Many of those who cheered her in work that I found abrasive or grossly exhibitionist now think that she has lost control by insisting on co-writing, directing, and producing her own film. For me, she has gained control, in both the literal and basically relevant senses. Her open declaration that she needs to run her own show indicates only that, at her own level, she has recognized what, for instance, Chaplin recognized: she cannot let anyone intervene between her and the audience. The resulting paradox is that in *Yentl* she seems less egotistical than ever, more at the service of her role and her fellow performers. In 1968, when she was acting in her first film, *Funny Girl*, her disagreements with the director, William Wyler, were notorious; the widespread story was that Wyler said to a friend, "Well, I have to be patient with her. After all, this is the first film she's directed." Wise Wyler apparently discerned a truth. On the evidence of *Yentl*, she is exactly the director she has needed. She ought never to permit anyone else to direct her again.

However, *Yentl* as a rendition of *shtetl* life in Eastern Europe in 1904 — the date assigned — is another matter. This film is to fact as *Fiddler on the Roof* was to fact except that, unlike *Fiddler*, it doesn't contain even one neatly choreographed little pogrom. *Yentl* takes place in a country populated entirely by Jews where prejudice and oppression do not exist, where one doesn't even see a soldier or a policeman. (The exteriors were shot in Czechoslovakia.) As an adaptation of I. B. Singer's story, it is both reduced and embroidered.* The dramatization by Leah Napolin and Singer, which was first presented off-Broadway in 1974, retained some of the sexual complexities. In the film these complexities are explored about as deeply as in *Charley's Aunt*. The screenplay that Streisand wrote with Jack Rosenthal gives grounds to those who want to complain of literary infidelity and historical inaccuracy. But did anyone complain that *Hello, Dolly!* was a distorted rendition of nineteenth-century New York and strayed from both Thornton Wilder and Johann Nestroy? Streisand, with Rosenthal, constructed a star vehicle for herself, with opportunities to get laughs, be hurt, be triumphant, and swell emotionally. Moreover, and surely most important, Streisand evolved a new way to use songs in film.

The story of *Yentl* is in the ancient line of woman-disguised-as-man narrative that doubtless antedates the *Arabian Nights* where it occurs. Yentl, the only daughter of a loving father, is intellectually ambitious and is not resigned to the female status that orthodox Judaism assigns her. She wants to study Torah, a privilege reserved to males. Her dying father foresees trouble for his rebellious child, and it begins at his grave when she — a girl! — insists on speaking the Kaddish, the prayer for the dead. (This moment was one of Streisand's scarce directorial slips. The play made much more of this heroic moment for Yentl.) She then cuts her hair, dons men's clothes, moves to another town, and, under the name Anshel, is accepted in a first-rank yeshiva.

In that yeshiva is another student, Avigdor, with whom she falls, very secret-

*See p. 296.

ly, in love. He is engaged to Hadass, a rich man's daughter, but he feels a disturbingly warm friendship for Anshel. Plot complications break off Avigdor's engagement to Hadass and force Anshel to marry Hadass in order to keep Avigdor from leaving town. Everything works out in the end—for Hadass and Avigdor, anyway—and Yentl, as Yentl, is off to a brave new life in America.

Nothing that this plot evokes is used seriously. Everything is used as a prop for Streisand's virtuosity; but, since she has the virtuosity, the exploitation is justified.

Her face never looked better. We all know that, anthropometrically speaking, there are no such absolutes as Jewish features. We also know that, by general acceptance, there are Jewish features. To deny this is to scant the most important element of Streisand's film success: that a woman with a Jewish face—or, if you like, a "Jewish" face—could rise to stardom without a nose job or a name change. And it would also scant the fact that she looks her best as Yentl. Her features help her as they have never done before, not even in *Funny Girl* and *Funny Lady* where she played Fanny Brice. (Brice was conventionally pretty—at least when she wanted to be.) Here Streisand is supposed to be one of a community, and looks it. This is not to ordain a future for her exclusively of Jewish roles, still in *Yentl* everything around her *supports* her looks, as against those films in which she behaved, and others behaved, as if she looked just like Miss Malted Milk from down the block.

The songs are handled in a way that I've never heard before: they are treated as private commentaries between Yentl and us, not musical numbers listened to by others in the cast. Often she starts a song alone, visibly singing, then moves through a scene with others while the song continues on the soundtrack under her dialogue with them; then the camera returns to her alone, visibly singing, to finish the song. A few lamebrains have complained that Streisand is now so conceited that she won't give a musical number to anyone else. How often does a diarist allow others to write entries in her diary?

The music is by Michel Legrand who has been striving for imaginative use of song in film ever since *The Umbrellas of Cherbourg* (1964). The lyrics, by Alan and Marilyn Bergman, successfully rise above Tin Pan Alley stock. I doubt that there will be singles hits from *Yentl*: this is theater music, integrated with the performance. As such, it's often moving and always apt, and the interwoven "private" use of it gives the whole picture an extra, novel dimension.

Streisand's direction is lucid enough without being distinguished, and sometimes leans on better film-musical moments. The last sequence, on a ship, is so imitative of a *Funny Girl* sequence that it must have been designed as a reminder. She has directed herself as actress very tightly and precisely. For instance, the moment when she is accepted by the yeshiva is handled in a throwaway style—"I'm a student," she says quietly—that zings.

And she does equally well by her fellow actors. Mandy Patinkin, who was splendid as Daniel's father in *Daniel*, is Avigdor and almost bursts the seams of the character with conviction. Various bearded elders, played by Nehemiah Persoff, Steven Hill, and David de Keyser, keep well this side of Rod Steigerism, which is a blessing. The one lump in the cast is Amy Irving as Hadass, inflexible and dull. David Watkin, the cinematographer, whose achievements run from *The Knack* to *Chariots of Fire*, seems stumped by Irving. *Yentl* is not Watkin's best work, anyway, but then the camera is here to provide settings, not evoke realities.

Terms of Endearment

(December 26, 1983)

When we say that, in his new film, Actor A gives his best performance since a film he made ten years ago, usually we're really saying that his new film gives him the best part he's had in ten years. In *Terms of Endearment* Shirley MacLaine has her best part since *Desperate Characters* (1974), and Jack Nicholson has his best part since *One Flew Over the Cuckoo's Nest* (1975). This is not to imply that any other actors could have done what they do here if the others had fallen into the parts; but when a performer gets a part that brings out his best, that extends his best, we tend to overlook the fact that talent means very little without adequate opportunity.

Another way to put this is that *Terms of Endearment* is well written, well cast, well directed. The screenplay by James L. Brooks is derived from a Larry McMurtry novel which I haven't read. I'm told reliably that the script retains much of the novel's dialogue, which on the evidence was sensible, and that Nicholson's character is a complete transmutation of a character in the book, which on the evidence was also sensible. Brooks demonstrates even more of his quality with the screenplay's venturous structure. The story covers about thirty years, and he has used ellipsis skillfully, leaving much of the scaffolding work to the viewer's imagination. The script relies, justifiably, on the collaboration of colleagues, including actors and director and audience, to fulfill it. Brooks is also the director, so the reliance was reasonable. This is the first time he has directed, so it was also brave. In any case, he was right.

Since TV is where Brooks has done most of his previous writing and since *Terms of Endearment* is a family drama, we're likely to hear that it is soap opera *in excelsis*. This is true, but only to the degree that soap opera is authentic drama in reduction. What Brooks has dared to try is what succeeded in such a gem as Passer's *Intimate Lighting* or, at the far pinnacle of such films, Ozu's *Tokyo Story*: a film whose drama comes from following the course of life, not from narrative conventions. *Terms of Endearment* does have a highly emotional conclusion, but it comes about quite arbitrarily, as highly emotional occurrences do in life. This arbitrariness has puzzled some reviewers who complain that the story starts as comedy-romance and ends dramatically, thus mixing genres. This is only to say that the story is lifelike: a young woman gets married and about ten years later (as readers of the novel know) develops cancer. Ought she not to have been blithe and frivolous ten years earlier on the chance that she might develop cancer? To complain of mixed genres about this reasonably lifelike picture is to complain that life mixes genres. One of the powers of art is that it can, if it chooses, clear up this confusion and give us unmixed comedy or drama, farce or tragedy. Another power of art is that, if it operates in good faith, it can reproduce the mixture.

Nicholson is not at the precise center of the story: MacLaine is. So is her daughter, acted in true terms of endearment by Debra Winger, who is witty, shrewd, warm. MacLaine is a well-to-do suburban Houston widow who rears her small daughter in a manner that is both concerned and resentful, neurotic and humorous. Her treatment of the girl is so challenging that the young woman grows up competent to deal with her. The grown daughter remarks, after an altercation, that she and the mother have always known that they loved each other. MacLaine is astonished: they fight all the time, she says. Winger replies, "It may have seemed like fighting from your end."

That's a fair sample of the dialogue, never awesomely profound, never tediously banal. It's the characters themselves, rather than the author, who seem to be avoiding banality. They seem conscious of the fact that most real-life dialogue in most real-life situations has been chewed over and over in print and on screen so often that it's difficult for an intelligent person to speak without hearing echoes of performance. In love or in hate, these people don't want to sound corny.

The plentiful humor is never impasted gag, as in Neil Simon: it's always either a character's credible wit or a "straight" line that comes out funny. In an Iowa supermarket a checkout girl behaves badly to a customer, and another customer tells her so. Checkout girl: "I don't think I behaved badly." Second customer: "You must come from New York."

MacLaine objects to her daughter's fiancé and won't attend the wedding. The objection isn't specified, but presumably it's because the man's financial pro-spects are poor—he's a college teacher—and because MacLaine is both secretly jealous and openly tyrannical. She might have been happy about her daughter's marriage if she herself had chosen the man. The daughter proceeds anyway, almost amused at her nutty, annoying mother. The bride and groom forgive MacLaine in a pattern that gets repeated throughout the film, argument and honesty resulting in a pact until the next argument. Children come, three of them; venues change. The husband gets a job in Iowa, then in Nebraska. Winger has an affair in Iowa without the soap-operatic motive of marital unhappiness. She is quite happily married: she has the affair simply because she likes the man sufficiently and wants the intimacy with him. When she learns that her husband is involved with a graduate student, she understandably refuses to take this as divine retribution and is furious. (The film's one hoked-up scene is a violent quarrel between wife and husband right out on the open campus.) Soon the medical news intervenes, which leads to the film's conclusion. The end ties up nothing neatly. Life is simply going to go on, which is all that life has been doing up to now.

Nicholson is MacLaine's neighbor, as he is neighbor to the story. He is an ex-astronaut whose life has peaked early and who knows it. He moves into the house next door and quickly earns MacLaine's dislike because he is noisy, drunk much of the time, and an unembarrassed womanizer. In the course of fifteen years, Nicholson's mere proximity, as he masculinizes away, piques MacLaine, and the pique results in an affair, so intense that it scares him off at the same time that it opens a new world of sex to her. The idea of the Nicholson character—an ass-chasing, heavy-drinking, pot-bellied ex-astronaut, with charm that is more overbearing that insinuating—is itself a ten-strike. All that remained was for it to be written well and acted well, which it was. And Brooks has resisted any temptation he may have had to make the affair "mean" something. It occurs at about the same time that the daughter is having her affair, but that simultaneity doesn't "mean" anything. The MacLaine-Nicholson affair is an experience that is absorbed and moved on from, like other experiences in the story.

Other good performances flower out of Brooks's casting choices and sympathy with actors: Jeff Daniels, as Winger's teacher-husband, with just the right combination of independence and subscription; Lisa Hart Carroll, as Winger's lifelong friend, covertly affectionate; John Lithgow, as Winger's sweet and slightly dull lover; and two boys, Troy Bishop and Huckleberry Fox, as Winger's two sons. The scene in which the boys, about nine and four, say good-bye to their mother in her hospital room is irresistible, especially since the smaller boy's heartbreak is mixed with the older boy's near-resentment of his mother's death, which Winger understands. Anyone who can work as well as Brooks does with veterans like Nicholson and MacLaine, with a relative beginner like Carroll, and with two children, has a right to call himself a director.

This is especially true because Brooks also shows a good eye for fittingly unusual composition and a good sense of tone. The sequence before the credits opens with voices coming out of a screen that is black except for a night light in the lower righthand corner. At one level, the night light assures us that the generally black screen isn't a blooper in the projection booth, and at another level it teases us into the film until MacLaine switches on the nursery lamp. The scene in MacLaine's summerhouse, when Nicholson tells her that the affair is over, is perfectly pitched, kept quiet and charged. Brooks holds the camera mostly in a low-angled two-shot with complete figures seated opposite each other. The Nicholson leaves gently and returns slowly to his house in the background while MacLaine remains seated in profile. It's all understated yet complete.

Andrzej Bartkowiak helps greatly. He is the cinematographer, born and trained in Poland, who was brought into American film by Sidney Lumet and who did such fine work in *The Verdict*, among others. Bartkowiak's lighting shows understanding of faces. The engaging music is by Michael Gore who, like the admirable Georges Delerue, uses classical forms with modern tartness.

Silkwood

(January 23, 1984)

Meryl Streep, as Karen Silkwood, drove her car through the gate of the plant where she worked, parked, then headed across the lot toward her job; and I felt snug. *Silkwood* was going to be all right. In those first ordinary actions, Streep had once again done the miraculous, which is the daily work of fine actors: she had changed the unchangeable. When I last saw her, in *Sophie's Choice**, the core of Sophie had been innate, immutable. Now she has transmuted to another immutable.

Streep does not let us down. But the film does, badly. Mike Nichols, returning to film direction after an eight-year absence, begins well enough. With his good cinematographer, Miroslav Ondricek, Nichols opens by laying in some quiet Oklahoma morning landscape, quiet, expectant. Then, prefiguring the finish, he picks up Streep's car on a lonely road as she drives with lover and friend to the plant where they all work. The stage is almost literally being set.

And in some ways the picture continues to disclose more good Nichols. He has cast the film unexceptionably. His use of space is cunning—such as the way he places Streep and Cher in different rooms, speaking through an open door, when there is a difference between them but they are united by a common roof over their heads. His use of camera motion and editing is more fluent than ever. These are matters that he has learned since he entered films. What seems numbed in *Silkwood* is what Nichols brought with him to films: his theatrical sense of dialogue—its rhythms and timing—which was exquisite. This film labors under longueurs, not of windy dialogue but of wind between the lines that bloats the film. No character can ask another to have a beer without enough time lapsing before the answer in which to drink the whole damned beer. (Incidentally, I'd like to see *one* film about proles in which a man in his undershirt on a hot day drinks beer and doesn't pour part of it over his head.) About twenty of the film's 128 minutes could have been eliminated by picking up cues, and the result would not have betrayed the idiomatic pace of the characters' speech. As is, the pace gets so draggy that it reflects on the actors. Audiences may think that Streep and colleagues are less gripping than they ought to be when the flaw is really Nichols's "conducting."

Some of the other good actors who suffer from this fault are Kurt Russell, as

---

*See p. 206.

Streep's lover, and E. Katherine Kerr and Fred Ward as co-workers. Cher suffers from it, too. I'm not yet sure about her acting (I saw her under the blight of Robert Altman's direction in a Broadway play), but here, as the housemate of Streep and Russell who has a lesbian interest in Streep, she is at least kept from false moves by Nichols.

Inexplicably, the gifted Georges Delerue was imported to write the score. It's hardly a score: not much music is used. Some of it is banjo stuff, to underline locale, and some of it is melodramatic underlining when nuclear dangers arise. Anyone could have written this music: Delerue was wasted.

But dissatisfactions go far past these matters of execution, bothersome as they are. The script by Nora Ephron and Alice Arlen is a compound of compromise, alteration, and misleading implication—all serious matters in what purports to be a true story. On the night of November 13, 1974, Silkwood was driving from Crescent City, Oklahoma, to Oklahoma City to meet a *New York Times* reporter. Silkwood was a lab worker in the Cimarron Plutonium Recycling Facility, in Crescent, owned by the Kerr-McGee Nuclear Corporation, and she is said to have been carrying revelatory documents to that meeting about safety conditions and quality control in the Cimarron plant. On her way to the meeting, her car ran off the road, and she was killed instantly. Speculation soon rose that she had been murdered to prevent her disclosures. Because no documents incriminating her employers were found, although there were other documents in the car, the murder suspicion seemed confirmed.

I am not remotely competent to sift all the evidence in this matter, but as far as I can make out, no irrefutable proof of murder or document theft has yet been produced although much time has been spent in trying to provide that proof. But this ambiguity has not deterred Ephron and Arlen—and of course Nichols and his producers—from implying heavily that Silkwood had incriminating evidence in the car and that another car came up behind hers on the road and forced her off. (In the film's worst sequence, Silkwood is "canonized" at the end. After we see her gravestone, we get the farewell scene between her and her lover, already viewed, done again in slow motion while on the soundtrack she sings "Amazing Grace.") Also, some published accounts indicate that facts about Silkwood's private life have been altered to make her more popularly acceptable and that her experiences in the plant, with safety practices and radiation tests, have been nudged a bit one way and another.

All these changes verge on the unethical, the deliberately misleading. E. L. Doctorow altered facts in the Rosenberg case for his novel *The Book of Daniel*, but he made no claim to be presenting that case factually. Quite the contrary: he was using elements of that case as he needed them for a work of art about the themes involved. No such rationale applies in *Silkwood*. The film was made with the clear intent to tell us the truth about a conspiratorial crime, and it apparently does not.

Conditions at the Cimarron plant seem to have been, according to Congressional testimony and news accounts, horrifyingly careless. No demurral about the "canonization" of Silkwood should be seen as exculpation of Kerr-McGee. (The plutonium plant was closed about a year after Silkwood's death.) But this film pretends to be fact, and the pretense is somewhat hollow.

Part of the fact manipulation comes, I think, not so much from social or political sympathies as from dramaturgic need, the need to make a cogent script out of a life that is hard to organize dramatically. The end of Silkwood's life is shocking, but in the life itself it's difficult to clarify themes without leaning on facts. The film does indeed show her growing awareness of her social situation and its connection with the physical condition caused by her job, but this is not the same as making her something akin to a labor Joan of Arc.

And the Ship Sails On

(February 13, 1984)

The screenplay of Federico Fellini's new film, *And the Ship Sails On*, which he wrote with Tonino Guerra, is transparently symbolic—by design. In July 1914 an Italian luxury liner called the *Gloria N.* sails on a special voyage. The ship carries the ashes of a great soprano, Edmea Tetua, who died fairly young and who had requested that her ashes be cast into the sea off the island where she was born. Accompanying the ashes are many notables of music, singers and conductors and impresarios from all over Europe. Also aboard are at least three of Tetua's lovers: a fat Egyptian who is accompanied by some veiled wives; a wan count who is accompanied by some newsreel film of his beloved; and a plump young Austrian duke who is accompanied by his blind sister and their retinue.

During the voyage, which starts shortly after the assassination at Sarajevo, a number of refugee Serbs are taken aboard. An Austro-Hungarian warship intercepts the *Gloria N.* and demands that the Serbs be handed over. The Italian captain refuses, and the warship threatens. The Austrian duke informs the warship that he is aboard the liner, and the *Gloria N.* is permitted to proceed to the island. During the funeral service, a phonograph plays a Tetua recording of an air from *Aida*, "O Patria mia." After the ashes are scattered, the duke sets out for the warship, and the Serbs are ordered into boats, also to be transferred to the warship. Before they are aboard the enemy, a Serb youth tosses a bomb onto the warship, which starts explosions. The Austro-Hungarians cannonade the *Gloria N.*, apparently considering the Italians responsible. Both ships are lost.

Add to this outline a few details. Opera, mostly Verdi, is not only prominent in the film score, it is part of the film's action: when the warship threatens, a conductor on the *Gloria N.* whips out a baton, and the passengers burst into an operatic chorus as a defense measure. Among the passengers, besides flirtations and romances and cherished romantic memories, are several strains of un-orthodox sexuality: an English woman is pantingly avid for men, and her husband relishes her avidity for others; a toothless old man likes little girls; a silent-film comic likes young men. As the *Gloria N.* founders, an Italian journalist, who has been our guide and confidant during the voyage, grabs the picture of Garibaldi in his stateroom and clambers into a rowboat; the last shot is of the correspondent making for shore, his sole companion a rhinoceros that had been destined for a zoo and whose stink has disturbed the passengers during the voyage.

Interpretation is unnecessary.

The symbolism is so transparent because we are meant to see through it to the film's real richness. Fellini, with Guerra, wrote the script, not for its meaning(s) but because of the way he wanted to film it. This is not the first time Fellini has made a film whose chief rewards are in its style, but this time he seems to have planned it that way.

His career, as I've noted before, divides in two: first, the so-called neorealistic films through *The Nights of Cabiria* (1957); second, those since *La Dolce Vita* (1960) that take the baroque as far, often gloriously so, as it has gone in film art. Excepting the masterworks 8½ and *Amarcord*, excepting too that lesser but lovely memoir-tribute *The Clowns*, the baroque films were conceived much in the manner of opera before this century: the stories were mere scaffoldings for stylistic display. The three autobiographical films cited above prove that pyrotechnics and thematic weight need not be mutually exclusive; his other baroque films dazzle but eventually disappoint, like fireworks that promise a change in the heavens but leave you in the dark. Of course Fellini's fireworks are repeatable, but so is the eventual letdown. Lately I saw *Juliet of the Spirits* again and was again delighted by its visual splendors; but the film promises some kind of enlightenment about the status of women in our society, on which subject it simply cops out.

And the Ship Sails On makes no corresponding promise. From the start, it is no more, and no less, than an ingenious arrangement of events that will give Fellini ample chance to exercise his filmmaking virtuosity. Which he does.

He began, as always, by choosing colleagues who are in temperamental harmony with him, virtual extensions of his own imagination. The art direction by Dante Ferretti (costumes by Maurizio Millenotti) is not quite at the level of the late Piero Gherardi's work for Fellini, but it is eccentrically gorgeous. The music by Gianfranco Plenizio, if it doesn't have the tunes with which the late Nino Rota stabbed our hearts, uses Verdi with understanding and wryness; and the rest of the time is pleasant ear-cushioning. Giuseppe Rotunno's cinematography is predictably superb, especially as he turns backgrounds into dreams and makes the moonlight his ally. Ruggero Mastroianni, Marcello's brother, has edited all Fellini films since *Juliet of the Spirits* and has almost become part of the director's persona.

Then there's Fellini's approach to casting. With some past exceptions, notably Marcello M., he chooses his actors for their faces and bodies; the voices are at his disposal, just as much a part of the sound track he will later put together as are the music and sound effects. As a view of acting, this is anathema to me, but Fellini is one of the rare exceptions that prove the rule. As far as I can tell, every performer in this new film has a voice that Fellini has chosen, usually humorously, for him or her. The faces-and-bodies are well up to his best—in a word, Daumier.

With his production and performance colleagues, Fellini has created a flow of images that transforms the material world into magic and eloquence. Here are only a few of the pictures that will stay with me: a group of opera singers on the visitors' gallery of the liner's boiler-room, performing for the huddled stokers far below who look up to them, like martyrs to saviors, in the glow of the furnaces; the fine-faced blind Austrian princess, smiling with secrets in the midst of tumult; the shot through the porthole of the wireless room that shows a skillet of spaghetti on the operator's table as he taps away for help; the water rushing through the corridors of the sinking *Gloria N.*, floating passengers' luggage along with it; the dead soprano's faithful lover sitting calmly in his suite on the doomed ship, watching a film of his beloved as the water rises around him.

Most of the recognizable faces are English: Janet Suzman as the dead diva in the newsreel shots; Barbara Jefford as a surviving diva; Philip Locke as the blind princess's lover; Freddie Jones (who was Sir in the London production of *The Dresser*) as the journalist. There is no protagonist. The interweaving of numerous stories is congenial to Fellini's style; he is the protagonist.

Some of the touches are familiar from his past work—e.g., the seance (*Juliet*), the Moslem with veiled wives (*Amarcord*)—but here these are more hallmarks than empty repetitions. One element, one set of elements, is bothersome. Throughout the film, Fellini uses camera awareness. The journalist frequently addresses the camera as if, anachronistically, he were making a sound-film record of the voyage; others see the camera, too. In *Amarcord* this camera awareness was poignant, the townsfolk of the past recording themselves to ward off oblivion. Here the device adds nothing. Fellini also uses some quaint old-fashioned theater touches: in the long shots of the two ships, the smoke coming from funnels is fixed, as in cardboard cutouts; in the last scene, the sea is rippling canvas. I couldn't see the value, esthetic or otherwise, of these small jokes, or of the glimpse near the end of the making of this very film. Such a moment occurs near the end of *Persona*, but in that great work about the complexities of consciousness, it is a last chilling touch that was prefigured from the start. Here it jars, as if Fellini just didn't want to miss any bets, was grabbing every chance for texture, whether it really helped or not.

But his *Ship* does indeed sail, even with a few barnacles. And, as usual, Fellini practices his wizardry with wit: from the extraordinary moustaches of the dining-room steward to the pomps of power and of romance.

One quality has resurged in him. Early Fellini was strongly marked by compassion: it was the chief impulse behind such films about poor people as *Il Bidone* and *I Vitelloni*. When he moved in part two to upper-class subjects, some of his films concentrated on disgust. In his new film, compassion figures strongly again, even for those who are bringing about the end of an era, for those willing to permit it. He hasn't forgotten that suffering is worse for the poor and powerless, but, older, he sees that disappointment and mortality are not class monopolies.

Entre Nous

(February 27, 1984)

The first two films by the French director Diane Kurys, born 1948, were *Peppermint Soda* and *Cocktail Molotov*, both of which were autobiographical. Her third film, *Entre Nous*, is biographical. Kurys has written and directed a film about her parents, though this is clear only at the end when she appends a closing note. The main characters are her father and mother, her mother's dear woman friend, and that woman's husband. The last shot, in 1952, is a four-year-old girl—Kurys under another name—watching silently as her parents finish their last conversation before a breach that was never healed. Those closing words tell us that her father left the next morning, that her parents never met again, that she dedicates *Entre Nous* to them and to her mother's woman friend. The film has given the reasons.

The mother, played by Isabelle Huppert, is first seen in 1942, still single, en route by bus to an internment camp in southern France. Only the music tells us that the bus is carrying Jews. In the camp a Foreign Legionnaire, Guy Marchand, on duty as a guard, smuggles a note to her, proposing marriage as a means of saving her. (He knows she will be shipped to Germany.) She accepts; marries; then discovers that he, too, is Jewish, though still unharrassed in Vichy France. The scene in which she discovers that she has married, not immunity but the possibility of further trouble, is perfectly balanced—outrage that is comic against a backdrop of dark fact. After the Germans move south, the pair escape, in great hazard, over the Alps to Italy.

Also in 1942 we see a young art student, Miou-Miou, and her lover, another artist, caught in a gunfight between partisans and French militia. Her lover is killed in her arms.

We leap forward to 1952, in Lyons. Huppert and Marchand now have two daughters. (The younger is Kurys's proxy.) After a rough time, Marchand has been able to start a garage, works hard, worships his family. Huppert, as far as she knows, is happy. Miou-Miou has married an unsuccessful, unscrupulous actor, Jean-Pierre Bacri, charming but not quite charming enough. They have a small son. Because of that son and Huppert's daughter, the two women meet, at a children's play. They become close friends. Eventually the two couples become friends, though not as close.

The need of each woman for the other is clear. Through Miou-Miou, who is a sculptor, Huppert finds reaches of imaginative response that Marchand can't open to her. From Huppert the other woman gets an emotional competency that her husband, the actor, can't provide. Very soon, each woman realizes that her life would seem empty without the other.

Each husband shows some sexual interest in the other wife but not for long. The actor makes moves toward Huppert virtually out of reflex, then quits. Marchand is almost sullenly excited by Miou-Miou; his feeling is converted to, or fuels, his resentment of her invasion of his wife's emotional being. He forbids Huppert to associate with the other woman. Huppert secretly persists, is found out, still persists. Huppert then opens a boutique, financed with difficulty by her husband. He later learns that Miou-Miou is a partner, and he smashes the shop to bits. This leads to the last scene—of nonreconciliation.

The focus of the film is women's love, not necessarily lesbianism. The lesbian possibility is gently suggested only once, by two scenes that come close together. On a train to Paris where she will meet Miou-Miou to shop for their boutique, Huppert allows a soldier she has just met to make love to her. When she meets Miou-Miou, she tells her friend about it and admits that the encounter produced her first orgasm. That night the women are in twin beds in a hotel. Huppert touches the other one's hand, then withdraws.

This picture is most impressive in the texture with which Kurys has woven her world. While the characters move through their lives to their meeting and its consequences, that progress is enriched by discursive episodes—like one in which Miou-Miou's little boy accidentally locks himself in a toilet—that don't advance the story yet are enriching. This means, of course, that the characters have been brought to a pitch of life where virtually anything they do is of some interest.

In purely filmic terms Kurys is now quite sure of herself, so that she understates, is almost laconic. This is particularly helpful in a film charged with high feeling, and it's particularly evident in the subtle pulse of her editing. Also, Kurys uses a commonplace device, period songs for a period picture, with some humor. A recurrent number is Perry Como's recording of "I Wonder Who's Kissing Her Now."

The picture's quality is lifted with the performances that Kurys gets from her three principals. (The actor fades.) Huppert has often been impressive, but in a tacitly suffering way, as in *The Lacemaker* and *The Judge and the Assassin*. Here she gives an outgoing performance, inflected in a range of colors, spontaneous and easy. I liked Miou-Miou in her first appearance here, in *Going Places*. (Huppert was also in that 1974 film.) She has grown tremendously and has certainly outgrown that cutesy name. She is a willowy beauty; she is also an actress of weight and wit, with a flavor of acceptance that is very far from resignation.

The most difficult of the three parts is Huppert's husband. As with all husbands in plays and films where our sympathy is meant to go to the wife, we must understand why she married him in the first place and stayed with him, or else the wife's character is diminished. Marchand creates winningly the man who would have offered marriage as he did when he did; who would quite literally have carried his wife across the snowy Alps to safety; who would have scrounged to make a postwar life for his family; would have adored them; and would have shortcomings of mind and spirit. The worst of it, for him, is that he perceives the gaps when someone else fills them for his wife. His rage, when he busts up the boutique, is not tyranny but impotence. He knows that he can't stop what will happen, either by barring his wife's way or by giving her what she gets from her friend. Marchand puts it all before us with warmth and vulnerability.

He is so good that he pushes to the front a question that, since the story is biographical, can't be a criticism of the script. It's a comment on behavior that is shown here as somewhat heroic, certainly worth approval. I couldn't help feeling—unpopularly, I suppose—that the Huppert character was cruel and selfish and ungrateful to leave her husband. Grant his patent deficiencies; grant that she loves her friend and will be happier with her. Out of what she had shared with her husband, not least the fact that twice he quite literally saved her life and the fact that he deeply loved her and the two children she was taking, it's possible to think that she might have put her satisfactions aside in obligation to a good and loving man.

Before any hoots of male chauvinism arise, I insist that I would have felt the same if the roles had been reversed (and know this from experience with friends and ex-friends). I'm not advocating a return to Victorian pietistic ideas of marriage. I share Bernard Shaw's anger at ritual domestic self-sacrifice. But we have gone from an era of corseted inhuman restriction to an era of self-indulgence, where self-satisfaction is the primary, sometimes sole, criterion. That seems to me equally inhuman and uncivilized. It disregards the idea of honor. In the circumstances of this marriage as given, I thought the wife had a debt of honor to her husband. I felt that Marchand deserved better from her, that she might well have borne the diminution of happiness that staying with him would have brought, borne it as payment of a debt of honor and love. What I especially dislike was the film's assumption that of course we would understand that she had to do it—even if it hurt him—because she wanted to do it.

No apologies for this moralist conclusion. The film presents some lives so well that it forces a reaction to those lives as such. *Entre Nous* says that self-satisfaction is all. I don't agree.

Seeing Red

(April 2, 1984)

Seeing Red is a well-made, 100-minute documentary, consisting mostly of interviews with surviving members and ex-members of the American Communist Party who joined during the 1930s. The filmmakers are James Klein and Julia Reichert, who previously did *Union Maids*, moving stories of the struggles to organize unions during the Depression, told by some of the women involved. At least one of those women is in the new film. For one viewer who is a contemporary of that woman and of the other people in *Seeing Red*, the film had an especially immediate effect, so perhaps a few personal notes may be allowed.

My own activity in support of the American Communist Party is quickly recounted. In the mid-1930s, Earl Browder, then head of the party, came to lecture at New York University, where I was a student. He spoke in a large theater. I arranged the lights and handled the curtain for his talk (of which I recall nothing but his Kansas accent). I was paid for my collaboration – not with Moscow gold but with university work-study funds.

That's it. The following May Day I was watching the immense Communist parade in Union Square when a couple of friends marched by and saw me on the curb. With a vehemence they must have learned from Soviet films, they called to me: "Intellectuals! Join our ranks!" Although tempted, as I had been recurringly tempted through the decade, I didn't join; I hadn't joined during my college years, and I stayed out until the temptation was dispelled. But my abstention was mostly a matter of luck. Not perception or prescience kept me out, not lack of interest in Marx or the world's troubles, only the fact that I was thoroughly engaged in other (nonpolitical) activity.

Still, from the time that I could begin to read and think politically, which was in the early 1930s, it seemed to me, as to almost all politically aware young people I knew, that the world faced only two alternatives: communism and fascism. Smile now if you like; it wasn't funny then, and it didn't seem remotely simplistic. The grinding of the Depression was all around us, in our homes and in the streets; the seemingly unstoppable rise of Italian and German fascism chilled our blood. (No one who did not witness that rise can truly know what it felt like.) When the Spanish Civil War erupted, I even looked into the possibility of joining the Abraham Lincoln Brigade to fight Franco. Creeping cowardice and parental horror deterred me, and, in this case, I've always been glad of both; but my impulse was a symptom of the time.

My recurrent temptation to join the party, from which other obligations protected me, evanesced toward the end of the decade. It's usually said that the first great disillusionment with communism was the German-Soviet pact of August 1939. My own shock came a bit earlier, with the verbatim report of the so-called Moscow trials in 1938. This eight-hundred-page book was published in English (presumably in other languages, too) by the Soviet government, apparently with pride; but it prepared me for the brutal expediency of the pact that came along soon after. Those American members of the party who survived both those shocks were, of course, confirmed in fervor when the Axis powers invaded the U.S.S.R. in June 1941. The heat of the war, with the Soviets as our allies and with the unsurpassed heroism of their forces, burned away political differences.

After the war, the various depredations of the Soviet government soon sharply restored those differences. Americans who remained members of the Communist Party seemed deformed by habit rather than courageous, no matter how much one despised the McCarthyism deployed against them. *Seeing Red* says that Khrushchev's "revelations" about Stalin in June 1956 caused eighty percent of the American party members to drop out. I don't see a great difference in intellectual or moral clarity between those who waited until then to drop out and those who remained.

However, none of this can seriously derogate the party enthusiasms of the early and middle 1930s: when support of exploited workers and farmers, campaigns against racial discrimination, organization against fascism, seemed to be led by Communists: when allegations of Moscow influence seemed either capitalist fantasy or, if true, quite logical. (After all, the influence of Hitler was terrifyingly present on the streets of Yorkville and at gigantic, uniformed rallies; why shouldn't the Soviet Union have wanted to countervail them?) The best hope for a humane future could easily be thought to rest with communism. For a localized example, look at *The Compound Cinema*, a collection of film criticism by Harry Alan Potamkin. He was a critic of exceptional mind and sensibility who wrote for only six years: he died in 1933 at the age of 33. In the first three years, his work was largely apolitical; with the onslaught of the Depression, he became a fiery Communist. His subsequent work was considerably burdened with doctrine and polemic (though it's far from worthless), and it has become the common opinion to dismiss all of his work, to dismiss Potamkin himself as a party hack. I see him rather as a valuable man who responded quite understandably to a change of climate, then had the ill fortune to die before he could go on to other responses. There are plentiful examples of artists and intellectuals who went through Potamkin's Stages One and Two, then lived to go through later stages; Potamkin's career was frozen by mortality in Stage Two. Because he didn't have the chance to go through those later stages, he is fixed in the historical movement of embracing communism as possibility, an embrace that I, only by dumb luck, escaped.

That leads to a salient omission in *Seeing Red*. I wouldn't have expected the film to be anything like a complete history, even a rounded synoptic history, of the party in the years covered. But it concentrates on workers and on people involved in labor movements and social work. Very few former or present Communist intellectuals are heard from. The omission makes even this little chronicle lopsided. In terms of visibility (at the time) and continuity (through histories), even an overview is impossible without some real knowledge of what artists and intellectuals were doing, saying, accepting at the time in relation to the party. Communist activity in aid of the poor and oppressed was clear and indisputable; in other fields, the activity was sometimes shadowy but equally indisputable. For example, it's not known generally or remembered widely that the party had a sort of cultural commissar—named V. J. Jerome—who wielded power through threats of party boycott. One instance of his power: John Houseman (as he himself tells it in *Run-Through*), along with Orson Welles, agreed to make changes in their 1938 production of *Danton's Death* to placate Jerome.

Seeing Red was intended, like some recent books, to explore the utterly human motives that impelled people to become Communists in the 1930s. It may also have intended to redress the past emphasis on artistic-intellectual Communist matters by concentrating on labor and social workers. But this concentration prevents the film from conveying the two criticisms which Klein has said that he and Reichert wanted to make: American Communists blindly followed another country's orders; the party was hierarchical and despotic. Almost all the people interviewed in *Seeing Red* either don't yet know those two points or won't discuss them.

The Good Fight

(April 23, 1984)

Reviewing *Seeing Red*, I mentioned the Abraham Lincoln Brigade. Now we get a documentary about that brigade, called *The Good Fight*. Like the earlier film, it consists chiefly of interviews with survivors, interwoven with newsreel footage and other material; like the earlier film, it is competently made and highly interesting. The filmmakers, Noel Buckner, Mary Dore, and Sam Sills, had aid from the National Endowment for the Humanities. Studs Terkel narrates.

Among the principal interviewees are Bill Bailey, the seaman in *Seeing Red* who was very visibly antifascist in the 1930s, and Milt Wolff, the former art student who at twenty-three became the commander of the brigade. Wolff and the other veterans speak of their experiences in the Spanish Civil War with pride and with affection for comrades. Rightly so. They went to Spain to fight fascism, and they risked their lives to do it. Many of their friends gave their lives.

I don't follow with a "but": no antithesis. Their political convictions then (and possibly now) are not up for judgment here. Every account I have read of the brigade has said that, among the Spanish Loyalists, the feeling at first was that these American volunteers were naive enthusiasts but that, after little training, they plunged into battle bravely, suffered severe losses, and kept fighting. Their casualties were so heavy that they soon had to be merged with another mauled American group, the virtually forgotten George Washington Brigade—not mentioned in the film.

Other matters are not mentioned. We hear that these brigades and others from other countries formed the International Brigade; we don't hear that the International Brigade was a project of the Comintern. We don't hear about the Soviet maneuverings of these dedicated volunteers, intrigues that are inscribed in history. (And in fiction—notably *For Whom the Bell Tolls*.) Hugh Thomas says in *The Spanish Civil War* that, after the Munich pact of September 1938, the Soviets, with Stalin's agreement, ordered the International Brigade to be disbanded and sent home so as to help clear the decks for a pact with Hitler, which followed in August 1939. The International Brigade was given a rousing farewell parade and was addressed in ringing phrases by La Pasionaria (some of them spoken here by Colleen Dewhurst), none of which mentioned the political reasons for the withdrawal.

Still the courage and sacrifice of these volunteer men and women are unassailable. *The Good Fight* is a good record of these matters.

L'Argent

(April 16, 1984)

Buffon was mistaken: style is not the man himself, it's the universe that is seen by the man. Many a disorderly person has been an orderly artist. But neither is style a separable system into which an artist feeds material. Van Gogh didn't look at the night sky and decide that it would be pretty to paint the constellations as whirls. Joyce didn't decide it would be clever to describe that same sky as "the heaventree of stars hung with humid nightblue fruit." Neither artist had, in a sense, much choice. The style was refined through a lifetime, but the temper and vision were given.

Thus it's impossible to imagine Robert Bresson *deciding* to make *L'Argent* as he did. On the basis of his career, we can assume that, at some time after he read Tolstoy's story, "The False Coupon," his mind and imagination shaped his film in ways that his mind and imagination have long been doing. It's a kind of fatalism, I believe. Not all fine artists work the same way all their lives: Ozu is one who did not. Some, like Bresson, do. At the age of seventy-six, he made his thirteenth film in essentially the same style that he used in *Les Anges du Péché* in 1943.

Consequently you know, if you know Bresson, that *L'Argent* was made with nonactors. He has rarely used professionals; he calls his cast "models." You know that if the subject is contemporary, the sounds of metropolitan life will probably be heard under the credits. You know that the story will be told with almost Trappist austerity; that the camera will fix on places a moment before characters enter and will remain a moment after they leave, not only to include environment as a character but also to signify that humans are transient in the world; that probably a chain of consequences will begin with an event seemingly unrelated to the conclusion. This style, which includes numerous other attributes, does not unfailingly produce engrossing films: *Four Nights of a Dreamer* and *Lancelot du Lac* say little more to me than that Bresson made them. *L'Argent*, though it has faults, enlightens. It's not of the quality of *A Man Escaped* and *Diary of a Country Priest* and *Mouchette*, but it's a film to be seen by every Bresson admirer, of whom I hope there are many.

The pattern is simple. A pebble is moved, and the eventual result is an avalanche. A teenage Parisian from a wealthy home asks his father for extra money, besides his weekly allowance, to repay a debt. The money is refused. The teenager consults a friend of his age and station; the other youth has counterfeit banknotes (no explanation of the source) and knows where to pass them (no explanation of the knowledge). The youths pass off a false note to a woman in a camera shop. When her husband discovers the fraud, he passes off the note to the driver of an oil delivery truck. The truckdriver is framed as a passer of counterfeits and goes to prison. (Prisons figure often in Bresson; he spent eighteen months in a German P.O.W. camp during World War II.) The story ends with the driver committing several murders.

The structure has patent holes. The accused driver could easily have proved, despite the shopowner's denials, that he had been there that day; he had a receipted bill. The shop assistant, whom the boss persuades to commit perjury, was evidently a bad egg even without that persuasion. And there's more. Yet, despite the weak seams, the story holds because the focus is not on the story, it's on matters of which we get only some visible-audible evidence. To the devoutly Catholic Bresson, evil is as much a part of life as good, and what happens here en route to God's judgment is not to be taken as proof or disproof of God's being. God does not prove, does not want to prove, his existence by making the good prosper and the wicked suffer, by aiding the morally weak or rescuing the misled. (The most religious person in the film becomes a murder victim.) "Grace is everywhere," says the country priest in Bernanos's novel and Bresson's film, just before he dies of cancer. This world is, after all, only this world, says *L'Argent*; God knows everything, the suffering of the faithful and also the suffering of the sinner.

The people in the film—as far as I can perceive—are not professional actors. Bresson hates acting, has often said so. He chooses people who have what he considers the right personal qualities for their roles, and he says that he never uses people twice because the second time they would try to give him what he wants instead of what they are. It's as if he were guided by Kleist's line: "Grace appears most purely in that human form which either has no consciousness or an infinite consciousness; that is, in the puppet or in the god." Since Bresson can't employ gods, he gets as close as possible to puppets—with nonactors.

They enact the story of *L'Argent* much as medieval townsfolk might have enacted a morality play, with little skill and much conviction.

Once, in conversation with an English playwright-screenwriter, I mentioned Bresson, and the Englishman said, "Ah, yes, the doorknob man." It's a funny, quick caricature. Bresson does often focus on a door through which a person passes or on a "headless" body approaching a door, turning the knob, and passing through. (His rare moving shots are usually reserved for that kind of traversal.) When it isn't doorknobs in this new film, it's cell doors—in prisons that are so clean and well-run, so much a part of society's organization, that they freeze the marrow. Bresson puts places, things, and people on virtually the same plane of importance. Other directors do this, too—Antonioni, for instance. But with Antonioni, it's to show that the world is inescapable, almost a prison itself; Bresson wants to show that the world and the things in it are as much a part of God's mind as the people in the world.

Bresson's view is well conveyed here by his two cinematographers, Emmanuel Machuel, whose previous work I don't know, and Pasqualino de Santis, who has worked for Bresson before, as well as for Visconti and Rosi. All the colors look pre-Raphaelite, the innocent idea of blue or red or whatever. This fits Bresson's elliptical "innocent" method: violence runs through this film but is never seen. When the driver commits a double murder, all we see of it is the tap water that runs red in a basin for a few moments as he washes his hands. When he commits ax killings, the only stroke we see is when he hits a lamp.

The last sequence of the film is its most piercing. The driver, who has killed off a family in an isolated country house, goes to an inn. He sits and has a cognac. Then he walks over to some policemen standing at the bar and confesses his crimes. In the next shot we are with the crowd outside the inn door. As they watch, the police come out, taking the driver away. The crowd still waits, watching the door, watching for more police, more prisoners. There will be no more, but they keep waiting and watching. The film ends.

We are that crowd.

Sugar Cane Alley

(April 30, 1984)

How desperately we need certain stories; how grateful we are when they recur. High among these nourishments for our morale is the epic of the poor boy, exceptionally bright, who by perseverance, luck, and the sacrifice of others, struggles upward out of the society in which he was born, then tells the story of his struggle—which means the story of those who are still down there because they have neither his brightness nor his luck. Two examples: *The Corn Is Green* by Emlyn Williams and *Aparajito* as filmed by Satyajit Ray from Bibhuti Banerji's novel.

I say "boy" because history has not allowed this to happen often to a girl. The latest example is again about a boy, but at least this time the film was made by a woman. *Rue cases Negres* (translated as *Black Shack Alley*) is a novel by Jose Zobel about a very poor 11-year-old black Martinique boy and the beginning of his movement upward. The film, called *Sugar Cane Alley*, was written and directed by a twenty-eight-year-old black Martinique woman named Euzhan Palcy. The very familiarity of the story enhances its loveliness in the hands of a filmmaker who understands absolutely everything about the lives she is touching.

It's 1930. Jose lives with his grandmother, who is aging and weakening but determined, in a shack in a street of shacks. Their town is a moderate riverboat trip away from the capital, Fort-de-France. Grandmother works in the cane fields, as do most of the other black people in the town, works brutally hard but is nonetheless, like others, in debt to the company store. Jose is affectionate, playful, troublesome, and extremely bright in school. The schoolmaster helps him get a scholarship to a higher school in Fort-de-France. Much excitement; then they find out that it's only a one-quarter scholarship. Grandmother is as gritty as she is weak. She insists that Jose have his chance, so the pair move to the capital and live in an auto crate in a lot on the outskirts of town while she does laundry and he goes to school. Just when his good work earns him a full scholarship, the old woman dies. Jose goes on with his schooling, resolved that some day he will tell the story of Sugar Cane Alley.

That (apparently) is what Zobel did; and Palcy has carried the work forward. Through Zobel, she gives us the fabric of life among these French-speaking blacks: the village sage, the funeral rites, the schoolmate whose white father supports his mother with whom he will not live, the squabbles and pranks and misery. It was the government of the whites that provided Jose with the education to write about this world; but that doesn't quite seem justification for the existence of that world.

Palcy herself began her career in radio and television on Martinique and made her first film there. She then went to Paris where she took degrees at the Sorbonne and at a film school. She has worked as a film editor and has made another short film. She also composes and records children's songs. Last year she made this first feature, and it establishes her in this profession.

I am not about to verify the authenticity of *Sugar Cane Alley*, but I can cite a recognition. I once spent a couple of weeks on the "other" island, Guadeloupe, and traveled from the hotel into town on the jitney, a rattletrap that held about twenty passengers, almost all of whom usually were black working people. Whenever the bus stopped and someone got on—known or unknown to the other passengers—he or she said, "Bonjour," and everyone on the bus answered. When someone got off, it was "Au'voir," answered by all. I soon found myself joining in; otherwise I'd have felt rude. And I found myself taking that jitney more often than I really needed to.

Palcy's fundamental achievement is to infuse her film with this communal spirit. Her people are joined by common interests, pleasures, hardships. *Everything* joins them together.

I don't know how many of the cast are professional actors, but under Palcy, each of them discloses what he or she knows about the character. Obviously Palcy has a particular concern for children, and she shows it with Garry Cadenat, who is replete with delicacy and deviltry. His pipe-smoking grand-mother is played by a wonderfully sweet, tough, rotund old woman named Darling Legitimus. I hope that she is in more films because I like to type her name.

Palcy and her cinematographer, Dominique Chapuis, have given the film a general tinge of sepia that suggests old photographs. Occasionally the narrative has a minor bump, even within a sequence, as if Palcy hadn't provided herself and her editor with absolutely all the footage that she needed; still, it's a compe-tent, controlled work, an affectionate restatement of a theme that needs con-tinual restating—the possibility of possibility.

The Bostonians

(August 6, 1984)

Obviously the idea of filming *The Bostonians* seemed particularly bright because of Henry James's theme, but there is no hand-rubbing cleverness in the result. At the last, success—meaning approximate re-creation of the novel's depths and reverberances—eludes the film, but a good deal of perception, taste, and skill have gone into it.

The screenplay is by Ruth Prawer Jhabvala, herself a noted novelist, who has been working with this producer and this director, Ismail Merchant and James Ivory, since 1961. I don't see how anyone could have done better than Jhab-vala, but she came up against two different kinds of stone walls: transmuting the book's visible drama and transmuting that drama's subtext.

Those who know the book, or who have at least read Josephine Hendin's enlightening essay on it, will recall that the novel deals centrally with the strug-gle between Olive Chancellor, a wealthy Boston feminist, and Basil Ransom, a Mississipian practicing law in New York, for the love and loyalty of an attrac-tive young woman, Verena Tarrant. Verena is drawn to Olive's cause and becomes an evangelist for it; then, without losing her faith, she is strongly drawn to Basil who wants her for a quite conventional life as his wife. Hendin observes that the novel can be seen as a "satiric replay of the Civil War on the battlefields of sex"—old Southern chivalric attitudes pitted against Northern progressivism (though, of course, these views were not confined to South and North). In the novel this visible struggle is enveloped in a texture of reaction and reflection. In the film, most of the texture had to be stripped away, so the effect is one of leaping from point to point of action. Eventually the picture becomes a succession of scenes in which Verena is embraced by Olive, then by Basil; renounces the institution of marriage to Olive, then melts in Basil's arms—a series of flip-flops rather than an agon.

Even more difficult to handle on film is the subtext, the invisible drama, which James couldn't make explicit: the basic struggle in Verena, conscious or not, between homosexuality and heterosexuality. James never suggests that feminism arbitrarily entails lesbianism. Olive—specifically Olive, not just any feminist—is emotionally drawn to Verena, and the younger woman responds. Basil senses this attraction and, we infer, thinks of himself as rescuing Verena not only from abnormal ideas but abnormal life. (James, however, warns us in his closing line that Verena's tears as she goes off to marry Basil are not the last she will shed.) The reader of the novel can perceive and be moved by the psychosexual struggle that had to be kept implicit in a novel written a century ago. Jhabvala could not possibly have made it explicit without vulgarizing James; only in one brief, highly agitated scene does Olive quickly caress Verena's body. But Jhabvala must have understood the unavoidable difficulty here: today's audience, viewing a work done today, is at least as conscious of the restraint being exercised by the filmmakers as of the matters that are being restrained.

This leads to the uncomfortable subject of Verena herself. I cannot think that she is one of James's better characterizations. Hendin says rightly that Verena is the only character who changes in the course of *The Bostonians*, and metamorphosis is one of the classic hallmarks of drama. But in my view Verena changes more because she is author-malleable than because she is, so to speak, inner-directed. She is more a composite of attributes—which change—than a creation. James wanted to explore the social-intellectual phenomenon of the public speaker in his day, and this interest coincided neatly with the subject of feminism. He makes Verena a smashing platform success on that subject, and he makes her the daughter of a public speaker to account for her affinity with the field. But her father is a charlatan; and her mother is a vulgarian. James never adequately explains the difference in character and breeding between daughter and parents.

More, this young woman who is so commanding in public is limp and ductile in private. Acknowledging that public and private selves are not necessarily identical, we can usually still see some connection, can believe the difference when it occurs. In Verena's case, her power on the platform is something we simply have to take on James's assurance because he and we need it for the story.

And, grimly enough, the film's greatest mistake is in the casting of Verena. A newcomer, Madeleine Potter, rudely underscores the doubts I have noted. She is not able to bolster the character in personality or talent or physical appeal. Her screen debut is worse than unimpressive, it damages the whole enterprise.

This miscasting is cruelly emphasized by the casting of Vanessa Redgrave as Olive. The simplest, truest statement to be made about Redgrave is that she is a great artist and a great beauty. As Olive, she is somewhat stronger and older than James's description, but she understands and creates the woman so completely that, in a sense, she overpowers James; from now on, Olive will be Redgrave for me. And to juxtapose this Olive with this Verena was unjust to both actresses. It makes Potter's inadequacies more vivid, and it gives Redgrave the added burden of making us believe her instant captivation by this flat young woman.

Christopher Reeve, hardly supple as Basil, is at least better than expected. With his columnar neck – almost as big around as Potter's waist – and his gigantic chest, he demonstrates his costumes rather than wearing them. It's difficult to understand how the Confederacy lost the war with him in its army. Still, Reeve has sufficient intelligence, if not talent, to sketch Basil for us.

Jessica Tandy, looking more and more like ivory, is Miss Birdseye and is serene, but the role illustrates one more difference between novel and film. James uses Miss Birdseye as a symbol of the continuity of New England egalitarianism and spunk; her presence is in itself a source of strength to her friends. But presence is not enough in a film – anyway, a film of a drama. Here Miss Birdseye is a character without motion or motive. In the book she fulfills her function; in the film she never begins to function. The difference between the forms converts living history into living décor.

The diminuitive Linda Hunt is Mary Prance, the "doctress" (James's word); Hunt's dignity and wit make her company a pleasure once again. Nancy Marchand, as Mrs. Burrage, the wealthy mother of one of Verena's suitors, plays her social cards shrewdly.

The confrontation betwen Marchand and Redgrave highlights the fine work of the costume designers, Jenny Beavan and John Bright. Compliments on costumes in period pictures are almost routine because such work is frequently good, but here it is even better – not just beautiful but apt. Note, in the scene cited, Redgrave's clean-lined jacket, vaguely masculine, and Marchand's ornate, fitted dress, with its wide lace collar emphasizing the maternal.

Walter Lassally, the veteran cinematographer who has long worked with Merchant and Ivory, has apparently profited by studying Thomas Eakins. Every frame of the film is exquisite with (as it seems) the light of 1875. Richard Robbins wrote the score with the collaboration of Wagner and Brahms.

The director, James Ivory, is serious and respectable. After that dreadful remark, I add that, without any great natural gift for directing – a gift that can be found in much less respectable directors – he applies and applies himself to the mysteries of making life on the screen, often with difficult material, and sometimes he succeeds. Not in much of The Bostonians. Except for occasional strong moments, most of them Redgrave's, Ivory has made a respectable film but not really a free-standing one.

Is this film any use, then? Yes, possibly: much more so, at least, than the Merchant-Ivory film of *The Europeans*. For those who haven't read *The Bostonians*, or haven't read it lately, this film can serve as an overture, much like an overture to an opera. A lot of the themes are stated, the atmosphere is signaled. Then the curtain rises (the book opens). But unlike some operatic preludes, this overture cannot stand alone.

Last Night at the Alamo

(August 27, 1984)

Houston, today. A young man and a young woman are driving along in a pickup. He is violently cursing the garage that didn't fix his car and forced him to borrow the truck; she is trying to restrain his anger and his language. They both speak in the Texan accent and diction that we non-Texans know so well from films.

That's the opening of *Last Night at the Alamo*, and it's discouraging: because we think we're going to see One More—another beer-guzzling, foulmouthed, southern-prole yarn. But that very discouragement soon leads to pleasure because it's deceptive: the film that follows is not just One More. It has the beer and the cussing and the proles, all right, but it's genuine, serious, somewhat daring.

The title, too, is deceptive, though wryly. The Alamo is the name of a bar, and this is its last night before demolition. The two young people are on their way to the Alamo where they cease to be principal characters and become members of a group. The rest of the story takes place in and around the bar, and all that happens is that the people who come in, most of them regulars, behave the way they usually behave. Except for one of them, their behavior is little touched by the fact that this is closing night. The taciturn patron is as monosyllabic as ever; the embattled husband is still quarreling with the wife who telephones him at the Alamo; the Mexican restaurant owner drops in for one of his drinking games; the barfly of the place continues to bum beers; the bitter guy looking for a fight is still looking; the two curvy young women who come in to "hang out" are familiar in type, even if not regulars; and the protagonist, as far as he can be called so, still struts, still prattles of going to Hollywood. (He is the one most concerned with the closing. He phones a legislator in order to get the demolition stopped but, as everyone knows, to no avail.)

This kind of script is familiar in the theater, and not only in America. (I once saw "this" play in Germany.) The bar is the center to which lives gravitate, where they reveal themselves, entangle, disentangle, and move on. The essence of the form is that, for most of the characters, nothing changes. The bar is like a spiritual fluoroscope behind which the characters pass, revealing their characters en route. As soon as we can see that *Last Night at the Alamo* is not going to be about the opening pair and that there's not going to be any plot, we ask ourselves—because it's a film—whether the piece is going to have the guts to stay the course. If it were a play (which, with very little revision, it could be), we probably wouldn't ask that question because the theater is the original habitat of the species. But, on the screen, a work of this kind requires courage because it controverts cinematic dicta; and *Last Night at the Alamo* does have the courage: to stick to its form and to accept the charge that this form lays on it these days.

The form is naturalistic. By now, as is increasingly recognized, naturalism has changed its historic function. Once it was primarily informational: naturalistic artists were chiefly concerned with telling harsh facts to a sheltered audience. But, in our information-drenched culture, what mere facts about our society do we need from films or plays? Today the function of naturalism is sheerly as one more option of style. And as with any other style, it exists as a means of conveyance, not as dramatized data. The naturalistic work now asks you to look, not at its veristic surface and its avoidance of maneuver, but beneath.

Eagle Pennell, who originated this film, and Kim Henkel, who wrote the script, recognize this. They want us to know as soon as possible that what we see and hear is only the means to reveal the invisible and unspoken. The filmmakers' daring is both in risking our initial false impression—with the first few minutes—and in accepting the charge that the "new" naturalism lays on them, to reveal and enrich below the nitty-gritty surface.

It's in that regard that this good film falters somewhat. Pennell and Henkel know these characters, know that their incessant vile language is no more than a canker of discontent with their lives, oblique evidence of hunger for something else, recognition of the spaces within them and around them. This much the film understands: but it does little with this understanding. We see people who, under their bluster, are hurting; but Pennell and Henkel convey little sense of why they are hurting, what they want. Certainly I don't ask for specifics, like planks in a party platform; in fact, what I miss is any suggestion of the unspecifiable, too large or ambiguous to articulate, buried under the barroom jawing. For contrast, take Horton Foote's *Tender Mercies*, which dealt with similar Texans. Admittedly, it is not a naturalistic work; but it moves past the details of its people's lives, even of their well-wrought drama, to glimpse a chilling truth—some intimation of Gloucester's vision: "As flies to wanton boys, are we to the gods." Pennell and Henkel stop short of anything comparable—any percept, whatever it might be, grim or heartening—to give their film completeness. They prove that they are serious, but they don't give much hint of what they are serious about.

Still, as far as they have gone, they have worked intensely. In the whole structure of *Last Night at the Alamo*, only one element seems contrived. About midway, two men peer through the windows of a trailer across from the bar and watch a young woman walking around half dressed. They know her as a "dirty lay"; and we know that a scene is coming in which one of the men will go in for a quick score and that the woman, despite her easiness in the past, will resent it with tears or with anger. It's the one plotty strophe in a script full of honest familiarities.

Pennell has directed with such fierce simplicity, so hot a concern for verity, that the film's pace and rhythm and editing seem to be governed by the characters. It was shot in 16mm black-and-white by Brian Huberman and Eric A. Edwards, is now blown up to 35mm, and looks comfortable in its new dimensions. I haven't seen Pennell's one previous film, *The Whole Shootin' Match*, but I'd like to see it—and more Pennell.

The film of Henkel's previous script, *The Texas Chainsaw Massacre*, I certainly have not seen and don't regret it. (He appears in *Alamo* as the taciturn man.) But he has a sharp ear and affectionate humor.

This is especially true in the writing of the sulphurous husband played by Louis Perryman. This man is, in stages, a conventional marriage-hating barroom grouse; a man who uses grousing to conceal affection for his wife because he thinks that affection saps his masculinity; and a man driven nearly nutty by this conflict. Perryman plays the role with bile and shame that seep right through the three levels.

Sonny Carl Davis, as Cowboy, the one who yatters about going to Hollywood and who wears a Stetson to conceal his premature baldness, is a strong conscious-defensive fake. But all the cast—with the exception of the barfly, who "acts"—are valid and vital, a tribute to Pennell's ability to choose actors and win their confidence.

Last Night at the Alamo was made in The Old Barn, a Houston bar. The shooting, which took just over three weeks and cost $50,000, was funded by three foundations, including the National Endowment for the Arts; Pennell had to scrounge for another $11,000 completion money. The difference between his film and all the expensive junk around us is not just that high budgets make everybody nervous. The difference is that almost all the expensive films, no matter how entertaining they may sometimes be, are corporate enterprises. *Last Night at the Alamo* exists for a basic reason: one man, Pennell, wanted to make it. For our country and our time, it helps to redefine the idea of the personal film.

Postscript. A few weeks later I saw *The Whole Shootin' Match*, Pennell's first film, which is much more crudely made than *Last Night at the Alamo* but which has the same true Texas tang, largely supplied by two of the same actors, Louis Perryman and Sonny Carl Davis. Pennell shot the film himself and was right to give up on photography; but his writing and directing point the way to his second film, which points further on.

Bizet's Carmen

(October 1, 1984)

Francesco Rosi's *Carmen* film completes a sort of tryptich. I don't mean a trio that includes Carlos Saura's danced *Carmen* and Godard's high-bouncing modernized version.* Rosi's film—which for identification is tagged *Bizet's Carmen*—stands with Bergman's *The Magic Flute* and Syberberg's *Parsifal* as representative of a third way to film opera.

Bergman, in a sense prefiguring *After the Rehearsal*, blended film and theater with mercurial interplay. Syberberg disregarded theater tradition; he used Wagner's score as the soundtrack for a visual exploration of everything that the music made happen in his imagination and fantasy. Now Rosi does the best "orthodox" filming of an opera that I know, not by shooting a staged performance but by transmuting a theatrical work into a film musical. Zeffirelli bungled this approach with *La Traviata*, as did Losey with *Don Giovanni*. In Rosi's hands, the result is exciting and gorgeous.

Bizet's Carmen was shot on location—notably the Spanish city of Ronda and its antique bullring—and in excellent settings, all under the fine eye of Enrico Job, the production and costume designer. (Job, who is Lina Wertmüller's husband, contributed much to the distinctive look of her films.) The cinematographer was Pasqualino De Santis, who does here the best work of his career. De Santis is known particularly for his work with Zeffirelli (*Romeo and Juliet*), Visconti (*Death in Venice*), and with Rosi (*The Mattei Affair, Christ Stopped at Eboli*). Here he blends the sumptuous qualities of the first two directors with Rosi's *verismo*. The immense Spanish sky, the romance of the old buildings and streets, the flare of passionate encounter, are held by De Santis within a palette of pastel, almost of watercolor. Obviously he and Rosi decided it would italicize matters to make *Carmen* look lurid. De Santis establishes a wonderful tension between the heat of what happens and the restrained colors in which we see it.

Rosi's directing models were, I'd guess, more in the Minnelli-Donen line than in either classical opera or dramatic film. He wanted to keep it all fluent, at ease on screen, without ever pretending that it's not being sung and danced. The film teems with his enlivening ideas. I cite just one: when the cigarette girls pour out of the factory in panic, after Carmen's knife fight, they frighten a horse that is just then pulling a carriage past the factory doors. And Rosi, with the aid of his chief editor, Ruggero Mastroianni, makes the most of the bullring mystique (which he once explored in *The Moment of Truth*, 1965). The last scene between Carmen and Don José takes place in a sandy circle outside the arena while Escamillo is triumphing in the larger sandy circle inside.

Rosi's one touch of excess is with his wonderful Carmen. (All the roles are

---

*See p. 230 and p. 231.

performed, I believe, by the people who sing them.) He urges or allows her to cut some bedroom capers that would have been just as clear without being so clarified. Julia Migenes-Johnson is a bombshell with a beautiful voice. Born in New York of Greek and Puerto Rican parentage, she has done pop work, musicals, and opera here and abroad—including at the Metropolitan, where she played Lulu. Migenes-Johnson has a cat face, a cat body, and feral timbre. The film needs virtually everything she can give it because Placido Domingo, singing well, plays Don José like a corseted tenor who has taken acting lessons; and Ruggero Raimondi, singing moderately well as Escamillo, looks like a matador on Geritol.

Antonio Gades, who designed the dancing for Saura's film and played the lead, did the sinuous choreography for this *Carmen*, too. Lorin Maazel conducts the Orchestre Nationale de France with energy, but occasionally he loses the countermelody—as in the prelude to Act Three or with the woodwinds near the close of the "Flower Song."

The end of the *Carmen* trail is not yet. *Variety* reports from Paris that a French director has just finished a version made directly from Mérimée. Well, Rosi's film only whets the appetite. *Bizet's Carmen*, despite the stockish acting of the two male leads, is a treat.

Stranger than Paradise

(October 29, 1984)

The slightest acquaintance with filmmaking compels us to wonder how tone and style can ever be sustained through that disjointed, nonsequential process. The slightest acquaintance with filmgoing shows how rarely tone and style are achieved.

Stranger than Paradise is one of those rarities. This American film was written and directed by Jim Jarmusch, thirty-one, who was trained at the N.Y.U. graduate film school, who has done various jobs—sound-recording, photography, acting, and music scoring—and who has made one previous eighty-minute film (*Permanent Vacation*, not seen by me). *Stranger than Paradise* is in three subtitled parts: *The New World*, *One Year Later*, and *Paradise*. That first part was shown separately at a Rotterdam festival in 1983, where it won a prize. The completed film won prizes this year at the Cannes and Locarno festivals, has just been shown at the New York festival, and is now released. Jarmusch's chief accomplishment was to know the tone and visualize the style before he began, then—through all the hassling of film financing as well as filmmaking—to realize them.

That tone (we'll come to the style) is the opposite of the strenuous and eager-to-impress: it's cool, unhurried. The film itself seems to be "hanging out" with its three characters, who are doing the same. *Stranger than Paradise* was shot in black and white (adequately, by Tom DiCillo), on a budget that seems mimetic of its characters' circumstances, and with the same touches of humor and poignancy that surface in their lives. The tonal relationship between what we see and how we see it is exactly balanced.

A young loafer, played by John Lurie, lives alone in a scruffy New York apartment. He came from Hungary ten years before, and now declines to speak Hungarian with his aunt when she phones, declines to do anything much except lounge about, wear a fedora something like Karl Malden's, bet the horses, and play cards, where he apparently cheats. His friend, Richard Edson, is not conspicuously Hungarian but is otherwise a reduced replica. Lurie's cousin, Eszter Balint, sixteen years old, arrives from Hungary, stays with him for a week, then moves on to join their aunt in Cleveland. A year later, Lurie and Edson win some money at cards, and decide to visit Balint at the aunt's (the elderly Cecelia Stark, who is the most vital person in the film, possibly because she's of an earlier generation). The two men leave for Florida, then decide to return to Cleveland and invite Balint to come south with them. She quickly accepts. In Florida they lose almost all their money at the dog races. Balint, because of a hat she has just bought, is handed an envelope full of money by a stranger who was waiting for a woman in a hat like that. The incident is as casually life-changing as most of the film is casually nonchanging. A mildly ironic ending follows.

The overall feeling of the film is of corks bobbing on a sluggish stream. The overall emotional tenor is expressed in one gesture: when the two men leave Balint in Cleveland (before they change their minds about inviting her), she almost—*almost*—waves goodbye. The very way that Jarmusch handles supposedly factual details—a ticket clerk in a small Florida airport says there's a nonstop flight to Budapest; when we see the plane, it looks just big enough to reach Jacksonville—is his comment on the demands of reality, mirroring his characters' attitudes.

The tone is neither hopeless nor pessimistic: either view would be too resolved. It's more as if these three people had acted out their lives before and are now doing a run-through for a director who wants to make sure they remember their parts in case of another performance. The effect of this approach, in contrast with the real world around them, is often funny. It's like lightweight Beckett, with the same patience on the part of tiny individuals toward a huge blundering universe, thus with glints of the same Beckettian humor.

Jarmusch's cinematic style gently but firmly completes the contradiction. The film is composed of episodes that finish with a moment of black before the next episode begins. It's a series of discrete utterances, like a series of proofs that the characters are still alive and moving. Further, more subtly yet equally affecting, each of these episodes is done in a single take. Sometimes the camera pans within an episode, but there is never a cut. This method, whose most famous practitioner is Jean Renoir and whose high priest is André Bazin, is closely

associated with humanism, the conviction that human life is the apex of creation and that the filmmaker's obligation is to present it whole, not to intrude
with fragmentation. Yet the lives shown here are not the apex of anything
much, and Jarmusch's wry twist is to treat them with Renoir's cinematic
reverence and then to do his idiosyncratic fragmenting between the uninter-
rupted "Renoir" episodes. It's an intelligent, witty, conceptually complete piece
of filmmaking, a dry commentary on the traditional view of glowing American
immigrants.

Paris, Texas

(December 3, 1984)

Paris, Texas is the latest, and perhaps the longest, product of America's impact on postwar European films. Almost all European countries reflect that
cultural impact in some of their films. The French New Wave welcomed the
postwar influx of American films as part of the liberation that came with victory. The younger Germans responded to American culture, especially films, as
if in rejection of their Nazi forebears; they pointedly embraced everything that
those forebears had decried in America. And no contemporary German director shows American influence more clearly than Wim Wenders (b. 1945) who
directed *Paris, Texas*.

When he was a film student in Munich in the late 1960s, Wenders made
shorts based on American pop music. His first feature (not widely released) had
an English title in Germany, *Summer in the City*, and also used American pop.
His next film was German, and it's no coincidence that this is his best—made
from a novel by his friend Peter Handke, *The Goalie's Anxiety at the Penalty
Kick*. (Several years later he produced *The Left-Handed Woman*, directed by
Handke.*) Then back Wenders went to American things with a version of *The
Scarlet Letter* that seemed to have been made under anesthesia, followed by
Alice in the Cities, a wandering story that wandered through America in its first
half. His next two films, *Wrong Movement* and *Kings of the Road*, were set in
Germany, but both strained to be American "road" pictures, trying to imply
American space. Then came a thriller called *The American Friend*: a leading
character was an American in Germany, and the cast included Samuel Fuller,
the American director who is idolized abroad. Wenders then went to San Francisco to make a picture, not widely released and unseen by me, called *Ham-
mett*, a fantasy about the author. This was followed by *The State of Things*, a
low-budget, black-and-white feature done in Europe and Los Angeles about
making a science fiction feature; in the cast were Viva, the Andy Warhol star,
and Samuel Fuller again. Now Wenders must feel that he reached his zenith:

---

*See p. 35.

Paris, Texas is two and a half hours, in color, and was shot entirely in western America, with a slide-guitar score by Ry Cooder.

But to me the picture is the biggest mistake that a talented man has so far made. Wenders collaborated on the story with Sam Shepard who then wrote the screenplay, which was worked on further by L. M. Kit Carson. Shepard, powerful dramatist and actor though he is, skids here as badly as he did in the script of *Zabriskie Point* for Antonioni. He was not sole author for Antonioni either, but the earlier script and the present one share Shepard's improvisatory feeling, a meandering intended as significance. Shepard says that the film form is beautiful when studios don't intrude. Apparently "intrusion" means a request for formal narrative; but who would complain about informality if the results were satisfying? *Paris, Texas* not only doesn't know where it's going when it starts, it doesn't know where it has arrived when it's finished. And there's a great deal of tedious stuffing in between. Shepard's freedom, plus Carson's polishings, produces only disproportion and—harsh but apt word—silliness. Even the dialogue, usually sharp in Shepard, is dull.

The beginning implies immensity. The protagonist, played by Harry Dean Stanton, is wandering through the Texas desert near Mexico, wearing a soiled suit and shirt and tie, unshaven, looking (which is untrue) as if he had walked out of an office some days before and headed into emptiness. To freight the situation even further, a vulture watches as he drains his last drop of water. At last he stumbles into a bar, which just happens to be in the middle of nowhere; he faints and wakes up in a clinic, also conveniently located in mid-desert, attended by an ominous German doctor. The doctor questions Stanton; he won't speak a word. The doctor finds a card in Stanton's wallet, calls a Los Angeles number, and reaches Stanton's brother, who hasn't heard from Stanton in four years. By the time the brother, Dean Stockwell, arrives at the clinic, Stanton has wandered into the desert again. Stockwell finds him and gets him into the car, but he remains mute. He wanders off again; Stockwell finds him again. At last Stanton speaks; and almost his first words are that he won't fly, so Stockwell has to drive him all the way home.

After this hugely portentous opening—desert, vulture, dogged muteness, attempts to flee back into the desert—we expect the revelation of nothing less than a Conradian mystery. What we get is, first, a tiny domestic drama of the reunion of a father (Stanton) and his small son that no TV producer would accept; then father and son set out on a search for the wife/mother who also disappeared four years ago. Finally Stanton finds her in a peep-show place in Houston. This runaway Texan wife is played by Nastassja Kinski, perhaps because her first film role was in Wenders's *Wrong Movement* ten years ago—there doesn't seem any other reason.

Kinski sits in a brightly lighted cubicle, facing a mirror; the customer, Stanton, sitting in a dark cubicle, can see her through the mirror. He proceeds to tell her a long story, almost every detail of which she already knows, just so that we can hear it, a story of domestic troubles that don't remotely justify the large-scale epic opening two hours and twenty minutes earlier. The film ends with a stupidly incredible reunion between Kinski and her son arranged by Stanton, who drives off alone again, leaving the viewer to wish that no one had found him the first time.

And the symbols! The oxymoronic title (the name of a real town, used here mythically); the brother wandering mute in the desert set against the brother whose vocation is building billboards that shout in a noisy city; the massive wind-carved rocks of the desert set against the massive man-carved skyscrapers of Houston; the pane of glass between the husband and wife who never communicated properly. As for the hitches in the narrative, they are so numerous and the film is so casual about them that it would be a waste to deal with them.

Apart from Kinski, egregiously miscast, the actors are all right. Stanton, moved from supporting roles to a lead, isn't sufficiently arresting to be at the center, but he does well enough at creating a sorely troubled man. Stockwell, who began as a child actor in 1945, tries to give the stable brother some warmth; then the film simply drops him and his wife, leaving their story unclarified. Stockwell's wife is played by a French actress, Aurore Clement. Why French? Possible to lend some resonance to the first half of the title.

Wenders's direction is, at its best, utterly ordinary. Sometimes he slips below that level: for instance, he shows Clement sitting up in bed naked in her Los Angeles home listening to Stanton downstairs, a shot with suggestions that don't materialize; and he uses the platitude of fitting Stanton's reflected face exactly over Kinski's on the glass between them. The editor, Peter Przygodda, cuts from face to face in the many question-and-answer scenes—tick-tock tick-tock—with a banality that italicizes the banal dialogue. And the way that the cinematographer, Robby Müller, shot Los Angeles and Houston made me think he must have studied the way that Alfio Contini shot *Zabriskie Point*.

Wenders, in my view, is committing prolonged artistic suicide. Most of his work shows him agonizing because he was not born American and cannot make American films from the inside. To compensate, he has spent the bulk of his career in absorbing Americana and trying to handle it like a native. His push to naturalize himself has only resulted in the degradation of the exceptional, very European sensibility that he showed early on. What lies beneath the many faults of *Paris, Texas* is that fundamentally he is insecure. His judgment of drama and growth is not finely tuned, his eye is looking for what he has seen in previous films. He arranges visual symbols as if they in themselves could make art, instead of being the perceptible data of deeper perceptions. *Kings of the Road* was a lesser film for me than for many, but at least it conveyed some sense of a director who knew his people, knew precisely what was troubling them, and could render it knowledgeably. *Paris, Texas* is crammed with the acquired and imitative, eager to pass as the real thing. Wenders is not the first European director to try to Americanize his films, but his career is one of the most melancholy wrecks along that road. I hope it's not too late for him to go home and be a German director again.

The Case Is Closed

(December 24, 1984)

Mrinal Sen, the Bengali director, is sixty-one and has made at least twenty-three films. Acclaimed in India, Sen has been widely shown in many countries but is hardly known in the United States. This ignorance is apparently now to be dented. His newest film, *The Ruins*, won first prize at this year's Chicago International Film Festival, and his twenty-second, *The Case Is Closed* (1982) — my first Sen film — has just had its American premiere at the Film Forum in New York.

Inarguably this delay in Sen's reception here has been an ill wind, but it may have blown a little good. Sen is a fervent Marxist, and his previous work is said to be polemic. It's also described as parochial. In the Autumn 1981 issue of the British journal *Sight and Sound*, Derek Malcolm wrote:

> What comes over from a study of his work is . . . that . . . he has traced the social and political ferment of India with greater resilience and audacity than any other contemporary Indian director. That may be why a knowledge of India is almost mandatory before his work can be appreciated to the full.

But recent writers have said that Sen's latest works are less polemic and less remote to foreigners. These statements are confirmed by *The Case Is Closed*. It's not overtly political, and it certainly doesn't require an extraordinary knowledge of India (or I couldn't have responded to it). I hope I may sometime see a half dozen of Sen's earlier films that I've read about, but I'm glad I saw *The Case Is Closed* first.

The temper of the film is watchful, implicative. Sen wrote his own screenplay from a story by Ramapada Chowdury; the pivotal event, which happens early, is an accidental death. We then follow the effect of that death on the people concerned, and it's like following a laboratory dye as it filters through tissues, staining them differently.

Calcutta during a cold spell in 1981 is the setting. Anjan and Mamata are a modestly comfortable couple with a small son. (The first names are the actors' own; Sen gives the family his last name.) Because the parents are busy and their child needs care, they do what many of their friends do: they engage a boy of twelve or so, a country boy from a poor family, to live with them as servant and baby-sitter. The boy's father turns him over to the couple reluctantly, tenderly.

The Calcutta winter lasts only two months, so the couple don't buy the boy warmer clothes. He is meant to sleep under the stairs, but because of the cold, he sleeps in the kitchen. One night there's a mishap with the small stove, and the boy asphyxiates.

No one is criminally to blame for the boy's death, but different sorts of blame, of guilt, are underscored by it. The film touches the conditions that made it necessary for the father to lease out his son (contrasted with the pampering—and probable future—of the couple's small boy) and the way the police treat the bereaved family, with more regulations than sympathy. But the focus is on Anjan and Mamata: how their initial shock and pain change, under the pressure of secret guilt, to self-protection, tinged with aggressive defense. The real closing of the case is the closing of the family circle, the clan against the world.

Only once does Sen let a blatancy obtrude: when the dead boy's father and his other relatives huddle around a fire in the street, waiting for morning and the chance to claim the body, the flames light up revolutionary graffiti on the wall behind them. Only a few times does Sen let cinema-consciousness obtrude: he uses a few freeze frames, and occasionally he lets the sound of the next scene begin under the current scene. For the most part, he achieves one sort of film purity: we are simply present, with no sense of manipulation by angles or editing or novel composition. The style is "no style," a *via negativa*, no pressure to admire the director. To make a film this way requires a lot of experience, and not just of filmmaking.

Sen gives his film an added twinge with another teenage boy from the apartment upstairs, who has the same job as the boy who died and who hovers outside doors and windows, watching and listening to what might have been his fate. The principal actors, guided by Sen of course, heighten our own feeling of espionage with the confidentiality of their performances. It's a kind of acting that precludes display and is thus easily underrated as mere "behaving," which it is not. There's a close parallel between the acting here and the look of the film itself: the actor needs skill—enough skill to ignore skill, to concentrate on congruence with the character, on permitting us to peep and eavesdrop rather than to project at us.

Mamata is Mamata Shankar, daughter of the dancer Uday Shankar and niece of the sitarist Ravi Shankar. She has played in three previous Sen films, but she is primarily a dancer; and her consummate grace is an irony added to the woman's change from silly householder hauteur to clawed defense of the home. Anjan is Anjan Dutt. I'm told reliably that he is not related to the renowned radical Bengali theater figure, Utpal Dutt, a point worth making because Utpal Dutt has himself worked with Sen. Anjan Dutt has had theater experience—has in fact performed in West Berlin—and he played the lead in the film that Sen made just before this one. Here it's fascinating to see how Dutt uses his continuing presence on the screen as a quiet journey into the interior, just as longer acquaintance with a person in life not only tells us more about him but often alters what we thought we knew about him.

The cinematography is by K. K. Mahajan, a graduate of the Film Institute of India (where Sen has taught) who has also worked with Sen before. Mahajan's palette is controlled to make every unquestionably real object before our eyes—a chair, a table, a bed—look almost as if it were a cutout, as if we were watching a realistic morality play. The cinematography helps this quiet film to linger in the mind, to return.

Thanks—once again—to the Film Forum, Sen at last begins to be visible in America.

It's noteworthy that this Bengali work is dedicated to the memory of Gene Moskowitz, the New Yorker who graduated from the Institut des Hautes Etudes Cinematographiques in Paris in 1948, who spent his life as a *Variety* correspondent based in Paris, who died last year, and who was a partisan of Sen's films.

Postscript. Subsequently I saw *Ten Days in Calcutta: A Portrait of Mrinal Sen*, a documentary by the German director, Reinhard Hauff. (Sen and Hauff converse in English.) It's a fascinating portrait of Sen, of a career dedicated to personal, compassionate filmmaking, of a man working through the years with a small group of colleagues in modest quarters to deal cinematically with his world. Sen takes Hauff through Calcutta and reveals how this brawling, impoverished, vital city has nourished him.

Beverly Hills Cop

(December 31, 1984)

Once past the incredible and violent opening of *Beverly Hills Cop*, which is tedious, we get the incredible and violent bulk of the picture, which is entertaining. The dialogue, by Daniel Petrie Jr., becomes springy. The familiar story idea is turned to good contemporary use.

That story idea is a Movieland antique. The hero is a smart but unorthodox detective. A friend of his is murdered, and the hero's chief warns him not to take revenge on his own. Guess whether the hero obeys.

However—and this is the contemporary use—the hero is played by Eddie Murphy. His blackness alters the tenor of every scene, and the fact that this particular black man is a comedian alters the tenor even further. This retelling of an old yarn doesn't mock the motives of loyalty and honor on which it has always been based, but the presence of Murphy in the lead takes the suspense down several pegs—it's much less likely that a comic will get killed than, say, Nick Nolte—and it turns the usually noble plot into a series of skits in which a clever, brave, cool, funny black man outwits both the hoods and his white colleagues.

Thus this seemingly routine "lone cop" film becomes, to some degree, a modern racial apotheosis. An enjoyable one. Murphy, scintillatingly talented, gets plenty of chance to scintillate. And all of us get pleasure in seeing—at least for the duration of the film—some historic imbalances slightly righted. This is only Murphy's third film (except for a misguided cameo in something called *Best Defense*), and, up to now, he has made a career out of social reversals. His first appearance, in *48 HRS.*, where he scored a smashing hit, was as a convict whose help was so badly needed by a detective that he had to be let out of jail. In *Trading Places*, he upset apple carts as a panhandler who became a financial whiz. His new film is constructed to let him upset other apple carts.

First, he is not a Beverly Hills cop, he is a Detroit cop—a detective who wears casual street clothes so that he can go underground in search of crime. His trail of personal (and disobedient) revenge leads him to Beverly Hills where all the detectives, including the black one, wear three-piece suits. To Murphy's defiance of his Detroit chief and his difference of dress in B. H. is added still another revolt: he's ordered out of town by the B. H. police, and he disobeys that order, too. Further, he lures several local detectives into aiding him in his quest. All these anarchies are justified—he is proved right about the respectable man he accuses of being an archcriminal—but a twist at the end hints at possible further anarchy.

Murphy's talent and success underscore a startling fact: in the entire history of American film, there have been only three black stars, and two of them, both currently working, are comedians. Before Richard Pryor and Murphy, the only black star was Sidney Poitier. Obviously there have been famous and popular black actors—Louise Beavers, Hattie McDaniel, and Clarence Muse, to name only three. Some black actors have been billed and treated as stars—- Diana Ross, Cicely Tyson, Billy Dee Williams, Jim Brown, for example—but none of them had the drawing power and longevity of stars. Poitier was the first real black star, rising perhaps on the surge of interest in integration during the 1960s but certainly not merely lucky: he was an extraordinarily taking actor who was primarily serious. Now comes the rise of two comic stars when—coincidentally?—integration and affirmative action have become more problematic issues. Pryor has shown in his one-man films that he can create and perform scathing satire; in his other films he has done subtle acting. Neither of these qualities is so far visible in Murphy's career—on theater screens, at least—but he has mercurial imagination, a fine cartoonist's ability to sketch varied types (something he does often), geysers of vitality, and a wide-grinning personality, almost aggressively pleasant but so well supported by talent that the grinning defiance transmutes into our own wide grin. He joins Pryor as one of the two reigning film blacks, both of them mockers of the status quo.

Martin Brest, the director, has made two previous films. I missed the first. His second, about three aged bank robbers and called *Going in Style*, went in very little style. This time Brest has his film firmly in hand and whips it along concisely. Yes, in the last shootout, dozens of machine-gun rounds are fired at the good guys who are out in the open yet are never touched. But who's complaining? In a picture like this, do we want to see good guys killed?

A Passage to India

(January 21, 1985)

First, the actors. I think first of them when I think of this film—something I expect to happen recurrently. The principals in *A Passage to India* do something more than embody what I had always imagined about E. M. Forster's characters. Their art goes some way toward re-creating in another medium the reticent strength of Forster's prose; their acting invites our collaboration in much the same manner as his prose.

Judy Davis, the Australian who linked arms with the world in *My Brilliant Career*,* is perfect as Adela Quested. An attractive woman, she is actress enough to convey an unattractive woman who becomes attractive through our experience of her. Temperamentally, she embodies the social conditioning intended as proof against uncertainties, along with the uncertainties that made the conditioning necessary.

Her prospective mother-in-law, Mrs. Moore, is Peggy Ashcroft. The highest tribute I can pay: her death in the film is not acting, it is loss. Ashcroft gives us an old woman now only partly in the world, who is impatient both with the world and with her persisting ignorance of it. She sweetly blends a pleasure in the best of living with a persuasion of its futility.

Victor Banerjee, the Dr. Aziz, is a figure in the Calcutta theater and in Indian film. He is new to me, but before he has been on screen a minute, he has little more to do in character creation: he is Aziz, warm, proud, vulnerable, extreme—his whole scale of reaction and emotion differently calibrated from that of the English people with whom he wants to be friends. From then on, it's just an enlightening matter of following this created character through his experiences.

Nigel Havers, who plays Ronny, Mrs. Moore's son and Adela's putative husband, was the wealthy aristocratic Olympian in *Chariots of Fire*.** Here he is subtly but completely different as the empire-conscious magistrate of Chandrapore. James Fox, remembered as the arrogant young master in *The Servant* (1963), spent a dozen subsequent years in a religious order and has only recently returned to acting. Here he is Fielding (whose first name is unaccountably changed from Cyril to Richard), the head of the local college. Fox gives the sort

*See p. 33.
**See p. 129.

of quietly humane performance that James Donald gave in *The Bridge on the River Kwai*, made by the same director, David Lean, in 1957.

Another veteran of *The River Kwai*, Alec Guinness, plays Dr. Godbole, the Hindu teacher and mystic. Surprisingly, Guinness is the one questionable member of the cast. He bears the burden of being the only non-Indian to play an Indian—the Indian actors are excellent—and his role consists of uttering wisdom. It would be a difficult job in any case, but Guinness is less convincing than an Indian actor might have been.

Forster's novel uses a traditional device: two people (Adela and Mrs. Moore) arrive in a strange place, and through the explanations to them, we learn what we need to know about the place. The duties and complexities, the stupidities and fumbled congeniality of British life in India in the 1920s are paraded before us in their various dazzles. Adela may or may not marry Ronny and has come from London to decide. First she says no, then changes her mind—a harbinger of her vacillation about the novel's crucial episode. That episode occurs when an expedition to the nearby Marabar caves is arranged by their Muslim friend, Dr. Aziz. When Adela was alone in one of the caves, she says, Aziz entered and tried to rape her. This accusation, which confirms the British reluctance to mingle with even the best-bred natives, results in a trial. Mrs. Moore, at her son's suggestion and her own wish, departs for England before the trial. She has been quite ill throughout, and she dies on shipboard. (The film shows us her death, touchingly, so we know of it during the trial. I think this an improvement over the novel where we learn of it later.)

At the trial, faced with the desperate and broken Aziz, Adela recants and withdraws her accusation. Despised by the British colony, her engagement broken, she returns to London. The novel continues in India; so does the film, with one telling exception.

The crucial episode—what happened in the Marabar cave—is treated with absolute clarity. I don't know why Lean talks of it, in interviews, as an open question. It's quite patent, both in the novel and in the film, that Adela's charge is (Lionel Trilling's phrase) "a frenzy of hallucination." Otherwise, if there really had been an attempted rape, Aziz's character, as drawn by Forster and by Forster-Lean, would be nonsense; and, which is basically more important, the whole thematic intent would be damaged. Surely what Forster meant to crystallize in Adela was a mixture of enthrallment and fear, of fierce racial superiority and secret curiosities, with the imagined rape attempt as a sexual epiphany of this tension. If the charge is not hallucinated, then the deepest truth of the situation is destroyed. That is fundamentally why the British colony is angered by Adela's retraction: it's a faint augury of the eventual decline of imperial sway.

Lean wrote his own screenplay, and a generally first-class job it is. His directing career began with some work on Shaw's *Major Barbara* in 1941 and has been largely concerned with adaptations ever since. (The egregious exception was his last film, *Ryan's Daughter*, which I missed and which is his least well regarded.) Of course Lean had to shear away much of the novel, including—for his structural purposes—the astonishing political prophecies at the end. But he hasn't merely condensed the book to manageable screen length; he has rearranged and has changed emphases, trying to fulfill Forster within a small compass, to dramatize compactly what the novel could handle discursively.

Lean favors two themes: the spiritual link between Mrs. Moore and Dr. Aziz and the idea in the title. Near the end Aziz learns that Fielding, on his return to England, had married Mrs. Moore's daughter, not (as Aziz had assumed) Adela. Aziz's discovery of the union between his friend, Fielding, and the daughter of his dead friend is an emotional peak. As for the title, in the very first sequence Adela is literally booking passage, in rainy London, for herself and Mrs. Moore. In the very last sequence (two hours and forty minutes later) Adela is back in London, reading a letter from Dr. Aziz. His home, we have seen, is now amidst snowy mountains; she sits in her little living room, with the rain beating down between her window and the brick houses across the way. The passage to India is completed, round trip.

For the script's fulfillment, the screenwriter relied on his director-editor. Lean, in his mid-seventies, did all three jobs himself. By now he is the superlative traditional filmmaker. Nothing that has happened in film esthetics since 1945 has had much effect on him, and in the light of the work he chooses to do, this is completely to the good. With all awe of the art of the postwar masters, I can only be delighted that Lean is still Lean, the director-editor who relies on conventional story forms, on character as the humanistic *scene* of drama, on editing as the pulse of the driving motion that to him is film vitality.

One example of the editing: in that first sequence, Adela is sitting at the desk of the steamship line's manager, booking tickets. He tells her that the voyage should be lively because the Viceroy will be on board. Lean cuts suddenly. Perhaps you remember the cut near the beginning of *Lawrence of Arabia* in which Peter O'Toole, close up, blows out a match sitting in a Cairo barracks and thus blows the whole shot off the screen; and Lean snaps onto the screen an immense vista of sun-drenched desert, the first such view in the film. The same sort of lovely shock ocurs here, as we cut from a drizzly London office to a vast high shot of a viceregal welcome in Bombay.

An example of the directing: in that scene near the end where Aziz learns that Fielding's wife is his friend's daughter, he turns away, raises his hands to the heavens and exclaims, "Mrs. Moore! Mrs. Moore!" Lean keeps the camera behind Aziz, so that we get the large graphic effect of his figure, rather than a mere tear-streaked face.

An example of Lean's attempt to replace Forster's prose with cinema: the top local British official gives a tremendous lawn party—a "bridge party" to try to close gaps between British and Indian society. Music is provided by a large Indian military band, seated in full scarlet fig. Slowly, ponderously, they play

"Tea for Two." It's funny, and it's epitomic.

Occasionally Lean underscores heavily. Inside the British club, the audience for an amateur performance stand to sing "God Save the King." Outside, in the middle of a peaceful moonlit river, a crocodile leaps and snaps. When Adela wanders into the ruins of a temple covered with erotic sculpture, the figures stimulate her, a helpful ingredient for the cave scene to come. But then temple monkeys teem over the sculptures and frighten her away. Eros degenerating in-to animality—in her mind—is italicized.

The heaviest underscoring is the score. Maurice Jarre has written the music for every Lean film since *Lawrence*, and it all sounds as if poured from the same toffee machine with slightly different flavors. Lean is apparently loyal to col-leagues, which has its price with Jarre but its rewards with Ernest Day. On the films since *Lawrence*, Day has been camera operator, second in command; here he is director of photography. Skillfully, he incises the crispness of the intimate scenes and evokes the languor of the Indian night.

Thus Day is a perfect collaborator with Lean's most striking gift, his ability to deal beautifully with the large scale and the intimate, his insistence on jux-taposing them. Lean makes the immense comprehensible, and he can see the world in a grain of sand. *A Passage to India* is a perfect choice for him, a fit com-panion to the Dickens and Shaw and Lawrence and Pasternak that he has previously filmed, and an opportunity for his particular power.

His best pictures affirm the very idea of adaptation at its best: to make a film that does not try to substitute for the original but is a valuable corollary to it, a film that enriches its own medium through this transmutation. An adaptation as good as this one makes us feel that not to have made it would have left un-mined some of the treasure in the original.

Lean, who works slowly, is now seventy-six. We would be lucky to get another film or two from him. If not, he is finishing his career without falter. Gratitude and cheers.

1984

(February 4, 1985)

The first person in the world to read George Orwell's *1984* was his British publisher, Fredric Warburg. In the course of a long report on the manuscript to his colleagues, Warburg said: "*1984* . . . might well be described as a horror novel, and would make a horror film which . . . might secure all countries threatened by communism for 1,000 years to come." A film came along only six years later, in 1955, which I haven't seen but which, by all reports, is negligible. Now there is a significant film of the book. Whether it will act as communism-insurance until 2985 I'm not quite qualified to say; but because this screen ver-sion was made with talent and understanding, it is, as Warburg meant it, a horror film, and it is sufficiently faithful to Orwell to raise again some of the questions that the novel originally raised.

When Diana Trilling reviewed the book on its American publication in 1949, she said:

> [It] is a brilliant and fascinating novel, but the nature of its fantasy is so final and relentless that I can recommend it only with a certain reservation . . . One cannot help being thrown off, I think, by something in the book's temper, a fierceness of intention, which seems to violate the very principles that Mr. Orwell would wish to preserve in the world . . . . To make this criticism is not to ask for quietism as a means of combating the passions which are destroying modern life. But it is to wish that there were more of what E. M. Forster calls the "relaxed will" in at least those of us who, like Mr. Orwell, are so acutely aware of the threats of power.

My own, highly personal view of the "fierceness" that Mrs. Trilling notes is that a dying man—dying in his mid-forties—was indulging in vendetta. (Orwell survived the completion of his book by only thirteen months, most of them in hospital.) Profoundly perceptive beyond question, he was nonetheless slashing some vengeance on the world for his disappointments in progressive politics, a vengeance very possibly further inflamed by bitterness at his personal fate. In fact he hit so hard at the dangers of social organization that he later had a qualm and issued a much-quoted statement:

> My recent novel is NOT intended as an attack on Socialism or on the British Labour Party (of which I am a supporter) but as a show-up of the perversions to which a centralised economy is liable and which has already been partly realized in Communism and Fascism. I do not believe that the kind of society I describe necessarily *will* arrive, but I believe (allowing of course for the fact that the book is a satire) that something resembling it *could* arrive.

This has always seemed to me an instance of fence-straddling in the career of a man passionate for truth. (How many of the book's millions of readers have thought of it as satire?) And indeed there is ambiguity in the novel itself. Several commentators have pointed out Orwell's curious attitude toward the proles in *1984*. The civil servants and bureaucrats, like the hero, Winston Smith, live under harsh rule and scrutiny. The proles, eighty-five percent of the population, are allowed relative freedom because the party thinks them subhuman. Orwell considers them a locus of hope, the "people who had never learned to think but who were storing up in their hearts and bellies and muscles the power that would one day overturn the world." Raymond Williams is quite right to label this as "stale revolutionary romanticism." Williams adds: " . . . if the tyranny of 1984 ever finally comes, one of the major elements of the ideological preparation will have been just this way of seeing 'the masses' . . . ."

The film concentrates on the bleakness of the supervised lives. Though some proles are visible, we get no hint of Orwell's (compensatory?) feelings about them. The filmmakers made their choice obviously because Orwell's ideas about the proles would be difficult to dramatize and are not the famous elements of the book; and because virtually all of the story, which is slim enough, concerns the supervised people.

Cinematically, it's clear that the producer, Simon Perry, the director, Michael Radford, and the cinematographer, Roger Deakins, began where they ought to have begun: with the look of the film. They wanted to fix the visual texture before they decided on anything else. What was evolved, with the aid of a laboratory, was a color film in which a gray-green tone predominates, cut through with exceptionally deep blacks—of shadow and of clothing. The result is an effect of combined dream and submersion, of underwater nightmare, lethargic but frightening. The few sequences in the countryside are shot in quite ordinary color, but by contrast they seem—as they must have seemed to Winston and Julia—gorgeous.

The settings by Allan Cameron, particularly the huge beehive offices, the eating rooms and meeting halls, are spare and austere, not slickly mechanized but bureaucratically grubby. The costumes by Emma Porteous suggest the robotistic without caricature. (It's never explained that the red sashes worn by the young women are emblems of the Junior Anti-Sex League.)

Radford wrote his own screenplay, and if you concede his concentration on the story, with minimum reference to the proles and the ideological discussion, it's competent. Winston (had his parents named him for Churchill?) works as a reviser of back newspapers to conform prophecies to events. His life is swathed in big-screen surveillance, programmed hates, continuous war bulletins; yet he manages a journal of secret feelings. Julia, a fellow-employee in the Ministry of Truth, contrives to slip him a note containing the words "I love you," a surprise to him and a piercing moment to us. They meet several times, make love, and are caught—the apt word because eroticism is to be stamped out. O'Brien, the party official interrogating and torturing Winston, wants to make him betray Julia, to make him replace his love for Julia with love for Big Brother, the head of state. My one substantive criticism of the screenplay—as Radford has chosen to craft it—is that the ending is left slightly open. The last line of the novel is "He loved Big Brother," as Winston looks at the telescreen in a café. In the film Julia has just left; Winston turns, looking after her, and says "I love you." He is sitting in front of B. B.'s immense face, but he looking, more or less, after Julia. A small fudge.

This is Radford's second feature film. Born in 1946, he was graduated from the British National Film School in 1974 and has made a number of documentaries. He both wrote and directed his first feature, *Another Time, Another Place*, also produced by Perry, which was released here last year. It was one more version of a conventional story, a P.O.W. and a local woman, this time an Italian assigned to a Scottish farm and the farmer's much younger wife—decently done but no kind of preparation for *1984*, which is filmmaking at a high imaginative level.

Suzanna Hamilton is Julia and has exactly the wiry, desperate sexuality that is needed. Kindly old Cyril Cusack is Charrington, and his kindliness helps the surprise of his duplicity. But it's the two leading men who set the final seal of quality on the film. John Hurt, principally remembered from *The Elephant Man* and the TV film of *The Naked Civil Servant* is Winston and is wonderful. His very face and voice suggest exile, banishment to this planet from some happier place, yet with resolve, with no slightest self-pity. Richard Burton is O'Brien, and the fact of Burton's death gives poignance even to his pensive sadism here. How easily he *fills* the character. When John Gielgud heard of Burton's death, he said (as I recall) that the news made him especially sad when he thought of all that this great talent had not done. That sadness haunts the screen here.

The music by Dominic Muldowney and the Eurythmics features two numbers called "Sexcrime" and "I Did It Just the Same." The temper of the music was intended, I guess, to suggest suppressed freedoms.

Reviewings

Que Viva Mexico

(November 24, 1979)

"The cinema's greatest artistic misfortune and its most celebrated scandal." So wrote Harry M. Geduld and Ronald Gottesman in the preface to *Sergei Eisenstein and Upton Sinclair: The Making and Unmaking of "Que Viva Mexico!"* (Indiana, 1970), a huge collection of relevant materials with commentary by the editors. The second part of their statement is inarguable: the first part is not.

The subject arises again because of a seven-film program to mark the anniversary of Soviet film, which was led off by still another version of the Eisenstein footage. Here's a very brief summary of the background: Sergei Eisenstein, deservedly world-famous at thirty-one, was permitted to leave the Soviet Union in 1929 to study film techniques abroad. Eventually he reached Hollywood where he was to make a film of *An American Tragedy*. This project dissolved. Then, with backing arranged by Upton Sinclair, Eisenstein went to Mexico to make a film there. With his assistant Grigory Alexandrov and his lifelong cinematographer Edouard Tissé, he arrived in Mexico in December 1930. He departed in March 1932, having shot hundreds of thousands of feet of film but without having finished. He and Sinclair had got into increasingly stormy broils, which are still being argued. (For a subjective portrait of Eisenstein, read the story "Hacienda" by Katherine Anne Porter. She knew the Russian group in Mexico and, using fictional names, expresses her preference for Alexandrov over his chief.) The director never edited his footage, which never reached Russia during his lifetime. A number of editings were done by different people, under various titles. The only previous one I've seen is called *Thunder Over Mexico* and was edited by Harry Chandlee, a name otherwise unknown to fame.

The new Soviet version is introduced by Alexandrov, now elderly, who also speaks an epilogue. He says that the footage was obtained after lengthy negotiations with the Museum of Modern Art in New York. (A member of the museum's film department confirms that the museum received about 600,000 feet of film from the Sinclair estate and made a copy which was sent to the Soviet Union.) Alexandrov says the material was edited according to Eisenstein's notes, scenarios, drawings. This could be true and still be a long way from what the director himself might have done; but there are reasons to believe that, though Eisenstein himself surely would have made the result better, he could not have put it in the front-line of his work—possibly could not even have made it good. It certainly is not good now.

The chief reason is intrinsic: in no other Eisenstein work is there such studied salon-photography estheticism. Everything seems to have been shot at 10:00 a.m. or 3:00 p.m.—never noon or early morning or late afternoon—so that the shadows will be just at the angle desired. A director can exercise his options, but after a while we feel that nothing happens in Mexico except for about fifteen minutes every morning and afternoon. Many, many of the shots are effectively composed but, with very few exceptions (three peons buried to the neck, for instance), they are undramatic, reminders of Paul Strand rather than Eisenstein. He seems to have been afflicted with the subtle virus that plagues directors abroad, a consciousness that he runs the risk of tourism and a desperate effort to perceive like a native. Antonioni in China behaved like a sophisticated tourist; Eisenstein in Mexico tried to see things from the inside out.

Most of the film is documentary. One episode is fictional, and it's foolish—as shot, not as edited. A peon starts an insurrection because his fiancée has been assaulted by his master's guest. The battle that follows, in which the master's daughter gaily takes part and is killed, is like a backyard parody of a Western.

Alexandrov's editing throughout, done with a large staff, may follow Eisenstein's intent. If so, all the more regrettable for Eisenstein. In one sequence, for instance, we see two lovers nestling in a hammock. This is immediately followed by a shot of two macaws billing on a branch above.

The rights and wrongs of the Eisenstein-Sinclair quarrel will probably remain in suspension forever. I certainly don't argue that Eisenstein should not have been permitted to edit his own film, but I simply can't see, on the evidence, that Sinclair's intransigence cheated the world of a masterpiece. Marie Seton, one of Eisenstein's biographers, prepared a version of the footage called *Time in the Sun*, which Otis Ferguson reviewed for *The New Republic* (September 30, 1940). I agree with his comments:

> The plain truth of the matter is that Eisenstein went to Mexico for some documentary stuff and there got drunk partly on his own reputation and partly on the million different things that could be photographed if you spent the rest of your life at it on subsidy; and that Upton Sinclair took a villainous drubbing for pulling him away in the end and trying to salvage some of that naive investment. A way to be a film critic for years was to holler about this rape of great art, though it should have taken no more critical equipment than common sense to see that whatever was cut out, its clumping repetitions and lack of film motion could not have been cut *in*.

L'Age d'Or

(May 17, 1980)

In 1928 Luis Buñuel, with Salvador Dali, made his first film, a twenty-four-minute silent surrealist work called *Un Chien andalou*. Subsequently Buñuel was offered financing for another film by the Viscount Charles de Noailles, and in 1930 Buñuel made another surrealist film, this time with sound, called *L'Age* d'Or. (Dali worked on it only a few days.) The second film caused an immense scandal. In 1934 the viscount and his wife withdrew it from circulation. Last year Allen Thiher wrote in *The Cinematic Muse* (University of Missouri Press): " . . . *Un Chien andalou* is undoubtedly the best-known work of surrealist cinema, and it will probably remain so until the family of Viscount Charles de Noailles decides that his soul will not roast in hell if *L'Age d'Or* . . . is ever released again." Evidently the family has made this eschatological decision: *L'Age d'Or* is now released and has just had its U.S. theatrical premiere at the Public Theater in New York.

Not many fifty-year-old scandals remain scandalous. *Le sacre du printemps* and *Ulysses* live by something more than the uproar they created when they were born. So must *L'Age d'Or*. I happened to see it in the 1960s at the Museum of Modern Art so I was braced for non-shock when I saw it again recently. Thiher says in his thoughtful book (critical essays on French film) that "the goal of all surrealist activity" was "to abolish the distinction between the objective and the subjective, between the repressive working of the reality principle and the pleasure principle." The distinction has been so steadily disregarded, if not worn away, during the last fifty years that the shocking disjunctures of sur-realism are now generally transformed to comedy. In *L'Age d'Or* when the man at a formal party slaps the face of the woman who accidentally spills wine on him, it doesn't seem much more socially anarchic than what Groucho did so often to Margaret Dumont. An even greater tamer of the "offenses" of *L'Age d'Or* is Buñuel himself, whose later works contain a lot of this film's elements refurbished, even amplified.

The three main assaults of the picture are on conventional love, piety, and social order. Buñuel said in 1955: "Dali and I would select gags and objects that would happen to come to mind. And we rejected without mercy everything that might mean something." "Mean" means, of course, some meaning in objec-tive reality. I won't try to list the episodes—which is what they are; not story—of the one-hour film. Here are a few samples. A mock founding of the ci-ty of Rome, on some seaside rocks, is interrupted by the sound of two lovers grappling in the mud. A grand party is interrupted by a horse-drawn cart pro-ceeding through the drawing room. A young woman discovers a cow sitting on her bed. A gamekeeper hugs his small son, then shoots the boy for jostling a cigarette he was rolling. The two lovers grapple again in a formal garden while an orchestra nearby plays a bit of *Tristan*, with a priest in the group. The man of the loving pair is summoned away; the frustrated woman sucks the toe of a statue. The conductor of the orchestra walks up the path, and the woman kisses him passionately. (Some accounts call the conductor her father.) A last episode refers to Sade's *120 Days of Sodom* with the Duke of Blangis dressed and bearded like Jesus. (The fact that Pasolini made a modernized, explicit film of the Sade novel, called *Salò*, is part of the cultural difference between 1930 and now.)

Two men in the cast link the picture closely to its era. Max Ernst, the dadaist/surrealist painter, has a small part; and Gaston Modot is one of the two lovers. Modot had a long career of secondary roles in French films (he died in 1970), the best-remembered of which probably is the jealous gamekeeper in Renoir's *The Rules of the Game*, but he began as a painter, was a friend of Picasso, and had his portrait painted by Modigliani in 1918.

No one who has seen *Saturday Night Live* or *Monty Python* is going to be greatly upset by *L'Age d'Or*, which is another way of saying that those programs are descendants of the surrealist movement in which Buñuel was active. But both in shock effect and intrinsically, I think this second film lesser than *Un Chien andalou*. One can see a daring, truly cinematic imagination in *L'Age d'Or*, but it is crudely photographed and acted, except for Lya Lys as the other lover. Buñuel's cruelty, his scatology, his linkages of sex and religion, of sex and death, have all become so familiar since 1930, have been used so much more diabolically, that this film is less a regained masterpiece than a regained sketchbook. Just think of *The Milky Way* (1969) and, quite apart from gains in technique, you see how Buñuel later made the conflict of the pleasure principle and the reality principle into a tense symbiosis rather than a mere juxtaposition.

The real shockers of 1930 these days are the films in which the reality of that period is *not* fractured, films that totally accept valentine-card love and *Saturday Evening Post* family life and hip-hoorah patriotism and the business world as evidence of divine order. Talk about surrealism!

Macbeth

(July 26, 1980)

I hadn't seen Orson Welles's *Macbeth* since it was first released in 1948, and I went to see it again recently because it's now available in a restored version. Bob Gitt, a film archivist at U.C.L.A., aided by the Folger Shakespeare Library, has found and put back twenty-one minutes that had been cut by Republic Studios, the producers, after some previews. Gitt has also restored some sequences that were in the released version but had originally been differently edited by Welles, and he has restored the first sound track, done with Scottish burrs, in place of the later track insisted upon by Republic. The opening of the first reel, with Welles's voice-over introduction, is apparently lost.

My opinion of this *Macbeth*, based on long-term remembrance, had nowhere to go but up, and up is certainly where it has gone. The sound track now has consistency, and the Scottish accents, though not needful, are no impediment. (The second, more familiar track is a patchwork—Welles had left for Europe and looped in some of his stuff from abroad.) I can't specify what the restorations are, but the previously released film ran only eighty-six minutes; an addition of almost twenty-five percent had to make a huge difference. Whatever the details of Gitt's job, Welles's *Macbeth* is now a bold, exciting, innovative film.

It is not Shakespeare's *Macbeth*. I'm not going to reopen the old critical hassle of whether or not there is an ideal *Macbeth* (or any other classic). I simply tell again the beads of my Shakespeare-on-film rosary: no film of a Shakespeare play can be that play because form is not incidental in a titan's creation and because film is primarily powerful in ways that are either secondary to Shakespeare's intent or else completely outside his knowledge. Shakespeare is in his language. Admittedly, very few theater productions of his plays are uncut, but few theater productions are as condensed as even the best Shakespeare films must be. Above and after all, these plays reside in their language, and that language has dynamics and being that are uncongenial to film.

But Welles knew all this. He said, "I use Shakespeare's words and characters to make motion pictures. They are variations on his themes . . . ." In *Macbeth* he used only about one-third of Shakespeare's words, and he rearranged sequences within that third. He also said of his Shakespeare films, "What I am trying to do is to see the outside, real world through the same eyes as the inside, fabricated one." So it's no surprise that his *Macbeth* has often been called expressionist. But in esthetic terms, the most striking aspect of this restored film is Welles's apparently quite conscious attempt to fuse a third form out of theater and film.

This *Macbeth* began on stage. Part of Republic's budget was allocated to a production of the play by and with Welles in Salt Lake City with some of the same people who were in the subsequent film. (Not Agnes Morehead who was the Lady in Utah and who would have helped the film). Then, with settings by Fred Ritter and camera by John L. Russell, with himself again in the title role, Welles shot the film at Republic in twenty-three days.

Before we get to the achievements, here are some of the oddities. First, there are textual oddities even for a particularized version. The witches are not agents of Fate, they themselves are made to seem malevolent toward Macbeth. An early line of theirs—"Peace! The charm's wound up"—is placed at the very end to make it seem as if they had accomplished what *they* set out to do. (That last shot, of Macbeth's castle on a hill, is a clear reminder of the end of *Citizen Kane*.) In Shakespeare the witches are both instruments of immensity and the voices of one man's buried desires and fears; in Welles they are merely evil. Banquo's speech, "Thou hast it now," plainly a soliloquy, is spoken right to Macbeth. Lady Macbeth's berating of her husband for his spasms of fear during the banquet—again plainly meant to be private—is shouted before all the guests. A character called a Holy Father was constructed out of some lines of the Old Man, Ross, and others, to serve, said Welles, as a moral referent for Macbeth's actions; this construct fails to achieve what Shakespeare had already done in some of the omitted text. The Porter is sliced to virtually nothing; if he was being sliced, why then add a line of Toby Belch's from *Twelfth Night*?

Notes on dress: Lady Macbeth wears very false eyelashes. Macbeth is apparently the only man in the Scotland of his day who had a twentieth-century barber; everyone else has long hair. All his headgear—his Mongolian helmet at the start, his square crown, his Statue of Liberty helmet at the end—seem designed to dare us to laugh. Also the Holy Father's braided wig.

Performances: All except Macbeth and Banquo (Edgar Barrier) are inadequate. Jeanette Nolan makes Lady Macbeth the sexy wife of a corporate vice president, fierce for hubby's promotion. Roddy McDowall flutes as Malcolm, Dan O'Herlihy is milky as Macduff. The worst scene in the film, possibly the worst in all of Welles, is the one where Macduff learns of his family's slaughter. Not just the acting, the direction as well.

But most of the standard objections to this film seem to me to miss the point. It's been dubbed the "pâpier-maché" Macbeth because of its sets, it's been castigated for its obvious studio lighting. These strictures, and more, grow out of the belief that film automatically equals realism; and they grow too out of hunger for the same kinds of cinematic virtuosity that Welles had shown in Citizen Kane and The Magnificent Ambersons, a poetic realism so prodigally inventive that it was almost as if he was making the first films ever and the world was lucky that the terrain was being discovered by a young man with genius.

In Macbeth he is moving past realism. The prior theater production in Utah shows that this movement is quite conscious. (In 1936 he had done a so-called "voodoo" Macbeth, transposed to Haiti, with an all-black cast in a Harlem theater. I saw it and can remember being disquieted by it.) The film settings are meant to look like settings, the way they would in a symbolic stage production. The lighting and photography are meant to evoke the atmosphere of the theater. This is not the "invisible" photography of most films, in which we are meant to see only the subject, nor the "visible" photography of German expressionist films (antecedents of Kane and Ambersons), in which we are meant to be aware of film's power to make visual texture a character in the drama. The lighting of Macbeth, in most shots, surrounds the subjects with the magic air that surrounds theater actors in non-realistic stage lighting, that strange feeling of the consecration of space. In Macbeth there is very little sense that Welles is trying to show that film can take things from the theater and do them better; he is taking from the theater and film and trying to do something else, to blend them, to give us a theater experience through film and vice versa, and therefore something different from a usual theater or film experience. The most comparable lighting that I know—call it theater/film style—occurs in much of what Fellini has been doing since La Dolce Vita.

With this general look of things, Welles has also worked for flowing motion. Whenever possible, a scene is led by the camera and the actors' movement into the next scene, which often means merely moving to another part of the huge multiple set, moving into changed lights. (Peter Brook did something like this in his film of Marat/Sade, 1967.) It's easy to say that Welles was going after the fluency of the Elizabethan stage, the speed that was such a big part of Granville Barker's theory of Shakespeare production, but doing it on film is more daring than on stage. On film it doesn't obey its medium, it challenges. It underscores artifice, rather than intensifying film realism, as the deep-focus and traveling shots of Renoir do.

Conceptually, scene after scene reminded me of drawings and photographs of the work of Gordon Craig and Robert Edmond Jones and Norman Bel Geddes: sculptural masses molded by the fall of light; a forest of spears rising, against a white background, out of a black blot of men; Birnam Wood floating through mist toward Dunsinane as the avenging army approaches, carrying boughs; the thick curve of old stone stairways; the fracturing of space to force the action toward the viewer. In one sense, seeing this *Macbeth* is seeing how a filmmaker profited from some of the most imaginative theater designers of the half-century before him.

In his union of theater and film—neither filmed play nor stagy film but an esthetic union—Welles is using ideas as revolutionary as those in *Kane*, though they have had much less influence. One clue to his intent is that remark of his, quoted earlier, about trying to see the outside world through the inside one. As in the theater, a double action is entailed. In a symbolically designed play, the non-real look tells us that the work's reality is internal; and, in turn, that inner reality is externalized in the physical abstractions of the production. The difference here from the theater is in the greater immediacy of that internal reality: a face, or some faces, sometimes as the whole of what we see; the voice-over soliloquies drifting up from inside; the almost palpable increase in envelopment by inner states.

I've left to last one of the best elements in the film, thrilling and also poignant in the light of Welles's subsequent career—his own performance of Macbeth. It is all *acted*, in every good sense of that battered term; it is all imagined, crafted, projected, realized. Nothing is ticked off to personality or booming or eccentric reading as a substitute for design. In every one of the big moments, Welles rises to the heroic. He doesn't try to slide around the edge as he did later in Othello and much later in Falstaff. When he bursts at the news that Banquo's son has escaped the assassins, when he assails the witches after he is king, he is in full fury, trying the measure of his spirit and his throat against the tragic event. And the haunted, doomed, futile touch is in him, too. His reading of "Tomorrow and tomorrow and tomorrow," during which we look only at one shot of swirling clouds, is the best I have ever heard.

We all owe thanks to Bob Gitt.

Unknown Chaplin

(June 20, 1983)

What's the point of investigating material that a great artist discarded? Much of the time, none. I don't like to hear the *Leonore Overture No. 2*: why get the piece half-baked when Beethoven did it better next time out? But once in a while, the discarded material is good in itself and is enlightening about the artist's known work. (Joyce's *Stephen Hero* vis-à-vis *A Portrait .of the Artist as a Young Man*.) And that's the case with *Unknown Chaplin*.

This is a three-part TV series made for Thames Television International of Britain — three fifty-two-minute programs, each of which is in two parts to allow for commercials, I guess. Kevin Brownlow and David Gill, well-known film historians and filmmakers, were researching another project when they came across this material. Lady Chaplin had permitted them access to Chaplin's vault for the initial project: they discovered this treasure and changed projects. The discoveries in the vault led to discoveries elsewhere. Sensitive editing, careful braiding of interviews with a few surviving Chaplin colleagues, an engagingly spoken narration by James Mason, and the result is a priceless addition to the Chaplin heritage.

Part One consists mainly of outtakes from the Mutual period, 1916-1917. But "outtakes" is not the precise word: this is not material omitted when the picture was being finally edited, it is progressive. The narration tells us truly that Chaplin rehearsed on film, revised on film. Costs, including his salary, were not negligible by the scale of the day, still he already had the power to use this method if he chose. What is artistically more relevant is that we see an experienced music-hall performer, accustomed to the tryout of new material before audiences with only their reactions to guide him, relishing the fact that here he could be in both positions: could do it, then could watch himself doing it. "This is too good to be true," we can almost hear him saying about this process as the takes of a scene increase and increase, as the scene gets better and better.

For instance, *The Cure*, done in April 1917. We see samples of the first seventy-six takes of a sequence shot in the courtyard of a spa hotel. When the slate goes to 76a, we have moved outside and a fountain has become a well. Through these takes, Chaplin has been a bellhop. By slate 84 he has become one of the guests, soused. By slate 622 we're back in the lobby, with the drunk as traffic cop in a jam of wheelchairs. Later, the sequence is dropped, but Chaplin keeps the role of the drunken guest.

The highlight of Part One is the development of my favorite Mutual film, *The Immigrant*, which followed *The Cure* and was finished only two months afterward. (The Mutual films were all two reels.) Many of us have thought so long of *The Immigrant* in a particular way that it's astonishing to see how Chaplin arrived at the finished film. He began, not with social commentary in mind, but with a sheerly comic restaurant scene. Stout, affable Henry Bergman, a

Chaplin familiar, is a supposedly ferocious waiter; Chaplin is the penniless, hungry Tramp watching Bergman rough up a customer who can't pay his bill. Bergman isn't scary enough. He is replaced by the even bigger and fiercer Chaplin familiar, Eric Campbell. Edna Purviance is seated at another table, and Chaplin eyes her adoringly as she ignores him. But the scene isn't coming together. Then Chaplin gets the key inspiration: what's needed is a prior sequence to give weight to this one. That opening sequence is on a ship: Chaplin and Purviance are fellow immigrants in steerage. (Bergman is a fat seasick woman.) When they accidentally meet again in the restaurant, they know each other. Her mother, whom we've seen on the ship, is now dead—information conveyed by a black-bordered handkerchief. To a gag situation have been added pathos, tenderness, and the chance for Chaplin to play the cavalier, which helps to build the Tramp's character and to make his difficulties funnier. (And Bergman is now an artist who sees the pair in the restaurant and offers them modeling work.)

What started as an attempt to get laughs out of a restaurant scene has evolved backwards into a romantic-ironic comedy about the Land of Opportunity.

Part Two covers the years 1918-1931. Jackie Coogan today comments on his experiences with Chaplin, and we see the boy Jackie do a shimmy, which Chaplin had taught him, to entertain a group of visiting exhibitors. Lita Grey Chaplin, very cordial considering the fact that Chaplin never even mentions her name in his autobiography, tells of the location work for *The Gold Rush* and how she had to quit the picture because of pregnancy. Georgia Hale, who replaced her and who was immortalized by the role, recalls how dissatisfied Chaplin was with Virginia Cherrill's work in *City Lights*. Cherrill herself frankly confirms this, and we see the last scene of that film with Hale replacing her as the blind girl. It's shocking. (A bit like the screen-test sequence in 8½ where we see other actors as the people whom we have been watching up to that point.) Hale, so fine as the dance-hall prostitute in *The Gold Rush*, may have had more talent than Cherrill, but she lacked the right personal quality for the blind flower seller.

For this and other reasons, Chaplin was forced to reengage Cherrill. She tells us that her friend Marion Davies convinced her that she had Chaplin over a barrel, that she could now ask for any salary she liked. So, she says, she asked for twice what she had been getting, and got it: $150 a week. (Chaplin, who spent freely on perfecting story and performance, was reputedly tight-fisted on salaries and on production elements like scenery.) Then we see that last scene as it became world famous, with Cherrill. She may not have been much of an actress, but Chaplin (like De Sica after him) was a wonderful director of non-actors who used the film medium like a hawk, to hover and to pounce on the one moment when the nonartist matched feeling with expression. I don't know what number the take was, but the last scene of *City Lights* is one of the glories of film history.

The pinnacle of Part Two is the sequence in which Chaplin refines the scene in *City Lights* where the Tramp first meets the flower girl, discovers that she is blind, and leaves her with the impression that he is a rich man. I won't give all the details of improvement (including the dousing that De Sica later paraphrased in *Miracle in Milan*). The making of the scene is an insight into two kinds of mastery, film and theater. This scene, like most of *City Lights*, like much else of Chaplin's work, was possible only to a man steeped in Victorian-Edwardian melodrama, who believed in it and knew how to perform it.

Part Three, called "Unshown Chaplin," includes some private footage, such as Chaplin doing the roll dance from *The Gold Rush* in his own persona. (Press notes say it was at a New York party in 1926.) And there's an early sequence about a manager of trained fleas, which he saved, and improved, for *Limelight*. But the high point of the section is a completely edited seven-minute sequence with which Chaplin planned, for a time, to begin *City Lights*. The shape is a classic of vaudeville and circus clowning, the inverted pyramid—a complex series of events building on a small action. The Tramp idly attempts to dislodge, with his cane, a small piece of wood stuck between the bars of a sidewalk grating outside a shop window. Eventually this involves other people, then a crowd, then window dressers inside the shop, then (naturally) the police. I'm glad of two things: that *City Lights* begins as it does (the Tramp discovered sleeping in the arms of a statue when it's unveiled); that this sequence has been rediscovered. It's a gem.

Chaplin, despite the glare of international publicity, was always somewhat mysterious, and his autobiography doesn't much help to clear things up. Besides the omission of projects that he started and dropped, sometimes finished and dropped, the book says very little about his working methods. In *Unknown Chaplin* one take of *City Lights* is slate 4,337. Doubtless the number applied to more than one sequence; still it demonstrates almost manic perfectionism. This TV series also exhibits his moodiness and broodiness. On *City Lights* the studio work sheets show that, in the first 83 days of production, the company was idle on 62 days: in the next 534 days, idle on 368. Chaplin was at home, perhaps thinking, perhaps being despondent, perhaps just at home.

These three programs, which really constitute a (nearly) three-hour film, don't begin to clear up all the mysteries about Chaplin. On the one hand, we can ask righteously: Why should all his secrets be explained? On the other, we know very well that we'd leap to see more—anything that would bring us closer to his genius, that would extend and widen his posthumous life. Thanks to Brownlow and Gill, to Lady Chaplin, to Thames Television and all others involved, more of Chaplin is now in the world.

The Leopard

(July 16 & 23, 1984)

For several months, a "new" version of this Visconti film—actually an earlier version—has been on view; so this note is belated. But the occasion is too important to overlook. When *The Leopard* was first shown here in 1963, it ran 161 minutes and was dubbed into English, except for Burt Lancaster as Lampedusa's Prince, who spoke his own lines. Visconti's original film ran 205 minutes and, to my knowledge, has not been shown outside Italy. The current version is in Italian. It runs 185 minutes (the length that was first shown in France) and is thus twenty-four minutes longer than the 1963 release. Also twenty-one years have passed. All these facts make a difference.

The blessing of not hearing Lancaster's voice has to be experienced to be appreciated. The Italian voice makes Lancaster *look* different. (Lillian Gish became a lesser actress, in beauty as well as talent, with the advent of sound. I've seen James Cagney in Italy, dubbed into Italian, and he moved differently.) Nothing that Lancaster says now can undercut what we are supposed to believe about the Prince. Other actors in the cast are also dubbed—Alain Delon, surely, as the Prince's fiery nephew, but with a voice that does not belie what I know of him from French films. My long-standing argument against dubbing has always been against intervention—between one part of an actor's equipment and another. When that intervention is unobtrusive (as with Delon here or with Jeanne Moreau in *La Notte*), the argument doesn't apply. When the intervention actually helps, as in Lancaster's case, the argument is stilled.

The Leopard never lacked splendor for the eye, and the restored twenty-four minutes—a long time in a film—makes the splendor even more splendid. (I can't specify where the cuts have been restored.) As I recall, the 1963 version seemed to lack climaxes and theatricality because it was worrying about climaxes and theatricality. Now it is more at ease with its existence as a chronicle, as a development in line and depth rather than a drama. The long, gorgeous, socially freighted grand ball that concludes the film is now both the cinematic and thematic statement that Visconti intended.

Also, a film viewer's experience in the last twenty-one years helped this new version. The latest and most relevant instance was Fassbinder's *Berlin Alexanderplatz,** which I had seen shortly before I saw *The Leopard* again. Fassbinder's sixteen-hour work affected our expectations of motion and time, of dimension, expanded the receptivity of film to narrative-as-drama, rather than a narrative struggling to *be* drama. Thus Fassbinder's later film influenced Visconti's earlier one. Borges said that Kafka modifies and refines our reading of Hawthorne: "A great writer creates his precursors." Proportionately, that has also been the case with these two filmmakers.

---

*See p. 183.

Comment

Domestic Troubles

(November 22, 1980)

The risk in writing about the trouble with American films is that something may come along next week to brighten the gloom. But even if something good comes along, I can't quite believe, for reasons below, that the gloom should stay lifted.

The poor state of our films is being talked about by everyone. ("Everyone" means the people I meet.) So I've looked back, just at 1980, since there had to be a cutoff date, ten months in which I reviewed exactly fifty U.S. pictures, many fewer than I saw, and I've come up feeling sad. Beneath the buzz of movie puffery, from both producers and press, beneath the torrential success of a few gigantic hits, it's been a drab time. Pickings can be slim in any ten-month period in any art, but I remember the past and there seem to be some factors that will affect the future. Here they are.

1. *Money.* Not only inflation but rising relative costs. A studio chief said recently that a U.S. picture must now gross $40 million at the box office to *break even.* His figure has been attacked as including padded overhead and leakage. All right, reduce it twenty-five percent, which seems too much. U.S. films would then have all the freedom of spirit and artistic adventure that a mere $30 million nut allows.

A possible palliative, the means used in almost every other filmmaking country, is government subsidy. The methods are usually direct grants or tax remissions or substantial prizes for work which is judged worthy by a professional jury and which has failed, after a year or so, to earn back costs. But the practicality of those ideas, I have to admit, is dim here. The size of U.S. film budgets, as compared to foreign ones, is so much greater that grants, to be really helpful, would stun Congress; because of that size and the larger spread of both film and government, the angles for corruption would be increased. Moreover, the fact that some people do reap immense fortunes out of film makes loss on a film—unlike loss on opera or ballet, where profit is impossible—seem like ineptness.

Ideally, subsidy would help. Ideally, subsidy is logical. But the real chance of significantly lowering that $40, or $30, million threshold by subsidy seems nebulous.

2. *Intrinsic artistic problems.* If costs were lowered, these problems would persist.

Not too simplistically, the history of U.S. film can be divided into three periods. First, the beginnings until about 1967, when the mass of Hollywood pictures, with shining exceptions, was entertainment and when that entertainment, at its best, was the best in the world. Second, post 1967 for about seven or eight years, when, under the influence of fine foreign films imported during the preceding decade and immediately spurred by the effect of *Blow-Up* and *The Graduate,* American film moved to respond directly to American life, to develop—within the still abundant entertainment flood—a strain of "personal" work. Third, the years since then. A lot of the "personal" work in Period Two was no more than well-intentioned: the pictures were not only poor, they lost money. Hollywood treated the "personal" film, which included the so-called youth film, as one more trend, like disaster pictures, and rushed out loads of junk whose only difference from other junk was its sincerity. The backlash came in Period Three. Some of the trappings of Two have been retained, like sexual frankness, like exploitative trips through social problems, like sophisticated cinema syntax, but reliable old-fashioned scripts have been slipped under the mod décor. (*Urban Cowboy*, for instance.)

Nowadays Hollywood seems to be saying, "OK, we gave those highminded types their chance, and they blew it. So we'll keep the mod décor because we paid for it, plenty, and because it helps us to stay a step ahead of TV; but we'll use it on proven stuff."

3. *Impulse.* A good work of art begins with the fact that someone wants to make it—out of himself. Put that thunderingly obvious fact next to the U.S. film situation where almost no one seems to have such an impulse, where everyone seems to be scurrying for a gimmick, a hot topic, or a best seller to adapt.

Art, in one aspect at least, is the transformation of experience through perception and imagination. The best films of the past exemplify that process; and the process seems to be continuing pretty well in some other American arts: dance, poetry, painting, even—though less than bruited—in fiction. But it's not happening much in film.

The filmmaker, under which tag I subsume director and writer and participating producer, doesn't seem to have much interest in that process. If he or she shows impulse at the start, shows interest in the process (Claudia Weill with *Girlfriends*), the industry washes him or her into the varnished-trash trade (Claudia Weill with *It's My Turn*). Or impulse, if it was at all visible initially, is from the beginning grafted with Movieland cleverness (Martin Scorsese, Paul Schrader). Either way, and other ways too, the filmmaker ends up as gimmick hunter.

4. *Lack of nourishment.* Compare our situation with that in some foreign countries—including their playwrights who, I'll show, are relevant. In several countries, notably Britain and West Germany, playwriting thrives. A strong element in this foreign strength is political urgency of one kind or another, though not always: one of the best of them all, Peter Handke, is apolitical, "merely" esthetically vigorous. In several foreign countries, West Germany oustandingly, some good film work goes on, nourished similarly.

It would seem that the American difference, leaving money aside, is in this cultural nourishment. Political vigor in art is difficult in a country that has no politics, that equates election campaigns with politics. Esthetic vigor in theater and film falters for different but linked antecedent reasons. Abroad the theater has always been one of several forms prized by the most serious writers (Goethe, Hugo, Chekhov, etc). In this country, we can infer that, until well into this century, a writer felt he was faced with a choice: between really serious writing or playwriting. This still puts the serious playwright in the implicit position of fighting for legitimacy, sensing that (in Eliot's terms) his individual talent doesn't fit into a tradition, as do the talents of American painters and poets. This can, possibly unconsciously, create a demoralizing situation for playwrights who show talent, and it may be one of the reasons why so many of them dribble away into silence or into film and TV job-hunting. Harold Clurman said, "America is lousy with talent," which I take to be his pungent version of Scott Fitzgerald's remark that in American lives there are no second acts. This century hasn't done much to foster a nourishing tradition for our playwrights. Despite all the conferences and college courses, that tradition has yet to thrive.

This lack of a strong artistic tradition in the U.S. theater affected U.S. film from the outset. When film began in Sweden or France or Germany or Italy, most of the work was of course pop, good or bad, but apparently some small proportion of people, in the profession and the public, wanted a small proportion of film work to reflect and extend their highly developed theatrical art. There was no equivalent pressure in the U.S. because there was no equivalent theatrical art: so virtually *all* our films were pop right from the start. Those films had, still have, tremendous influence abroad; the converse influence of foreign filmmakers is demonstrable—I've demonstrated it elsewhere—but it's neither equivalent nor basic. It couldn't be, because of the differences in cultural history. So the newer country has had no rivulet of serious film flowing along near its flood of entertainment. And the American filmmaker, of possible serious intentions, is generally unsustained, is more or less on his own; and his own is not often enough. (I'm ignoring hundreds of serious American filmmakers who work in documentary or animation or non-theatrical forms: they are not my subject.)

The financial crunch has exacerbated all these matters.

On the other hand—and I'm glad to say there is another hand—two points. First, history doesn't give us the right to expect a predominance of good work at any time in art. The rich periods in any art are the exceptions, and even during the rich periods, most of the work is lean. (Thousands of hack operas were written in Italy during the lifetimes of Bellini and Verdi.) Still, no one is asking for Eden, just for sustenance.

Second, occasional good films do appear even now in the time of the crunch. I can't write off as zero a year that saw *The Outsider* and *Airplane!* In the former, an American director named Tony Luraschi won through to make a film about an American in the current Irish troubles, a picture that, barring its brief prologue and epilogue, is authentic and alive. In the latter, three young men named Jim Abrahams, David Zucker, and Jerry Zucker won through to make a satire of unflagging effervescence, full of not-too-good-natured ridicule. (*Airplane!* was especially refreshing because the year was littered with inane or compromised attempts in the same vein.)

These days the most inspiriting event in any art anywhere is the appearance of a good new film. Which is another way of saying that the odds against good work are greater in film than in other arts. But it does appear, even—despite the handicaps I've cited—in the U.S. Two respectable pictures in a year can keep hope alive. On the other hand (again!) real hope only makes one intolerant and impatient.

Takashi Shimura

(March 17, 1982)

Takashi Shimura died in Tokyo on February 11, just one month before his seventy-seventh birthday. He had long been ill. His acting career had begun in the theater, then he had moved into films and had played in many, including most of Akira Kurosawa's, beginning with that director's debut in 1943. Shimura is doubtless best known in the U.S. for three Kurosawa roles: the woodcutter in *Rashomon*, the leader of the samurai in *The Seven Samurai*, and the civil servant doomed by cancer in *Ikiru*. Just to remember those performances is once again to feel tingles between the shoulder blades.

Last winter Kurosawa announced at a press luncheon in New York that he plans to make a version of *King Lear*, and I asked him whether Shimura would be in it. He replied that there was a large part for Shimura but that the actor was hospitalized and the prognosis was not good. The film will be made, I hope, but one role in it, however well played, will not be played as well as it might have been.

If we feel that we "know" Chekhov and Mark Twain and Rembrandt and Haydn—to name some of the artists who have the peculiar power to evoke a sense of personal acquaintance—it's not surprising that we should have that feeling about some film actors, since their physical beings are the medium of their art. Once in Zagreb a Yugoslavian director told me that his brother and Gary Cooper had died in the same week; he hadn't seen his brother in twenty years and Cooper's death had affected him much more. But Cooper was a star, a real star, who was sometimes a good actor. Shimura was never a star and was always a wonderful actor.

It's tempting to talk about universality and immortality when discussing film artists, but I can't think of a better reason to yield to that temptation than the occasion of Shimura's death. Three times I sent greetings to him through men I met in New York: his colleague Toshiro Mifune in 1969, the great cinematographer Kazuo Miyagawa about a year ago, and Kurosawa a few months ago. I don't know whether he got the greeting, and if he did, I can't imagine that it meant much to him: I'm talking about what it meant to me. I felt an urge, an ache, to reach around the globe to someone I knew and had never met. My perceptions of myself and my life have been in some degree touched because Shimura lived and worked, and the attempt at a greeting was confirmation of that strange, commonplace truth.

Film is supposed to be permanent. It isn't. It's supposed to be universally available. It isn't. When it *is* preserved and available, it often isn't even "textually" correct: snips and muddiness make us groan. But if there is anything at all to the ideal of film preservation and continuance, then there are people to come—some, at least, in many parts of the world—who will be affected by the humanity of the human being who died in Tokyo last month.

Powers That Be

(November 15, 1982)

Last month I met the gifted Hungarian director Károly Makk, who was in New York because the Film Festival showed his latest film. *Another Way* deals with two lesbians in the troubled days of 1956, and, whatever else may be said of it, it's beautifully acted. The two women were played by Poles, and I asked Makk why, fine though these Polish actresses were, he had not cast this picture about Budapest troubles with Hungarian actresses. He replied that he wanted people who knew political danger firsthand. Conditions are relatively calm in Hungary now; in Poland, as the world knows, they are not. He wanted two young women who could bring to these roles, not recreations of an atmosphere they could not themselves have known but immediate knowledge of political crisis.

The more I thought about Makk's reply, the more it seemed to dovetail, basically, with Werner Herzog's insistence on spending years in the Peruvian hinterlands to make *Fitzcarraldo.** Widely different as the instances are in scale, the impulses behind them are much the same. Makk wanted verity of background brought into his fiction; Herzog wanted verity of place and ordeal brought into his fiction.

Are these impulses naive? I'm aware that many of the most wonderful experiences I've had in film came from actors who, in their personal lives, had nothing to do with the characters they were portraying. I'm aware that many of the most thrilling spectacles I've seen were artifices contrived by technical ingenuity. "You see films like *Star Wars* and whatever and there are always tricks," Herzog said in a recent interview. "The audience has lost a basic faith in that they don't believe their eyes. I would like to get people to trust their eyes again." Leaving the *Star Wars* sort of film out of it—who would expect even Herzog to make a film of that sort in outer space?—I think his remark, as edict,

---

*See p. 191.

is hogwash.

Still, there *is* a power in films that has been there from the beginning, used from the beginning (I'm speaking only of fiction films), that Makk and Herzog are employing. To simplify, let's call it the Third Power. Power One: the film can use realism in ways that had not previously been possible, even though the realism is achieved in studio circumstances. Power Two: the film can use imaginative devices—devices that play with time and place and substantiality—in ways that had not previously been possible. But there is also Power Three: reality. The film can use reality (as opposed to fabricated realism) so intense that it goes past verisimilitude into a territory of the imagination. D. W. Griffith refined and extended the vocabulary of film, and he did much of his pioneering in studios, with artificial light and canvas walls. But he also recognized the Third Power. He shot the blizzard scenes of *Way Down East* in an actual snowstorm, so fierce that, says Lillian Gish in her autobiography, "a small fire burned directly beneath the camera to keep the oil from freezing." He shot the ice scenes on White River, Vermont, with Gish lying on an ice floe, one hand trailing in the water. "My hair froze," says Gish, "and I felt as if my hand were in a flame. To this day, it aches if I am out in the cold for very long." No one would contend that these sequences could not possibly have been done otherwise, but anyone who has seen the film can understand why Griffith wanted to make it as he did.

Is Power Three literalism? Does it contradict Powers One and Two? I think not. King Vidor, one of the sturdiest American directors, told a story about his early career that is now part of film lore: he wanted to take a company out on location to get the right background for a sequence, and the producer, budget-conscious, said that a tree was a tree and Vidor could shoot the scene in the Los Angeles city park. But Power Three, Vidor apparently felt, would see through the trees in the park, would be searching for the right trees. Those directors who want to use this power—and almost no director has ever wanted to use it continuously—are not looking for greater realism: the difference, I believe, goes past the idea of realism, to a belief that the camera can penetrate, can find essences. Leave out of the discussion the location work that's essential because the scene couldn't be credibly be done any other way (like the shot in *Stagecoach* of the coach rolling out of the town into immensity). Consider only those shots and sequences that could conceivably be done otherwise. Some directors believe that the camera's ability to go to actual places carries with it the ability to move beneath surfaces to distillation.

With Makk, mutatis mutandis, the same idea prevailed. He knows what actors can do and how he can help them to do it. (One instance. Lili Darvas, in his exquisite film *Love*, was magnificent as an Austrian-born, very old, bed-ridden invalid, though she herself was none of these things.) But in *Another Way* he wanted the camera to go beneath his actors' art to what had helped to shape their art, because—*in this instance*—he felt that those pressures would support the performances that he wanted.

It's no help to argue against Power Three on the ground that films are illusion. All art is illusion; and in the film art, every director, Griffith and Herzog and Makk and everyone else, has been aware of that commonplace. The question is: At what point do they want the illusion to begin? I have considerable interest in acting as a high and complex art, and I've often objected to pointless literalism. Nevertheless (therefore?) I don't want to proscribe—in my own mind anyway—any truly artistic options that are open to film. The visionary psychologist-philosopher Hugo Münsterberg wrote in *The Film* (1916): "In every respect the film is further away from physical reality than the drama, and in every respect this greater distance from the physical world brings it nearer to the mental world." All of us would shudder if Power Three were to become the iron law of the film universe. But the Griffith-Makk-Herzog belief cannot be dismissed as mere literalism. It's quite the reverse. Fundamentally, it's a quasimetaphysical belief in the camera's power to reveal one more kind of truth.

Outraged Virtue

(March 5, 1984)

I. B. Singer tells us in a self-interview (*The New York Times*, January 29, 1984) that he has seen the Streisand film made from his story, "Yentl the Yeshiva Boy," and that he doesn't like it.* What a surprise. He tells us himself that his story "was in no way material for a musical." Would he also tell us the name of the person who put a gun to his head and, despite his foreboding, forced him to sell the story to Streisand?

Singer now joins a club I wish he had stayed out of, the authors who take the money and do not run, who stay to complain about what Hollywood did to their work. Other members include William Styron, E. L. Doctorow, and Judith Rossner, all of whom told a literary luncheon last November how their writings had suffered in film transformation. None of them said anything—at least as reported—about who forced them to sell their film rights or about asking that their names be removed from the desecrating films.

It's such a stale ploy. These writers, and dozens before them, have known quite well what Hollywood would almost certainly do to their work. (Doctorow himself wrote the screenplay of *Daniel* and served as executive producer.) They want the money; and, after they get it, they want to play up to literary luncheons as ravished virgins. Possibly it takes their mewlings too seriously to point out that films of novels are not necessarily desecrations: Pudovkin's *Mother*, Ford's *The Grapes of Wrath*, Rohmer's *The Marquise of O. . .*, for a few examples. (The first two are improvements over their originals.) But the real point is not that film automatically despoils but that these writers play the straight money game and then complain because the purchasers play it too.

---

*See p. 233.

How differently some writers look at the relationship between literature and film. Last November 18, about the same time that the bruised millionaires were carrying on at the New York literary luncheon, the (London) *Times Literary Supplement* featured a symposium on "Writers and the Cinema." Ruth Prawer Jhabvala, admitting that her long-term partnership with the director James Ivory and the producer Ismail Merchant protected her from what she calls "the real world of films," nonetheless said about screenwriting:

> It has been a two-way traffic for me—what I have learned in films I have put back into my books, and what I have learned about . . . writing fiction I've put to use in my films. I've needed both to keep going—I mean imaginatively as well as financially.

Malcolm Bradbury compares the emergence of film in this century with that of the novel in the eighteenth century:

> The novel, like film, emerged as a "low" form, and its very codes and systems were thought vulgar. Yet increasingly they penetrated into literary activity, shaping all the forms of writing. Much the same has been true of the impact of film on twentieth-century fiction; many of the devices and coding systems that we identify as radical and experimental in the modern novel therefore have an implicit film source.

This is not precisely the same subject that the Americans were anguishing about. (Among the latter, only Doctorow said a word about the formal influence of film on fiction.) And the *TLS* contributors did not disavow the conflict between most film writing and serious writing. But at least the symposium added something to the much-chewed topic of fiction-and-film, and at least it was free of that tedious hypocrisy by well-paid hustlers of film rights pretending to be victims of rape.

Allowing for Exceptions

(March 26, 1984)

What is the domain of the film critic? Two recent statements offer definitions.
Last autumn the National Association of Theater Owners had a trade show in California, prominent in which was a display of the candy, pop, and popcorn available for theater concession stands. According to *The New York Times* of November 5, 1983, the sale of such items was expected to reach approximately $750 million last year. One president of a theater chain said that, without the sales at concession stands, theaters could not remain in business. Theaters expected to sell more than $3.6 billion in tickets last year, but more than half of that money would go to the distributors and makers of the films. The money

earned at the concession stand belongs to the theater owners, and that money would be the profit margin.

So: the film critic's job is to comment on the material that provides the occasion for selling candy, pop, and popcorn. If the critic were to put first financial things first, he or she would criticize the items on sale at the concession stand; they are what keep the theater going, not the stuff inside on the screen, which is only a lure to draw people in to buy the refreshments.

Another candid statement comes from Ned Tanen, who recently resigned as head of Universal Pictures. Interviewed in the British film journal *Sight and Sound* (Winter 1983/84), Tanen says that, of the eighteen or twenty pictures a year produced by a major studio, with luck two or three will make a profit. He is asked about the Classics divisions that most major studios have instituted to release "quality or foreign or independent films." He admits that this operation has some assets: it gives the studio a good image, it opens doors to people you might want to do business with, "It's a source of supplementary income so long as you don't kid yourself that it'll amount to much . . . . If one of those movies runs for forty weeks on the East Side of New York or thirty weeks in L.A. and the critics love it, what does it mean? Who the hell *cares?*" Later he says: "The audience has gotten older and I think that's good news. It'll allow you to make a few more movies which aren't about car racing or rites of passage, God help us. Basically, your audience is around eighteen-twenty, but it's not fourteen anymore."

So: the critic, who spends time concentrating on the stuff that sells the popcorn, is expending enthusiasm, when possible, that has absolutely no effect on the people who make the decisions about film production. What's more, the maximum average intellectual age of the audience in general, whose discrimination the critic hopes to reach, is twenty. (A new high.)

To me, those statements from the trade show and Tanen are bracing.

First, the consolations of cold comfort. Compare the literary critic who writes regularly for a journal and who concentrates on fiction (which is the closest analogy to most film). That critic has to pick his or her way through mounds and mounds of novels that are figurative popcorn-sellers, the very novels that keep the bookshops and the wholesalers and the publishers in business. The current *New York Times* best-seller list of fifteen hardbound novels contains only three that would appeal to those of a mental age higher than twenty; the current paperbound best-seller list of fifteen includes eleven that I wouldn't read if they were the only books washed up with me on a desert island.

The theater situation in New York is even worse for the theater critic (which, elsewhere, I also am). The number of trumpery new productions, on and off Broadway, is proportionately at least as high as the number of trumpery new films; the targeted intellectual level of most productions, especially on Broadway, cannot be higher than twenty, even if it's in the heads of people two or three times that age. Most of the people I know whose minds I respect go to the New York theater with decreasing frequency, and I don't often have a reason to urge them otherwise.

The film critic's domain, therefore, doesn't seem to me arbitrarily more circumscribed or more dismal than that of the fiction or theater critic. Dross for dross, all the fields weigh in about the same. In possible effect on taste and on producers' ambitions, criticism in all three fields seems equal. The salutary effect of the popcorn statement and the Tanen bluntness is to make us see that some other fields, thought relatively sacrosanct, are not really superior to film.

But let's leave the negative, the defensive. In proportion of good work, the film world certainly does not lag behind the many new plays I see and those new novels that I have time to read. Limiting comment to the past year, I'd say that, excepting three new short plays by Samuel Beckett, I've seen no new play and have read no new novel that I'd rank as high as, let alone higher than, *Tender Mercies*, *Ways in the Night*, *The Draughtsman's Contract*, or *Monty Python's The Meaning of Life*. I don't put *Berlin Alexanderplatz* and *Parsifal* on the list because they were based on renowned works, though, as sheerly cinematic achievements, they tower above any sheerly theatrical achievement of the year. And not all of these pictures have been failures by the popcorn or Tanen standards.

The fact of the film matter is that experience contradicts theory, even theory derived from experience. Good films do get made, and not only abroad where costs are still much lower. Possibly some of last year's good films—I haven't listed all, domestic or foreign—were mistakes by the Tanen standard, were either failures or trivial successes. But even films made solely to make money often fail of their purpose, as Tanen tells us; and there *is* the occasional exception, the film made for some other reasons as well. (No film, Bergman or Bugs Bunny, is made without intent to earn money.)

The serious critic thrives on the exceptions. He or she enjoys, I hope, the enjoyable pictures of lesser intent: the viewer who gets no fun out of *Tootsie* or *The Grey Fox* isn't fully equipped to appreciate the films noted above. Still, the exceptions are what the serious critic hopes for.

But then the human race thrives and survives by its exceptions. Any god, looking down from Olympus or Valhalla and judging by the general level of character and action, would have to conclude that humankind is a depressing spectacle. Its justification is in its exceptions; but the whole, generally sorry species has to exist in order to get the exceptions. Within one minuscule area of humankind's actions, film, the same ratio holds. The popcorn principle and the Tanen candor only underscore that the film microcosm conforms to the macrocosm.

Index